OECD Reviews of Innovation Policy: Malaysia 2016

OECD
BETTER POLICIES FOR BETTER LIVES

Please cite this publication as:
OECD (2016), *OECD Reviews of Innovation Policy: Malaysia 2016*, OECD Reviews of Innovation Policy, OECD Publishing, Paris.
http://dx.doi.org/10.1787/9789264255340-en

ISBN 978-92-64-25533-3 (print)
ISBN 978-92-64-25534-0 (PDF)

Series: OECD Reviews of Innovation Policy
ISSN 1993-4203 (print)
ISSN 1993-4211 (online)

Photo credits: Cover © Photo by Philippe Larrue

Corrigenda to OECD publications may be found on line at: *www.oecd.org/about/publishing/corrigenda.htm*.

Foreword

The OECD review of Malaysia's innovation policy is part of a series of OECD country reviews of innovation policy.* It was requested by the Malaysian authorities, represented by the Science Advisor of the Prime Minister, Dr Zakri Abdul Hamid, and the Malaysian Industry-Government Group for High Technology (MIGHT) and was carried out by the OECD Directorate for Science, Technology and Industry (DSTI) under the auspices of the Committee for Scientific and Technological Policy (CSTP).

The Steering Committee, co-chaired by Dato Lee Yee Cheong and Datuk Dr. Mohd Yusoff Sulaiman (President and CEO, MIGHT), provided invaluable guidance for the review.

The purpose of this review is to obtain a comprehensive understanding of the key elements, relationships and dynamics that drive the Malaysian innovation system and the opportunities to enhance it through government policy. More specifically, the review:

- provides an independent and comparative assessment of the overall performance of the Malaysian innovation system
- recommends where improvements can be made in the system
- formulates recommendations on how government policies can contribute to such improvements, drawing on the experience of other OECD countries and evidence on innovation processes, systems and policies.

The review is relevant to a wide range of stakeholders in Malaysia, including government officials, entrepreneurs and researchers, as well as the general public. It also aims to provide a comprehensive presentation of the Malaysian innovation system and policy to a global audience through the OECD communication channels.

A draft version of the "Overall Assessment and Recommendations", containing key issues and recommendations, was presented for a peer review to the Working Party for Innovation and Technology Policy (TIP) of the CSTP in June 2015. DSTI Director Andrew Wyckoff presented emerging results of the review at the meeting of the Global Science an Innovation Advisory Council (GSIAC) held in New York City in September 2015 and chaired by Prime Minister Dato Sri Mohd Najib bin Tun Abdul Razak. The Minister of Science, Technology and Innovation (MOSTI), Datuk Wilfred Madius Tengau, and MOSTI's Secretary-General Dato Sri Dr Noorul Ainur Mohd received presentations during their respective visits to OECD headquarters in September 2015 and April 2016. The review also received the supportive endorsement by the former Ambassador of Malaysia to France, HE Tan Sri Ismail Omar, and the present Ambassador of Malaysia to France, HE Dato Ibrahim Abdullah.

* www.oecd.org/sti/innovation/reviews.

The review was led by Gernot Hutschenreiter, Head, Country Innovation Policy Reviews Unit, (Science and Technology Policy Division [STP], DSTI, OECD). Gang Zhang (STP, DSTI, OECD) played an instrumental role in its initiation and in liaising with key stakeholders in the review process. The review report was drafted by Philippe Larrue, with contributions of Pluvia Zuniga (both STP, DSTI, OECD) and Frédéric Sgard (Global Science Forum Secretariat [STP, DSTI, OECD]), under the supervision of and with contributions from Gernot Hutschenreiter (STP, DSTI, OECD). Dimitrios Pontikakis participated in the first fact-finding mission to Malaysia and, together with Michael Keenan, provided valuable input at the early stage of the review. The review also benefited from contributions by Dieter Ernst (consultant to the OECD; Senior Fellow, East-West Center, United States) and Keith Smith (consultant to the OECD; Senior Research Fellow, Imperial College, United Kingdom) during the initial phase of the review, including the first fact-finding mission. Yana Vaziakova (STP, DSTI, OECD), Marion Robert and Maria Anokhina (both working at DSTI at the time of their contribution) provided valuable input, statistical support and web-based research.

The review draws heavily on the results of a series of interviews with a wide range of major stakeholders of the Malaysian innovation system during the two fact-finding missions (see the acknowledgement in Annex A).

The review owes much to the support and co-operation of the Malaysian counterparts from MIGHT: in particular Dr Raslan Ahmad (Senior Vice President), supported by Ahmad Razif Mohamed, and Rushdi Abdul Rahim (Senior Vice President) were key in facilitating the review. Mohd Nasir Md Ibrahim supported the review in numerous ways, both in Malaysia and during his secondment at OECD headquarters in Paris in 2015. Anusha Magendram – as well as Rozita Abdul Rahim and Nik Sufini Nik Mohamed – provided essential organisational and logistical support for the two fact-finding missions to Malaysia and through other communications. Robert Tai provided support and input during the first fact-finding mission. The Malaysian authorities also provided a Background Report.

The report has benefited from comments and additional information received from stakeholders in Malaysia, the TIP peer review and distinguished experts in the field – in particular Ian Hughes (Senior Policy Advisor, Department of Jobs, Enterprise and Innovation, Ireland) and Xiaoyong Shi (Senior Evaluator, National Centre for Science and Technology Evaluation, People's Republic of China) who contributed by acting as peer reviewers at the TIP meeting and, at the invitation of the Malaysian authorities, participated in the second fact-finding mission to Malaysia, and provided valuable contributions to the final report. Lennart Stenberg (Senior Advisor, Sweden's innovation agency – Vinnova, Sweden) contributed empirical, notably bibliometric, information.

Table of contents

Acronyms and abbreviations 11

Executive summary 15

Chapter 1. Overall assessment and recommendations 19

Achievements and challenges 20
Strengths and weaknesses of the Malaysian innovation system 22
Strategic tasks and guiding principles of science, technology and innovation policy 22
Key issues and recommendations 24

Chapter 2. Macroeconomic performance and framework conditions for innovation in Malaysia 41

Economic performance and structural change 42
Challenges to becoming a high-income economy 46
Malaysia's trade performance and participation in global value chains 53
Framework conditions for innovation 57
Notes 69
References 71

Chapter 3. Innovation performance in Malaysia 75

A significant increase in R&D effort… 76
Insufficient and uneven R&D investment 77
Mixed innovation performance 80
Notes 88
References 89

Chapter 4. Innovation actors in Malaysia 91

Business sector 92
Higher education institutions 114
Public research institutes 128
Notes 136
References 140

Chapter 5. Innovation policy and governance in Malaysia 147

Science, technology and innovation policy in Malaysia: A historical perspective 148
Main policy actors 156
Overall national plans and strategies currently in action 159
Support to R&D 166
Special support to industry and services 178
Enhancing the contribution of higher education institutions and public research institutes to innovation 193
Supporting system transition 202

Strengths and weaknesses of STI governance and the policy mix 207
Notes 219
References 223
Annex 5.A1. SME support measures in the Eleventh Malaysia Plan 231
Annex 5.A2 Main actions of the Malaysia Education Blueprint 2015-2025 (Higher Education)....232
Annex 5.A3 Main ongoing sectoral and thematic strategies, plans and roadmaps 234
Annex 5.A4 Malaysia's national innovation system: Main actors and STI functions 235
Annex 5.A5. Recent initiatives to support social innovation 236

Annex A. **List of people interviewed during fact-finding missions** 239

Tables

Table 1.1. SWOT analysis of the Malaysian innovation system 22
Table 2.1. Transitions between the World Bank income categories since 1950, selected Asian countries 48
Table 2.2. Inward foreign direct investment flows as a share of gross fixed capital formation 53
Table 2.3. Average annual growth rate of exports of goods and services, Malaysia, ASEAN, China and the United States, 1970-2014 54
Table 2.4. Top ten export commodities, Malaysia, 2013 55
Table 2.5. Highest Revealed Comparative Advantage of ASEAN countries, 2012 56
Table 2.6. Infrastructure indicators in Malaysia, 2010 and 2015 68
Table 3.1. R&D intensity goals and achievements in Malaysia, 1986-2020 79
Table 3.2. International comparisons of bibliometric indicators, selected Asian countries, 2001-11 82
Table 3.3. Global Competitiveness Report – innovation pillar indexes, Malaysia, 2010-16 86
Table 4.1. Share of small and medium-sized enterprises in the total number of firms and GDP, Malaysia, 2011 and 2014 93
Table 4.2. Business R&D expenditures by manufacturing sector, Malaysia 96
Table 4.3. Top ten Malaysian PCT applicants, publication year 2012 99
Table 4.4. Top 30 Malaysian European Patent Office patent applicants, filing years 2000-11 100
Table 4.5. Share of sub-sectors in total services value added, 1990 and 2010 104
Table 4.6. Top 15 business USPTO patent applicants, Malaysian inventors, 2010-14 112
Table 4.7. Factors hampering innovation activities, average results by factor type 112
Table 4.8. Higher education landscape of Malaysia 115
Table 4.9. Size and type of public universities in Malaysia 116
Table 4.10. Local patent applications by type of applicant, 2005-12 121
Table 4.11. Selected public research institutes in Malaysia 129
Table 5.1. Main science, technology and innovation governance-related initiatives and events in Malaysia, 1985-2010 152
Table 5.2. Role of government and focus of the science, technology and innovation system according to development stages, Malaysia 153
Table 5.3. Main non-sectoral science, technology and innovation councils and committees in Malaysia 160
Table 5.4. Objectives of the National Policy on Science, Technology and Innovation 2013-2020 163
Table 5.5. Main initiatives to support research and innovation under the Eleventh Malaysia Plan 165

Table 5.6. Main ongoing science, technology and innovation-related strategies and plans in Malaysia 167
Table 5.7. Main funding schemes to support research and innovation in Malaysia 174
Table 5.8. Main support schemes for small and medium-sized enterprises in Malaysia 180
Table 5.9. The twofold mission of local innovation centres in Malaysia 186
Table 5.10. Green growth initiatives under the Tenth and Eleventh Malaysia Plans 204
Table 5.A1.1. SME support measures in the Eleventh Malaysia Plan 231
Table 5.A2.1. Main actions of the Malaysia Education Blueprint 2015-2025 (Higher Education) 232
Table 5.A3.1. Main ongoing sectoral and thematic strategies, plans and roadmaps 234
Table 5.A4.1. Recent initiatives to support social innovation 235

Figures

Figure 2.1. Growth of GDP, Malaysia, 1960-2014 43
Figure 2.2. GDP per capita of Southeast Asian countries, 2005 and 2014 43
Figure 2.3. GDP by sector, Malaysia and ASEAN countries, 1960-2013 45
Figure 2.4. Evolution of the share of manufacturing in GDP, Malaysia and selected world regions, 1980-2013 46
Figure 2.5. Share of sectors in GDP, Malaysia, 1990-2014 47
Figure 2.6. Share of services in GDP, Malaysia and selected countries, 2000 and 2014 47
Figure 2.7. Gap between Malaysia's GNI per capital and the United States and the high-income threshold, 1987-2013 47
Figure 2.8. Income gap relative to the United States, 2013 49
Figure 2.9. Levels of labour productivity per hour worked, selected Asian countries, 1970-2013 51
Figure 2.10. Contributions and shares of labour, capital and total factor productivity to GDP growth in Malaysia, in comparison with China and the United States, 1970-2013 52
Figure 2.11. Revealed Comparative Advantage by industry type, Malaysia, 1995-2012 55
Figure 2.12. Revealed Comparative Advantage by industry type, China, 1995-2012 55
Figure 2.13. Domestic value added in exports, 1995 and 2011 57
Figure 2.14. Distance to frontier scores on Doing Business 2016: Malaysia 60
Figure 2.15. Most problematic factors for doing business, Malaysia, 2010-16 61
Figure 2.16. Sources of finance for investment projects of small and medium-sized enterprises, East Asia and OECD 62
Figure 2.17. OECD FDI Regulatory Restrictiveness Index, selected industries and sectors, Malaysia, 1997-2014 65
Figure 2.18. Intellectual property protection rates and ranking, 2015-16 66
Figure 2.19. Internet users, per 100 inhabitants, 1990-2014 68
Figure 3.1. R&D expenditure by institutional sector, Malaysia, 1988-2014 77
Figure 3.2. R&D expenditure by source of funds, Malaysia, 1998-2012 77
Figure 3.3. BERD by source of funds, Malaysia, 1992-2012 77
Figure 3.4. GERD by type of research, Malaysia (amount) 78
Figure 3.5. GERD by type of research, Malaysia (percentage) 78
Figure 3.6. Researchers in R&D, headcounts, Malaysia, OECD and selected Asian countries, 1996-2012 78
Figure 3.7. R&D intensity, Malaysia and selected Asian countries and OECD average, top and bottom five, 1990-2012 79

Figure 3.8. GERD on GDP, Malaysia and selected Southeast Asian countries, 2002 and latest available year 79
Figure 3.9. GERD by type of research, OECD average and Malaysia, 1992-2012 80
Figure 3.10. GERD by type of research, Singapore, 1994-2012 80
Figure 3.11. Number and annual increase of scientific publications, Malaysia, 2001-14 81
Figure 3.12. Number of publications, citations per document and share of international collaboration, Malaysia, 1996-2014 82
Figure 3.13. Share of world total and world's 10% most cited articles (purely domestic articles in all fields), 1990-2010 82
Figure 3.14. Share of articles among world's 10% most cited articles in the respective field (purely domestic articles in all fields), 1990-2010 83
Figure 3.15. Share of articles among world's 10% most cited articles in the respective field (articles with authors from at least 5 countries in all fields), 1990-2010 83
Figure 3.16. Share of articles among world's 10% most cited articles by field (purely domestic articles in all fields), 1990-2010 84
Figure 3.17. Patent applications by residents and non-residents, Malaysia, 1994-2013 84
Figure 3.18. Patent applications by residents and non-residents, ASEAN countries, 2013 85
Figure 3.19. Patent applications by residents, Malaysia and selected ASEAN countries, 1994-2012 85
Figure 3.20. Royalties and licensing fee receipts, Malaysia, 2005-13 86
Figure 3.21. Royalties and licensing fee receipts, selected countries, 2013 86
Figure 4.1. Productivity of small and medium-sized enterprises and large firms, Malaysia 94
Figure 4.2. BERD, total amount and share of total by type of research, Malaysia, 1992-2014 96
Figure 4.3. Number of top 500 corporate R&D investors, per GDP, 2013 or latest year available 97
Figure 4.4. Business R&D personnel, total number and share of total by type of post, Malaysia 99
Figure 4.5. Schematic question tree for analysing the upgrade of the manufacturing and service sectors in Malaysia 101
Figure 4.6. Sector share of total manufacturing value added in selected Asian countries, 2000 and 2011 (or closest year available) 102
Figure 4.7. Different types of upgrading in global value chains 106
Figure 4.8. Factors hampering innovation activities, all factors 113
Figure 4.9. Evolution of R&D expenditure in higher education institutions 118
Figure 4.10. Evolution of R&D personnel and researchers (FTE and headcount) in higher education institutions 118
Figure 4.11. Total researchers in higher education institutions, 2002 and 2012 119
Figure 4.12. R&D expenditure per researcher in higher education institutions, 2002 and 2012 119
Figure 4.13. Sources of funding for R&D performed by higher education institutions, evolution over the period 2006-16 119
Figure 4.14. Sources of funding for R&D performed by higher education institutions in 2013 or latest available 119
Figure 4.15. International collaboration in science: International co-publication ratio (relative to total publications), 2000-14 120
Figure 4.16. Patenting by universities and public research organisations in PCT applications, 1980-2010 121
Figure 4.17. Evolution in the number of scientific papers by public research institutes in Malaysia 134

Figure 5.1. Main public actors of the Malaysian science, technology and innovation system, 2015 159
Figure 5.2. Total amount and breakdown of financial support for R&D by Malaysia Plan period 170
Figure 5.3. Amounts allocated and selection rate of the ScienceFund and Pre-commercialisation Fund, 2006-15 171
Figure 5.4. Breakdown of allocations of the ScienceFund and Pre-commercialisation Fund, 2006-15 172
Figure 5.5. Total amount and breakdown of R&D support scheme financing in Malaysia, 2012 173
Figure 5.6. Total amount allocated by scheme, 2008-12 173
Figure 5.7. Number of projects applying for double-deduction on R&D expenditures and amount of deduction, Malaysia, 1999-2011 177
Figure 5.8. Number of applicants for double-deduction on R&D expenditures and export promotion, Malaysia, 2000-06 177
Figure 5.9. Number of R&D projects by type of R&D incentives, Malaysia 177
Figure 5.10. SME Policy Index, all policy dimensions, Malaysia and ASEAN 183
Figure 5.11. SME Policy Index, institutional framework 184
Figure 5.12. "Staircase" for developing company capabilities 185
Figure 5.13. Top ten PCT applicant OECD partner economies in selected environmental-related technologies 204
Figure 5.14. Policy development, co-ordination, planification and implementation in Malaysia 215

Boxes

Box 2.1. Intersectoral reallocation of labour in the development process 45
Box 2.2. Malaysia and the middle-income trap 50
Box 2.3. The evolution of global value chains in Southeast Asia 58
Box 2.4. Competition from a new cohort of catching-up economies: The example of Viet Nam 59
Box 4.1. The interaction between knowledge-intensive services and high-tech manufacturing 103
Box 4.2. The development of Islamic finance and insurance in Malaysia 105
Box 4.3. A typology of global value chain upgrading 106
Box 4.4. An emergent new source of growth: The Malaysian solar industry 109
Box 4.5. Performance-based funding of higher education institutions: Current reforms 126
Box 5.1. Mixed results of government policies supporting the upgrade of the Malaysian economy (1970-2000): Lessons from the literature 155
Box 5.2. The Investment Committee for Public Funds (ICPF/JKPDA) 158
Box 5.3. Malaysia's New Economic Model: Leveraging global value chains for structural transformation 161
Box 5.4. Science, technology and innovation in the national development budget process in Malaysia 164
Box 5.5. Summary of recommendations on investment promotion and facilitation from the 2013 *OECD Investment Policy Review of Malaysia* 178
Box 5.6. Technology extension services 186
Box 5.7. Key features of the Chilean Supplier Development Programme 190
Box 5.8. International examples of programmes to foster linkages between multinational enterprises and local firms 192

Box 5.9. State-owned enterprises as development agents: Lessons drawn from emerging countries' experiences 194
Box 5.10. Recommendations from the GLC Innovation Survey 2012 for government-linked companies to improve innovation capabilities 195
Box 5.11. Recommendations of the 2013 PRA performance assessment concerning public research institutes 200
Box 5.12. Restructuring public research institutes in Sweden: The creation of the Research Institutes of Sweden (RISE) 203
Box 5.13. An example of an integrated strategic policy framework: The National Green Technology Policy 205
Box 5.14. Lessons learnt from international comparisons of national science, technology and innovation councils 211
Box 5.15. Selected extracts from recent reports recommending a reform to improve prioritisation and co-ordination of science, technology and innovation policy in Malaysia 214
Box 5.16. An ongoing reform – Streamlining China's STI governance and funding system 216
Box 5.17. Lessons on R&D grant schemes from the Public Research Assets (PRA) Performance Evaluation 218

Acronyms and abbreviations

AIM	Malaysian Innovation Agency *Agensi Inovasi Malaysia*
ASEAN	Association of Southeast Asian Nations
BAP	Business Accelerator Programme
BERD	Business expenditure on research and development
CRDF	Commercialisation of R&D Fund
CREST	Collaborative Research in Engineering, Science & Technology
E&E	Electrical and electronics
EPU	Economic Planning Unit; Prime Minister's Department
ERGS	Exploratory Research Grant Scheme
FDI	Foreign direct investment
FRIM	Forest Research Institutions Malaysia
FTE	Full-time equivalent
GDP	Gross domestic product
GERD	Gross expenditures on research and development
GLC	Government-linked company
GNI	Gross national income
GSIAC	Global Science and Innovation Advisory Council
GVC	Global value chain
HDI	Human Development Index
HEI	Higher education institutions
HICoE	Higher institution centre of excellence
ICT	Information and communication technologies
IGS	Industry R&D Grant Scheme
IMP	Industrial Master Plan
INCEIF	International Islamic Financial Centre
IP	Intellectual property
IPR	Intellectual property rights
IRPA	Research in Priority Areas programme
JKPDA/ICPF	Investment Committee for Public Funds *Jawatankuasa Pelaburan Dana Awam*
KPI	Key performance indicator

LRGS	Long Term Research Grant Scheme
MaGIC	Malaysian Global Innovation & Creativity Centre
MARA	Council of Trust for the Bumiputera *Majlis Amanah Rakyat*
MARDI	Malaysian Agricultural Research and Development Institute
MASTIC	Malaysian Science and Technology Information Centre
MATRADE	Malaysia External Trade Development Corporation
MCB	Malaysian Cocoa Board
MGS	Multimedia Super Corridor R&D Grant Scheme
MIDA	Malaysian Investment Development Authority, previously known as the Malaysian Industrial Development Authority
MIGHT	Malaysian Industry-Government Group for High Technology; Prime Minister's Department
MIMOS	National R&D Centre in ICT of Malaysia
MITI	Ministry of International Trade and Industry
MNE	Multinational enterprise
MOE	Ministry of Education
MOF	Ministry of Finance
MOHE	Ministry of Higher Education
MOSTE	Ministry of Science, Technology and Environment
MOSTI	Ministry of Science, Technology and Innovation
MPC	Malaysia Productivity Corporation
MPOB	Malaysian Palm Oil Board
MRB	Malaysian Rubber Board
MSC	Multimedia Super Corridor
MTDC	Malaysian Technology Development Corporation
MyCC	Malaysian Competition Commission
MyIPO	Intellectual Property Corporation of Malaysia
NCSRD	National Council for Scientific Research and Development
NEM	New Economic Model
NHESP	National Higher Education Strategic Plan
NKEA	National key economic area
NPSTI	National Policy on Science, Technology and Innovation
NSC	National Science Council
NSRC	National Science and Research Council
NSTIP	National Science, Technology and Innovation Policy
OECD	Organisation for Economic Co-operation and Development
PCT	Patent Cooperation Treaty

PEMANDU	Performance Management and Delivery Unit; Prime Minister's Department
PhD	Doctor of Philosophy
PPP	Purchasing power parity
PPRN	Public-Private Research Network
PRA	Public research asset
PRGS	Prototype Development Grant Scheme
PRI	Public research institute
PTPTN	National Higher Education Fund Corporation *Perbadanan Tabung Pendidikan Tinggi Nasional*
R&D	Research and development
R,D&C	Research, development and commercialisation
RMA	Research Management Agency
S&T	Science and technology
S2A	Science to Action
SIRIM	Standards and Industrial Research Institute of Malaysia
SME	Small and medium-sized enterprise
SOE	State-owned enterprise
STI	Science, technology and innovation
TAF	Technology Acquisition Fund
TES	Technology extension services
TFP	Total factor productivity
TVET	Technical and vocational education training
UIAM	International Islamic University Malaysia
UiTM	Universiti Teknologi Mara
UKM	National University of Malaysia *Universiti Kebangsaan Malaysia*
UM	Universiti Malaya
UMT	Universiti Malaysia Terengganu
UN	United Nations
UNDP	United Nations Development Programme
UNIMAS	Universiti Malaysia Sarawak
UPM	Universiti Putra Malaysia
USIM	Universiti Sains Islam Malaysia
USM	University Sains Malaysia
UTeM	Universiti Teknikal Malaysia Melaka
UTM	Universiti Tecknologi Malaysia
UUM	Universiti Utara Malaysia
VDP	Vendor Development Programme
WoS	Web of Science

Executive summary

Malaysia's achievements and challenges

Malaysia is one of Asia's great success stories. Its economic and social development since independence has been impressive. High economic performance was based on a profound transformation into a diversified economy. Malaysia has climbed the income-per-capita ladder and is now close to achieving its goal of becoming a high-income country. It succeeded in poverty reduction and many other aspects of human development. This has meant better lives for many.

However, Malaysia has also been facing challenges. Economic growth has slowed in the aftermath of the 1990s Asian financial crisis, the rate of investment dropped, productivity growth slowed and some export market shares declined. Comparative advantage based on low labour costs has dwindled as the economy matured. The East Asian region has been undergoing rapid change and Malaysian firms are facing new competition.

Malaysia has benefited much from the integration in global value chains (GVCs). It could benefit even more through accelerated upgrading towards sophisticated goods and tradable services of high knowledge content. This would help raise the comparatively low share of domestic value added in gross exports.

Malaysia's innovation imperative

To respond to these challenges, Malaysia needs to rely more on innovation-driven productivity gains. As the examples of Korea and others have shown, improvements in domestic innovation capabilities can translate into sustained growth in productivity and gross domestic product (GDP).

Malaysia has recognised the challenge: it has done much to advance its science, technology and innovation (STI) capabilities and invested much in education. Research and development (R&D) expenditure has grown from 0.2% of GDP in 1996 to nearly 1.3% in 2014. Building a well-performing innovation system requires persistent commitment.

Improving public governance of the innovation system

Malaysia's STI governance is characterised by a multiplicity of advisory committees and councils as well as ministries, agencies, etc. engaged in STI policy making, funding and implementation, each of which is equipped with its own strategic framework and policy instruments. A rationalisation of Malaysia's STI governance structures is needed to achieve better co-ordination across government and, ultimately, higher impact at lower cost.

A continued effort has been made to create a simplified and efficient architecture of STI governance. The newly created National Science Council (NSC) should provide consistent mid- to long-term strategic orientation and government-wide co-ordination. A new Research Management Agency (RMA) should manage the allocation of research funding based on an efficient and transparent selection of research proposals and evaluation of results. This reform should now be implemented.

Drawing lessons from previous experience, it is important to i) assign clear roles to the NSC relative to already existing institutions with related mandates; ii) ensure a clear and consistent relation between the NSC and the RMA, and separating strategic and operational functions, and iii) ensure efficient information flows between the NSC and the relevant ministries and agencies, including the RMA. The RMA should be built upon an organisational model which allows it to fulfil its mission with sufficient resources and autonomy.

Fostering innovation in the business sector – Upgrading in value chains

Raising business firms' in-house innovation capabilities should be a central priority of Malaysia's STI policy. This priority should extend to a broad range of businesses, including domestic small and medium-sized enterprises (SMEs) which barely innovate and do not engage in R&D, often for lack of skills or funding.

Fostering business innovation requires a transparent set of public support measures which is at the same time accessible, effective and coherent and meets the needs of different types of firms – in particular those of SMEs, which need continuous and hands-on support. Regional innovation centres, in conjunction with already existing measures, could provide SMEs easy access to critical resources for innovation capacity building.

The upgrading of Malaysian enterprises in GVCs can be supported by fostering relations between multinational enterprises (MNEs) and domestic suppliers, including SMEs, through dedicated initiatives and incentives beyond the support already in place. Support networks and collaborative platforms – such as the Collaborative Research in Engineering, Science and Technology platform (CREST) – provide useful experience.

Enhancing the contribution of higher education institutions (HEIs) to innovation

The contributions of HEIs to innovation are manifold and comprise the provision of skilled human resources, the generation of knowledge through R&D and the commercialisation of research results. Malaysia has profoundly expanded, diversified and reformed its university system over the last decades.

While some outcomes are encouraging, a number of expectations have not yet been met. The overall contribution of HEIs to innovation could be increased by emphasising the provision of high-quality education and skills which are needed to nurture and grow innovative businesses and often are in short supply. In order to provide the right set of incentives, the corresponding monitoring and performance metrics need to be reviewed.

At the same time, the effort to strengthen the quality and relevance of research needs to be maintained as impact of research tends to be low and much of the intellectual property generated remains on laboratory shelves, un-commercialised. High-quality research carries an enhanced potential for commercialisation and relevance in tackling societal challenges. Focus and impact of university research can be improved by priority setting and creating critical mass through larger-scale collaborative programmes.

The Malaysian research system would also benefit from clear policies for strengthening, developing and maintaining research infrastructure and from a national research infrastructure plan and periodical inventory assessments.

Strengthening the contribution of public research institutes (PRIs) to innovation

PRIs play an important role in Malaysia's innovation system through their applied research, technology transfer and information services. However they vary and have seen their R&D funding fluctuate widely. Exceptions are cess-funded (commodity-oriented statuary) PRIs. Overall, the research and technology transfer capacity of PRIs remains underdeveloped.

The PRIs are in need of reform and modernisation based on an assessment of their respective mission and competences. Those assessed favourably with regard to their potential should be encouraged to develop their research strengths and technology transfer capacity by complementing own revenues by a healthy mix of competitive and institutional funding, subject to regular evaluation. For the remaining institutes other options – including their merger, downsizing or, discontinuation, if required – should be considered.

Efficiency gains can be reaped by enhancing linkages between universities and PRIs, e.g. through joint formation of advanced human resources (PhD programmes and training), research collaboration and sharing of equipment.

Strengthening the human resource base and skills for innovation

Human resources are the key to innovation. Accordingly, education has been a major focus of Malaysia's development effort: literacy rates are comparable to the OECD level, and an increasing share of the population is receiving tertiary education. Businesses (especially innovative ones) still find the lack of suitable skills an important barrier. A shortage of skills prevails in numerous domains, including university graduates and specialised technicians.

There is a need to improve the relevance and quality of skills across the board – in both tertiary education and technical and vocational education and training (TVET). The match between the supply of skills and the needs of industry should be improved, e.g. by including industry in curricula development, improving the delivery of the TVET system, and increasing the attractiveness of TVET courses.

Malaysia has developed a number of initiatives and strategies such as the Human Capital Development Strategic Reform Initiative and the Higher Education Blueprint 2015-25 to address human resources issues. The focus should now be put on the implementation of these various blueprints and plans and on setting up a mandatory schedule to evaluate the outcomes of these initiatives.

Malaysia faces a number of challenges. But there are immense opportunities to be seized, if these are tackled successfully: Malaysia is located in one of the most dynamic regions of the world, in the proximity of the world's largest, most populous and dynamic emerging economies, the People's Republic of China and India. For a country of about 30 million and the potential of its diverse population, this environment offers great opportunities of exploring and developing niches that are capable of generating prosperity in a sustainable manner.

Main recommendations

- Implement the continued effort to create a simplified and efficient architecture of STI governance with the NSC providing consistent mid- to long-term strategic orientation and government-wide co-ordination, and the RMA managing the allocation of research funding based on an efficient and transparent selection of research proposals and evaluation of results.
- Make raising business firms' innovation capabilities a central priority of Malaysia's innovation policy and implement an accessible, effective and coherent set of public support measures designed to best meet the varied needs of different kinds of firms, in particular those of SMEs, which need continuous and hands-on support.
- Enhance the higher education institutions' contribution to research and innovation by emphasising the provision of high-quality education and skills needed to upgrade businesses, while continuing efforts to strengthen excellence and relevance of research with enhanced potential for commercialisation and for addressing societal challenges.
- Reform and modernise the public research institutes based on an assessment of their respective mission, competences and governance. Enable those assessed favourably to develop their strengths by complementing their own revenues through a healthy mix of competitive and institutional funding, subject to regular evaluation. For the remaining institutes consider other options, including their merger, downsizing or discontinuation, if required.
- Improve the match between the supply of skills and the needs of industry, inter alia by including industry in curricula development, improving the delivery of the TVET system and increasing the attractiveness of TVET courses. Focus at this stage on the implementation of the various blueprints and plans and set up a mandatory schedule to evaluate the outcomes of these initiatives.

Chapter 1.

Overall assessment and recommendations

This chapter presents an overall assessment of Malaysia's innovation system and policy, reflecting key findings of the review. It identifies strengths and weaknesses of the innovation system, sets out strategic tasks for innovation policy and develops specific policy recommendations for improving Malaysia's research and innovation performance.

Achievements and challenges

Strong development performance …

Malaysia is one of Asia's great success stories. Its economic and social development since independence has been impressive. Over an extended period of time, Malaysia has achieved robust growth in gross domestic product (GDP), exceeding 7% per year. Today, with a gross national income (GNI) of USD 11 200 per capita in 2014, Malaysia places well in the upper middle-income range, and is now close to becoming a high-income country according to the World Bank definition. Malaysia enjoys the third-highest GDP per head among the ten countries making up the Association of Southeast Asian Nations (ASEAN), exceeded only by the city-state of Singapore and oil-rich Brunei Darussalam. To achieve this level of economic development, Malaysia – like other countries in the East Asian region – used export-led manufacturing based to a large extent on foreign direct investment (FDI) to emulate the success of the first wave of East Asian Tigers (including Hong Kong [China], Korea, Singapore and Chinese Taipei).

Malaysia's success has not been confined to the economic sphere. It can also be demonstrated in a much broader set of indicators on areas impinging on many important aspects of life. This is reflected, for example, by Malaysia's position in the United Nations Development Programme's (UNDP) Human Development Index (HDI). Among the 185 UN member countries listed in the Human Development Index, Malaysia ranks 64th – above Turkey, Mexico and Brazil. Moreover, during the past half-century it has built world-class physical infrastructures (roads, air transport facilities, rail, energy and water supplies) and major knowledge infrastructures (notably an extensive system of universities and research institutes) that bode well for the future.

… underpinned by structural change

Malaysia's economic success would not have been possible without the profound transformation of its economy. Since its independence, Malaysia has moved from an economy based on primary commodities to one driven by manufacturing and services. Throughout the colonial period, and into independence, Malaysia's economy was based on a number of resource-based industries: tin mining and processing, rubber, cocoa, timber and rice. Since then, new resource-based industries have emerged, namely oil and natural gas, and palm oil. Post-independence development has maintained the growth of resource-based industries but added major manufacturing capacity, especially in electrical and electronic products (E&E). During this process Malaysia became a major global exporter of electronic components. Other significant manufacturing activities are chemicals, food and beverages, metal products and machines. The service sector has developed, among others, around the expansion of financial services and a large tourism sector.

Challenges: Losing dynamism over time

While Malaysia has been expanding rapidly for a prolonged period of time, it has also experienced episodes of turbulence. A period of robust high growth that started in the late 1980s was brutally interrupted by the Asian financial crisis that began in 1997 and which had lasting effects. While the Malaysian economy recovered from the crisis, pre-crisis levels of economic growth remained out of reach. In the 2000s, Malaysia also lost ground to other Southeast Asian economies, with economic growth averaging close to 5% over the decade 2000-09. Malaysia was hit again by the global financial and economic crisis of the second half of the 2000s, with GDP contracting in 2009, albeit less severely than a decade earlier.

Overall, the dynamism of the Malaysian economy has lessened over time. In summary, economic growth slowed in the aftermath of the Asian financial crisis while powerful sources of growth have dwindled: the rate of investment dropped, productivity growth slowed and some export market shares declined. Malaysia has fallen short of the dynamism of the People's Republic of China (hereafter "China"), India and newly emerging Southeast Asian countries such as Viet Nam – which have recently embarked on a process of catching up, starting from very low levels of income per capita – as well as the dynamism achieved by much more advanced East Asian economies such as Korea.

These developments illustrate that in a long-term perspective, the previous "virtuous cycle" – driven by a combination of comparative advantage of low labour costs, conducive framework conditions, and well-developed infrastructure and targeted incentives to attract FDI – which transformed Malaysia into a thriving manufacturing export platform has lost momentum as its economy matured moved up the income scale.

While Malaysia has greatly gained from a close integration in global value chains (GVCs), it has not fully reaped the benefits of participating in such GVCs. Upgrading in value chains turned out to be slower in some areas, such as E&E, especially when compared to the best performing economies in Asia (e.g. Korea and Chinese Taipei). This makes Malaysia more vulnerable to fiercer competition in higher-end products and services on the one hand, e.g. from China which has been gaining in manufacturing strength through backward integration and upgrading final products, and, on the other hand, to competition from a new cohort of emerging economies which compete on low labour costs (e.g. Viet Nam). In order to prepare for the future, Malaysia has to become a more innovative economy and society.

Malaysia's innovation imperative

To respond to these challenges, the Malaysian economy will have to rely more on innovation-driven productivity gains. As the examples of Korea and others have shown, continuous improvements in domestic innovation capabilities can be translated into sustained growth in productivity and GDP, even in a high-income context.

Malaysia has recognised the challenge: it has made many efforts to advance its science, technology and innovation (STI) base and capabilities and important investments in education and research. Malaysia's research and development (R&D) expenditure grew from 0.2% in 1996 to 1.13% in 2012 and 1.26% of GDP in 2014. There has been a strong increase in the number of researchers, and new universities have been created. However, the results of this effort have not lived up to the high expectations that were set. Continued efforts will be needed to build a mature innovation system.

As recent OECD work demonstrates, innovation has become an important arena of policy making in many countries – including both advanced and emerging economies – in recent years. Policy makers today see innovation as central to achieving a wide range of economic and social objectives. There are three broad reasons for the new centrality of innovation in development policy. First, innovation generates qualitative improvements in products and processes, and through this it produces output and productivity growth. Second, real incomes and economic welfare are affected by the ways innovation shapes levels of technology. Third, innovation is central to establishing and maintaining competitive trade positions that both accompany and enable domestic growth strategies. Because of these wide effects, innovation is central not only to economic performance, but in the long term to the financial position of the government and the welfare of the population as well. At the same time, innovation policy involves multiple challenges across a range of policy arenas, including education, research, finance and organisational development. This makes innovation policy making a demanding, cross-cutting endeavour.

Strengths and weaknesses of the Malaysian innovation system

Table 1.1 presents the results of a SWOT analysis of the Malaysian innovation system.

Table 1.1. **SWOT analysis of the Malaysian innovation system**

Strengths	Opportunities
– Successful socio-economic development trajectory – Good business environment and well-developed infrastructure – Rich natural resource endowment and biodiversity – A coherent vision for the country; well-designed and comprehensive strategic plans – Capacity to launch comprehensive and ambitious (cross-)sectoral reforms – Embracing consultation processes for policy making and experimentation – Research capabilities in certain areas, e.g. agricultural commodities – Islamic banking and finance centre – A sizable R&D system	– Strengthened innovation capabilities within business firms, including small and medium-sized enterprises (SMEs) – Learning and upgrading in global value chains towards higher value-adding activities – Newly emerging industries (e.g. in green technologies) and services (sustainable tourism, hub for higher education) – Enhanced and better aligned technical education and training – Enhanced governance of the higher education and research institutes sector – Stronger contributions of public research institutes (PRIs) and universities to business innovation – Opportunities to lead ASEAN integration, including in science, technology and innovation (STI) (R&D co-operation, research infrastructure) – Cultural diversity
Weaknesses	**Threats**
– Mismatch of skills, shortcomings in education – Low R&D and innovative capacity, notably in domestic firms and SMEs – Weak connections between innovation actors – Lack of co-ordination of science and technology policy and overlapping policies and initiatives – Weak implementation of strategies – Lack of prioritisation, critical mass and stability of funding for research – Weak evaluation culture and practices – Institutional fragmentation in STI governance – High disparity in research capacity and performance across PRIs and universities – Weak incentives to innovate in some sectors	– Increasing sustainability challenges – Instability in the international political and macroeconomic environment – Growing exposure and loss of opportunities due to failure to upgrade to higher value-adding activities – Political and social polarisation – Brain drain

Strategic tasks and guiding principles of science, technology and innovation policy

Strategic tasks

Science, technology and innovation (STI) is the most important driver of sustainable growth and improving living standards in the long term, and is indispensable for tackling societal challenges effectively. The overall task of Malaysia's STI policy today is to contribute to the country's goal of becoming a fully developed economy, to narrow the gap with the advanced economies, and achieve the economic, societal and sustainability objectives the country has set for itself more broadly.

To achieve these goals, Malaysia has to strengthen its domestic innovation capabilities and build an innovation system which can contribute effectively to these goals. These capabilities are critical for driving the productivity growth of enterprises in manufacturing as well as in services industries – a high priority of the Eleventh Malaysia

Plan – and improving their competitiveness in local and international markets. Improved innovation capabilities are indispensable for upgrading towards higher value-added activities which often take place within GVCs. The challenges in this regard are manifold: one is the need to transform industries, including the erstwhile predominant and still very large E&E industry, by moving along the value chain, from simple high-volume assembly operations and component manufacturing towards higher value-adding activities. The second is the need to initiate and facilitate new development dynamics in resource-based and traditional industries, extending upstream and downstream and into areas of high potential. The third is in fostering the reallocation of resources to new and emergent industries, including in advanced manufacturing and knowledge-intensive services.

Implementing an innovation-based development strategy that can achieve the required transformations calls for action in several domains:

- Continued attention to and investment in developing the human resources and skills which are at the core of STI capabilities.
- Gradually building a mature, well-performing national innovation system with healthy interactions between its constituent parts and Malaysia's international environment. This entails:
  - Fostering the innovation capabilities of business firms through innovation-friendly framework conditions, complemented by a set of dedicated and responsive innovation policies that help Malaysian firms across sectors to become more innovative.
  - Strengthening the contribution of universities and research institutes, notably though improved mechanisms of steering and funding, taking due account of the full range of these institutions' functions (from educating skilled personnel for STI to performing advanced research and commercialisation).
- More effective overall STI governance arrangements and mechanisms, including both a streamlined framework and institutional setup as well as efficient processes to strengthen policy co-ordination and implementation, sending clear signals and incentives for innovation in businesses, universities and government research institutes.

Guiding principles

In formulating and implementing policies to carry out the strategic tasks of innovation policy, the Malaysian government should consider applying or continue to apply the following guiding principles:

- **Long-term commitment.** Sustained commitment at the highest level of government and broad stakeholder consensus are key factors of success of STI policy. This was demonstrated impressively by a series of countries in East Asia, from Japan and Korea, to a number of smaller Southeast Asian countries, and lately China, which has maintained a persistent financial and political effort to transform and upgrade its innovation system over some decades now.
- **Business at the centre of the innovation system.** It is the innovation undertaken by business enterprises and other producers – often in interaction with other businesses and drawing on knowledge inputs from universities and public research institutes – that generates more and better jobs, income and welfare. Policy priority should therefore be given to improving the innovation performance of a greater number

and variety of enterprises, and accompanying policy measures tuned to developing a well-integrated innovation system that responds to their needs.

- **Broad approach to innovation.** Taking a broad approach means addressing not only technological but also non-R&D-based forms of innovation that draw on all types of creativity, such as organisational and marketing innovation, new business models, innovation in services, and social innovation. Care should be taken to avoid too narrowly focusing policy on "high technology", as can be observed in other countries. Malaysia has a good track record of research and innovation in "traditional" sectors.
- **Effective STI governance.** The effectiveness of STI governance can be improved by simplifying and streamlining the institutional configuration and the processes applied. Better co-ordination across government (both between line ministries and different levels of government), its agencies and public research institutions is an important part of this effort. International experience provides numerous examples of how to implement effectiveness-enhancing arrangements, such as separating strategy and operational functions.
- **Participatory approach to STI policy.** Greater interaction and better information exchange within the policy-making community needs to be accompanied by dialogue and the active involvement of all relevant stakeholders of the innovation system, including businesses, in policy formulation, implementation and assessment. While there are already good practice examples in Malaysia, policy making and implementation still tend to be fragmented and there remains scope for greater stakeholder involvement.
- **Evidence-based policy making.** A sound basis for policy makers to take decisions to improve the performance of the innovation system requires systematic evidence on the performance of the innovation system and its actors in the form of statistics, qualitative analysis and feedback from (independent) evaluations on the effectiveness of policy interventions. These elements should become an integral part of national practices.
- **Objective, independent and transparent resource-allocation processes.** A variety of resource-allocation mechanisms are used for research and innovation policy purposes. These processes used should be objective, independent and transparent as clarity and the use of decision criteria that reward projects and institutions of high quality and relevance tend to result in greater efficiency than allocation processes based on other criteria. Objective and transparent processes are also conducive to building trust in the innovation system.
- **Inclusiveness of the innovation system.** Inclusiveness is desirable not only in itself but also because it generally supports effective and efficient innovation. Malaysia has made much progress in this regard, e.g. through wide access to education. Social inclusiveness also helps, e.g. in fully mobilising the pool of talent for R&D and innovation and better translating societal needs into signals about innovation needs and eventual demand.

Key issues and recommendations

Taking due account of Malaysia's innovation-related strengths, weaknesses, opportunities and threats (see Table 1.1), a number of key issues have been identified.

The recommendations relating to each of these issues are in line with the strategic tasks and guiding principles outlined in the previous section.

Improving the public governance of science, technology and innovation

The government has played an important role in guiding and fostering Malaysia's transformation at different stages of its development. Malaysia has proven its strengths in identifying major challenges and producing the diagnostics for an ambitious set of interlinked economic and innovation strategies. These strategic frameworks are most often well-designed, comprehensive and formally innovative, in some cases even paving the way to the creation of genuine integrated "thematic innovation systems" (e.g. in the area of green technologies). Against this backdrop, the five-year Malaysia plans have diversified the national portfolio of policy instruments to cover all the needs of research and innovation performers from higher education institutions (HEIs) and public research institutions (PRIs) to multinational enterprises (MNEs), small and medium-sized enterprises (SMEs) and, more recently, various communities.

Malaysia's STI governance is characterised by a multiplicity of institutions (e.g. horizontal, thematic and sectorial advisory committees and councils) and organisations of various types (ministries, agencies, government-linked corporations, etc.) engaged in STI policy making, funding and implementation, each of which is equipped with its own strategic framework and policy instruments. To some extent this is a reflection of the cross-cutting and multi-faceted nature of innovation. This has, however, rendered the governance of science, technology and innovation dysfunctional and hinders it from fulfilling its objectives, as the multiplicity of actors and support instruments entail excessive fragmentation and overlapping competencies. This is exacerbated by a lack of co-operation and information exchange across "governance silos".

The advisory committees have set priorities, devised roadmaps or strategic research agendas, most often derived from multi-staged processes involving wide-ranging consultations. Not only has the wealth of priorities run the risk of conflicting guidance, but it has also rendered unclear how these priorities could be turned into action through the various programmes and policy instruments available. The links between research priorities and key sectors also remain blurred.

The multitude of institutional actors and overlapping responsibilities and the ensuing lack of co-ordination and direction have made policy implementation a difficult task. Furthermore, weak monitoring and evaluation, excessive bureaucracy, and a lack of middle-management skills in various parts of the administration have limited the capacity to deliver on well-crafted strategic plans. Most of these systemic failures have been identified repeatedly since the beginning of Malaysian STI policy in the mid-1980s and are echoed in various policy areas.

The proliferation of STI-related strategic frameworks, organisations and policy tools is also partly responsible for the significant fluctuations of funding assigned to each of them, in particular over the last 15 years. The lack of long-term stability in funding has had a negative impact on the research system as its objectives can only be achieved over a longer time horizon.

The government has made attempts to address these issues through the creation of new government agencies, strengthening centre of government STI prerogatives, the launch of comprehensive cross-sectoral programmes, as well as the establishment of co-ordination councils and committees. However, many of these initiatives have failed or succeeded only partially, and have further added to the system's complexity.

A rationalisation of Malaysia's STI governance structures is therefore urgently needed in order to ensure better co-ordination across government, provide stable funding, improve policy implementation and, ultimately, achieve higher impact at lower cost. A new reform of the STI governance architecture was brought on the way in the recent past. The three main strands of this reform have been new STI legislation, the establishment of a high-level committee in charge of STI strategy and policy orientation, and the creation of a central research agency. After intense discussions, the Science Act was put on hold. The National Science Council (NSC), chaired by the Prime Minister, held its first meeting in early 2016, and is meant to streamline the various STI committees. The establishment of a national Research Management Agency (RMA) was endorsed by the Eleventh Malaysia Plan, in line with recommendations made in the Public Research Assets (PRA) Performance Evaluation undertaken under the National Science and Research Council (NSRC) in 2013.

The NSC and RMA have the potential to significantly improve the co-ordination of STI activities, provided that some principles drawn from international experience are observed: a clear separation of the strategy and implementation functions; realistic and distinct mandates for the organisations in charge of these two functions, both in terms of tasks and the range of research or broader STI activities covered; the establishment of efficient information loops between these two functions; the consistency between the mandate of these organisations and their organisational, legal and budgetary status; systematic monitoring and *ex post* evaluation of activities.

Main recommendation

Implement the continued effort to create a simplified and efficient architecture of STI governance with the NSC providing consistent mid- to long-term strategic orientation and government-wide co-ordination, and the RMA managing the allocation of research funding based on an efficient and transparent selection of research proposals and evaluation of results.

Other recommendations

- *Task the NSC with setting the mid- to long-term strategic priorities which feed into the planning process of the Malaysia plans and guide the immediate operations of the RMA and STI-related ministries and agencies.*

  The NSC includes representatives of all ministries involved in a significant way in research and innovation; its decisions and recommendations regarding strategic orientation and co-ordination should encompass the entire STI system and policy spectrum. Previous experience suggests that the following three conditions are necessary for it to succeed: 1) the remit and the authority given to the NSC should reflect a commitment to change at the level of the whole research and innovation system; 2) the implementation of the NSC's recommendations, even if non-binding, by the agencies in charge should be systematically monitored; 3) priorities set by the NSC should not consist simply of a list of themes, areas or sectors but should clearly identify the ministries and agencies in charge of implementation, including a "lead body", and the injunction to devise an action plan within a certain period of time, which will be submitted to the NSC.

- *Task the RMA with focusing on the efficient and transparent management of the competitive allocation of funding for research projects, from fundamental to applied research and development, and the commercialisation of research results.*

  The RMA should have a clearly defined mission to address the main research weaknesses identified in the PRA assessment and other studies (lack of efficiency and transparency of R&D and commercialisation programmes and instruments, overlap, weak monitoring and *ex post* evaluation, insufficient linkages with industry, etc.). The remit of the RMA's mandate includes the allocation of research funds through competitive mechanisms, and the monitoring and *ex post* evaluation of research activities at project, thematic programme or "call" levels. The task of initiating and designing top-down strategic programmes to address issues of national interest can be either managed by the RMA or left with the relevant ministries. In the latter case, co-ordination with the related research projects managed by the RMA should be ensured, as necessary.

- *Improve the alignment between the R&D support instruments and the current and future needs of key industries and sectors.*

  A better alignment of publicly funded research and demand from industry can be achieved in different ways. The RMA could better match research calls with the needs of industries and sectors based on industrial/technology road mapping and other types of technology foresight exercises. Balancing the representation of academia and industry on selection panels plays an essential part in improving the relevance of the R&D policy instruments. Finally, the government could initiate and support the creation of selected top-down strategic and targeted programmes operated by consortia of actors (universities, PRIs, small and large firms) around issues of national interest, following a collectively agreed upon research and innovation agenda. These programmes could be either managed by the RMA or left with the relevant ministries/agencies. In the latter case, co-ordination with the related research projects managed by the RMA should be ensured.

- *Ensure efficient information flows between the NSC and the various ministries and agencies, including the RMA, in charge of implementing its decisions and recommendations.*

  Ministries and agencies implement the priorities defined by the NSC and feed information back to it, drawing in particular on monitoring and evaluation results. The ministries have an essential role in maintaining a clear and consistent relation between the strategic orientation and implementation functions since they are represented in the NSC and are regularly in contact with their agencies. They can therefore provide essential inputs that feed into the NSC's decisions and set the appropriate conditions (budget, information, incentives) for their implementation by the agencies and departments under their remit.

- *Ensure that the RMA is built upon an organisational model which allows it to fulfil its mission with sufficient resources and autonomy.*

  This would imply that the RMA has a stable annual budget of its own, or clearly earmarked funds originating from various ministries. More generally, all of the necessary conditions should be met to ensure high legitimacy of the new agency *vis-à-vis* the other public institutions as well as public and private research performers. A study has been commissioned to propose an appropriate model and governance structure for the RMA.

- *Seek co-operation between the RMA and the relevant ministries and other specialised agencies as required and seize all opportunities for synergies.*

  Entrusting the delivery of programmes of different ministries to the RMA could facilitate and provide an incentive for joint programming and streamlining programme portfolios, and lead to economies of scale; it could facilitate informal co-ordination and break up "silos".

- *Assign clear roles to the NSC and RMA relative to already existing institutions with related mandates. This includes,* inter alia, *the Investment Committee for Public Funds (ICPF/JKPDA), the NSRC, the National Innovation Agency of Malaysia (AIM) and all other committees not under the purview of the NSC.*

- *Ensure that all strategic frameworks include an action plan to guide their implementation.*

  The action plan should feature budget indications (if not appropriations), clearly assigned tasks to the various public research actors as well as concrete monitoring and evaluation principles (i.e. timeline, process and performance indicators to be monitored, succinct and precise qualitative progress report by action, etc.).

- *Set an annual evaluation plan (at least endorsed by the NSC) covering all STI policy instruments (or even a broader scope, for instance in relation to the Malaysia plans process).*

  The implementation of the evaluations under this plan should follow international best practices and their results should be available online.

Fostering innovation in the business sector – Upgrading in value chains

Developing innovation capabilities is critical for Malaysia's future economic development and for responding to growing sustainability challenges. Business enterprises that thrive on innovation – and leverage R&D performed in universities and public research institutes (PRIs) – are at the centre of all national innovation systems that successfully drive growth and development. Improving in-house innovation capabilities – which requires skills to engage in design, engineering, marketing, information technology and R&D – in a broad range of enterprises should be an overarching priority. Malaysia already stands out: it is among the emerging economies where the business enterprise sector is a major performer and funder of R&D. However, there is a continued need to strengthen the R&D and innovation capabilities of domestic businesses, including SMEs. The bulk of domestic SMEs barely innovates and do not engage in R&D.

Considerable effort has been devoted to attracting and supporting business R&D activities, particularly in "high" and "medium technology" sectors. A number of measures have been introduced to promote industrial R&D and innovation, including fiscal incentives, support to consortia and clusters, public-private partnerships, and the promotion of science-industry linkages and knowledge transfer. Despite some success in specific clusters and industries, the upgrading of the electrical and electronic (E&E) industry, which was previously a pioneer and catalyst of structural change, has slowed down in the 2000s. Rapid changes in GVCs, especially in Asia, add urgency to investing in R&D and advanced technological capabilities. Strong innovation capabilities are essential for enterprises to achieve a more favourable position in GVCs. MNEs are restructuring their global activities – and hence GVCs – using the evolving comparative advantages of newly emerging economies such as Viet Nam. It is therefore important that

Malaysia's human resources and innovation capabilities stay abreast of these important new developments. A lack of adequate skills is an obstacle for the growth of innovative domestic enterprises, especially SMEs, and the expansion of higher value-adding activities in MNEs. As for emerging sectors that build upon the E&E resources, such as the solar panel sector, their recent impressive growth remains fragile and dependent on the international context. Some resource-based industries in which Malaysia has strong comparative advantages, such as rubber and palm oil, have made significant progress in moving "downstream" in order to increase value added and remain competitive on export markets. Notable success has also been achieved in sectors like composite materials and services such as Islamic finance.

As noted, very few domestic SMEs engage in innovation, either for lack of adequate skills, funding or incentives to change their traditional business model. With only limited in-house innovation capabilities, SMEs rarely co-operate with academia, do not take part in collaborative R&D with MNEs and barely use shared equipment at universities, while at the same time the Ministry of Science, Technology and Innovation's collaborative grants are short of high-quality applications and equipment at universities is often underutilised. The government has long acknowledged this issue and has taken action to address it, which places Malaysia's SME policy ahead of that of other countries in the region. However, greater efforts to monitor, evaluate and streamline the plethora of instruments available to support the upgrade of SMEs, in particular in the context of the SME Masterplan 2012-20 and the governance architecture set up for its implementation, would help improve its cost-effectiveness.

Recent initiatives to provide SMEs with external technological and managerial expertise (e.g. AIM's Steinbeis Foundation Malaysia, the SIRIM-Fraunhofer partnership and the Ministry of Higher Education's Public-Private Research Network – PPRN) recognise that the first steps towards innovation in SMEs often involve on-demand problem-solving and require collaboration with experienced academics or industrial experts. In order to be effective, support to SMEs, especially those with low innovation capabilities, has to be continuous, affordable and readily accessible in facilities located in their proximity. Several countries have set up such local innovation centres which are fulfilling on the one hand a public mission (provision of information, awareness-raising, promotion of innovation, general capability building, etc.) while, on the other hand, providing project-based support to individual (or groups of) SMEs and initiating collaborative innovation on a more permanent basis.

Supporting SMEs, especially in traditional industries, calls for a broad notion of innovation, including incremental and non-technical innovation – as recognised for example by the creation of the Malaysian Global Innovation and Creativity Centre (MaGIC), the broadening of eligibility criteria of existing support instruments and the creation of new ones. Local innovation centres can be instrumental in establishing links between the relevant firms and communities and these initiatives.

Enhancing domestic firms' innovation capabilities contributes to upgrading their position in GVCs through a shift into higher value-added products and/or processes (product and process upgrading) as well as via the extension of activities from production – upwards to design and R&D or downwards to marketing and services, such as advertising and aftersales (functional upgrading). The latter implies, or calls for if carried out externally, the development of knowledge-intensive services. The Service Sector Blueprint launched in 2015 contains a wide range of actions to support these developments.

Main recommendation

Make raising business firms' innovation capabilities a central priority of Malaysia's innovation policy and implement an accessible, effective and coherent set of public support measures designed to best meet the varied needs of different kinds of firms, in particular those of SMEs, which need continuous and hands-on support.

Other recommendations

- *Ensure that a sufficiently differentiated set of instruments is in place to meet varied needs of firms while taking provisions for maintaining the coherence of the policy mix as a whole.*

  Malaysia will continue exploring, assessing and scaling up policy instruments if they are proven to be effective (for instance low-barrier instruments such as vouchers, public procurement schemes in support of innovative SMEs, co-operative research, or – at the high end – PPPs for research and innovation). To keep the overall policy mix coherent, effective and transparent, instruments with low recorded impact need to be phased out. A priority for the SME support infrastructure should be to address the lack of innovation capability in the vast majority of these enterprises, and strengthen those which have already started to innovate. This entails taking into account firms' evolving needs along all stages of the research and innovation process, from fundamental research to commercialisation, and ensuring the continuity of support over time, helping SMEs to gradually move up the innovation ladder. Supporting SMEs calls, in most cases, for a broad notion of innovation, including incremental and non-technical (e.g. organisational) innovation.

- *Set up local innovation centres to provide domestic SMEs easy access to critical resources for upgrading their innovation capabilities (information, expertise, specific equipment, etc.).*

  SMEs often lack financial, technological and strategic capability to access support in the area of STI. They are in need of specific hands-on support based on proximity and the mid- to long-term commitment of competent experts. Emulating the best international practices of intermediary organisations such as, for example, technical centres, extension services, the local innovation centres should clearly distinguish between and ensure the continuity of their public mission (provision of information, awareness-raising, promotion of innovation, general capability building, etc.) and their specific support activities to individual (or groups of) SMEs (technical assistance and consulting, interface between experts, from academia and industry). These activities should be aligned and in co-operation with existing and newly established organisations and initiatives (SME Corp, AIM, Steinbeis Foundation Malaysia, PPRN, SIRIM-Fraunhofer).

- *Foster relations between MNEs and domestic suppliers, including SMEs, through dedicated schemes and incentives beyond the support already in place, such as the vendor development and technology procurement programmes.*

  Priority should be given to a hands-on approach whereby SMEs are supported financially and non-financially throughout the process of learning and transfer involving the three main stakeholders of these initiatives, i.e. MNEs, SMEs and the state. Successful regional and/or thematic cluster initiatives, in Malaysia and internationally, could serve as examples to adapt and adopt.

- *Encourage and support networks and collaborative platforms.*

  Such networks and platforms "on the ground" typically include a range of stakeholders from the business sector (including MNEs and domestic firms), public research institutes, universities, government and agencies involved in policy implementation, end users, etc. They can undertake a wide range of activities, from the co-ordination of R&D to capability building and advocacy. The Collaborative Research in Engineering, Science and Technology platform (CREST) in Penang provides a good example, along with the rich OECD experience with sectoral, regional and technology-based networks/platforms. CREST should be assessed to derive concrete lessons for other platforms.

- *Foster the role of government-linked companies (GLCs) in promoting and enhancing innovation, within the scope of their own activities and that of their partners (suppliers and clients).*

  This could include, for instance, setting corresponding objectives, monitored by new key performance indicators (KPIs) and/or developing innovation programmes specific for each GLC.

- *Mobilise resources (both financial and human) to strengthen and upgrade standard-setting organisations, especially for priority products.*

  As a key mechanism for the diffusion of technological knowledge, standards contribute to productivity growth and should be considered as an important component of a growth strategy which seeks to create high-quality jobs in higher value-adding manufacturing and services. Standards should be set at high quality levels, both to ensure safety and to create a source of incentives for local firms, which will have to meet such stringent quality standards to increase their competitiveness by upgrading their capabilities.

Enhancing the contribution of higher education institutions to innovation

Malaysia has profoundly expanded, diversified and reformed its university system over the last decades with some encouraging outcomes, although a number of expectations have not yet been met. Important reforms were introduced with the launch in 2007 of the National Higher Education Strategic Plan (NHESP) – Beyond 2020 and the National Higher Education Action Plan 2007-10. More recently the *Malaysia Education Blueprint 2015-2025 (Higher Education)* (hereafter "Higher Education Blueprint 2015-25") set the roadmap and action plan for the transformation of the higher education sector. The government has increased public expenditure for education consistently over the years. Today, Malaysia invests much more in tertiary education than its peers in the region.

Several regulatory reforms have been enacted to enhance the autonomy of institutions and improve the governance of the sector, and new monitoring and performance evaluation instruments have recently been adopted. Mechanisms for quality monitoring and accreditation have been reinforced and public funding for R&D has expanded substantially through the introduction of new performance-based block funding schemes (e.g. Research University Programme) and competitive funding for projects (e.g. Science Fund).

New funding regulations now require HEIs to diversify their sources of finance and increase revenue generation. The best performing universities have been granted more autonomy in exchange for a commitment to raise a significant share of funding externally. A comprehensive, multi-layered system of monitoring increasingly determines the level of block funding allocated to universities and government research institutes. While this is a positive development, overly tight financial constraints might create difficulties, at least for some universities – especially new and smaller ones which lack capabilities and experience in revenue generation.

The national plans mentioned above resulted in improvements in higher education in a relatively short period of time. The sector has expanded significantly, which reflects growing demand, and quality control mechanisms have been reinforced, enrolment ratios and number of graduates have expanded at all levels of tertiary education. As regards the democratisation of education and raising the number of university graduates and post-graduates, important results have been achieved. However, in terms of overall quality Malaysia stills lags behind. Responsiveness to industry needs remains an area of concern, as is ensuring quality education in private universities. No Malaysian institution is on the list of the top 100 in the Asian QS University Rankings – in contrast to universities from Singapore, Hong Kong (China) or India, who have recently joined this list. The quality and supply of science and technology graduates needs to improve to respond to the business sector's growing demand for such skills.

In recent years, efforts have been bolstered to foster university excellence, increase funding for research and improve technology transfer. HEIs saw their R&D expenditure multiply by a factor of 11 between 2000 and 2012 and the number of researchers expand five-fold between 2006 and 2012 – from 12 152 to 64 962 researchers. However, most of the new funding for R&D has remained concentrated in a small number of research universities, while other, more recently established HEIs are confined to their mission in higher education, with very limited research activity. This expansion has been driven by enhanced public support through a variety of competitive funding instruments and the creation of the Research University programme. The latter, however, has had a varying level of funding over the last three years.

So far, results from increasing investment in research are mixed – although it has to be recognised that it takes time for results in investment in R&D to materialise. Research and innovation capabilities at HEIs show signs of improving, but mostly in terms of quantity of publications rather than quality and impact. While there has been an unprecedented surge in the number of publications (owing partly to new research evaluation criteria), their impact measured by citations has been very low. Similarly, the number of HEIs' patents has increased very rapidly, including those resulting from residents' research, but a lot of the intellectual property created by research remains uncommercialised. The attractiveness of university patents to industry and their practical applicability seems weak; this is in part due to the lack of relevance of research to industry and weak communication between the two sectors. The quality of these patents remains a concern given the high costs of patenting and renewing intellectual property rights (at both national and international levels).

In spite of new public support mechanisms for technology transfer and more enabling intellectual property regulatory frameworks, results are yet to materialise. Collaboration with the business sector remains underdeveloped. Only a few universities have started to collaborate with industry in R&D and technology transfer activities. Overall, enhancing interaction/consultation with the business sector in the definition of curricula and education programmes or in research agendas remains an important challenge for most universities.

While universities have taken steps in articulating research policies and research management offices, research efforts remain fragmented both across and within universities and lack effective strategic prioritisation. There are many economic priority and research areas – and their inter-linkages are often not clearly established. Currently there are many small research centres (centres of excellence) spread across universities. A lack of critical mass in many scientific areas reduces the potential impact of research in areas of importance for the Malaysian economy and society, as well as its international visibility. Malaysia also lacks platforms or programmes that encourage interdisciplinarity and multi-perspective approaches.

An additional handicap to universities' research excellence is the lack of research infrastructure management and policy. Malaysia has not developed a national policy in this regard – neither an inventory nor roadmaps have been formally set up. The Ministry of Science, Technology and Innovation has begun efforts to conduct a national inventory but no co-ordination mechanisms are yet in place. Guidelines for the collective use of infrastructure also need to be established to ensure a cost-efficient use of infrastructure and equipment. A competitive and well-managed research infrastructure is critical to foster research excellence, enhance the quality of research and attract talented young researchers, including from abroad.

Main recommendation

Enhance the higher education institutions' contribution to research and innovation by emphasising the provision of high-quality education and skills needed to upgrade businesses, while continuing efforts to strengthen excellence and relevance of research with enhanced potential for commercialisation and for addressing societal challenges.

Other recommendations

- *Put human capital formation at the heart of the priorities of universities.*

  Universities should not be detracted, e.g. by the focus on commercialisation, from progressing in their contribution to innovation through the formation of highly qualified graduates with skills relevant to the Malaysian economy. In doing so, the higher education sector needs to address the challenge of ensuring a better balance between quantity and quality, reinforcing the quality of higher education – as stressed in the Higher Education Blueprint 2015-25. This will require improving and updating curricula to reflect the demand for new skills as well as improving methodologies and pedagogy to encourage creative thinking, problem solving and a more entrepreneurial culture. Enhancing the quality and supply of science and technology graduates remains an important priority in this area.

- *Review and streamline monitoring and performance metrics, taking into account the whole range of contributions HEIs may make to innovation and development.*

  The monitoring system should contribute to achieving an adequate balance of education, knowledge generation, and technology and knowledge transfer. The monitoring system should allow HEIs sufficient flexibility to be able to innovate and develop their own strategies to respond to the overall objectives.

- *Enhance stability in research funding by providing appropriate time horizons for research (e.g. at least five years for the Research University programme; three to four years for basic research projects), especially in collaborative schemes and fundamental research.*

  Based on this new framework, evaluate the results of research activities in HEIs on a multi-annual basis. This should allow pursuing the efforts toward a performance-based allocation of research funds while providing institutions with sufficient stability to engage in multi-annual research programmes and projects.

- *Consider strengthening research through larger scale collaborative programmes, e.g. by consolidating certain centres of excellence under a single entity.*

  An option in the strategy to foster critical mass in key areas could be to merge/consolidate certain centres of excellence. These may perform multi-disciplinary research addressing an agreed agenda (corresponding to national demands) and engage in collaboration with industry through research consortia. Larger initiatives would require an adjustment of funding, timelines and performance criteria.

- *Improve the focus and impact of university research. It is important to involve the higher education sector in the priority-setting process to better align demands with current research competences (and their future development).*

  It is important to provide more clarity regarding priority areas and the linkages between science (public research) and the research requirements of key economic areas and sectors. Priority setting should be streamlined and simplified – and the connections between scientific and economic priorities better aligned. In doing so, research capacity and competences should be assessed and compared against industry necessities. It must be acknowledged that academic research might not currently have all of the competences and will need to concentrate in a few key strategic areas while at the same time reinforcing multi-disciplinary research.

  Sectorial research programmes could be launched in priority areas with specific thematic lines of research, and bringing together public stakeholders as well as industry to achieve agreed-upon common objectives. The development of technology roadmaps (taking into account lessons learnt from roadmaps carried out previously in the health, biotechnology and cybersecurity sectors/areas) and consultation with stakeholders will help define research necessities in priority sectors. This, in turn, should become the thematic lines of research in sectorial competitive research calls. It is fundamental to ensure the appropriate allocation of resources for the implementation of sectorial (industry/sector or technology-focused) agendas.

- *Support and encourage universities to develop clear strategies guiding their research and technology transfer activities.*

  Specific financial support could be provided to encourage HEIs which commit to develop and implement institutional strategies (e.g. the Institutional Strategies scheme under the Excellence Initiative in Germany). Some of them, in particular smaller sized local universities, could play a pivotal role in developing technology transfer projects in co-operation with local producers, including SMEs and service providers, and in close contact with local public authorities (e.g. through innovation centres – as proposed earlier). These universities should also have access to public support for their technology diffusion activities. They could become key partners of the regional innovation centres proposed earlier.

- *Widen the approach to university technology transfer and recognise this diversity of channels in performance evaluations for both research organisations and scientists.*

  A better balance is needed between intellectual property-based technology commercialisation and traditional technology transfer activities such as R&D collaboration and contracting research for industry, training, technology extension services, two-way mobility of researchers or joint PhD programmes. Given the low level of R&D in the business sector, these traditional modes of technology transfer should potentially have a higher impact on industrial innovation than intellectual property.

- *Adopt clear policies for strengthening research infrastructure, its development and maintenance, establish a national research infrastructure plan and conduct periodical inventory assessments.*

  Developing a national strategy for research infrastructure could facilitate the development of regional to world-class research groups in selected and strategic areas, as research infrastructures act as focal points to attract top scientists wishing to benefit from unique facilities. In the Malaysian case, medium-sized research infrastructure could optionally be developed in various domains such as health (e.g. biobanks related to selective diseases), agronomy (e.g. seeds and biodiversity collections), nanotechnologies (e.g. clean facilities), computing (e.g. super computer node). This could put Malaysia in a privileged position to participate in the possible development of an ASEAN research infrastructure roadmap and lead collaborative projects on research infrastructures at regional level.

Enhancing the contribution of public research institutes to innovation

PRIs play an important role in Malaysia's innovation system, basically through their activities in applied research, technology transfer, or information and monitoring services. There is no unique profile of a PRI; their level of development and types of activities vary widely, reflecting differences in mission, governance and funding structures. The degree of autonomy differs as well but is weak in many cases, particularly in ministry-related PRIs. For these, the governing ministry has complete oversight regarding the management, funding and regulatory issues governing the individual institutions. In an effort to enhance the efficacy and efficiency of public sector organisations, the government has initiated the corporatisation of several public research-related institutions since the 1990s, such as the Standards and Industrial Research Institute of Malaysia (SIRIM), the Malaysia Institute of Microlectronics System (MIMOS) and Technology Park Malaysia.

Overall, the research and technology transfer capacity of these institutions remains underdeveloped – which reflects difficulties in funding and a lack of strategy. The government is the main source of finance for R&D in PRIs, providing, on average, more than 90% of funding. Research funding is distributed through a multitude of sources, including managing ministries (in the case of sectorial PRIs with a public good orientation), the Economic Planning Unit (EPU), the Ministry of Finance, etc. Often, the

EPU in the Prime Minister's Department provides block grants to various PRIs to carry out top-down directed research.

PRIs have seen their R&D funding and personnel vary drastically over time. Exceptions are cess-funded (commodity-oriented statuary) PRIs, which seem better funded than the rest. Cess-funded PRIs like the Malaysian Palm Oil Board (MPOB), the Malaysian Cocoa Board (MCB) and the Malaysian Rubber Board (MRB) have higher R&D budgets – their expenditure is twice the expenditure on agricultural research conducted by the Malaysian Agricultural Research and Development Institute (MARDI), the main agriculture research agency.

As stated in the PRA assessment, a number of PRIs still do not have the critical mass to make a significant contribution and fulfil their mandate. Infrastructure and the quality of equipment widely differ across organisations, and some PRIs have not seen their equipment updated in years. Over the years, several PRIs have expanded their scope by engaging in new activities and disciplines, although somewhat missing the focus of the original mission for which they were created. Changing policy priorities and regulations, the multiplication of funding sources and agencies, as well as the pressure to strengthen commercialisation, have contributed to this trend.

The purpose and role of PRIs (develop tools for policies, monitor regulations, facilitate technology transfer, etc.) is, in fact, not always clearly defined in missions and this situation in part reflects weak guidance from the part of stakeholders – in the case of statutory PRIs – or weak stakeholder/client relations. The lack of guidance of national strategic plans regarding the role that these institutions should play in deploying new efforts has undermined the visibility and funding of PRIs. This has also left ambiguity on how they should relate to national efforts.

Although a number of PRIs have demonstrated their capacity to develop technologies useful to stakeholders, particularly statutory PRIs with industry orientation, connection with the business sector remains very uneven and unsatisfactory overall. A recent assessment has noted some improvements in performance, but also highlighted some overlaps and institutional inflexibilities (e.g. hiring of new personal – ministry and statuary PRIs are subject to Public Service Department regulations) that prevent scale-dependent research and more long-term collaboration with industry.

Some exceptions apart, research institutes seem to be less prepared to pursue commercialisation and intellectual property (IP) activity than universities. PRIs face larger administrative barriers, budget cuts on research and a less adaptive culture that until recently put little emphasis on collaboration with the private sector or on producing IP. These institutions, however, have very different profiles, and this situation calls for a careful appreciation of their outcomes and achievements.

In conjunction with stakeholders and governing agencies, a comprehensive modernisation and reorganisation of PRIs is needed – as recognised in the PRA assessment. This process will entail first assessing the potential of each public research institute to contribute to innovation and the ways in which they might do so. In a second stage – for those showing a potential for change – an in-depth revision of their mission and objectives should be undertaken followed by a new injection of resources based on performance-based funding mechanisms.

Action plans and funding should follow, with a more healthy balance between block funding and project funding and enhanced use of performance-based funding mechanisms. In the articulation of modernisation plans, legal and regulatory frameworks need to be revisited as well as accountability frameworks – in line with performance engagements and resource utilisation.

Main recommendation

Reform and modernise the public research institutes based on an assessment of their respective mission, competences and governance. Enable those assessed favourably to develop their strengths by complementing their own revenues through a healthy mix of competitive and institutional funding, subject to regular evaluation. For the remaining institutes consider other options, including their merger, downsizing or discontinuation, if required.

Other recommendations

- *Conduct an in-depth assessment of individual PRI's technological competences and management in order to define their potential for change and the extent of the modernisation needed.*

  The NSRC's 2013 PRA assessment showed the diversity of PRIs and identified common challenges and bottlenecks – especially in terms of regulatory frameworks and governance. Building on the results of this study, a review of each PRI's technological competences (research capacity and portfolio, as well as outcomes including intellectual property portfolio) and resources (e.g. staff, qualifications and infrastructure), and the way resources are obtained and used will help redefine their respective focus and evolution, and identify the best ways to improve their results in terms of transfer of knowledge and technology, and support to the domestic industry.

- *Sharpen PRIs' mission under the leadership of directing agencies and stakeholders.*

  For many PRIs, especially those with weak autonomy or limited decision making, modernisation or reform might not occur without a strong leadership and direction of managing or governing agencies or ministries – to which they are attached or related. For some PRIs, this revision will require refocusing core competencies and areas where they perform the best or have the potential to improve. The type of activities and engagements might also change across PRIs – depending upon the directions and agendas agreed with stakeholders. The results of the assessment should help clarify the PRI's roles and engagements. For some PRIs, traditional forms of knowledge transfer, such as advisory services and technology extension (e.g. adaptation of existing technologies and their diffusion), might remain a priority while for others enhancing technology commercialisation through IP and licensing (those with growing research capacity) might become a new formal engagement.

- *Consider the different options available for PRIs' governance reform and efficiency improvement.*

  Among the options for restructuring are: 1) merging institutions with the potential for synergies; 2) corporatisation of PRIs; 3) transformation of certain ministry/division PRIs into statutory organisations; internal restructuring with no governance change or liquidation/closure. These options are not exclusive of one another; a combination of them could be considered.

- *For those PRIs with enhanced potential for improvement, augment funding through performance-based mechanisms to implement modernisation plans and expand research and technology transfer capacity.*

  One example is the use of performance contracts, which are widely applied in OECD countries. These are comprehensive contracts reflecting an "agreement" between parties (typically universities or PRIs and funding ministries/departments) regarding the activities to be delivered, resources, and timelines and result metrics. Performance-based contracts therefore contribute to a more efficient allocation of resources through steering (at least at the margin) and encourage institutions to set goals and develop their own strategies to achieve them. This instrument can be applied in conjunction with the sectorial policy of the "principal" ministry/department of the PRI, or the industry stakeholders to which the PRI are associated (statutory PRIs).

- *Define and implement performance evaluation of PRIs periodically, following best practices.*

  Although the mission and objectives of PRIs might vary, these institutions should be subject to periodical performance evaluation by their funding agencies. Evaluation helps assess the use of research outcomes and progress in the achievement of agendas. At the institutional level, international peer review may be useful as it helps benchmark with global practice.

- *Enable PRIs to better access competitive research funding.*

  Ensure that PRIs are able to compete and access resources available through competitive schemes for research and technology commercialisation. This will entail training for drafting research proposals, improving research agendas internally, as well as revisiting eligibility criteria in calls for proposals.

- *Enhance linkages between universities and PRIs through joint formation of advanced human resources (PhD programmes and training), research collaboration and sharing of equipment.*

  Increasing the interaction between the two types of core research actors will foster synergies and efficiency of public investment, and contribute to higher quality research and improve its impact.

Strengthening the human resource base and skills for innovation

Over the last decade, Malaysia has undertaken important efforts to improve the national human capital base and the level of skills in order to respond to the evolving human and economic development needs. While important steps have been made to improve the level of education and the quality and supply of competences, access to qualified personnel and lack of skills are still among the important bottlenecks firms encounter in their attempts to invest in innovation and improve productivity.

According to the World Bank Enterprise Survey, the inadequate workforce is the most important obstacle in the business environment (quoted by 33% of firms in Malaysia, as opposed to the average of 10% of firms in Southeast Asian countries). The *Global Competitiveness Report* (2015-16) also stresses human capital and training as one of the weakest pillars of national competitiveness as perceived by firms.

This situation reflects a combination of challenges. First, a shortage of skills prevails in numerous domains and this gap concerns not only the demand for university graduates but also for specialised technicians. The still relatively low share of science and engineering students in Malaysian higher education remains an important handicap to boosting innovation in industry. Migration of graduates and post-graduates accentuated the lack of qualified professionals for local industry.

Second, an important mismatch prevails between supply and demand for skills whilst the quality of higher education remains a great concern. Malaysia needs to improve the relevance and quality of skills across the board – in both tertiary education and technical and vocational education and training (TVET). In quantitative terms, the levels of education and number of graduates have improved dramatically over the last decade but quality is often questioned, as reflected in the dissatisfaction of companies and the unemployment among graduates. In terms of highly skilled human capital, those with masters and doctorate degrees are still weakly integrated in the business sector. This reflects deficiencies in terms of information and weak connections of industry and higher education and research.

Improving and expanding TVET for industry needs remains an important task on the higher education agenda. The number of students undertaking TVET courses remains far below mainstream higher education. For a long time, TVET remained poorly considered and underfunded compared to mainstream higher education. The need to raise its status to that of higher academic education was well identified in the review of the Higher Education Blueprint 2015-25. Nevertheless, a number of challenges remain, including the need for improved relationships with business, the sometimes insufficient skills of the staff and the lack of identified pathways for bright TVET students to pass to high-quality mainstream HEIs.

There has been a significant increase in the number of institutions and students in the area of TVET. However, the diversity of the number of institutions combined with the absence of a unified system of accreditation *ex ante* and evaluation *ex post* has led to problems of quality and relevance of training programmes. An insufficient level of capabilities of instructors and their limited linkages with industry have hindered the TVET system to respond adequately to rapidly evolving needs for skills.

Mainstreaming and broadening access to TVET were at the heart of the main actions undertaken during the Tenth Malaysia Plan to increase the relevance and impact of the sector. Further efforts are foreseen in the Eleventh Malaysia Plan to better address industry demands by improving system delivery and increasing the attractiveness of TVET courses as an option.

Addressing these challenges will require continued strengthening of Malaysia's skills and education system – in line with the different human development engagements defined in the Higher Education Blueprint 2015-25, the Eleventh Malaysia Plan and the Human Capital Development (HCD) Strategic Reform Initiative (SRI) contained in the Economic Transformation Programme. This will also involve activating skills supply by removing regulatory barriers to hiring and mobility and using skills effectively – making full use of skills in the workplace to strengthen productivity and better matching supply with demand.

Some of these issues are currently addressed in the HCD SRI, led by the Ministry of Human Resources. This strategy focuses on enhancing and addressing the human capital capabilities and needs of the 12 national key economic areas (NKEAs) as well as strengthening the skills of Malaysia's workforce. A series of regulatory reforms (e.g. current update of the Industrial Relations Act 1967 and the Employment Act 1955) and support programmes are currently in the process of being implemented. Among its initiatives are upskilling and upgrading of the workforce (in the 12 NKEAs) and strengthening the human resource management of Malaysian SMEs. The former comprise implementing sector-specific manpower training programmes.

The main challenge in ensuring the performance of these plans is not to fine-tune the diagnostics or devise new actions, but to put in place adequate implementation procedures, monitor their results in a clear and transparent way, and adapt and pursue efforts accordingly. A second institutional challenge key to their success is ensuring the linkages between the different strategic programmes to ensure synergies and efficiency in the allocation of resources. The linkages are not always clear and the relationships to the innovation agenda (and national science and technology plans) are not always clearly defined.

Equally fundamental is making headway in setting up sectorial skills agendas for the NKEAs for which co-ordination across stakeholders is a key to success. As foreseen in the HCD, this requires engaging industry, educational institutions and the government to develop sustainable sector-led approaches to address skills necessities in each priority sector. A first exercise was carried out in 2012 for the oil, gas and energy NKEA. Lessons from this exercise can nourish new developments.

Main recommendation

Improve the match between the supply of skills and the needs of industry, *inter alia* by including industry in curricula development, improving the delivery of the TVET system and increasing the attractiveness of TVET courses. Focus at this stage on the implementation of the various blueprints and plans and set up a mandatory schedule to evaluate the outcomes of these initiatives.

Other recommendations

- *Establish synergies* (collaborative mechanisms such as joint launching of funding programmes and joint work in the preparation of sectorial agendas) *between the Human Capital Development Strategic Reform Initiative and the other national strategy plans related to skills development and qualification, such as the Higher Education Blueprint 2015-25 and the Eleventh Malaysia Plan.*
- *Improve the match with industry demands by involving business representatives in the development of education curricula, and better align the composition of graduate output across disciplines with evolving demand.*
- *Enhance mobility programmes and funding for the placement of highly skilled human capital – such as Masters of Science and PhDs – to support their integration in the productive sector.*
- *Implement, monitor and evaluate regularly against objectives to allow policy makers to measure progress and adjust programmes if needed.*
- *Ensure adequate inter-ministerial co-ordination of the various initiatives addressing issues in higher education and TVET.*

Chapter 2.

Macroeconomic performance and framework conditions for innovation in Malaysia

This chapter provides an overview of Malaysia's macroeconomic performance. It begins with an examination of Malaysia's rapid growth and structural change in the context of its long-term economic trajectory since its independence. It next looks at the significant challenges the country has been facing since the 1997 Asian financial crisis, in particular due to the weakening of two of the main sources of growth: capital accumulation and productivity. The chapter then considers the current state of framework conditions for innovation.

Malaysia is one of Asia's great success stories. It has succeeded in developing into an upper middle-income country, and is now close to passing the high-income threshold. It has shown robust growth over most of the period since its independence, while transforming the structure of its economy and integrating into the global economy, not least through foreign direct investment (FDI) and participation in global value chains (GVCs). However, while Malaysia has been growing robustly for an extended period of time, growth has not always been smooth. The period of high growth in the 1990s was brutally interrupted by the Asian financial crisis of 1997, and with lasting effects. While the Malaysian economy recovered from the crisis, economic growth has not since achieved pre-crisis levels. Following the Asian financial crisis, Malaysia also lost some ground to other Southeast Asian economies with economic growth averaging 4.6% over the decade 2000-09. Malaysia was hit hard again by the global financial and economic crisis, with gross domestic product (GDP) dropping significantly in 2009, albeit less severely than a decade earlier. Current official forecasts are in the range of 4-5%. This is well below the average growth rate recorded during the four decades since Malaysia's independence, and is also below the growth target of 6.5% per year set in 2010 in the New Economic Model for the period 2011-20 (NEAC, 2010).

Furthermore, per capita income gaps *vis-à-vis* advanced countries are still high. There are clear signs that the dynamism of the Malaysian economy has considerably lessened over time. Two of the main sources of growth, capital accumulation and productivity, have shown signs of exhaustion further to the 1997 Asian financial crisis. The contribution of labour productivity to per capita GDP growth has dropped, from 3.7 percentage points (1990-00) to 2.1 percentage points (2000-12). The growth of multi-factor productivity – which measures the overall efficiency of the use of factors of production – was relatively weak in 2000-13, notably when seen in an Asian context. The rate of investment has also dropped drastically since the pre-crisis 1990s. The rates of investment achieved in the post-crisis years could not have sustained growth at the rates achieved before the crisis. Finally, Malaysia has also shown weaknesses in its export performance, indicated in some loss of market shares.

Economic performance and structural change

Economic development

Since its independence in 1957, Malaysia's economic performance has for the most part been impressive, with the result that Malaysia long ago entered the group of middle-income countries. Over an extended period of time Malaysia achieved robust annual growth in GDP, exceeding 7% in the 1970s and 1990s (Figure 2.1). Malaysia's economic growth even passed the 10% benchmark in some years. Since the end of the 1990s, the GDP trend growth has been around 5% per year (punctuated by the recession in 2009). Short-term official forecasts for 2016 are in the range of 4-5%.

With a gross national income (GNI) of USD 11 120 per capita (using current USD) in 2014,[1] Malaysia places well in the upper middle-income range, not distant from the high-income threshold.[2] Apart from Singapore (a city state and *entrepôt* economy with specific characteristics) and Brunei Darussalam (an economy largely based on oil resources), Malaysia has achieved the highest level of GDP per capita among the ten Association of Southeast Asian Nations (ASEAN)[3] countries, ahead of Thailand and Indonesia (Figure 2.2).

Figure 2.1. **Growth of GDP, Malaysia, 1960-2014**

Average annual rate

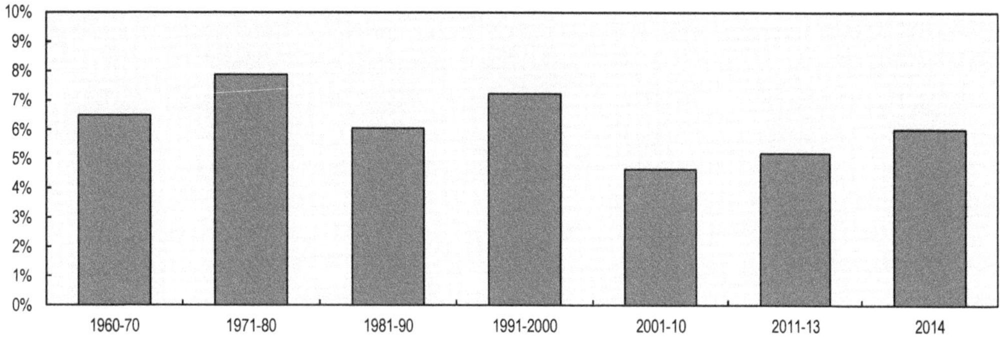

Source: World Bank (2015b), *World Development Indicators* (database), http://data.worldbank.org/data-catalog/world-development-indicators.

To achieve this level of per capita income, Malaysia – like other countries in East Asia – used export-led manufacturing based to a large extent on FDI to emulate the success of the first wave of "Asian Tigers"[4] to build manufacturing capacity, which was at the core of its export-led model (Yusuf and Nabeshima, 2009). The government was instrumental in attracting multinational enterprises (MNEs) to locate in Malaysia, including by offering generous incentives, tax relief and subsidised investment loans.

Figure 2.2. **GDP per capita of Southeast Asian countries, 2005 and 2014**

Current USD PPP

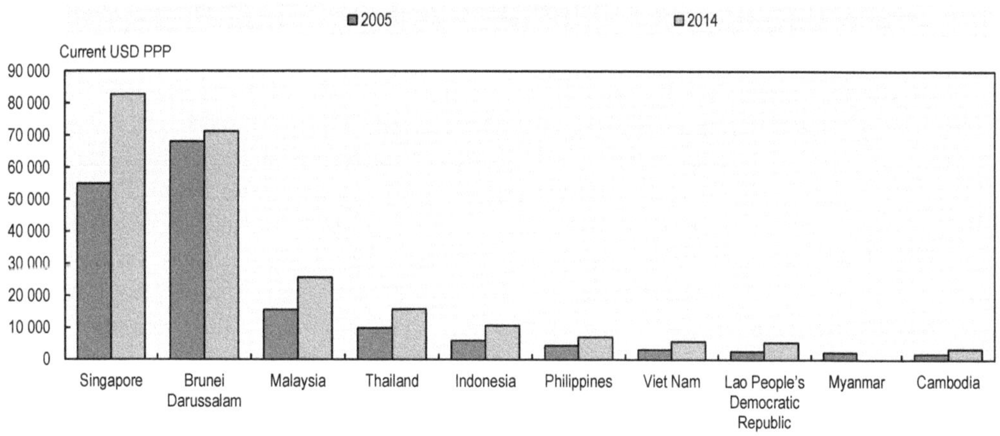

Source: World Bank (2015b), *World Development Indicators* (database), http://data.worldbank.org/data-catalog/world-development-indicators.

Wider social progress

Malaysia's success is not confined to the economic dimension. It can also be demonstrated in a much broader set of indicators on areas impinging on many important aspects of life. This is reflected, for example, by Malaysia's "high human development" according to the 2013 United Nations Development Programme's (UNDP) Human Development Index (HDI).[5] Among the 185 UN member countries listed in the HDI, Malaysia ranks 64th – like Libya and Serbia, above Turkey, Mexico and Brazil, and marginally below such countries as Argentina, the Russian Federation and Latvia.[6] The emergence of a middle class has strengthened domestic demand for more sophisticated consumer goods and services which, in turn, may help stimulate manufacturing capabilities and services innovation. Moreover, during the past half-century Malaysia has built world-class physical infrastructures (roads, air transport facilities, rail, energy and water supplies; see the section on framework conditions below) and major knowledge infrastructures (notably an extensive system of universities and research institutes) that bode well for the future. There has been very significant urbanisation with some problems of transport congestion but none of the slum development or heavy environmental damage seen in many other cities.

Structural change

Malaysia's economic success would not have been possible without a profound transformation of its economy. Since independence, Malaysia has moved from an economy based on primary commodities to one driven by manufacturing and, increasingly, services. Throughout the colonial period, and for some time after independence, Malaysia's economy was based on a number of resource-based industries: tin mining and processing, rubber, cocoa, timber and rice. Later on, as a dedicated government effort to diversify, new resource-based industries were encouraged and developed rapidly, notably oil and gas,[7] as well as palm oil. Post-independence development has maintained the growth of these industries. The most important change was the development of manufacturing, especially in electronic and electrical (E&E) products, which became the motor of Malaysia's export-led growth. Government policy to attract MNEs through favourable framework conditions, specific incentives and the provision of infrastructure was an important factor contributing to this success. The government's industrialisation programme of the first half of the 1980s favoured, with mixed success, large-scale and capital-intensive projects including in steel, machinery and equipment, petrochemicals, cement and automobile manufacturing.

As a result, industry value added increased from 19% of GDP in 1960 to 40% in 2014, largely mirrored by a decline in the share of agriculture from 34% to 8.9%, while the share of services has recorded a mildly increasing trend since the first half of the 1970s, to 51% today (Figure 2.3). Malaysia has undergone a more profound structural transformation than the ASEAN region, which follows similar secular trends. The share of employment in agriculture in Malaysia (13% in 2012) is significantly lower than in ASEAN countries (apart from Singapore, for obvious reasons), which concur with the argument that the potential for the reallocation of labour from agriculture to other sectors has become limited (Box 2.1). This argument plays an important role in assessing scenarios of Malaysia's future economic development.

Between 1960 and 2000, Malaysia's manufacturing sector recorded a strong expansion, from 8% of GDP to a peak of 31%. By 2014, the manufacturing share declined to 23%, however. Seen over the past 35 years, Malaysia differs markedly from developments observed in other countries and world regions. In Southeast Asia overall, the expansion of the share of manufacturing in GDP was less pronounced than in Malaysia but lasted until the mid-2000s, when it also started to decline (Figure 2.4). In line with considerations of economic theory, in the European Union the relative weight of manufacturing showed a declining trend during the 1980s, and an accelerated pace since 1990. The same applies to the United States; advanced Asian countries also followed that pattern. A number of countries in Latin American and other world regions underwent a process that has been termed "premature deindustrialisation" (see, for example, OECD, 2014b).

Figure 2.3. **GDP by sector, Malaysia and ASEAN countries, 1960-2013**

Malaysia | ASEAN average

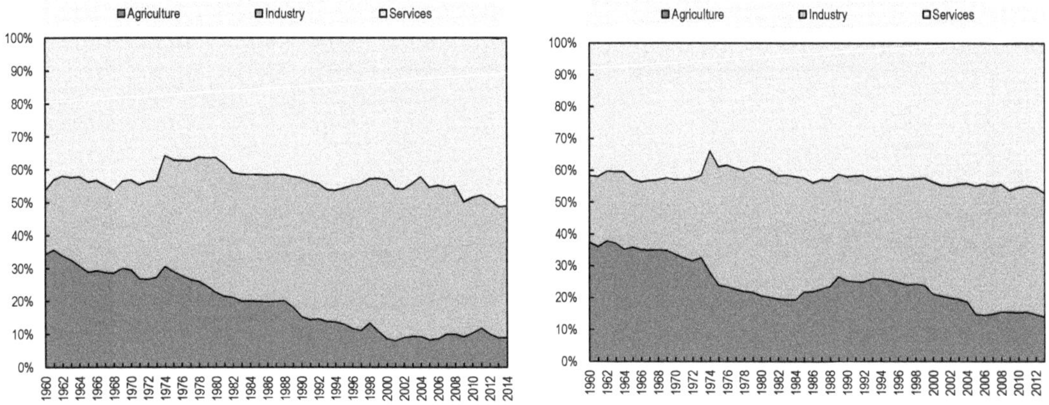

Source: World Bank (2015b), *World Development Indicators* (database), http://data.worldbank.org/data-catalog/world-development-indicators.

Box 2.1. **Intersectoral reallocation of labour in the development process**

In the early stages of industrial development, it is structural change – the evolution of the sectoral composition of the economy – that provides most of the initial gains in total factor productivity. The transfer of labour and resources from low-productivity employment in subsistence farming and small-scale rural industry to urban industry and services results in a leap in factor productivity. This continues until much of the excess rural workforce is depleted or, to use different terminology, until the economy has reached the Lewis turning point as agricultural labour becomes scarcer and agricultural productivity and wages rise (Lewis, 1954). Herrendorf, Rogerson and Valentinyi (2013) provide a detailed review of the literature, analysing the process of structural change and its relationship to growth. Effectively, the turning point arrives when the mobile population in the 18-45 age group has migrated to urban areas. The People's Republic of China (hereafter "China") is rapidly approaching this point.

This process can last for two decades or more depending on growth in demand for labour in the urban sector. Viet Nam is still some distance from that turning point (45% of the population was still engaged in primary activities in 2010, down from 59% in 2002). China may be approaching the turning point, and India may still be a long way from completing the transition. The urbanisation of the economy can confer productivity gains through agglomeration economies (Glaeser and Gottlieb, 2009) and a greening of urban development with an eye to the implications of global warming, rising energy prices and emerging technological opportunities. As intersectoral resource transfers stabilise and a country begins approaching the technology frontier, home-grown innovation acquires a more important role. Sustaining rapid growth depends more on promoting innovative activity and on the commercial success of innovations. To maintain economic growth, the economy will have to rely more on within-industry productivity growth.

According to the OECD (2014c), middle-income countries such as Malaysia, and to a greater extent India and Indonesia, still have (varying) margins to shift labour from lower productivity sectors (agricultural) to higher productivity sectors (agricultural, industry and service). It was still an important factor of labour productivity growth in many countries between 2000 and 2009, including in India, Indonesia, Mexico and Turkey.

Source: Adapted from OECD and World Bank (2014), *Science, Technology and Innovation in Viet Nam*, http://dx.doi.org/10.1787/9789264213500-en.

Figure 2.4. **Evolution of the share of manufacturing in GDP, Malaysia and selected world regions, 1980-2013**

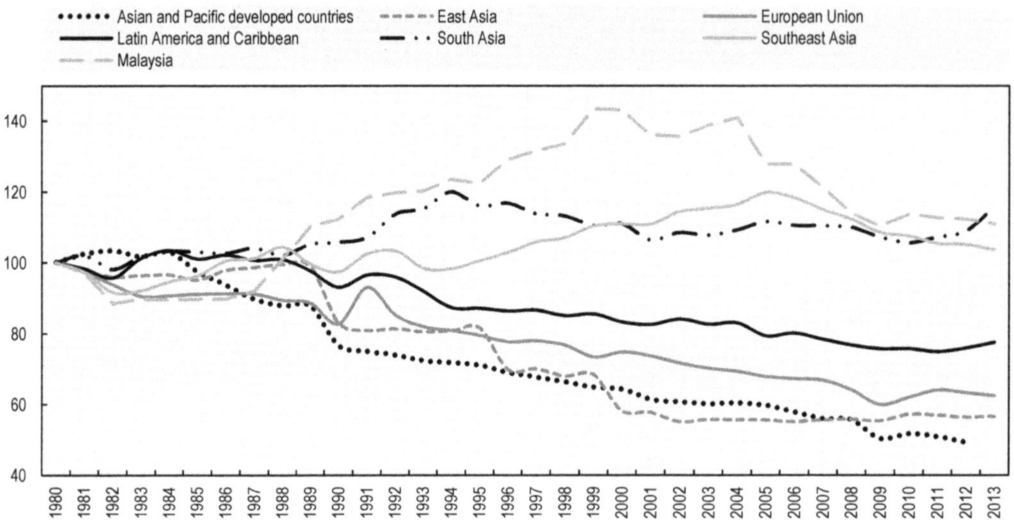

Note: 1980=100.

Source: World Bank (2015b), *World Development Indicators* (database), http://data.worldbank.org/data-catalog/world-development-indicators.

Since 2000 the share of manufacturing in value added has decreased while the weight in services has increased (Figure 2.5). The service sector now accounts for more than half of Malaysia's GDP (51.2% in 2014) and is continuing to grow (Figure 2.6); in recent years, the service sector's value added has grown at a faster pace than value added in manufacturing.[8] As could be expected, this trend contrasts with the transformation of other, more recently emerging ASEAN economies such as Cambodia, Lao PDR, Myanmar and Viet Nam, where the share of industry in total value added increased markedly (ERIA, 2014). Only recently – and to a lesser extent – has the share of services become more prominent in Southeast Asian countries, reaching 31% of GDP in Brunei Darussalam and 75% in Singapore in 2014 (close to the level of the most advanced countries, e.g. 78% in the United States and 73% in Japan in 2013).

Challenges to becoming a high-income economy

Persisting gap with advanced economies and the "middle-income trap"

Notwithstanding Malaysia's robust growth performance, the gap *vis-à-vis* the advanced economies in terms of GDP per head is still large (Figure 2.7). In fact, the gap *vis-à-vis* the average and, even more, the top-performing OECD countries, increased. In addition, there have been concerns over the slow pace at which Malaysia has been advancing towards the high-income threshold. At a level of GNI per capita at USD 11 120 (current USD, Atlas method) in 2013, Malaysia reached the lower middle-income threshold in 1969 and crossed the higher middle-income threshold in 1996 (i.e. 27 years later). The optimism of the authorities at the beginning of the 2000s, forecasting average annual growth at 7.5% (supported by a total factor productivity [TFP] contribution of 3.2%) over the 2000s, growth remained in the range of 5% (Woo, 2009). As of 2015, Malaysia has thus spent 46 years in the middle-income category, including 19 years in its upper tier. By comparison, Korea, which joined the middle-income group of countries the same year as Malaysia, reached the upper middle-income level as early as 1988 (i.e. within 19 years) and achieved high-income status in 1995 (i.e. within another 7 years; see Table 2.1). China has achieved the most rapid transition since the 1950s, advancing from lower (1992) to upper middle-income (2009) status within 17 years (Felipe, 2012). These delays and signs of weakening economic dynamism – some of which have been mentioned above – have nourished concerns that Malaysia may be facing what has become to be known as the "middle-income trap" (Box 2.2). According to Felipe (2012),[9] Malaysia was, as of 2010, the only Asian country in the "upper middle-income trap".

Figure 2.5. **Share of sectors in GDP, Malaysia, 1990-2014**

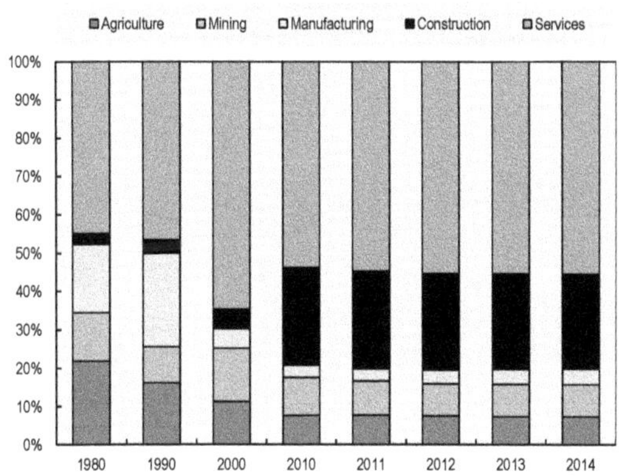

Source: APO (2014), *APO Productivity Databook 2014.*

Figure 2.6. **Share of services in GDP, Malaysia and selected countries, 2000 and 2014**

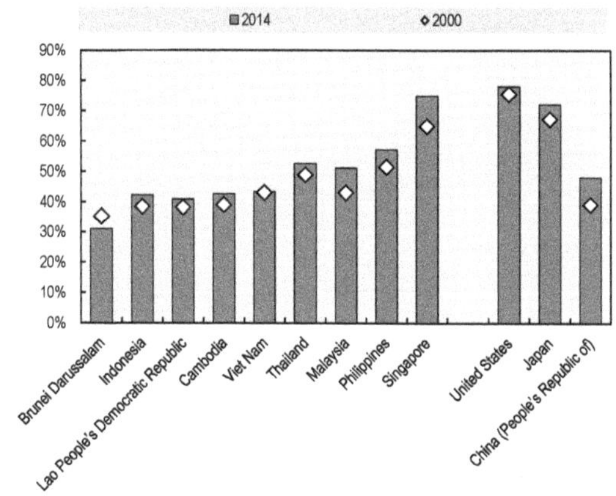

Note: Data for Brunei Darussalam, Japan and the United States are for 2013.

Source: World Bank (2015b), *World Development Indicators* (database), http://data.worldbank.org/data-catalog/world-development-indicators.

Figure 2.7. **Gap between Malaysia's GNI per capital and the United States and the high-income threshold, 1987-2013**

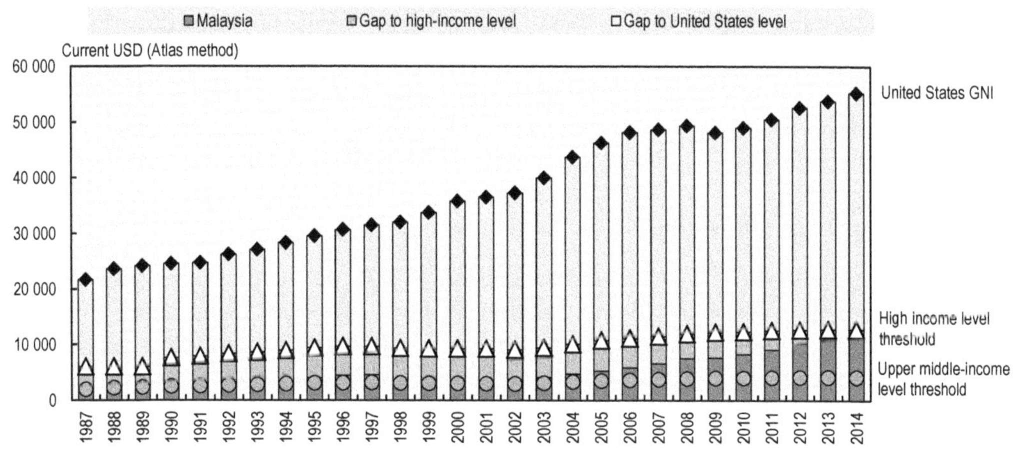

Source: World Bank (2015b), *World Development Indicators* (database), http://data.worldbank.org/data-catalog/world-development-indicators.

Table 2.1. **Transitions between the World Bank income categories since 1950, selected Asian countries**

	1950s	1960s	1970s	1980s	1990s	2000s
Upper middle-income to high-income			Japan (1977)	Hong Kong (China) (1983) Singapore (1988)	Chinese Taipei (1993) Korea (1995)	
Lower middle-income to upper middle-income		Hong Kong (China) (1976) Japan (1968)	Singapore (1978)	Chinese Taipei (1986) Korea (1988)	**Malaysia (1996)**	Thailand (2004) China (People's Republic of) (2009)
Low-income to lower middle-income	Japan (1951)	**Malaysia (1969)** Korea (1969) Chinese Taipei (1967)	Thailand (1976) Philippines (1976)	Indonesia (1986)	China (People's Republic of) (1992)	
Low-income	Lao People's Democratic Republic Cambodia Myanmar Viet Nam					

According to Ohno (2009), neither Malaysia nor Thailand have succeeded so far in breaking through the divide between the stage of "technology absorption" – characterised by a situation where a domestic supplier base has emerged but MNEs still dominate the industry – and the stage of "creativity" – where the country has internalised skills and knowledge and acquired the capacity to create new products. Yusuf and Nabeshima (2009) found that in the important electronics industry, there is little evidence of technological deepening and rising value added despite some success stories. Rasiah (2010) provides a more nuanced assessment. According to his findings, the technological capabilities of Malaysian electronics firms have increased significantly, but he also states that their participation in the most technology-intensive activities is still very low. For a further discussion on this point, see Chapter 4.

However, Malaysia is approaching the high-income threshold[10] and can be expected to cross it in due time. According to the "best scenario" projection based on historical growth trends, achieving high-income status by 2020 is well within reach for Malaysia (OECD, 2014a).[11] This is a major achievement and a good occasion to look beyond 2020. There is a continuing challenge to transform and revitalise the Malaysian economy in order to continue the catch-up process vigorously, with innovation playing a major part.

Productivity growth slowdown

The difference between the level of Malaysia's GDP per capita and that of the United States – and more generally in relation to most advanced economies – can be attributed to a combination of differences in labour productivity and, to a small part, labour utilisation. Figure 2.8 shows that the income gap of Southeast Asian countries to the United States can indeed be almost entirely attributed to lagging labour productivity. The gap in relation to the United States increased between 2000 and 2008 for large emerging economies such as Brazil, Mexico and Turkey (OECD, 2014a). This is not the case for Malaysia, where the gap in GDP per capita to that of the United States has been narrowing compared to 1995 as a result of decreasing differences in both labour utilisation and productivity. Malaysia reduced its gap in labour productivity from -56 to -51. While Singapore reversed the gap to its advantage from -2 to +19 and Thailand reduced it from -87 to -82, other Southeast Asian countries recorded a widening gap (APO, 2015).

Figure 2.8. **Income gap relative to the United States, 2013**

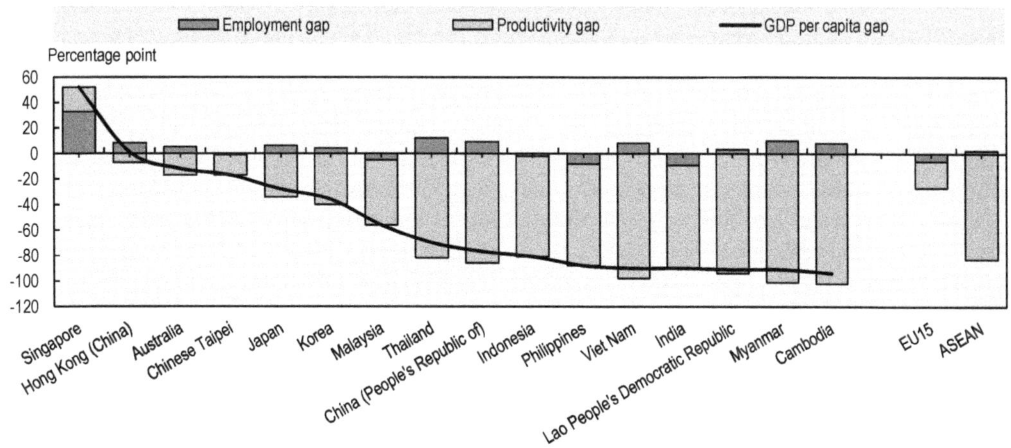

Note: Labour productivity is defined as real GDP per worker; the employment rate is measured as the number of workers relative to the population. Decomposition of per capita GDP gap at constant market prices using 2005 PPPs.

Source: APO (2015), *APO Productivity Databook 2015*.

While Malaysia has been catching up, it has yet to reach the level of productivity[12] achieved by the United States in the 1970s, and is currently lagging 20 years behind Japan and 25 behind Singapore (Figure 2.9). At the same time, Malaysian productivity levels are significantly higher than in most other Southeast Asian countries. However, there have been signs of weakening. Malaysia saw its labour productivity growth decrease from 3.3% during the 1990s to 2.3% over the period 2000-12 (APO, 2014).[13]

The decomposition of growth into the contribution of accumulation of factors of production – (various types of) labour and capital – and TFP sheds light on some of the characteristics of Malaysia's development trajectory since the 1970s (Figure 2.10). Like in other catching-up economies, Malaysia's rapid growth over the period 1970-2000 was mainly driven by non-IT capital accumulation (accounting for more than half of the recorded growth during this period) and, to a lesser extent, by labour input (in the range of 20% in the 1970s and 1980s, then decreasing to about 10% in the 1980s) and TFP (increasing from 1% in the period 1970-85 to 6% in the period 1985-2000). IT capital[14] played a minor role during these three decades. In the aftermath of the Asian financial crisis, Malaysia has experienced not only a significant growth deceleration, but also important shifts in growth patterns. In particular, IT capital inputs have become more important, accounting for 13% of growth between 2000 and 2013, while the contribution of physical capital decreased by about half compared to the earlier period.[15] The contribution of TFP, however, decreased to 6% in 2010-13 (APO, 2015).[16]

Box 2.2. Malaysia and the middle-income trap

The so-called middle-income trap can be defined as a stage characterised by a slowdown in growth due to an inability to move up the value chain, away from factor-driven, export-dependent growth and into new innovation-driven industries.

According to development theories, the model of development of economies having achieved the transition from a low-income to a high-income status contains its own limitations at its very core. Besides national specificities, this growth model relies in many cases upon the transfer of labour inputs from low productivity, resource-based sectors to higher productivity industry and service sectors, and the accumulation of physical capital allowing important economies of scale in manufacturing. High volumes of production, consisting to a large part of low value-added final products and goods assembled from imported components, are mainly intended for exports. As the volume of potential transfer of labour diminishes, the average wages increase and, consequently, hinder these countries' comparative advantage in labour-intensive industries. Other economies formerly lagging behind but currently entering the process of industrialisation would then conquer increasing market shares in regional and global value chains based on their greater labour availability and, therefore, lower labour cost. This shift in regional production is reinforced by FDI flowing toward the newly emerging countries, partly at the expense of the development of the formerly fast-growing economies.

Middle-income countries are therefore compelled to carry out micro and macroeconomic, structural and institutional reforms in order to shift from an intrinsic/quantitative growth model based on factor accumulation, toward an extrinsic/qualitative growth model based on improvement of labour skills, ICT capital, production organisation and corresponding higher value-added services. However, besides their own domestic barriers hindering such a transition, these countries also face fierce competition from advanced economies in the high value-added manufacturing and service sectors. As it is argued by the precursors of this concept, the countries in the middle-income trap that do not grow fast enough to reach the high-income category find themselves "squeezed between the low-wage poor-country competitors that dominate in mature industries and the rich-country innovators that dominate in industries undergoing rapid technological change" (Gill and Kharas, 2007).

There are ongoing debates about what could be considered a reliable marker of an income "trap". Recent research has found that the slowdown tends to occur at different income levels (one around USD 10 000 and another around USD 15 000 of GDP per capita, constant PPP dollars) rather than at one single point in the country's development trajectory (Eichengreen, Park and Shin, 2013). Other scholars have argued that there is no such "trap", claiming that slowdowns can occur at any level of a developing country's per capita income. Recent history shows that several middle-income countries have experienced persistent difficulties in moving up the value chain, which keeps them at an upper middle-income level. This is, in particular, the case of several Latin American countries which reached the middle-income level decades ago.[1] Of the 13 countries which have succeeded in making the transition from middle- to high-income status since the 1960s, five were from East Asia – pioneering Japan and the four "Asian Tigers" of Hong Kong (China), Korea, Singapore and Chinese Taipei. However, the extent to which these countries' trajectories could offer a model for the "second generation" of Asian Tigers is a matter of debate since the geopolitical and institutional contexts have changed significantly in the last two decades (OECD, 2013a). In particular, international competition on product markets and the "market" for FDI has become more vigorous, not least due to the rapid rise of China and the evolution of global value chains, based on the fragmentation of production. In addition to the change in context, their initial conditions are different in the sense that the economy of newly emerging countries was mainly resource-based, with little prior industrialisation. This has further extended the time of transition, as it required building the intrinsic engine of growth almost "from scratch" and provided less incentives for private actors to do so in the absence of a strong policy. Ohno (2009) also argues that the catching up of latecomers appears more complicated than it was for the first wave of emerging economies for several reasons: these countries have fewer possibilities to protect their nascent industries; they lack a strong private sector comparable to those of Japan and Korea; and their governments fall short of having the industrial policy vision and capabilities to steer the development process.

1. According to Zhuang, Vandenberg and. Huang (2012), 28 countries have remained in the middle-income category since at least 1987, among them 14 are in Latin America (including Argentina, Brazil and Costa Rica) and 3 are in Asia (Malaysia, the Philippines and Thailand).

Figure 2.9. **Levels of labour productivity per hour worked, selected Asian countries, 1970-2013**

In constant market prices, 2011 PPPs

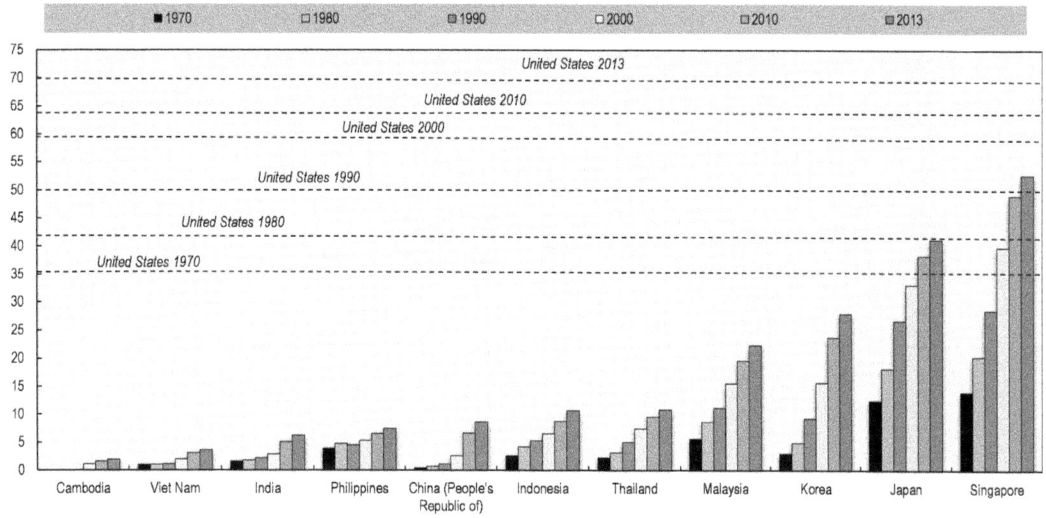

Source: APO (2015), *APO Productivity Databook 2015.*

The bulk of the contribution of the two traditional production factors to growth is made through factor accumulation rather than through a qualitative change: the improvement of labour quality only contributed 0.1% (out of the total 1.1% contribution of labour) to the 5.1% GDP growth over the period 2011-13. It accounted for a share of 2.4% of GDP, compared with 12.6% in Japan, 8.8% in Singapore, 8.4% in Korea and 7% in the United States (MPC, 2014). Despite its increase, non-IT capital exceeds by far the contribution of IT capital (35% versus 10% in 2010-12).

The evolution of the two determinants of labour productivity, TFP and capital intensity ("capital deepening"), during the period 1970-2013 shows that capital intensity remained high and TFP performance modest, both in terms of contribution (in percentage points) to growth and share in growth (0.5% growth, contributing 17% to the country's GDP growth between 1970 and 2012). While in the medium to long term capital deepening should translate into higher TFP and, as a result, an increase in labour productivity, this has yet to happen in Malaysia. This may relate to the fact that a large share of investment went into construction (between 45% and 47%), which contributes less to improving labour productivity. ICT and machinery and equipment accounted for only 9% and 14%, respectively, of total investment during this period, and the investment in intellectual property (IP) products represented at most 1.7% (MPC, 2014).

The manufacturing sector is crucial to the development of middle-income countries as it is often the main recipient of foreign technology, which can be then adopted and progressively adapted using domestic innovation capabilities. Between 1990 and 2000, Malaysia's manufacturing sector was the main contributor to economic growth (2.4% per year on average) and at a greater level than in any other Asian country – with the notable exception of China (4.4%). Over the period 2000-13, however, Malaysia's manufacturing growth – at an average annual growth rate of 1% – lagged behind that of several emerging economies. This concerns not only newly catching-up economies such as Myanmar (2.3%), Cambodia (1.8%) and Viet Nam (1.7%), but also Thailand (1.3%) and Chinese Taipei (1.8%) (APO, 2015).

Figure 2.10. **Contributions and shares of labour, capital and total factor productivity to GDP growth in Malaysia, in comparison with China and the United States, 1970-2013**

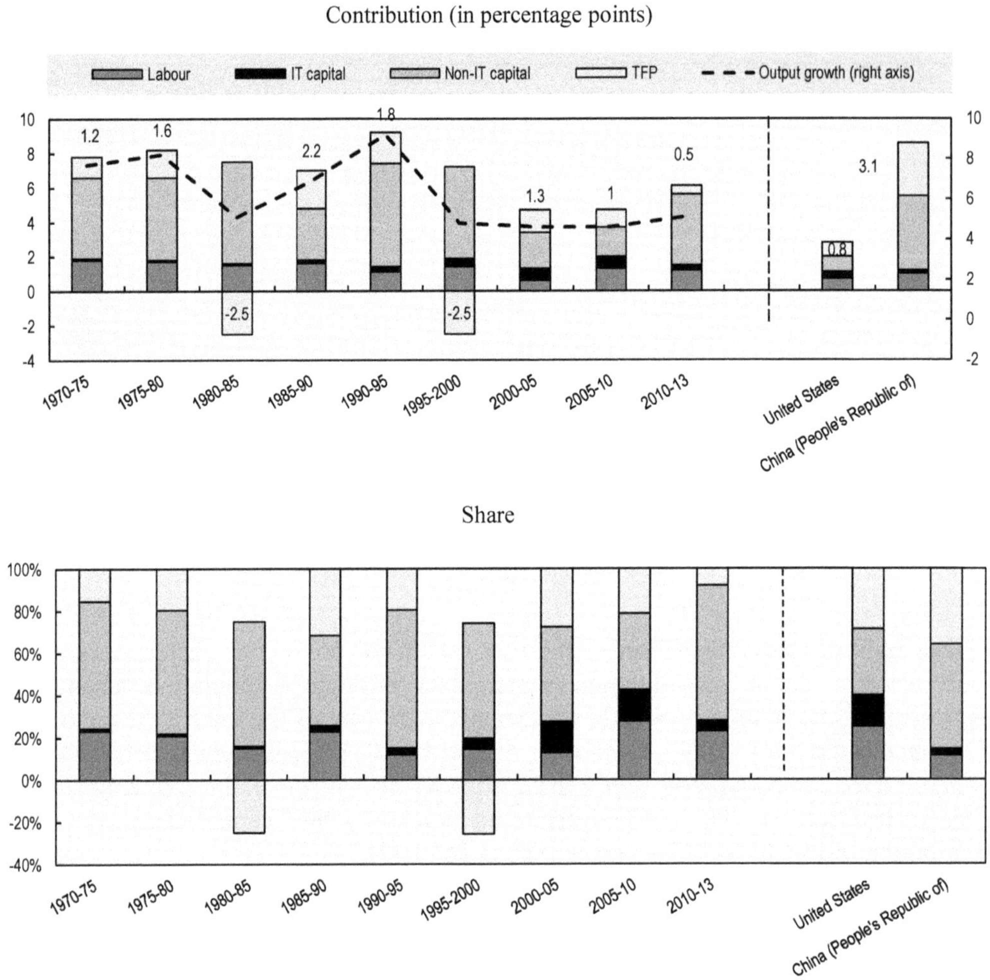

Notes: TFP = total factor productivity. Data for China and the United States are for 1970-2013.

Source: APO (2015), *APO Productivity Databook 2015*.

While the weight of value added in services in Southeast Asian economies increased rapidly, labour productivity in this sector remains low. With the exception of Hong Kong (China) and Singapore, the gap in relation to the level of service sector labour productivity achieved in advanced economies is even wider than in the respective gap in the manufacturing sector (Noland, Park and Estrada, 2012). This can be explained by the fact that most of these growing activities still consist of labour-intensive, "low-tech" services, such as often inefficient activities in wholesale and retail trade, and hotels and restaurants (OECD, 2014a). Labour productivity growth in the Malaysian service sector has accelerated, from 0.9% between 1980 and 2000 to 2.1% between 2000 and 2010, exceeding the growth achieved by other ASEAN countries (Park and Shin, 2012). It is, however, far below the productivity growth in major emerging Asian economies (8.1% in China and 5.4% in India).

The drop in gross capital formation

As mentioned above, growth of the Malaysian economy was largely supported by capital accumulation, including through FDI. However, the 1997 Asian financial crisis led to a dramatic slump of investment, from a record high of almost 45% of GDP in 1998 to about 22% in 2000. Investment has remained at a low level since and reached a low during the crisis in 2009. Since then the rate of investment has rebounded to levels above those recorded in the 2000s but still far below pre-crisis levels (25% of GDP in 2014).

FDI represents a significant but varying share of investment in Southeast Asia (Table 2.2). It has been predominant notably in Singapore, Cambodia, Brunei Darussalam and, to a lesser extent, Viet Nam. In Malaysia, the share of FDI in overall investment has remained in the middle range, above 15% of gross fixed capital formation in the 1990s and 2010s and around 12% in the 2000s (with an all-time low in 2001 at 2.1%) and again around 15% during the period 2010-14. The Asian financial crisis in 1997, and again the financial crisis in 2008, were associated with large outflows of FDI as investors repatriated part of their investment.

Table 2.2. **Inward foreign direct investment flows as a share of gross fixed capital formation**

In %

Country	1990-99	2000-09	2010-14
Malaysia	**15.9**	**12.1**	**14.8**
Brunei Darussalam	22.4	68.9	29.9
Cambodia	37.8	27.5	56.9
Indonesia	3.9	1.3	6.7
Lao People's Democratic Republic	20.5	9.8	x
Myanmar	38.7	20.6	22.9
Philippines	6.8	6.9	5.8
Singapore	35.3	68.7	79.6
Thailand	9.0	13.8	9.6
Viet Nam	31.1	16.3	21.7
China (People's Republic of)	11.1	7.7	3.3

Note: x = not applicable.

Source: UNCTAD (2015), *FDI Statistics Division on Investment and Enterprise* (database), http://unctad.org/en/Pages/DIAE/FDI%20Statistics/FDI-Statistics.aspx.

Asia and Europe are the most important sources of FDI in Malaysia (accounting respectively for 41% and 34% in 2011). The largest investors are Singapore, followed by Japan and the United States (OECD, 2013b). About half of these investments are in the manufacturing sector, in particular in the electronics industry, and one-quarter in the financial sector. The latter benefited from the government support designed to make Malaysia a global leader in Islamic finance (OECD, 2013b). The evolution and structure of FDI flows is all the more important as it is linked to the manufacturing performance. Empirical evidence suggests that there is a strong correlation between FDI (stocks) and manufacturing value added since building and maintaining manufacturing capabilities need sustained investment (ERIA, 2014).

Malaysia's trade performance and participation in global value chains

Through export-led industrialisation Malaysia transformed itself into Asia's third most open economy. The value of exports reached a peak at about 120% of GDP in 1999. Although the relative weight of Malaysian gross exports in its economy declined after that date, it still exceeds that of ASEAN economies on average (2013) and expectedly those of large economies such as China.

In contrast to past decades, however, exports are now increasing at a slower rate, which indicates that the model might be reaching its limits (Table 2.3). Over the period 1970 to 2000, exports of goods and services expanded steadily, at an average annual growth rate of about 10%. A similar expansion took place in other ASEAN countries, though with an average growth rate of exports of 9.5% over the same period. However, in more recent years, Malaysia's exports have been growing at a slower pace (on average 4.5% annually over the 2000s) and 5.1% over the period 2013-14.

Table 2.3. **Average annual growth rate of exports of goods and services, Malaysia, ASEAN, China and the United States, 1970-2014**

In %

Country/region	1970-79	1980-89	1990-99	2000-09	2010-12	2013-14
Malaysia	8.2	9.2	12.7	4.5	3.6	5.1
ASEAN	9.3	8.0	11.1	7.9	7.6	-0.48[1]
China (People's Republic of)	..	8.6	16.5	15.9	13.4	4.0
United States	7.4	6.0	7.2	3.4	6.3	2.81[1]

Note: .. = not available.

1. Data are for 2013.

Source: World Bank (2015b), *World Development Indicators* (database), http://data.worldbank.org/data-catalog/world-development-indicators.

The composition of the Malaysian export basket has changed radically compared to four decades ago. The part of the resource-based sector has been declining over time while the part of electrical appliances and goods has been expanding. Pre-independence Malaysia was one of the world's largest producers and exporters of tin and rubber (accounting for some 95% of total exports). Since the early 1980s, electrical goods and appliances and electronic goods, particularly semiconductor devices, came to represent a large portion (some 40% at some times) of total exports – while natural resources now only account for about 30%.

Malaysia remains at the top globally in terms of its share of "high-technology" exports in total manufacturing exports. However, this performance has deteriorated. While it was well above the level achieved on average by OECD top-performers in 2000, its share of total manufacturing exports has decreased markedly since then. Indicators pertaining to production or trade in goods classified as "high-technology" should be interpreted with caution, however, as the corresponding domestic activity is not necessarily of a knowledge (R&D)-intensive, high value-adding character. High-technology content may well pertain to imported components, not to the tasks performed locally. Most of the activity in high-tech manufacturing remains assembling imported parts with relatively low domestic value added. This is the case of assembly manufacturing platforms, including in China (which has embarked on a dynamic process of upgrading), and recently Viet Nam.

Malaysia's export specialisation in "high-technology" products is evidenced by a breakdown of exports into finer product groups (Table 2.4). Electrical machinery, apparatus and appliances are the most important commodities exported from Malaysia and in particular electronic integrated circuits and micro-assemblies. More generally, six out of ten top export items at this level are E&E products. Liquefied gas is the third, palm oil the fourth and crude petroleum the fifth most important export commodities.

Table 2.4. **Top ten export commodities, Malaysia, 2013**

Class	Commodity (4-digit heading of harmonised system 2007)	Rank in exports	Export value (USD million)	Share of total exports (%)	Share of world exports (%)
7764	Electronic integrated circuits and micro-assemblies	1	24.9	10.9	5.1
9310	Special transactions and commodities not classified according to kind	2	23.7	10.4	1.4
3431	Natural gas, liquefied	3	18.9	8.3	11.2
4222	Palm oil and its fractions	4	12.3	5.4	37.6
3330	Crude petroleum	5	10.2	4.5	0.8
7763	Diodes, transistors and similar semiconductor devices; photosensitive semiconductor devices	6	6.0	2.6	6.7
7599	Parts and accessories, data-processing machines	7	5.4	2.4	4.3
7768	Piezoelectric crystals, mounted; parts of the electronic components	8	4.5	2.0	13.4
7527	Storage units, whether or not presented with the rest of a data-processing machine	9	4.3	1.9	5.9
7611	Television receivers, colour (including video monitors and video projectors)	10	3.6	1.6	4.4

Source: UNcomtrade (2015), *United Nations Commodity Trade Statistics Database* (database), http://comtrade.un.org/db/default.aspx.

The Revealed Comparative Advantage (RCA)[17] Index reveals Malaysia's strong export specialisation in "high-technology" products (Figure 2.11). This specialisation has, however, decreased significantly, from 2.5 in 2005 to 2 in 2010 and 1.5 in 2012. By contrast, China's specialisation in high-tech products has been slightly increasing (Figure 2.12).

Figure 2.11. **Revealed Comparative Advantage by industry type, Malaysia, 1995-2012**

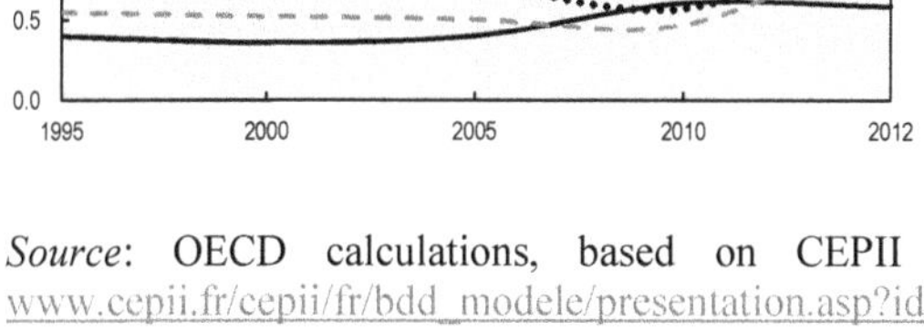

Figure 2.12. **Revealed Comparative Advantage by industry type, China, 1995-2012**

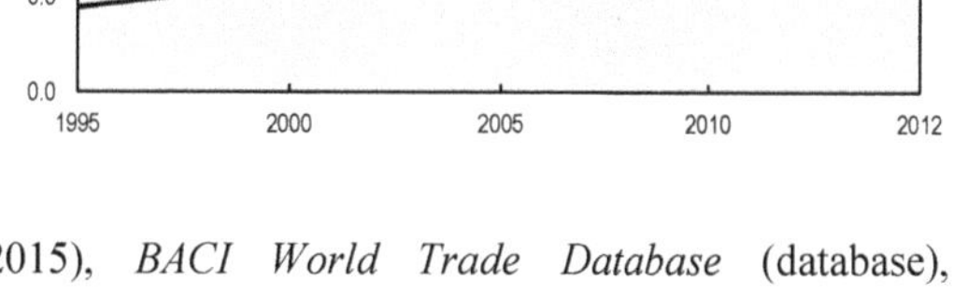

Source: OECD calculations, based on CEPII (2015), *BACI World Trade Database* (database), www.cepii.fr/cepii/fr/bdd_modele/presentation.asp?id=1.

However, in a world where fragmented production in global value chains (GVCs) has become widespread, these gross export statistics can lead to misinterpretation of the patterns of specialisation as one country can import most of the goods that it exports after having performed some low value-adding assembly tasks.

Table 2.5 classifies East Asian economies according to constellations of RCA values, taking both exports and imports into account.[18] It shows that Malaysia is not only exporting a higher share of "high-technology" products than the world average (i.e. enjoys an RCA in this class of products), but that it also imports a disproportionate share of intermediary high-technology products (components). For instance, several of the top ten export products pertaining to the E&E industry are also among the top ten import products.[19] Other indicators confirm that Malaysia's technology-based export products have high import content.

Table 2.5. **Highest Revealed Comparative Advantage of ASEAN countries, 2012**

	High-technology exports	Medium-high-technology exports	Medium-low-technology exports	Low-technology exports
High-technology imports	China (People's Republic of) **Malaysia**		Hong Kong (China)	
Medium-high-technology imports				
Medium-low-technology imports	Singapore			Indonesia Thailand
Low-technology imports			Lao People's Democratic Republic	Cambodia Myanmar Viet Nam

Note: Grey zones indicate profiles where countries have a higher Revealed Comparative Advantage in higher technology product categories in imports than in exports.

Source: OECD calculations, based on CEPII (2015), *CEPII BACI World Trade Database* (database), www.cepii.fr/cepii/fr/bdd_modele/presentation.asp?id=1.

This is also reflected in statistics of domestic content in exports. In the case of Malaysia, this ratio has not changed significantly between the mid-1990s and today (Figure 2.13). This means that Malaysia has not reaped the full benefits of GVC integration. Domestic content in exports (of both final and intermediate products) has actually decreased, from 69.5% in 1995 to 59.4% in 2011. In contrast, it expanded in the Philippines, moving from 70% to 76.4% while it remained more or less at the same level in Indonesia and China (88% and 67.8%, respectively) in 2011.

The domestic contribution in exports of final products (as a share of gross exports) decreased from 27% in 1995 to 21% in 2011 (Figure 2.13). A slight contraction is also recorded for domestic value added in exports of intermediate products. The latter is considered a measure of "forward linkages", or how much exports are connected to a secondary stage of production in another country. In this sense, forward integration did not change substantially in Malaysia in the 16 years shown in Figure 2.13.

Overall, the GVC integration of Malaysia is mostly driven by a high backward participation – a high import content of exports (40.6% of total gross exports) – which is about twice as high as the average in both developing and developed countries. In contrast, the forward ratio (part of gross exports that are used as inputs in a forward value chain stage) displays levels close to the world average (19.8%). The top GVC importing industries are computer and electronics (40.5), food and beverage (7.2), and chemical products (5.9).[20]

At 60.4% of gross exports in 2011, Malaysia's total GVC participation remains higher than the world average as measured by the GVC participation index. The average in developing and developed countries was 48.6% and 48% respectively. Although this intensity in global integration has been growing, this expansion is similar to (rather slightly lower than) the average in developing countries. Over the period 1995-2011, Malaysia recorded an annual percent change of 11% in the GVC participation index while the average in developing countries was 12%.

Figure 2.13. **Domestic value added in exports, 1995 and 2011**

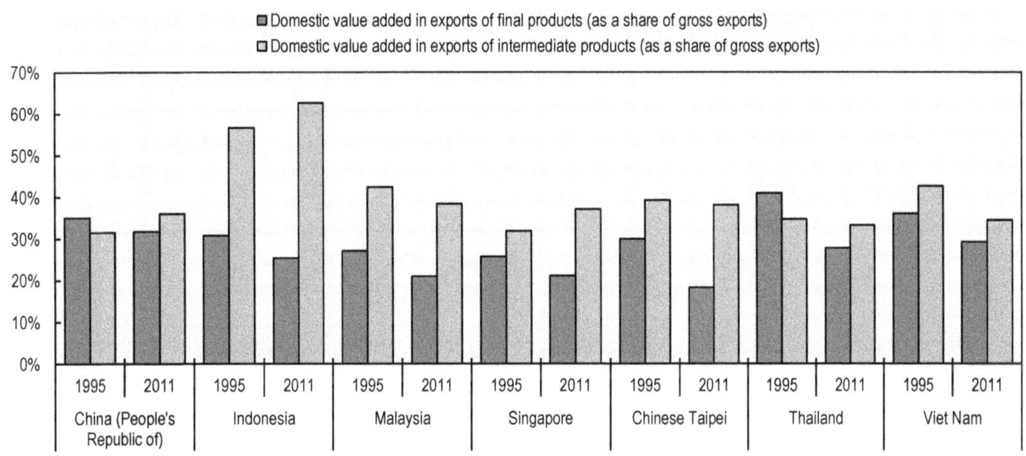

Source: OECD/WTO (2016), "Trade in value added", *OECD-WTO: Statistics on Trade in Value Added* (database), http://dx.doi.org/10.1787/data-00648-en.

Malaysia's strong export performance has largely been driven by a successful integration in GVCs, but this performance currently faces growing competition by other countries from the region and China. While China's increasing demand for a broad range of exports has evidently benefited Southeast Asian countries, its growing performance in manufacturing also presents a challenge. The pace at which it upgrades its economy and raises productivity can be expected to further raise competitive pressures and to some extent replace imports of components that are currently manufactured in Southeast Asian countries (Box 2.3). In addition, a new cohort of catching-up economies is emerging in global trade, notably in the Southeast Asian region; Viet Nam, which is rapidly expanding its participation in global manufacturing trade is one example (Box 2.4).

Framework conditions for innovation

The role of framework conditions

The macroeconomic and general business environment, the product and labour market regulations, competition intensity, the accessibility and quality of business financing, the tax system, the level and quality of entrepreneurship, and the quality of infrastructure all influence a country's innovation performance. Good framework conditions stimulate firms to engage in innovation and R&D, and support the diffusion of innovations throughout the economy and society at large. Thus, conducive framework conditions and a healthy business environment are key prerequisites for strong innovation performance of individual innovation actors and the innovation system as a whole. Moreover, framework conditions for innovation have gained importance in recent decades as businesses and capital have become more mobile and select the most favourable operating environments. Framework conditions are important for several reasons:

- Innovation activity requires a medium- or long-term horizon and a sufficiently stable operating environment. This is particularly important for R&D, as well as for more fundamental and costly types of innovation activity.
- The regulatory framework is crucial to generating and speeding up the diffusion of new technologies. A favourable regulatory framework critically accelerates the reallocation of labour and capital to innovative firms and industries, which in turn stimulate investment in knowledge-based capital by raising its return (Andrews and Criscuolo, 2013).
- Vigorous competitive pressure provides a powerful incentive for business innovation. By contrast, a lack of competition allows inefficient firms and technologies to remain in the market.

Box 2.3. The evolution of global value chains in Southeast Asia

The economies of Southeast Asia continue to undergo profound changes and are becoming ever more closely integrated into fast-evolving regional and global production and knowledge networks. Advances in technology, including transportation and communication technologies, together with lower barriers to international trade and investment, have allowed production to become increasingly fragmented, and to spread geographically and across political borders. This has given rise to today's global value chains (GVCs). Southeast Asian economies have increasingly become involved in GVCs, which have boosted, reshaped and redirected the trade flows they are engaging in. Based on a fragmentation of production, GVCs link geographically dispersed activities. They have strengthened comparative advantages in certain industries through the country-specific location of tasks. Centres of gravity such as the attractors of trade in intermediate products have shifted, especially with the emergence of China as the largest manufacturing platform globally.

The rise of China is impacting the Southeast Asian economies via increasing bilateral trade and investment, and also cross-border flows of various types of knowledge related to GVCs. It also has an impact through competition in third markets. To date, the economies of Southeast Asia have gained overall from China's increasing demand for a broad range of exports from this region. At the same time, competition from China has also challenged Malaysian producers. The ongoing improvement of China's manufacturing capabilities and the pace at which it upgrades its economy and raises productivity can be expected to further raise competitive pressure on, and to some extent replace imports of, components that are currently manufactured in Southeast Asian countries. This is a challenge, notably for "middle-income" countries, such as Malaysia. In addition, there is a new cohort of catching-up economies, notably in the Southeast Asian region, for instance Viet Nam, which have lower income levels than Malaysia and currently also possess a lower level and range of manufacturing capabilities. These countries are moving into areas of production that have been important for Malaysia's own catch-up but are no longer feasible at its current state of development. They have attracted some production even from China's coastal areas. Some countries in this new cohort of catching-up economies will also gradually evolve and try to improve their innovation capabilities to upgrade and escape a lock-in to low value-adding activities.

Source: OECD (2013a), *Innovation in Southeast Asia*, http://dx.doi.org/10.1787/9789264128712-en.

When framework conditions are deficient, they are likely to reduce the effectiveness of policies designed to foster innovation. Favourable framework conditions facilitate innovation throughout the economy. At the same time, OECD experience shows that "dedicated" policy measures are also needed to address specific market or systemic failures that hamper R&D and innovation. Empirical OECD work has found that framework conditions and dedicated science, technology and innovation (STI) policies affect innovation performance, both separately and in combination; it has helped identify the policies, institutions and framework conditions that support innovation effectively (Jaumotte and Pain, 2005a, 2005b; Westmore, 2013).

Box 2.4. Competition from a new cohort of catching-up economies: The example of Viet Nam

A new cohort of countries has arrived, taking on activities previously performed by countries that have meanwhile moved up the income ladder, such as Malaysia. Investment by East Asian and western firms has enabled producers located in Viet Nam to link to buyer-driven global value chains (GVCs). In a little more than a decade, Viet Nam has entered GVCs in clothing, furniture and electronics. Although Viet Nam is a latecomer, its participation in GVCs (50%) is similar to that of Thailand (51%), but less than that of Malaysia, the Philippines, Singapore and Chinese Taipei. While exports have grown, changes in the mix of the top export items have been limited for some time. Petroleum, rice, coffee and seafood have remained among these, together with furniture, garments and footwear during the 2000s. Domestic firms lacked the technological capabilities to upgrade or diversify their manufacturing activities. Viet Nam's Revealed Comparative Advantage (RCA) – a widely used indicator of trade specialisation – is still predominantly in low-technology items, but changes are occurring. The RCA Index for exports is the highest in textiles and clothing, food and wood products (although it has decreased over the past decade), followed by other manufacturing. This is mirrored by China's loss of comparative advantage in the assembly of textiles and clothing.

While much of Viet Nam's productive capacity is still in low value-added and low-technology processing and assembly manufacturing as well as low-end tradable services, a number of high-technology MNEs have recently arrived, e.g. from Japan, Korea and the United States. Viet Nam's export basket is changing accordingly: the RCA value for this product category increased slowly, from 0.07 in 1995, 0.22 in 2000, 0.32 in 2005 and was still only 0.37 in 2010, but up to 1.26 in 2012. Exports of "high-technology" products (which typically do not have high domestic knowledge or value-added content) expanded very rapidly; for example exports of cell phones and accessories doubled in both 2011 and 2012. Exports of electronics and computers, and transport vehicles and parts also achieved high growth. Phones and parts (11.1%) and electronics and computers (6.8%) had become an important component of Viet Nam's export basket by 2012, and further expansion is imminent. According to OECD and World Bank (2014), Viet Nam exported cell phones and accessories worth USD 12.7 billion in 2012, and was expected to export USD 18 billion, overtaking garments as Viet Nam's largest export item, in 2013. In parallel to exports, imports of "high-tech intermediates" have increased steeply as Viet Nam is becoming a platform for assembling.

Source: OECD and World Bank (2014), *Science, Technology and Innovation in Viet Nam*, http://dx.doi.org/10.1787/9789264213500-en.

Overall business environment

Malaysia has been improving the business regulatory framework substantially over the last decade. Several important reforms have been introduced since 2005. The World Bank Ease of Doing Business, which captures various dimensions of the broader business environment, shows the extent of the progress it has made. Malaysia improved its overall score from 20th position in 2009 to 18th in 2016 (out of 189 economies). It ranks well above China (84th), Indonesia (109th), and the regional average for East Asia and the Pacific (109th) (World Bank, 2016a).

Malaysia ranks high in terms of protecting minority investors, starting a business, getting electricity and dealing with construction permits – all ranking within the top 15 (out of 189) positions. In terms of new business regulation, for example, Malaysia since 2010 took a series of steps to ease the burden for local entrepreneurs, such as easing business start-up by introducing more online services; merging the company, tax, social security and employment fund registrations at a one-stop shop; and providing same-day registration. Efforts such as these have reduced the time required to start a business from 37 days in 2005 to less than 6 days today – less time than in Brazil or Ireland. Resolving insolvency and enforcing contracts are the less advanced areas – although they still rank relatively high (within the top 50).

Compared to international practice, starting a business, getting electricity and trading across borders are the top three areas best aligned to international regulatory practice (Figure 2.14). In contrast, enforcing contracts and resolving insolvency appear again as the less advanced areas of Malaysia's business regulatory framework compared to global standards. There is hence still significant room for improving the business regulatory framework. Updating the legal framework for insolvency procedures in line with international standards will allow "viable businesses" to be rebuilt.[21]

Figure 2.14. **Distance to frontier scores on Doing Business 2016: Malaysia**

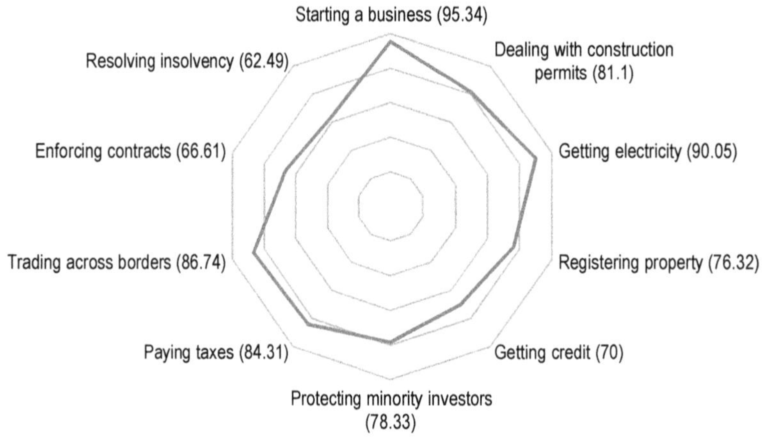

Note: The rankings are benchmarked to June 2015 and based on the average of each economy's distance to frontier (DTF) scores for the ten topics included in this year's aggregate ranking. An economy's DTF score is indicated on a scale of 0 to 100, where 0 represents the worst performance and 100 the frontier. Scale: Score 0 centre, Score 100 outer edge. For the economies for which the data cover two cities, scores are a population-weighted average for the two cities.

Source: World Bank (2016b), *Doing Business Data* (database), www.doingbusiness.org/data.

According to the 2016 World Economic Forum's Global Competitiveness Index, Malaysia also needs to improve several government-related competences, such as efficiency in bureaucracy and eradication of corruption (Figure 2.15). Crime and theft were also considered important factors constraining competitiveness.

In terms of overall quality of regulation, Malaysia scores high compared to the average in the ASEAN region. According to the Fraser Institute, in 2013 Malaysia was one of the regional leaders in terms of favourable business regulations and overall regulation. That year marked a turning point in the government's approach to regulation when it launched the National Policy on the Development and Implementation of

Regulations (NPDIR), aimed at improving the Malaysian rule-making process. This marked a transition from deregulation to a whole-of-government approach on good regulatory practice, which is in line both with the OECD Recommendation of the Council on Regulatory Policy and Governance (OECD, 2015b) and international good practice.[22] An institutional infrastructure has been set up to implement the NPDIR, led by the Malaysia Productivity Corporation (MPC). According to the Eleventh Malaysia Plan (2016-20), 16 public agencies already implement 31 good regulatory practices following the OECD principles (EPU, 2015).

Figure 2.15. **Most problematic factors for doing business, Malaysia, 2010-16**

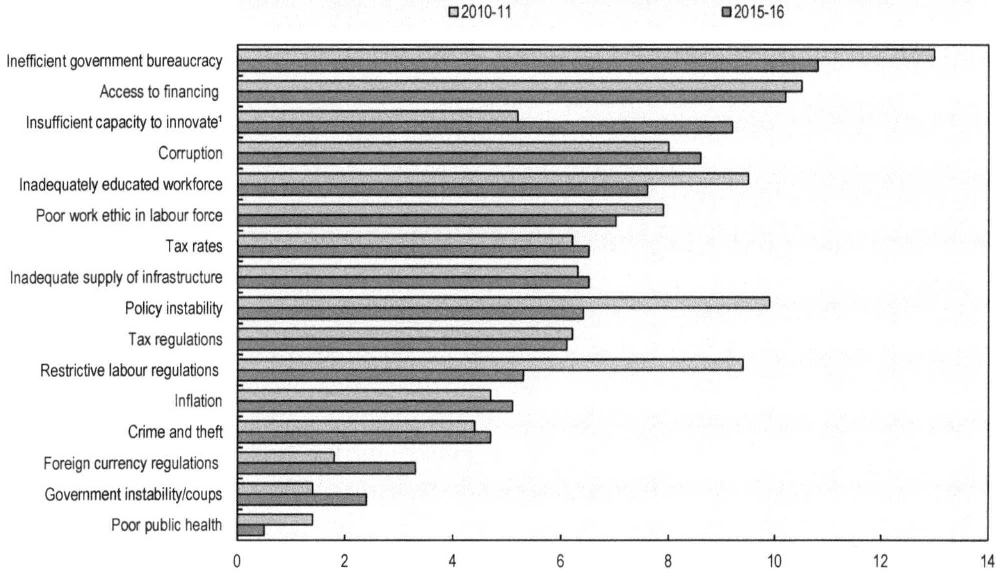

Notes: This assessment is the result of a survey of Malaysian business companies. From a list of factors, respondents were asked to rate them between 1 (most problematic) and 5 (not problematic). The bars in the figure show the responses weighted according to their rankings.

1. 2012-13 data instead of 2010-11.

Source: World Economic Forum (2015), *Global Competitiveness Report Dataset* (database), http://reports.weforum.org/global-competitiveness-report-2014-2015/downloads; World Economic Forum (2016), *Global Competitiveness Report 2016*, http://reports.weforum.org/global-competitiveness-report-2015-2016.

Access to finance

Access to finance is fundamental for firms to invest in productive resources – such as capital and innovation – and enhance their competitiveness. Difficulties in accessing finance (bank credit or other forms of finance such as equity) are closely associated to firm size. Recurrently, in business surveys worldwide, firms and in particular small and medium-sized enterprises (SMEs), consider financial constraints among the most important handicaps for competitiveness and innovation investment.

The lack of, or difficulties in accessing, finance are related to various factors. On the demand side these include: limited collateral capacity and economies of scale – inherent to size, as well as technical deficiencies of firms that prevent them from managing and/or implementing sustainable investment projects, among others. On the supply side, limited medium- and long-term sources of funding in the domestic market and lack of transparency and information to conduct proper credit risk assessments lead to a reduced appetite on the part of banks to serve the SME market segment.

For innovation investment, market failures related to asymmetric information and moral hazard (in repayment by the agent) are exacerbated due to the intangible nature of innovation and uncertainty surrounding research and development efforts, among other reasons. In the case of young firms and start-ups, the lack of collateral further inhibits access to external finance.

Despite the government's actions to improve access to finance for SMEs – as reflected by the proliferation of loans, grants, guarantee schemes, venture capital and government loan schemes introduced in recent years – financial constraints continue to be one of the key barriers to firm productivity and innovation in Malaysia. Several macro-level indicators suggest that Malaysia is lagging behind some peers in terms of access to credit and firms' use of external sources of finance. It has been estimated that the total credit gap (the difference between formal credit provided to SMEs and total estimated potential need for formal credit) recorded for 2010 was about USD 8 billion – twice the credit gap of Viet Nam and four times that of the Philippines (IFC, 2011). This gap is higher in Thailand (USD 11.8 billion) but lower in Singapore (USD 7.1 billion).

Malaysian SMEs rely mainly on internal funds to finance investment projects (Figure 2.16). The use of external finance is weak and mainly consists of bank finance. For manufacturing SMEs, 46% of investments are financed with internal sources while 33% are financed with bank credits. In this type of funding, Malaysian firms rely more strongly on bank credits than most countries in the region – Cambodia, China, Indonesia or the Philippines; firms in Thailand or Sri Lanka display higher ratios. The use of finance by supplier credits or through equity and stock markets remains low, as in other countries in the region, representing less than 5% of the investment being covered through this type of funding.

Figure 2.16. **Sources of finance for investment projects of small and medium-sized enterprises, East Asia and OECD**

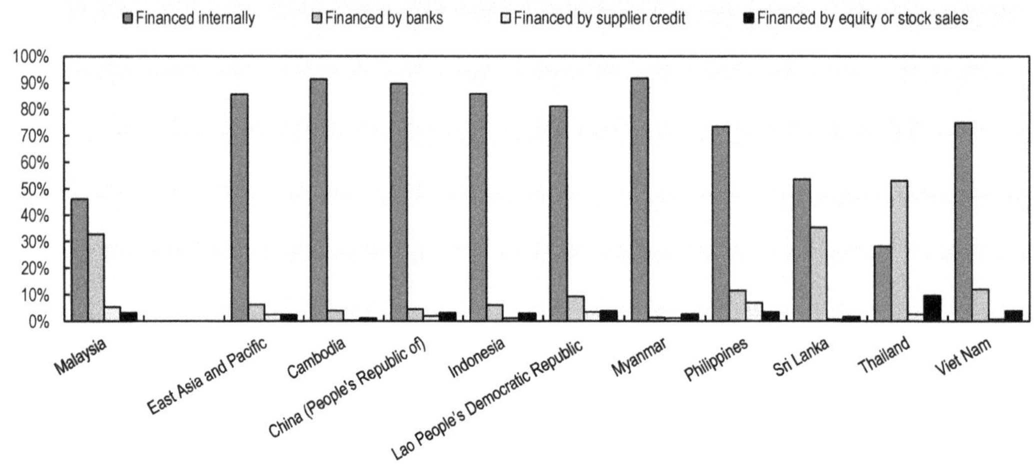

Notes: An SME is defined as a firm with less than 100 employees. The most recent available data are for 2007 for Malaysia, 2013 for Cambodia, 2012 for China, 2009 for Indonesia, 2012 for Lao People's Democratic Republic, 2014 for Myanmar, 2009 for the Philippines, 2011 for Sri Lanka, 2006 for Thailand and 2009 for Viet Nam.

Source: World Bank (2015a), *Enterprise Survey Data* (database), www.enterprisesurveys.org/data/survey-datasets.

In terms of early-stage funding, several initiatives have been set up but they are still in the early stages. Venture capital is still embryonic and is often linked to public funding. The first venture capital Berhad fund of MYR 13.8 million was created in 1984. In the 1990s, an important step toward the liberalisation of venture capital was made: companies were allowed to invest up to 75% in high-tech or risk projects in order to qualify for tax holidays or pioneer status. Since 2009, venture capitals investing at least 30% of their funds in start-up or early-stage companies benefit from a five-year tax exemption. However, restrictive investment criteria, poorly communicated business plans, low public awareness, general disconnect between the potential entrepreneurs and the venture capital industry as well as lack of skilled personnel to manage the funds are still the main obstacles for many companies in Malaysia.[23]

During the Tenth Malaysia Plan, the financing of companies at the development and growth stage slightly accelerated. For example, Malaysia Technology Development Corporation (MTDC), Malaysia Venture Capital Management Berhad, Malaysia Debt Ventures Bhd and Multimedia Development Corporation (MDeC) provided about MYR 495.2 million of grants, loans and venture capital for technology development to 760 *Bumiputera*[24] SMEs owned by the bottom 40% household income group (the so-called "B40"). Efforts to improve finance for innovative start-ups continued with the creation of PlaTCOM Ventures (in 2012) under the SME Master Plan 2012-20. This programme currently provides help to new innovative business, entrepreneurs and academics at all stages of product or service creation.

The Eleventh Malaysia Plan will introduce new ways of early-stage business financing through the SME Investment Partner (SIP) programme. SIP will combine equity and loan financing features and provide up to 100% margin of financing. It is supposed to complement the existing venture capital, private equity and angel financing landscape. SMEs will be encouraged to pool resources, utilise shared services and purchase inputs, raw materials and services in bulk to reduce costs (EPU, 2015).

Competition conditions

Competition and market structure are central to innovation. While the relation is certainly not linear (Aghion et al., 2005), competition encourages companies to invest in innovation in order for them to gain market shares and/or stay in the market. The incentive to innovate (additional profit) is stronger, particularly in the case of highly concentrated industries or markets (or those characterised by neck-to-neck technological competition).[25] In this sense, artificially maintaining incumbency (e.g. preserving monopolies and/or oligopolies) keeps favoured firms working at productivity levels that are lower than optimal and with weak incentives to innovate as they know they will preserve their market leadership.

Competition is fundamental for the effectiveness of public policies for innovation and productivity. It has recently been shown that productivity policies, such as subsidies and grants directed to firms in competitive sectors or industries with healthy competition, lead to productivity growth in those sectors. In contrast, public policies in industries with low levels of competition may prove to be ineffective. Measures to foster competition include policies that are more dispersed across firms in a sector or measures that encourage younger and more productive enterprises (Aghion et al., 2005).

In Malaysia, competition conditions are not exactly fair and equal for firms and may vary substantially across industries and markets. This reduces companies' incentives to innovate, with the corresponding detrimental effects in prices, and product quality and variety. The most prevalent issue pertaining to competitive neutrality is the issue of preferential treatment of GLCs (OECD, 2015b).[26] There have been instances of outright subsidies, preferential access to financing and loan guarantees, preferential treatment in public procurement, selective enforcement of competition law, or even administrative intervention to protect or advantage state-owned enterprises (SOEs).

Malaysian estate enterprises receive various subsidies and financial assistance from the government and other SOEs. The government also provides a guarantee of the debts, although this practice has been on the decline. In 2012, the Auditor General found that between 2009 and 2011, 18 of the SOEs audited had received loans from the government. For instance, IWK, the national sewage company, received substantial government subsidies for its operation. In fact, the 2012 Auditor General report noted that the company was too reliant on government subsidies to cover its operational expenses (OECD, 2015b).

Steps have been taken to improve competition regulation and enforcement. A major improvement was made in competition policy in Malaysia with the adoption of the National Competition Act – the first comprehensive national competition law. The Malaysian Competition Commission (MyCC) has been successful in enforcement activities, especially in price-fixing cases involving trade associations (Lee, 2014). Future work will require reviewing public sector regulations touching competition, merger control and regional integration regulation.

Market openness and foreign direct investment regulations

In addition to general macroeconomic conditions, integration into global markets through trade and foreign direct investment (FDI) is key to an innovation-friendly environment. Trade openness may lead to scale economies by providing more opportunities for growth, and may encourage innovation through competition and learning (learning-by-exporting) from partners. Firms that participate in global markets are subject to increased exigencies in product quality and novelty compared to domestic markets – which in turn fosters innovation efforts.

FDI is potentially also a major source of knowledge transfer and spill-overs to the local economy through the channels of employee turnover (or spinoffs) and business linkages with domestic firms. For developing countries, in particular those building an absorption capacity, trade and foreign investment can be seen as important instruments to the process of productivity catch-up.

Like other countries in the region, Malaysia is a highly open economy displaying an intensity of trade (exports plus imports relative to GDP) superior to the size of the national economy. Trade represented 138.4% of GDP in 2014 – an important decrease from 2004 when this ratio was twice the value of GDP. The decrease in trade openness is to some extent related to demand contractions in global markets and increases in non-trade related GDP. In spite of this drop, the level of openness remains high and hence presents an important opportunity for learning and knowledge transfer for Malaysian companies.

FDI has also played an important role in the Malaysian economy, given the country's model of development over the last two decades. Foreign firms have played a major role in the process of growth and diversification and foreign investment has been a key part of the outward-oriented development strategies of successive governments (OECD, 2013a).

FDI has continued to rise in absolute terms but has declined significantly as a share of both GDP and total FDI in ASEAN countries since the pre-crisis 1990s (ibid.). By the early 1990s, FDI represented 8% of GDP, but in more recent years this participation has been shrinking – down to 3.1% of GDP in 2014 (World Bank, 2015). A large share of FDI inflows involves reinvested earnings of existing foreign affiliates, which suggest that while established foreign investors are not leaving the country, there are fewer new arrivals compared to earlier decades. In more recent years, the delocalisation trends involving a number of MNEs have also affected the spread of FDI across Southeast Asia and its location in Malaysia. The government attributes this shift in inflow FDI to the refocusing of FDI strategy towards more knowledge-intensive investment (OECD, 2013b).

The nature and type of FDI have also been changing. Outward FDI has gained in importance. Since the mid-2000s, FDI outflows have exceeded inflows, and this is in part related to fiscal reforms and the development of some domestic sectors.[27] Mergers and acquisitions have gained in importance with the introduction of a five-year tax deduction for mergers and acquisitions abroad, leading to high-technology production in the Malaysian territory or gains in new export markets for local products (OECD, 2013b).

Malaysia is continuing its efforts to attract and enhance local linkages with FDI. Figure 2.17 shows that Malaysia made some important efforts to reduce FDI restrictions over the period 1997-2014, including on services. For manufacturing and, more specifically the E&E sector, Malaysia has even opened its economy to a higher degree than the OECD average. The key sector of business services is now at par with the OECD average level of restrictions. As an example, in 2009, Malaysia removed its former Foreign Investment Committee (FIC) investment guidelines, enabling transactions for acquisitions of interests, mergers and takeovers of local companies by domestic or foreign parties without approval by the FIC.

Figure 2.17. **OECD FDI Regulatory Restrictiveness Index, selected industries and sectors, Malaysia, 1997-2014**

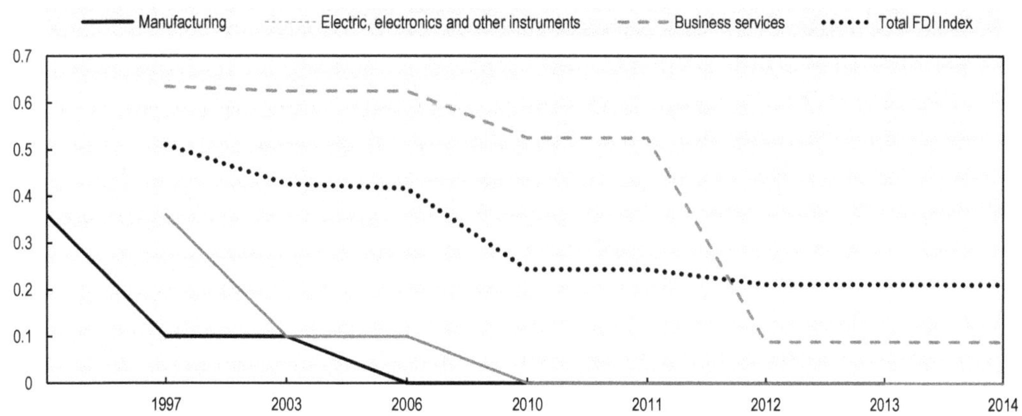

Note: The FDI Regulatory Restrictiveness Index (FDI Index) measures statutory restrictions on foreign direct investment across 22 economic sectors. It gauges the restrictiveness of a country's FDI rules by looking at the four main types of restrictions on FDI: 1) foreign equity limitations; 2) discriminatory screening or approval mechanisms; 3) restrictions on the employment of foreigners as key personnel; and 4) other operational restrictions, e.g. restrictions on branching and on capital repatriation or on land ownership by foreign-owned enterprises. Restrictions are evaluated on a 0 (open) to 1 (closed) scale.

Source: OECD (2016), "OECD FDI regulatory restrictiveness index", *OECD International Direct Investment Statistics* (database), http://dx.doi.org/10.1787/g2g55501-en.

Intellectual property[28]

Improving the intellectual property rights (IPR) legal framework and functioning is important for innovation and business development, particularly for countries moving up in the development cycle and starting to invest in frontier innovation capacity.[29] As economies develop and acquire valuable knowledge assets, local firms begin to develop a vested interest in building IPR institutions and protecting intellectual creations to foster competitiveness. An effective IPR system is also ancillary in the development and organisation of markets by helping consumers scrutinise the quality of products and services and their origins, e.g. signalling quality of a brand is the main attribute of trademarks, origin designations and geographic indications.

An in-depth analysis carried out by the OECD (2015a) has shown the maturation of Malaysia's national intellectual property (IP) system in the past decades, notably with regards to its legal and operational aspects. This positive evolution has allowed the role of the Malaysia Intellectual Property Office (MyIPO) to be enhanced in the national innovation system.

Malaysia ranks well in international benchmarks in terms of IP protection. It positioned 23rd out of 140 in the Global Competitiveness Report for Intellectual Property Protection, with a score of 5.4 out of 7 in 2015-16 (Figure 2.18). This ranking has slightly improved in recent years[30] and compares well with other countries in the region. These developments were also acknowledged by the Fraser Institute, where the protection of property rights score went from 4.23 in 2000 to 7.16 in 2013 on a scale of 1-10 (Gwartney, Lawson and Hall, 2014; 2015).

Figure 2.18. **Intellectual property protection rates and ranking, 2015-16**

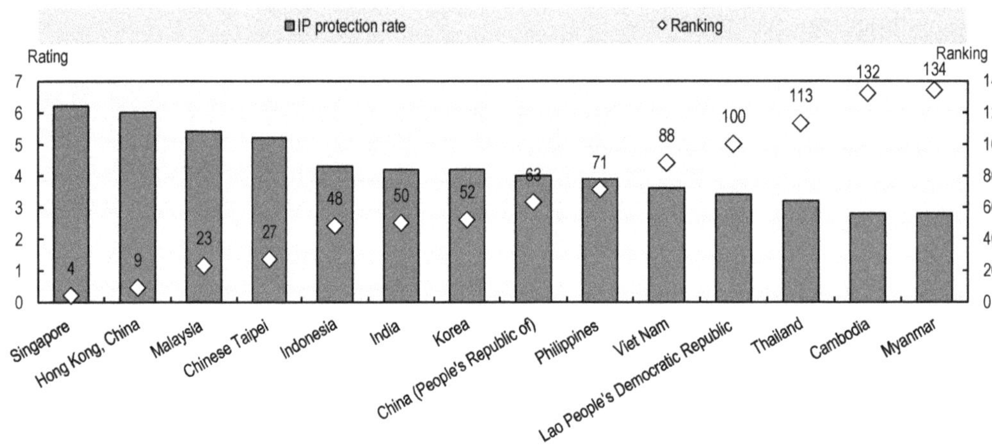

Note: Average rating provided to the question "In your country, to what extent is intellectual property protected? [1 = not at all; 7 = to a great extent]" in the framework of the World Economic Forum survey, carried out in 140 countries.

Source: World Economic Forum (2016), *Global Competitiveness Report 2016*, http://reports.weforum.org/global-competitiveness-report-2015-2016.

A number of reforms to IP laws have brought policies in line with international standards underscored in the WTO Trade-Related Intellectual Property Rights (TRIPS) agreement. Malaysia has signed additional IP-related commitments under the Association of Southeast Asian Nations (ASEAN) and other international IP treaties, including the Patent Cooperation Treaty (PCT) system in 2006. The corporatisation of the MyIPO in 2003 helped improve institutional capacities to deal with legal and administrative matters related to IP rights. Management reforms and examiner reward programmes for high productivity have contributed to this achievement. Today, the processing of IP titles is very efficient by international standards. Application fees compare favourably with international fees, although small companies perceive maintenance fees as costly. Enforcement has been improved, and in 2007 a new system of IP High Courts was introduced to ensure that titles obtained are enforced.

Malaysia's IP policy has started playing a more proactive role by taking steps to improve markets for IP and therefore the diffusion of innovation, by facilitating the trading of IP titles and providing financing opportunities for IP. An additional approach to raise the contributions of IP consists of finding ways for IP to serve as collateral for loans to finance innovation activities. The policy measure, which is implemented by Malaysia Debt Ventures (MDV), is still in its initial phase, and is led entirely by the government. The government is creating the technology platforms and subsidising the credit rates for the loans using IP as collateral. However, for it to consolidate and succeed in the future it needs to be taken up by Malaysia's private banks and operate internationally.

Several weaknesses of the IP system remain, as emphasised in the previous OECD review. The national IP system is still best characterised as one of multiple institutions that implement separate policies aimed at incentivising the uptake and effective use of IP policies (OECD, 2015a). The MyIPO itself implements some, but not all, of these policies. Although the diversity allows for policy experimentation, initiatives could benefit from greater co-ordination between the IP policy agencies, namely the NIPP Action Council and National IP Committee – which focus mainly on legal and enforcement matters, and the MyIPO. Improving the awareness of the importance of IP protection in the private sector is also a pending task.

ICT and transport infrastructure

Improving infrastructure was one of the selling assets in the promotion of the export-oriented economic model. In international benchmarks, Malaysia ranks well in overall infrastructure, with particularly high scores in the quality of roads, railroads, ports and airports. The country performs less well in terms of telephony, particularly fixed telephone lines (per 100 population) according to the *Global Competitiveness Report* (World Economic Forum, 2016) (Table 2.6).

In the last five years, Malaysia has succeeded in improving all its infrastructure indicators and climbed 11 positions in this international ranking (World Economic Forum, 2016). The Malaysian population now has good access to basic services such as electricity and water. However, major issues remain in the field of energy and supportive infrastructure. The problem of immoderate use of natural gas, coal and hydropower to produce electricity and the underdevelopment of renewable sources of energy remains a challenge.

During the high growth years – until the early 1990s, the infrastructure sector received an important share of public investments in line with the Malaysia plans that always put infrastructure development high on the agenda. However, the deceleration of the growth rates in the last 15 years shifted the funding role to the private sector. Following Vision 2020 in 1991, the Malaysian government facilitated this transition by launching the Master Privatisation Plan of telecommunications, ports, airports, roads, railways as well as power generation and supply.[31]

Private participation led to positive results, Malaysia's Ports Klang and Tanjung Pelepas are now considered to be among the most productive ports in the region, only lagging behind the Chinese city of Shenzhen and Hong Kong (China). The launch of the Multimedia Super Corridor (MSC) project in 1996 was one of the crucial steps in the strengthening of infrastructure in Malaysia. Huge investments were made in the improvement of transport, telecommunications and power-generation technologies. The construction of Kuala Lumpur International Airport in 1998, located close to the MSC, facilitated the access of new companies and investors. Between 2006 and 2009, 31 ports, 5 international airports and 5 economic corridors were created in Malaysia.

Table 2.6. **Infrastructure indicators in Malaysia, 2010 and 2015**

Indicators	2015-16 (out of 140 countries)	2010-11 (out of 139 countries)
Quality of overall infrastructure	16	27
Quality of roads	15	21
Quality of railroads	13	20
Quality of ports	16	19
Quality of airports	21	29
Quality of electricity supply	36	40
Mobile telephone subscriptions/100 population	24	47
Fixed telephone lines/100 population	73	80
Individuals using Internet	45	39

Sources: World Economic Forum (2015), *Global Competitiveness Report Dataset* (database), http://reports.weforum.org/global-competitiveness-report-2014-2015/downloads; World Economic Forum (2016), *Global Competitiveness Report 2016*, http://reports.weforum.org/global-competitiveness-report-2015-2016.

Figure 2.19. **Internet users, per 100 inhabitants, 1990-2014**

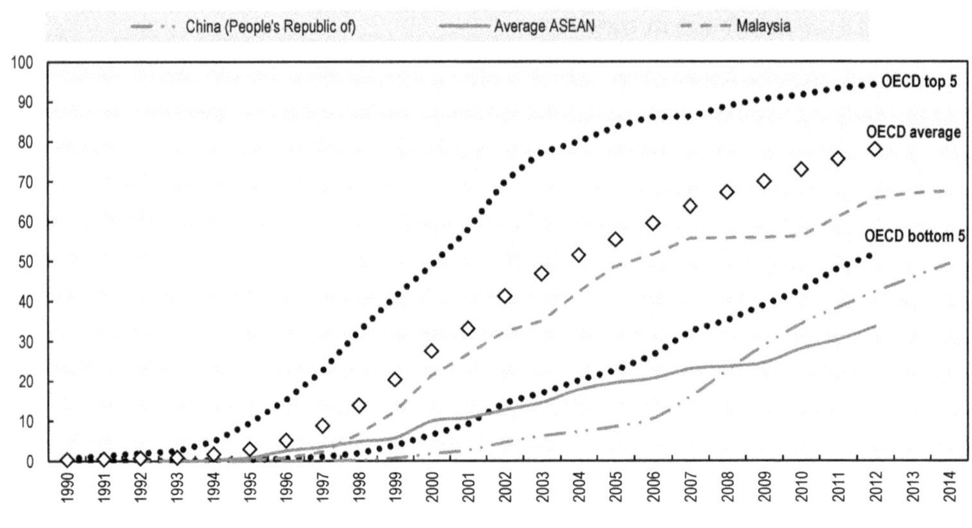

Source: OECD calculation based on World Bank (2015b), *World Development Indicators* (database), http://data.worldbank.org/data-catalog/world-development-indicators.

In terms of Internet infrastructure and penetration, Malaysia has also made improvements. Internet penetration has grown quickly in recent years (Figure 2.19), from 21% in 2010 to 67.5% in 2014, representing the second highest level in the region after Singapore. Mobile phone penetration is very high (149%), with more than one mobile phone per person on average. This rate is higher than Indonesia or the United States. 4G connection is widespread and more than 90% of Malaysians are using e-commerce. At the same time, the level of field telephone subscriptions or broadband is very low (14.6% and 10.1% accordingly) and unpopular among Malaysians. Broadband penetration therefore remains an important area for improvement.

Notes

1. Using the World Bank's Atlas method this corresponds to 24 770 PPP international dollars, as used in Figure 2.7 (see: http://databank.worldbank.org/data/download/GNIPC.pdf for a measure of GNI per capita using the two exchange rates). In terms of GNI per capita at current USD, Malaysia ranks 82nd and 62nd using PPP international dollars.

2. Viet Nam, for example, at a GNI per capita which is just about one-seventh of that of Malaysia (USD 1 730 in 2013), has only recently entered the lower middle-income range. The World Bank (for the 2016 fiscal year) defines middle-income economies as those with a GNI per capita of more than USD 1 045 but less than USD 12 736; lower middle-income and upper middle-income economies are separated at a GNI per capita of USD 4 125. Accordingly, low-income countries are those with a GNI per capita of USD 1 045 or less, whereas high-income economies are those with a GNI per capita of USD 12 736 or more (http://data.worldbank.org/about/country-and-lending-groups).

3. ASEAN was established on 8 August 1967 by five member countries, including Malaysia. It now has ten member countries: Brunei Darussalam, Cambodia, Indonesia, Lao People's Democratic Republic (hereafter "Lao PDR"), Malaysia, Myanmar, the Philippines, Singapore, Thailand and Viet Nam.

4. Hong Kong (China), Korea, Singapore and Chinese Taipei.

5. The HDI goes beyond the purely economic dimension, and in addition to GNI per capita includes data on health (life expectancy) and education (years of schooling); the *Human Development Report* also provides supplementary information on progress towards gender equality, income equality, poverty, development of competences, personal security, environmental quality and perceptions of well-being. Economic data cover investment, international integration and infrastructures (especially communications).

6. Between 1980 and 2012, Malaysia's HDI value increased from 0.563 to 0.769. The rise of this index reflects significant progress in multiple dimensions: during this 32-year period, the life expectancy at birth of its population increased by 7.1 years, mean years of schooling increased by 5.1 years, expected years of schooling increased by 3.6 years and GNI per capita increased by about 191% (UNDP, 2013).

7. In 2015 Malaysia was the world's second-largest exporter of liquefied natural gas after Qatar and the second-largest oil producer in Southeast Asia behind Indonesia (IGU, 2015). The country indirectly also plays a role in the production of biofuels as palm oil is used as a raw material in biodiesel production.

8. The service sector in Malaysia contributed to over one-half of the growth of GDP between 2000 and 2010. This was also the case in Indonesia, the Philippines and Singapore (Noland, Park and Estrada, 2012).

9. Considering the track record of countries having already achieved the transition, a country is considered to be in the lower/upper middle-income trap today if it has been in the lower/upper middle-income group longer than the historical experience.

10. Defined as GNI per capita above USD 12 736 in 2016.

11. According to the "best scenario", China would reach the threshold in 2026, Thailand in 2031, Indonesia in 2042 and India in 2059 (OECD, 2014a).

12 Labour productivity here is measured by output per hour worked. Similar results are obtained for Malaysia when using productivity as defined by output per worker.

13. According to the latest data available, labour productivity increased by 2.3% in 2013, against an annual average of 3% during the period 2008-12, and less than in Asian countries such as China, Indonesia, Thailand and Viet Nam (MPC, 2014).

14. IT capital includes IT hardware and software as well as communications equipment.

15. According to national data, investment in ICT almost doubled between 2006 and 2010 (period of the Ninth Malaysia Plan) and 2011-13, i.e. the three first years of the Tenth Malaysia Plan (MPC, 2014).

16. TFP growth during the Tenth Malaysia Plan (2011-14, 1.1%) was slower than during the Ninth Plan (2006-10, 1.5%), the Eighth Plan (2001-05, 1.4%) and the Seventh Plan (1996-2000, 1.2%), with little variation overall (MPC, 2015).

17 The index of Revealed Comparative Advantage (RCA(X)) of total exports is calculated as RCA(X)i,c = (Xi,c/Xi,world)/(Xeconomy,c /Xeconomy,world) where Xi,c and Xi,world are respectively exports in industry i by country c and the world, while Xeconomy,c and Xeconomy,world are economy-wide exports by country and the world.

18. Electronic integrated circuits and micro-assemblies, crude petroleum, parts and accessories, data-processing machines, diodes, transistors and similar semiconductor devices; photosensitive semiconductor devices are, respectively the first, third and fourth largest commodity groups for imports in 2013 (UNcomtrade, 2015).

19. Malaysia is the third largest importer of intermediates as a share of its production (25% in 2009), following the logistics hubs of Singapore and Luxemburg. Imported products also represent an important share of its final domestic demand.

20. A part of a country's exports participate in GVCs either through upstream (forward) links – that is looking back along the value chain and measuring foreign inputs/value added included in a country's exports – or downstream links – i.e. measuring the domestic inputs/value added of the country contained in the exports of other countries by looking forward along the value chain.

21. For instance, revisiting bankruptcy time – in several OECD countries it does not last longer than three years (e.g. Canada or Singapore) – and recognition of firm restructuring could find a better balance between creditor protection and the entrepreneur's recovery.

22. According to this taskforce, practices such as identifying policy objectives to regulatory design to implementation; articulating regulatory policy goals, strategies and benefits clearly; and considering the impacts of regulation on competitiveness and economic growth, are key goals for Malaysia.

23. Despite the fact that the Malaysian and Singapore venture capital sectors were created almost at the same time, Malaysia has an important lag in terms of venture capital utilisation.

24. *Bumiputera* is the Malaysian term to describe the Malay race and other indigenous peoples of Southeast Asia.

25. The incentive to innovate relates to the increase in profit that a firm can earn if it invests in R&D – and this will depend on the type of innovation (product or process), the size of this technological novelty (how radical it is), the degree of product differentiation and technological competition, as well as the extent to which innovation is protected through formal means (IPRs).

26. Government-linked corporations (GLCs) account for 36.8% of the agriculture, forestry and fishing sector; 59.6% of the banking sector; 43.7% of the communications sector; 72.3% of the transportation and warehousing sector; and 98.2% of the utilities sector.

27. FDI-related fiscal reforms were initiated in 1992 with a first tax abatement on income generated overseas, followed in 1995 by a full tax exemption on income remitted by Malaysian firms investing abroad.

28. This section draws primarily on the dedicated intellectual property review performed by the OECD in 2015 (OECD, 2015a).

29. For these reasons, IPR is central to competitiveness and business growth, particularly in countries which have started to move up in the curve of development (middle-income countries) and intending to move towards higher levels of development.

30. Malaysia was 25th (out of 144) in 2014-15, 30th (out of 148) in 2013-14, 31st in 2012-13 (out of 144) and 2011-12 (out of 142).

31. A large number of SOEs were privatised, notably Klang Port, Telecom Malaysia and the Tenaga Nasional (electricity utility company). As a result, by 2008, private sector and government-linked companies were investing more in infrastructure than the public sector.

References

Aghion, P. et al. (2005), "Competition and innovation: An inverted U relationship", *Quarterly Journal of Economics*, Vol. 120/2, pp. 701-728, Oxford University Press, Cambridge, Massachusetts, http://dx.doi.org/10.1093/qje/120.2.701.

Andrews, D. and C. Criscuolo (2013), "Knowledge-based capital, innovation and resource allocation", *OECD Economics Department Working Papers*, No. 1 046, OECD Publishing, Paris, http://dx.doi.org/10.1787/5k46bj546kzs-en.

APO (2015), *APO Productivity Databook 2015*, Asian Productivity Organisation, Tokyo.

APO (2014), *APO Productivity Databook 2014*, Asian Productivity Organisation, Tokyo.

CEPII (2015), *CEPII BACI World Trade Database* (database), www.cepii.fr/cepii/fr/bdd_modele/presentation.asp?id=1.

Eichengreen, B., D. Park and K. Shin (2013), "Growth slowdowns redux: New evidence on the middle-income trap", *NBER Working Paper*, National Bureau of Economic Research, Cambridge, Massachusetts, No. 18 673, http://dx.doi.org/10.3386/w18673.

EPU (2015), *Eleventh Malaysia Plan*, Economic Planning Unit, Prime Minister's Department, Putrajaya, http://rmk11.epu.gov.my/index.php/en.

ERIA (2014), *ASEAN Rising: ASEAN and AEC Beyond 2015*, Economic Research Institute for ASEAN and East Asia, www.eria.org/ASEAN_RISING-ASEAN_and_AEC_Beyond_2015.pdf.

Felipe, J. (2012), "Tracking the middle-income trap: What is it, who is in it, and why?", *ADB Economics Working Paper Series*, No. 306, March, Asian Development Bank, Manila, www.adb.org/sites/default/files/publication/29804/economics-wp-306.pdf.

Gill, I. and H. Kharas (2007), *An East Asian Renaissance, Ideas for Growth*, The World Bank, Washington, DC, http://siteresources.worldbank.org/INTEASTASIAPACIFIC/Resources/226262-1158536715202/EA_Renaissance_full.pdf.

Glaeser, E.L. and J.D. Gottlieb (2009), "The wealth of cities: Agglomeration economies and spatial equilibrium in the United States", *Journal of Economic Literature*, Vol. 47/4, American Economic Association, Nashville, Tennessee, pp. 983-1 028, http://dx.doi.org/10.1257/jel.47.4.983.

Gwartney, J., R. Lawson and J. Hall (2015), *Economic Freedom of the World: 2015 Annual Report*, Fraser Institute, www.fraserinstitute.org/sites/default/files/economic-freedom-of-the-world-2015.pdf.

Gwartney, J., R. Lawson and J. Hall (2014), *Economic Freedom of the World: 2014 Annual Report*, Fraser Institute, www.fraserinstitute.org/sites/default/files/economic-freedom-of-the-world-2014.pdf.

Herrendorf, B., R. Rogerson and A. Valentinyi (2013), "Growth and structural transformation", *NBER Working Papers*, No. 18 996, National Bureau of Economic Research, Cambridge Massachusetts, www.nber.org/papers/w18996.

IFC (2011), *IFC Enterprise Finance Gap Database*, https://finances.worldbank.org/fr/Enterprise-Finance/IFC-Enterprise-Finance-Gap-Database-Raw-Data/2ppx-k958.

IGU (2015), *World LNG Report – 2015 Edition*, International Gas Union, Fornebu, Norway.

Jaumotte, F. and N. Pain (2005a), "Innovation in the business sector", *OECD Economics Department Working Papers*, No. 459, OECD Publishing, Paris, http://dx.doi.org/0.1787/688727757285.

Jaumotte, F. and N. Pain (2005b), "An overview of public policies to support innovation", *OECD Economics Department Working Papers*, No. 456, OECD Publishing, Paris, http://dx.doi.org/10.1787/707375561288.

Lee, C. (2014), "Competition law enforcement in Malaysia: Some recent developments", *Malaysian Journal of Economic Studies*, Vol. 51 (Special Issue), Emerald, Bingley, pp. 77-88.

Lewis, W.A. (1954), "Economic development with unlimited supplies of labour", *The Manchester School*, Vol. 22/2, Wiley, Hoboken, New Jersey, pp. 139-191, http://dx.doi.org/10.1111/j.1467-9957.1954.tb00021.x.

MPC (2015), *22nd Productivity Report 2014/2015*, Malaysia Productivity Corporation, Petaling Jaya, www.mpc.gov.my/mpc/images/file/APR/APR20142015.pdf.

MPC (2014), *21st Productivity Report 2013/2014*, Malaysia Productivity Corporation, Petaling Jaya, www.mpc.gov.my/mpc/images/file/APR%202013%202014/Cover.pdf.

NEAC (2010), *New Economic Model for Malaysia*, National Economic Advisory Council, Putrajaya.

Noland, M., D. Park and G.B. Estrada (2012), "Developing the service sector as engine of growth for Asia: An overview", *ADB Economics Working Paper Series*, No. 320, Asian Development Bank, Manila, www.adb.org/sites/default/files/publication/31114/developing-service-sector-engine-growth-asia.pdf.

OECD (2016), "OECD FDI regulatory restrictiveness index", *OECD International Direct Investment Statistics* (database), http://dx.doi.org/10.1787/g2g55501-en.

OECD (2015a), *Boosting Malaysia National Intellectual Property System for Innovation*, OECD Publishing, Paris, http://dx.doi.org/10.1787/9789264239227-en.

OECD (2015b), *Implementing Good Regulatory Practice in Malaysia*, OECD Publishing, Paris, http://dx.doi.org/10.1787/9789264230620-en.

OECD (2014a), *Economic Outlook for Southeast Asia, China and India 2014: Beyond the Middle-Income Trap*, OECD Publishing, Paris, http://dx.doi.org/10.1787/saeo-2014-en.

OECD (2014b), *OECD Reviews of Innovation Policy: Colombia 2014*, OECD Publishing, Paris, http://dx.doi.org/10.1787/9789264204638-en.

OECD (2014c), *Perspectives on Global Development 2014: Boosting Productivity to Meet the Middle-Income Challenge*, OECD Publishing, Paris, http://dx.doi.org/10.1787/persp_glob_dev-2014-en.

OECD (2013a), *Innovation in Southeast Asia*, OECD Publishing, Paris, http://dx.doi.org/10.1787/9789264128712-en.

OECD (2013b), *OECD Investment Policy Reviews: Malaysia 2013*, OECD Publishing, Paris, http://dx.doi.org/10.1787/9789264194588-en.

OECD and World Bank (2014), *Science, Technology and Innovation in Viet Nam*, OECD Publishing, Paris, http://dx.doi.org/10.1787/9789264213500-en.

OECD/WTO (2016), "Trade in value added", *OECD-WTO: Statistics on Trade in Value Added* (database), http://dx.doi.org/10.1787/data-00648-en.

Ohno, K. (2009), "Avoiding the middle-income trap: Renovating industrial policy formulation in Vietnam", *ASEAN Economic Bulletin*, Vol. 26/1, Institute of Southeast Asian Studies (ISEAS), Singapore pp. 25-43.

Park, D. and K. Shin (2012), "The service sector in Asia: Is it an engine of growth?", *ADB Economics Working Papers*, No. 322, Asian Development Bank, Manila.

PEMANDU (2014), *Economic Transformation Programme: Annual Report 2014*, http://etp.pemandu.gov.my/annualreport2014.

Rasiah, R. (2010), "Are electronics firms in Malaysia catching up in the technology ladder?", *Journal of the Asia Pacific Economy*, Vol. 15/3, Special Issue: Innovation and Catch-Up Experiences in Automotive and Electronics Industries in Asia, pp. 301-319, http://dx.doi.org/10.1080/13547860.2010.494910.

Thiruchelvam, K. et al. (2011b), "Innovation financing in Asia: The experience of Malaysia", report prepared for the International Development Research Centre, Ottawa.

UNcomtrade (2015), *United Nations Commodity Trade Statistics Database* (database), http://comtrade.un.org/db/default.aspx.

UNCTAD (2015), *FDI Statistics Division on Investment and Enterprise* (database), http://unctad.org/en/Pages/DIAE/FDI%20Statistics/FDI-Statistics.aspx.

UNDP (2013), *Human Development Report 2013: The Rise of the South: Human Progress in a Diverse World*, United Nations Development Programme, New York, http://hdr.undp.org/sites/default/files/reports/14/hdr2013_en_complete.pdf.

Westmore, B. (2013), "R&D, patenting and growth: The role of public policy", *OECD Economics Department Working Papers*, No. 1 047, OECD Publishing, Paris, http://dx.doi.org/10.1787/5k46h2rfb4f3-en.

Woo, W.T. (2009), "Getting Malaysia out of the middle-income trap", University of California, Davis, Economics Department, 13 August, http://ssrn.com/abstract=1534454.

World Bank (2016a), *Doing Business 2016 – Measuring Regulatory Quality and Efficiency*, The World Bank, Washington, DC, www.doingbusiness.org/~/media/GIAWB/Doing%20Business/Documents/Annual-Reports/English/DB16-Full-Report.pdf.

World Bank (2016b), *Doing Business Data* (database), www.doingbusiness.org/data.

World Bank (2015a), *Enterprise Survey Data* (database), www.enterprisesurveys.org/data/survey-datasets.

World Bank (2015b), *World Development Indicators* (database), http://data.worldbank.org/data-catalog/world-development-indicators.

World Bank (2014), *Malaysia Economic Monitor: Boosting Trade Competitiveness*, No. 89 102, The World Bank, Bangkok, www-wds.worldbank.org/external/default/WDSContentServer/WDSP/IB/2014/06/27/000350881_20140627082245/Rendered/PDF/891020WP0P14640B00PUBLIC00MEM100web.pdf.

World Bank (2013), *Taking Stock. An Update of Vietnam's Recent Economic Developments*, The World Bank, Hanoi, 8 July.

World Bank (2010), *Malaysia Economic Monitor: Growth through Innovation*, The World Bank, Bangkok, http://siteresources.worldbank.org/INTMALAYSIA/Resources/324392-1271308532887/mem_april2010_fullreport.pdf.

World Economic Forum (2016), *Global Competitiveness Report 2016*, The World Economic Forum, Geneva, http://reports.weforum.org/global-competitiveness-report-2015-2016.

World Economic Forum (2015), *Global Competitiveness Report Dataset* (database), http://reports.weforum.org/global-competitiveness-report-2014-2015/downloads.

Yusuf, S. and K. Nabeshima (2009), "Tiger economies under threat. A comparative analysis of Malaysia's industrial prospects and policy options", *Knowledge Economy Study*, No. 51 278, The World Bank, Washington, DC, http://dx.doi.org/10.1596/978-0-8213-7880-9.

Zhuang, J., P. Vandenberg and Y. Huang (2012), *Growing Beyond the Low-cost Advantage*, Asian Development Bank, Manila.

Chapter 3.

Innovation performance in Malaysia

This chapter examines the innovation capabilities and performance of the business and public research sectors. It begins with a review of the significant increase in R&D efforts, as evidenced by the increase in STI expenditures and personnel, although still insufficient and uneven. It then examines the mixed results of these efforts, from direct outputs to commercialisation.

A significant increase in R&D effort…

At the time of its independence, Malaysia had a handful of historical universities and public research institutes (PRIs), which were mainly dedicated to supporting the leading primary sectors (palm oil, minerals, etc.). The surge of foreign direct investment (FDI) generated a growing demand for domestic technical expertise and skills to maintain and adapt manufacturing equipment and master industrial processes. Malaysia gradually adapted to this surge of FDI. However, its R&D efforts remained at a low level until well into the 1990s. Malaysia's economic growth trajectory was punctuated by the Asian financial crisis and slowed in its aftermath. Malaysia, in response, started to search for new sources of growth and stepped up its investments in intangible assets, including R&D. In 2012, the R&D expenditure of higher learning institutions, government research institutes and business enterprises taken together was 20 times higher than in 1996, reaching MYR 10.6 billion (about USD 3.4 billion) in 2012.[1]

An important hurdle for many middle-income countries aspiring to build a stronger innovation system is a fundamental imbalance in, or even distortion of, their existing innovation system. In most cases, R&D in these countries is largely performed in public institutions (universities or government research institutes), whereas R&D activity in the business sector is very low. Furthermore, domestic public research institutes and universities often have little interaction with businesses which exert little effective demand for their R&D-related services. In contrast, Malaysia has reached a considerable level of business R&D activity, accounting for about 0.73% of gross domestic product (GDP) in 2012, in the same range as the People's Republic of China (hereafter "China") in 2002 or, more recently, Brazil and the Russian Federation. In addition, businesses account for the majority of Malaysia's domestic R&D expenditures. The impressive increase in R&D expenditure from 1992 to 2006 was led almost exclusively by companies' spending (Figure 3.1, Panel A). R&D expenditure started to slow down in 2006 and even, as of 2010, to decline in absolute[2] and relative terms. The fall in the share of business R&D expenditures, which represented over 80% of the GDP on R&D (GERD) in 2006, was accentuated by the increase of R&D activities in universities and, more recently, PRIs following a long period of decline of the latter. This trend has led to a more even distribution of public and private actors' expenditures, with the public research organisations accounting for 54% of total expenditures in 2014 (Figure 3.1, Panel B).[3]

Business enterprises have historically been the main funders of R&D in Malaysia. However, their share has decreased since 2006 (Figure 3.2). In 2014 it reached its all-time lowest share of GERD (MASTIC, 2016a). Most business R&D expenditure is self-financed (Figure 3.3); the financial support provided by the government to business R&D remains very small despite a large portfolio of policy instruments dedicated to stimulate business investment in research. The data for 2014 show a significant increase of the amount of BERD financed by the government.

Most of the business R&D expenditure is for applied and, to a lesser extent, experimental development (Figure 3.4). These two types of R&D represent a large proportion of total R&D expenditure. Along with the overall trend of business R&D expenditure, the growth of R&D expenditure for applied research has slowed down in recent years (Figure 3.5), whereas basic research has slightly increased since 2006 – and radically in 2012 (34% of GERD). Applied research has, however, remained at a high level (more than 66% in 2010 and 2011 and 50% in 2012). The data for 2014 show some unexpected trends, with applied research increasing to 76% and basic research decreasing by half to 17% of GERD.[4] The bulk of R&D funding is allocated to the fields of ICT, engineering sciences and biotechnologies.

Figure 3.1. **R&D expenditure by institutional sector, Malaysia, 1988-2014**

Panel A

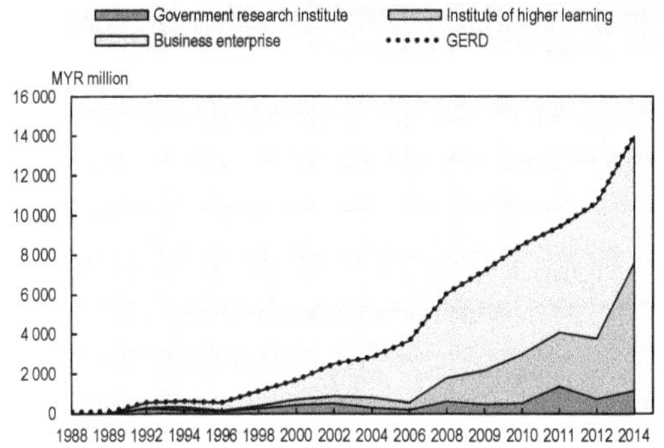

Source: MASTIC (2001, 2005, 2009, 2013, 2016a), *National Surveys of Research and Development.*

Panel B

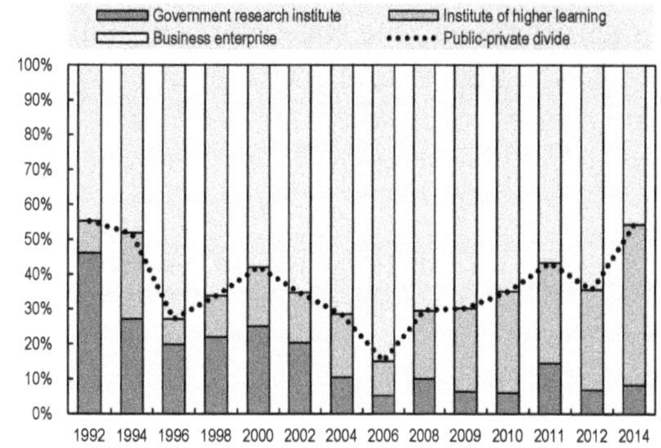

Source: MASTIC (2001, 2005, 2009, 2013, 2016a), *National Surveys of Research and Development.*

Figure 3.2. **R&D expenditure by source of funds, Malaysia, 1998-2012**

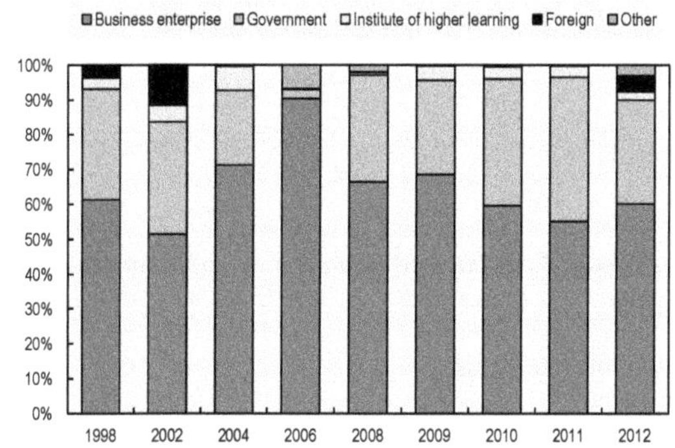

Sources: UNESCO; MASTIC (2001, 2005, 2009, 2013, 2016a), *National Surveys of Research and Development.*

Figure 3.3. **BERD by source of funds, Malaysia, 1992-2012**

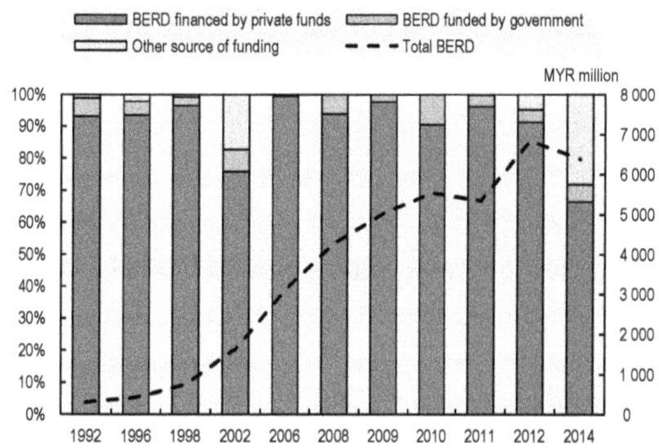

Sources: MASTIC (2001, 2005, 2009, 2013, 2016a), *National Surveys of Research and Development.*

In line with the increase in expenditures, there has been a strong increase in the number of R&D personnel since 2006. This concerns mainly researchers, but the number of technicians and support staff has also increased significantly. Twenty-one percent had a PhD in 2014 (45% in 2012), however, only 0.4% of those who had a PhD work in business companies, whereas 98% are employed in institutes of higher learning (MASTIC, 2016a). Moreover, the proportion of researchers, although superior to all Association of Southeast Asian Nations (ASEAN) countries with the exception of Singapore, remains low according to developed countries' standards (which is at the level of the bottom five OECD countries; Figure 3.6).

Insufficient and uneven R&D investment

Aggregate R&D intensity (GERD over GDP) has increased significantly, in particular between 1996 and 2002 and again from 2006 to 2009. During the whole period for which data are available, it rose from somewhat below 0.5% in 1990 to 1.13% in 2012 and 1.26% in 2014, which represents a significant achievement given the GDP growth Malaysia recorded during these 25 years. Yet this level of R&D intensity still falls short of the national goals set by the government in its national STI-related plans (Table 3.1). In the context of a changed global economic environment, the Malaysian government lowered its target from 1.5% (for 2010) to 1% (for 2015). In another revision of the R&D intensity target,[5] the latest National Policy on Science, Technology and Innovation set the bar at a higher level, *viz.* at 2% of GDP for 2020 (MOSTI, 2013). Achieving this ambitious target when the country is meant to join the high-income group of nations would require tremendous efforts from both public and private actors.[6]

Figure 3.4. **GERD by type of research, Malaysia (amount)**

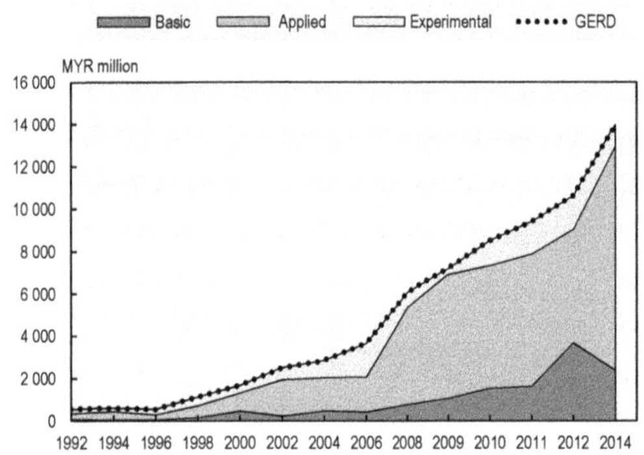

Sources: MASTIC (2001, 2005, 2009, 2013, 2016a), *National Surveys of Research and Development.*

Figure 3.5. **GERD by type of research, Malaysia (percentage)**

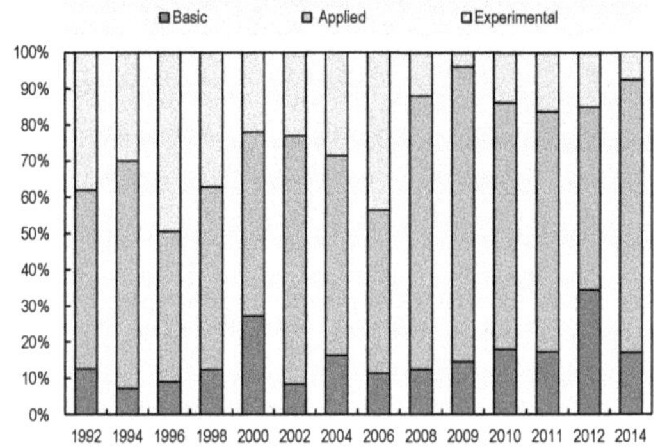

Sources: MASTIC (2001, 2005, 2009, 2013, 2016a), *National Surveys of Research and Development.*

Figure 3.6. **Researchers in R&D, headcounts, Malaysia, OECD and selected Asian countries, 1996-2012**

Number of researchers per million people

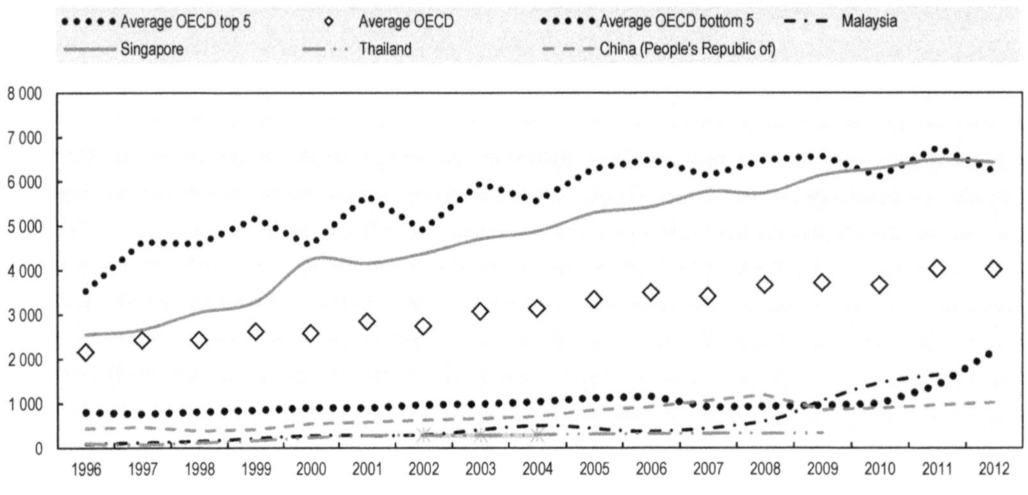

Source: World Bank (2015), *World Development Indicators* (database), http://data.worldbank.org/data-catalog/world-development-indicators.

Table 3.1. **R&D intensity goals and achievements in Malaysia, 1986-2020**

Science, technology and innovation national plans	Timeframe	R&D intensity goal	R&D intensity achieved during/at the end of the period
National Science and Technology Policy (NSPT1)	1986-89	1.5% in 1989	0.38% in 1992
Ninth Malaysia Plan	2006-10	1.5% in 2010	1.07% in 2010
Second National Science and Technology Policy (NSPT2)	2002-10	1.5% in 2010	
Tenth Malaysia Plan	2011-15	1% in 2015	1.26% in 2014
National Policy on Science, Technology and Innovation (NPSTI)	2013-20	2% in 2020	

Malaysia's achievements notwithstanding, its level of R&D still compares rather poorly with that of developed countries overall. It is slightly above the level of R&D intensity of the bottom five OECD countries, but still far below the OECD average (Figure 3.7).[7] In emerging Asia, Malaysia is below the level achieved by Singapore and China (slightly above and below the OECD average, respectively). Whereas Singapore has reduced its R&D intensity, China has steadily increased its investment in R&D at a high pace, allowing it to rise from the level of the OECD bottom five to the OECD average in terms of R&D intensity in only 15 years, despite high GDP growth (Figure 3.8). At the same time, Malaysia is far ahead of most Southeast Asian countries both in terms of the level of R&D intensity achieved and evolution of this key indicator. The countries are very heterogeneous, owing to their respective state of development and the priority they give to research and innovation.

Figure 3.7. **R&D intensity, Malaysia and selected Asian countries and OECD average, top and bottom five, 1990-2012**

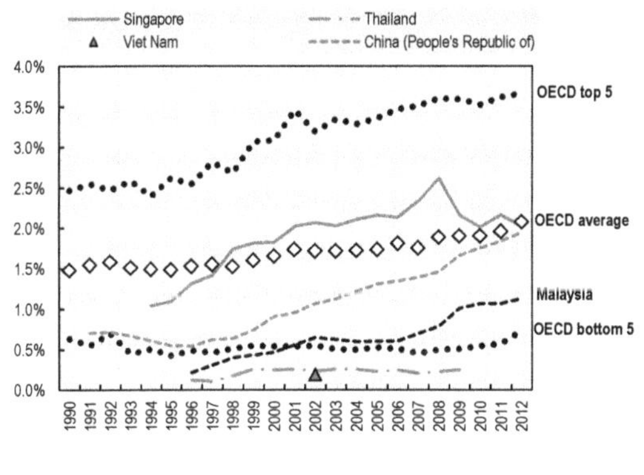

Sources: MASTIC National R&D Surveys; OECD (2016), "Main science and technology indicators", *OECD Science, Technology and R&D Statistics* (database), http://dx.doi.org/10.1787/data-00182-en.

Figure 3.8. **GERD on GDP, Malaysia and selected Southeast Asian countries, 2002 and latest available year**

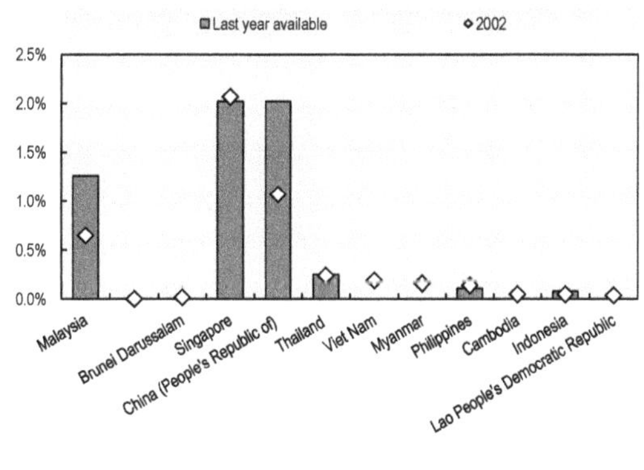

Note: Latest available year is 2014 for Malaysia, 2012 for Singapore, 2013 for China, 2009 for Thailand, 2007 for the Philippines and 2009 for Indonesia.

Sources: MASTIC National R&D Surveys; OECD (2016), "Main science and technology indicators", *OECD Science, Technology and R&D Statistics* (database), http://dx.doi.org/10.1787/data-00182-en.

The focus was on applied research mirrored by both low experimental development and basic research, which have been throughout the whole period below the OECD average despite significant annual variations (Figure 3.9). The composition of Malaysian R&D is also in sharp contrast to other Asian countries, where experimental development is dominant, as is the case in China (84% of GERD in 2012), Chinese Taipei (67% in 2012) or, to a lesser extent, Singapore and Thailand (both 48% in 2012 and 2009).

This is particularly meaningful considering the trajectory of top-performing countries such as Korea or Chinese Taipei, where applied research accounted for the largest share of total R&D expenditures in the early stages of their development. As those countries reached high-income levels, experimental research and – later on in most cases – basic research increased. More recently, the evolution of Singapore's research portfolio over the last two decades or so, and in particular the gradual increase of the share of basic research while maintaining a high share of experimental development, is also notable in that regard (Figure 3.10).

Figure 3.9. **GERD by type of research, OECD average and Malaysia, 1992-2012**

OECD average | Malaysia

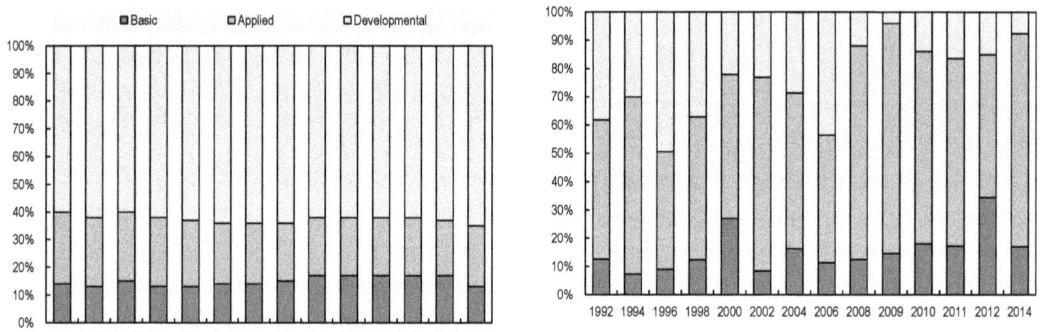

Source: MASTIC National R&D Surveys; OECD (2016), "Main science and technology indicators", *OECD Science, Technology and R&D Statistics* (database), http://dx.doi.org/10.1787/data-00182-en.

Figure 3.10. **GERD by type of research, Singapore, 1994-2012**

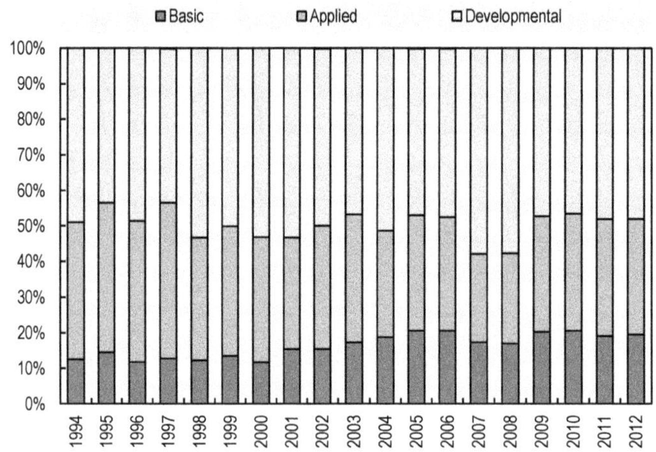

Source: OECD (2016), "Main science and technology indicators", *OECD Science, Technology and R&D Statistics* (database), http://dx.doi.org/10.1787/data-00182-en.

Mixed innovation performance

Research outputs

Starting from very modest levels, the number of scientific publications increased almost seven-fold between 2001 and 2011. Malaysia recorded the world's fastest growth in the number of publications over the period 2005-09 (NSRC, 2013). The peak in 2008 was at least partly triggered by both a significant increase in R&D government funding and a change in the criteria used by the Ministry of Education for evaluating institutes of higher learning, factoring in the number of publications (Figure 3.11).[8] More than half of these publications were produced by only two universities: the University of Malaya and the Universiti Sains Malaysia (MASTIC, 2012c). More generally, the universities that were awarded the status of research universities accounted for about 70% of publications during the period 2005-09 (NSRC, 2013) and 62% in 2014 (MASTIC, 2016b).

Figure 3.11. **Number and annual increase of scientific publications, Malaysia, 2001-14**

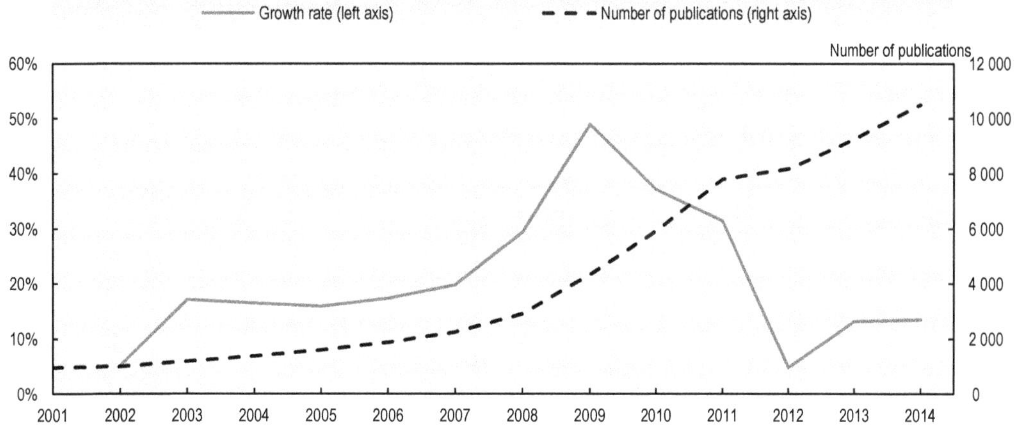

Source: MASTIC (2016b), *Bibliometric Study 2015*.

Despite the surge in publications up to 2010, Malaysia remains behind Singapore and Thailand over the period 2009-11 (MASTIC, 2012c), as was already the case between 1996 and 2008.[9]

Performance in terms of number of citations and international collaboration is also mixed. The proportion of international collaborations has remained rather stable, between 30% and 45% of publications. The number of citations, a widely used indicator of the impact of research, has also been stable and decreased in recent years, which can be partly attributed to the mechanics of citations (Figure 3.12).

Using the number of publications and citations during the period 2001-11, Malaysia ranked, respectively, 45th and 50th, behind Singapore and Thailand. However, Malaysia only ranks 136th out of 147 countries when the number of citations by publication is taken into account, far behind any other ASEAN country (Table 3.2). This gap raises concerns about the quality and usefulness of Malaysian publications. In many regards, it seems the quality has not followed the increase in the quantity of publications.

The country share of the world's top cited articles is another commonly used proxy of scientific excellence. The analysis of this indicator over the period 1990-2010 confirms and deepens the results set out above.

The quality of the articles with only Malaysian authors, i.e. excluding all articles published in collaboration with foreign authors, has considerably increased during the period. The share of the world's top 10% most cited articles in their respective fields by these "purely domestic articles" rose from 0.01% in 1990-92 to 0.22% in 2008-10 (Figure 3.13). The gap between the share of all articles and the share of the best (most cited) articles has become smaller over time, which tends to show a move toward scientific quality rather than quantity.

Figure 3.12. **Number of publications, citations per document and share of international collaboration, Malaysia, 1996-2014**

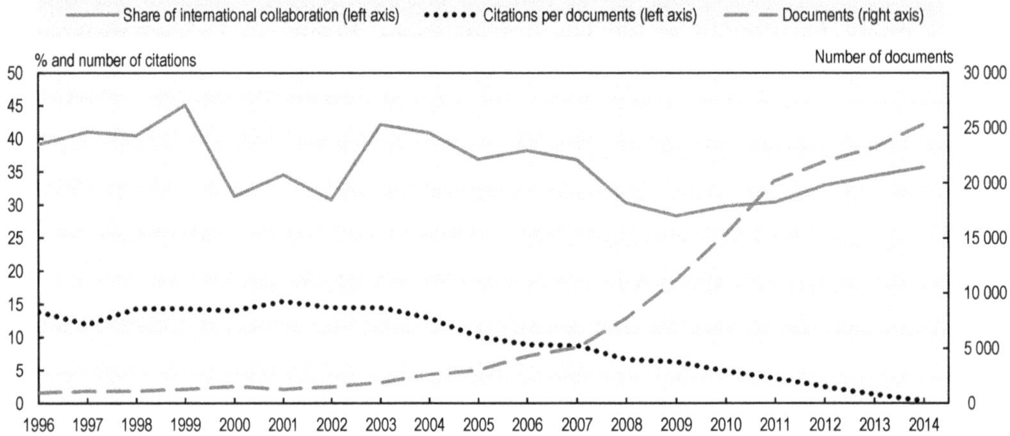

Source: SCImago (2014), *Country Rankings* (database), www.scimagojr.com/countryrank.php.

Table 3.2. **International comparisons of bibliometric indicators, selected Asian countries, 2001-11**

	Rank by number of publications	Rank by number of citations	Rank by number of citations per publication
Malaysia	50	45	136
China (People's Republic of)	7	2	106
Indonesia	61	67	73
Philippines	64	70	59
Singapore	29	32	46
Thailand	41	44	75
Viet Nam	63	65	87

Source: MASTIC (2012c), *Bibliometric Study 2012*.

Figure 3.13. **Share of world total and world's 10% most cited articles (purely domestic articles in all fields), 1990-2010**

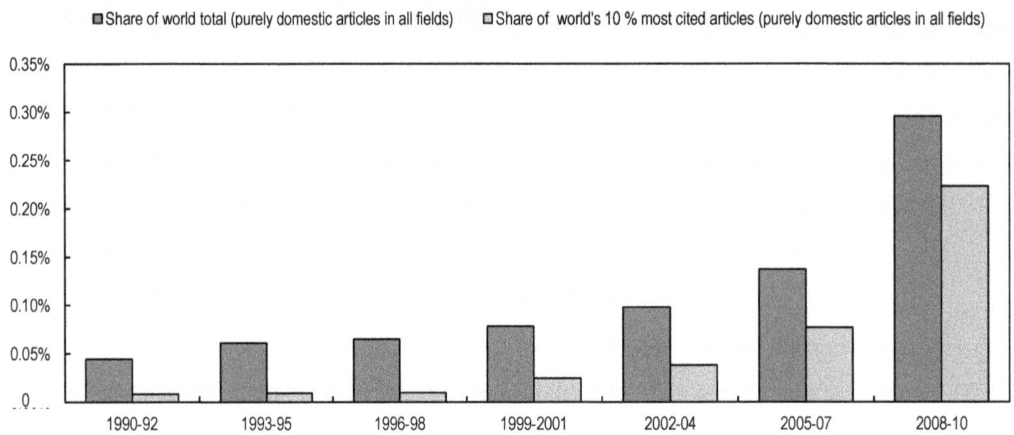

Source: Thomson Reuters Web of Science (WoS), based on calculations made for IVA (2013), *Sweden's Global Connectivity in Research: An Analysis of International Co-authorship*, www.iva.se/globalassets/rapporter/agenda-for-forskning/agenda-for-forskning-swedens-global-connectivity-in-research.pdf.

Countries such as Thailand and Viet Nam began a similar surge a few years later than Malaysia and their domestic scientists have now reached almost the same level of excellence (Figures 3.14 and 3.15).

Articles produced in the framework of an international collaboration have a level of quality far higher than the purely domestic ones. In international comparison, Malaysia performs less favourably than other Southeast Asian countries, in particular in the most recent years.[10]

Figure 3.14. **Share of articles among world's 10% most cited articles in the respective field (purely domestic articles in all fields), 1990-2010**

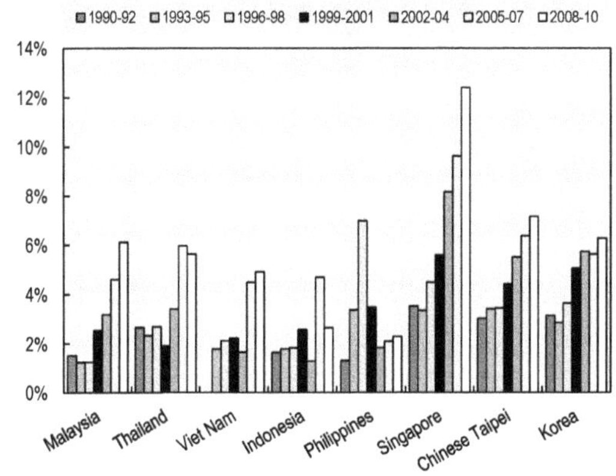

Figure 3.15. **Share of articles among world's 10% most cited articles in the respective field (articles with authors from at least 5 countries in all fields), 1990-2010**

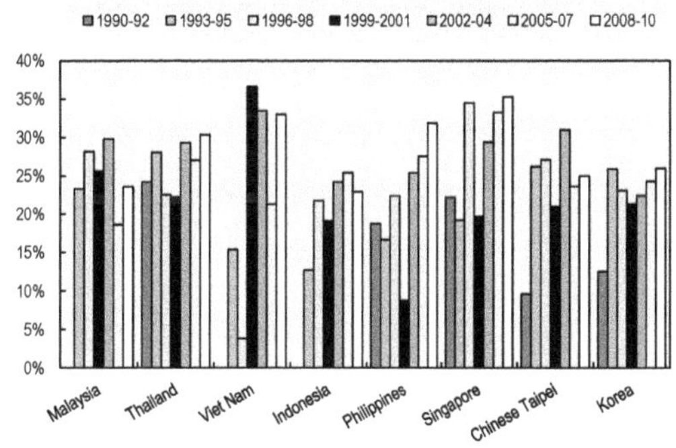

Source: Thomson Reuters Web of Science (WoS), based on calculations made for IVA (2013), *Sweden's Global Connectivity in Research: An Analysis of International Co-authorship*, www.iva.se/globalassets/rapporter/agenda-for-forskning/agenda-for-forskning-swedens-global-connectivity-in-research.pdf.

Medicine, which used to be the top ranking scientific fields in terms of number of publications (13% of all publications), has now been overtaken by engineering (26%) (OECD, 2015a). In a national bibliometric study covering the period 2001-14, the field of material science ranked first, closely followed by crystallography and, further behind, electrical and electronic engineering (MASTIC, 2016b). The analysis of top-cited articles demonstrates the strength of Malaysia's scientists in mathematics, engineering and agriculture (Figure 3.16).

The number of patent applications has also increased significantly over the last two decades. Between 1994 and 2013, the number of applications doubled, from approximately 4 000 to more than 8 300. However, the country has moved down a few positions in the world ranking, from 33rd in 2003 to 37th in 2012 (OECD, 2015a). While the bulk of these patents are applications filed by non-residents – mainly multinational enterprises located in Malaysia – the share of resident applicants has increased significantly since 2001, up to 17% of total applications in 2013. The number of applications filed abroad by residents has also increased significantly since 2003 (Figure 3.17). The share of residents' applications, which can be considered an indicator of progress in developing the domestic science and technology base, is the second highest among ASEAN countries, after Thailand (Figure 3.18).

Figure 3.16. **Share of articles among world's 10% most cited articles by field (purely domestic articles in all fields), 1990-2010**

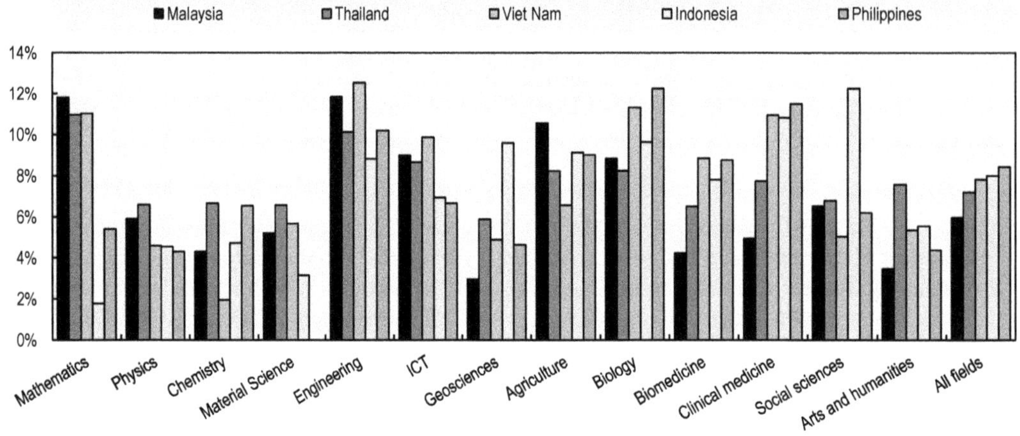

Source: Thomson Reuters Web of Science (WoS), based on calculations made for IVA (2013), *Sweden's Global Connectivity in Research: An Analysis of International Co-authorship*, www.iva.se/globalassets/rapporter/agenda-for-forskning/agenda-for-forskning-swedens-global-connectivity-in-research.pdf.

Figure 3.17. **Patent applications by residents and non-residents, Malaysia, 1994-2013**

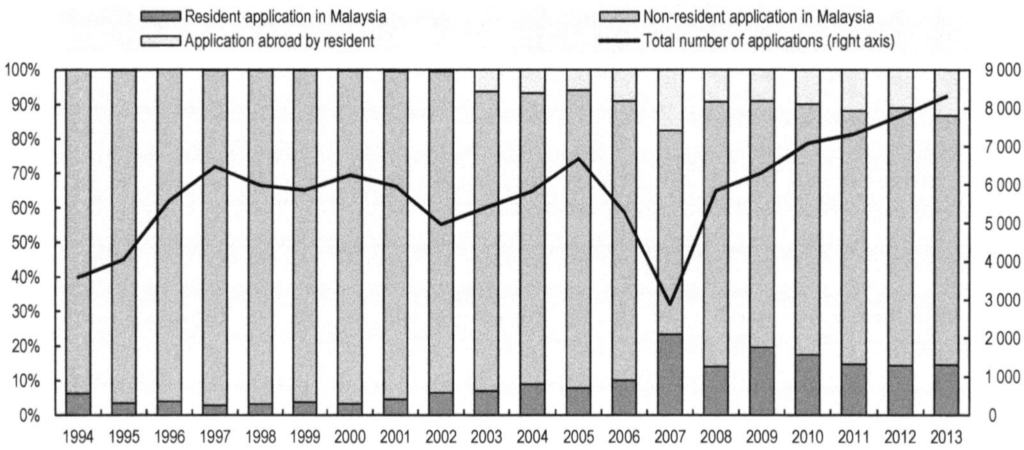

Notes: A resident application is an application filed with an intellectual property office by an applicant residing in the country in which that office has jurisdiction. A non-resident application is an application filed with a patent office of a given country/jurisdiction by an applicant residing in another country. An application abroad is an application filed by a resident of a given country/jurisdiction with a patent office of another country/jurisdiction.

Source: WIPO (2015), *WIPO IP Statistics Data Center* (database), http://ipstats.wipo.int/ipstatv2.

The evolution of the number of resident applications has accelerated, in particular between 2006 and 2009, outpacing Thailand and Singapore around 2008 (Figure 3.19). This indicator is all the more important as there appears to be a correlation between the number of resident applications and a country's level of development. By comparison, the share of resident applications was, on average, 63% in OECD countries and 82% in China in 2012. In China, the share of resident applications followed a U-shaped trajectory, as residents were the only applicants before the country adopted its "open door" policy which attracted technologically active non-residents. Around 2000, this trend was reversed as the country built its own domestic scientific capabilities.

Figure 3.18. **Patent applications by residents and non-residents, ASEAN countries, 2013**

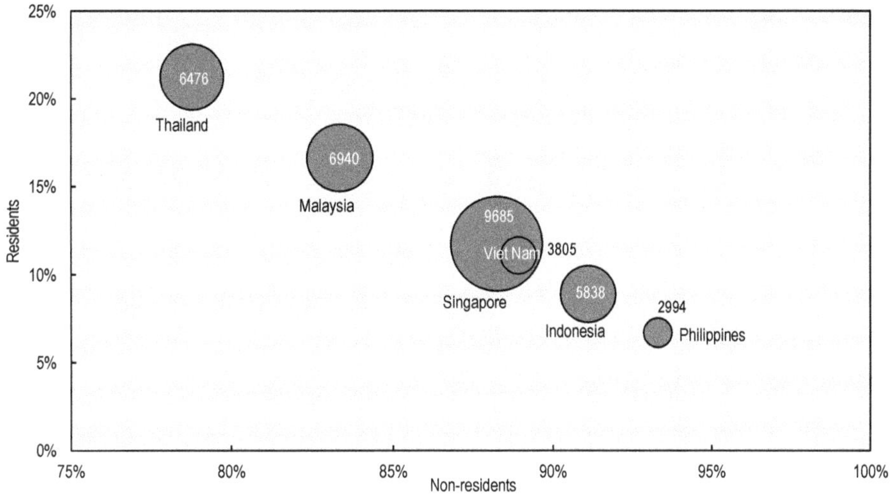

Notes: The numbers in the circles indicate total patent applications filed through the Patent Cooperation Treaty procedure or with a national patent office.

Source: World Bank (2015), *World Development Indicators* (database), http://data.worldbank.org/data-catalog/world-development-indicators.

Figure 3.19. **Patent applications by residents, Malaysia and selected ASEAN countries, 1994-2012**

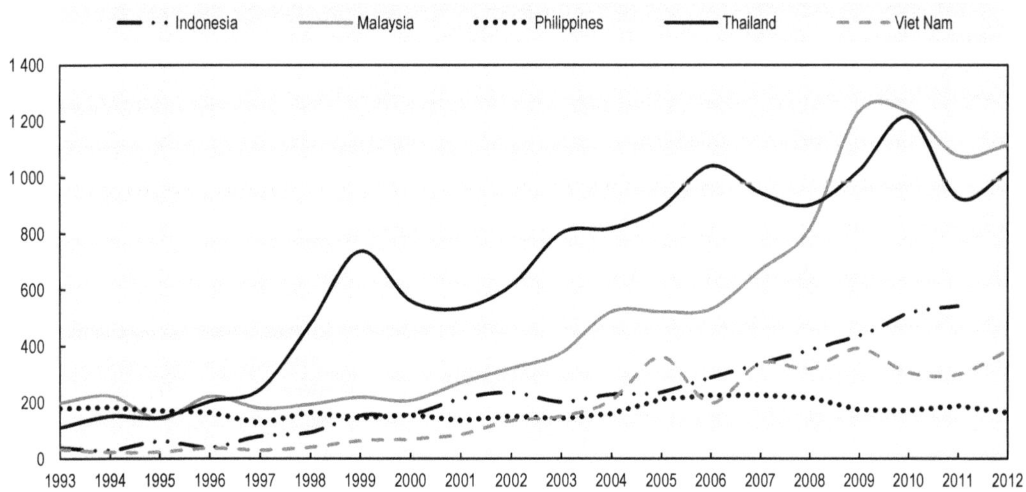

Notes: A resident application is an application filed with an intellectual property office by an applicant residing in the country in which that office has jurisdiction. A non-resident application is an application filed with a patent office of a given country/jurisdiction by an applicant residing in another country. An application abroad is an application filed by a resident of a given country/jurisdiction with a patent office of another country/jurisdiction.

Source: WIPO (2015), *WIPO IP Statistics Data Center* (database), http://ipstats.wipo.int/ipstatv2.

Research commercialisation

Malaysia's innovation performance is mixed. Although there is little doubt that it has improved in the last two decades – in line with the increase in both R&D spending and patent applications by residents – the extent of this progress is still debated. It has, for instance, improved significantly in the rankings of innovation-related indexes of the World Economic Forum's *Global Competitiveness Report*. In 2015-16, Malaysia's global ranking on capacity for innovation improved from 25th to 7th place and it is now ranked 1st among Southeast Asian countries (Table 3.3).

Table 3.3. **Global Competitiveness Report – innovation pillar indexes, Malaysia, 2010-16**

	2010-11		2015-16	
	Rank		Rank	
	Global	Southeast Asia	Global	Southeast Asia
Capacity for innovation	25	2	7	1
University-industry collaboration in R&D	22	2	12	2

Note: Out of 139 countries in the 2010-11 report; out of 144 countries in the 2014-15 report.

Source: World Economic Forum (2016), *Global Competitiveness Report 2016*, http://reports.weforum.org/global-competitiveness-report-2015-2016; World Economic Forum (2015), *Global Competitiveness Report Dataset* (database), http://reports.weforum.org/global-competitiveness-report-2014-2015/downloads.

Malaysia is a net importer of intellectual property rights, paying USD 1.42 billion in royalties and receiving USD 101 million in return in 2013. The gap between payments and receipts has increased since 2009, revealing that Malaysia captures even more foreign technologies, while its intellectual property (IP) licensing has stagnated or even decreased. In absolute terms, the amounts involved are rather small compared to China, Singapore and, to a lesser extent, Thailand (Figures 3.20 and 3.21).

Figure 3.20. **Royalties and licensing fee receipts, Malaysia, 2005-13**

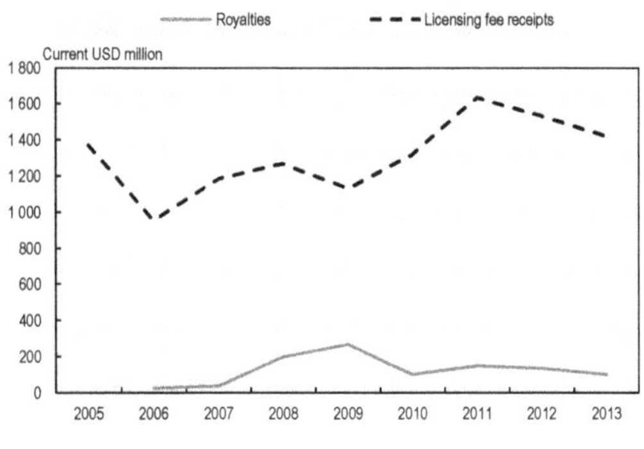

Figure 3.21. **Royalties and licensing fee receipts, selected countries, 2013**

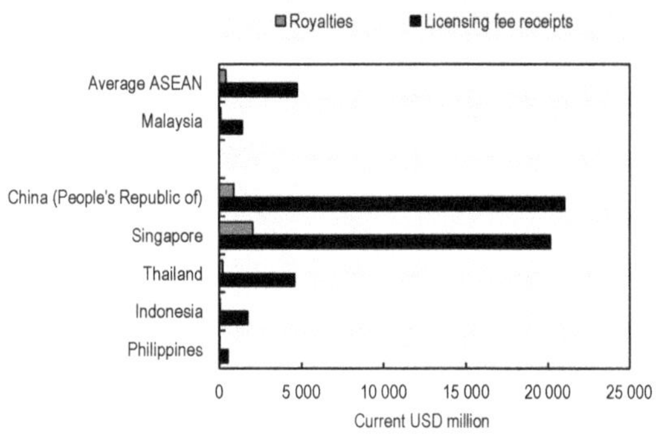

Source: World Bank (2015), *World Development Indicators* (database), http://data.worldbank.org/data-catalog/world-development-indicators.

Although the number of patent applications is increasing, the commercialisation rate of research from public research institutions has until recently remained low. While the data on that matter have to be treated with caution, there is some evidence supporting this argument:

- In a review of R&D commercialisation challenges for Malaysia, Chandran (2010) analyses a survey of 5 232 projects implemented by the public research institutions and universities over 1991-99. The share of these projects identified as candidates for commercialisation was 14.1%; 5.1% were commercialised subsequently.[11] The author notes that the commercialisation rate was even lower, at 3.4% for 2000-05.
- A more recent assessment of R&D undertaken in the primary commodity sector indicated that the percentage of commercialisation of R&D in industrial agricultural commodities was 8.9%. In this regard, the palm oil sector contributed the highest commercialisation rate of 12.1% (EPU, 2006).
- An evaluation of R&D projects funded under the Intensification of Research in Priority Areas (IRPA) Programme, funded by the Ministry of Science, Technology and Innovation (MOSTI) during the Seventh Malaysia Plan, revealed that only 3.4% of the projects were commercialised during the Eighth Malaysia Plan period (EPU, 2006).

Much of IP-protected research in Malaysia is therefore never commercialised. Exceptions are to be found in the IP portfolio of key Malaysian research actors, such as the Universiti Sains Malaysia and the Universiti Putra Malaysia (UPM), as well as, on the public research institute side, the Malaysia Palm Oil Board (MPOB) and the Rubber Research Institute of Malaysia (RRIM) (Chandran, 2010). For instance, the MPOB generated USD 1.43 billion and has the highest commercialisation rate, at 30.6%.

The main barriers to improving the rate of commercialisation are the insufficient industry-relevant R&D projects and the lack of funding at the various stages of the commercialisation process (Chandran, 2010). This is confirmed by the results of the National R&D Survey 2012, where the lack of funding for and the high costs of innovation activities are considered by innovating Malaysian companies to be the main factors hampering innovation activities.[12] Among the knowledge factors, the limited pool of qualified personnel is also seen as particularly detrimental to innovation activities (MASTIC, 2016c).

In general, research institutes in many cases seem less prepared for commercialisation than universities, facing larger administrative barriers, budgetary constraints on research and a culture that until recently put little emphasis either on collaboration with the business sector or on IP.

The number of IP titles held by universities is one of the required quantitative performance measurements used in performance evaluations which influence funding. Such efforts have successfully introduced universities to a different way of operating, to tackling challenges involved in registering and obtaining IP, and to creating incentive programmes that encourage researchers to engage in IP ventures and look for effective partnerships with industry.

As an attempt to provide an incentive for commercialisation, the Ministry of Education required universities and public research institutes to generate a share of their revenues. Another, more qualitative approach, consisted in the creation of platforms for technology, where patents held by universities and public research institutes are displayed and promoted to generate sales. The two main platforms are PlatCOM Ventures, which provides a strong legal infrastructure and effective administration regime to enhance greater creativity and exploitation of intellectual property, and MyIPO (Intellectual Property Corporation of Malaysia), charged with the provision of technical information.

Both platforms aim to give research institutions the opportunity to display their technologies to potential licensors or purchasers. The OECD (2015a) recommends combining both initiatives to raise interest among IP owners to feature on platforms.

There is also an initiative by Malaysia Debt Ventures to accept IP as collateral for loans to finance innovation activities. However, this initiative is still in its initial stage and will require legal adjustments that would allow patents to function as collateral.

As part of efforts to accelerate the commercialisation of R&D findings, many schemes and grants are available, such as the Biotechnology Commercialisation Fund. However, apart from fiscal incentives, such as the pioneer status for ten years and tax deductions equivalent to actual investment, companies are barely using – and for a majority of them are barely aware of – the support initiatives put in place by the government.[13]

Notes

1. The latest year for which data are currently available.
2. Decrease from 2 708 to 2 479 constant USD PPPs (IPP data).
3. Above 40% in 2011. However, as of 2012, five government research institutes have been reclassified as business enterprises: SIRIM Berhad, Cyber Security Malaysia, Sarawak Biodiversity Centre, Astronautic Technology Sdn Bhd and Craun Research (MASTIC, 2014).
4. It will be important in the coming years to verify whether this evolution reflects a new trend or the change of survey methodology (the mode of data collection and the databases used were significantly modified in the latest R&D Survey) (MASTIC, 2016a).
5. In their survey on Malaysia, the quality of survey-based STI indicators, including GERD, is put into question by Day and Muhammad (2011). The response rate has, however, increased significantly in the latest national R&D surveys (MASTIC, 2016a).
6. Although this type of projection should be taken with caution, an extrapolation of the data from 2000 through 2014 indicates that Malaysia could only achieve 1.83% of GERD per GDP in 2020 (MASTIC, 2016a).
7. The total OECD R&D intensity was 2.4 in 2013 (OECD, 2015b).
8. The number of publications in 2011 should be considered with caution as the year was truncated because of the data collection schedule (MASTIC, 2012c).
9. According to Day and Muhammad's analysis of the *Scopus database* (2011), Malaysia ranked 48th in the world in terms of publications, while Thailand ranked 42nd and Singapore 31st.
10. Only the statistics for large co-operation (authors from at least five countries) are shown here. Malaysia's performance compares even more poorly when considering the statistics for publications with two to four foreign co-authors.

11. This represents about 260 projects in nine years. For comparison, in the 2015 Budget, the government has set a target for MOSTI to commercialise 360 high-impact innovative products within the next five years.

12. This proportion has increased in the most recent surveys (EPU, 2010).

13. As shown by the results of the *National Survey of Innovation 2012* (MASTIC, 2013) as well as data on the beneficiaries of research grants (MASTIC, 2016c).

References

Chandran, V.G.R. (2010), "R&D commercialization challenges for developing countries: The case of Malaysia", *Tech Monitor*, Nov-Dec, pp. 25-30, www.techmonitor.net/tm/images/d/dd/10nov_dec_sf3.pdf.

Day, N. and A. Muhammad (2011), *Malaysia: The Atlas of Islamic-world Science and Innovation*, Country Case Study No. 1, Royal Society of London for Promoting Natural Knowledge, London, http://hdl.handle.net/10625/48146.

EPU (2010), *Tenth Malaysia Plan 2011-2015*, Economic Planning Unit, Prime Minister's Department, Putrajaya, www.epu.gov.my/en/tenth-malaysia-plan-10th-mp-.

EPU (2006), *Ninth Malaysia Plan 2006-2010*, Economic Planning Unit, Prime Minister's Department, Putrajaya, www.epu.gov.my/epu-theme/rm9/html/english.htm.

IVA (2013), *Sweden's Global Connectivity in Research: An Analysis of International Co-authorship*, Royal Swedish Academy of Engineering Sciences, Stockholm, www.iva.se/globalassets/rapporter/agenda-for-forskning/agenda-for-forskning-swedens-global-connectivity-in-research.pdf.

MASTIC (2016b), *Bibliometric Study 2015*, Ministry of Science, Technology and Innovation, Putrajaya.

MASTIC (2016c), *National Survey of Innovation 2015*, Ministry of Science, Technology and Innovation, Putrajaya.

MASTIC (2014), *Malaysian Science and Technology Indicators Report 2013*, Ministry of Science, Technology and Innovation, Putrajaya.

MASTIC (2012c), *Bibliometric Study 2012*, Ministry of Science, Technology and Innovation, Putrajaya.

MASTIC (2001, 2005, 2009, 2013, 2016a), *National Surveys of Research and Development*, Ministry of Science, Technology and Innovation, Putrajaya.

MOSTI (2013), *National Policy on Science, Technology and Innovation*, Ministry of Science, Technology and Innovation, Putrajaya.

NSRC (2013), *PRA Performance Evaluation. Unlocking Vast Potentials, Fast-Tracking the Future*, UiTM Press, National Science and Research Council, Shah Alam, http://umexpert.um.edu.my/file/publication/00012427_86127.pdf.

OECD (2016), "Main science and technology indicators", *OECD Science, Technology and R&D Statistics* (database), http://dx.doi.org/10.1787/data-00182-en.

OECD (2015a), *Boosting Malaysia's National Intellectual Property System for Innovation*, OECD Publishing, Paris, http://dx.doi.org/10.1787/9789264239227-en.

OECD (2015b), *OECD Science, Technology and Industry Scoreboard 2015: Innovation for Growth and Society*, OECD Publishing, Paris, http://dx.doi.org/10.1787/sti_scoreboard-2015-en.

SCImago (2007), *Country Rankings* (database), www.scimagojr.com/countryrank.php.

WIPO (2015), *WIPO IP Statistics Data Center* (database), http://ipstats.wipo.int/ipstatv2.

World Bank (2015), *World Development Indicators* (database), http://data.worldbank.org/data-catalog/world-development-indicators.

World Economic Forum (2016), *Global Competitiveness Report 2016*, World Economic Forum, Geneva, http://reports.weforum.org/global-competitiveness-report-2015-2016.

World Economic Forum (2015), *Global Competitiveness Report Dataset* (database), http://reports.weforum.org/global-competitiveness-report-2014-2015/downloads.

Chapter 4.

Innovation actors in Malaysia

This chapter describes the main actors in the Malaysian innovation system: business enterprises, higher education institutions and public research institutes, highlighting their respective roles in the development of the innovation system in recent years. It reviews scientific, technological and related functions carried out by the main actors within the system and their contributions to innovation.

The statistical data for Israel are supplied by and under the responsibility of the relevant Israeli authorities. The use of such data by the OECD is without prejudice to the status of the Golan Heights, East Jerusalem and Israeli settlements in the West Bank under the terms of international law.

This chapter examines successively the role and performance of the main public and private research and innovation actors in the development of the Malaysian innovation system in recent years: business enterprises, higher education institutions and public research institutes.

Business sector

Due to the small size of its domestic markets and its limited investment capacity, following an initial period characterised by export substitution, independent Malaysia has relied heavily on international trade and foreign direct investment (FDI) to stimulate and feed its rapid development. This strategy has proven successful and resulted in a set of diversified and fast-growing manufacturing and, more recently, service industries. The electrical and electronic (E&E) industry in particular has acted as a pioneer and catalyst of structural change towards high-technology manufacturing and allowed Malaysia's industry to connect to and integrate in global value chains (GVCs), focusing on the assembly and testing of different types and generations of components. Malaysia has now diversified well beyond the semiconductors and hard-drive companies established in the 1970s. Despite some remarkable successes in specific clusters, industries and firms, the perceived slowdown of the upgrading process in the 2000s triggered a debate about Malaysia's ability to fully move its manufacturing and services industries to the next "knowledge-intensive" stage. This transition is hampered by bottlenecks related above all to the lack of adequate skills. This is an obstacle for the growth of innovative domestic enterprises, especially small and medium-sized enterprises (SMEs), and makes multinational enterprises (MNEs) reluctant to expand higher value-adding activities in Malaysia.

Structure of the business sector

Overall industry profile

Even more than in other countries of "factory Asia", manufacturing has been a pillar of Malaysia's development success, in particular since the 1980s. Although its weight in the economy peaked in 2000 and has gradually decreased since then, this sector has kept growing in recent years (4.8% per year on average during the Tenth Malaysia Plan 2011-15), contributing 23% of gross domestic product (GDP) in 2015. It also accounted for 18% of employment and 81.8% of total exports in 2015 (compared to 17% and 76.6%, respectively, in 2010) (EPU, 2015a). The E&E industry remains the largest contributor to the manufacturing value added in Malaysia at 25.7% (2014),[1] followed by two other largely export-oriented industries, *viz.* refined petroleum (12.7%) and chemicals and chemicals products (10.9%). E&E represented 42.7% of the manufacturing sector's gross exports and 33.4% of the country's total exports in 2014 (MPC, 2015).

The largest contributor to Malaysia's GDP (at 54%), however, is the service sector, which expanded at a rate of 6.3% per year over the period from 2011 to 2015 (EPU, 2015a; MPC, 2015). Wholesale, retail trade, and restaurants and accommodation account for 61.6% of the contribution of services to GDP; finance, insurance, real estate and business services for 20.6% (SME Corporation, 2015). Like in other Asian economies, manufacturing was a major driving force behind Malaysia's economic and labour productivity growth. Since about 2000, a profound shift has occurred: following secular development trends and enhanced by new ICTs, the service sector's contribution to both output and labour productivity increased at the same or higher rate than the contribution of manufacturing. The manufacturing sector's contribution to economic growth in Asian economies was at 29% between 2000 and 2013, compared to 32% during the preceding decade (APO, 2015).

The importance of the primary and resource-based sectors[2] in the country's exports declined from about 95% at the time of Malaysia's independence to some 43% in 1990, and 17% in 2000 (World Bank, 2014). However, these sectors still play an important role in the Malaysian economy since most of them, in particular palm oil and rubber, and to a lesser extent forestry, have gone through a process of moving "downstream". The manufactured products derived from these resources[3] account for a growing share of exports (from 5.4% in 2002 to 23.3% in 2012) and were the most powerful driver of growth of the manufacturing sector over the period 2002-12 (Bank Negara Malaysia, 2013). By 2013, the share of exports of the resource-based and primary sectors rose to 33%.[4]

Small and large private companies

The vast majority of Malaysian manufacturing and service enterprises are privately-owned SMEs. They represent 97.3% of business establishments according to the census conducted in 2011; most of them operate in the service sector (90% of SMEs) according to the new definition introduced in 2014[5] (Table 4.1). Whereas large firms account for only 2.7% of establishments, they contributed 64.1% to GDP in 2014.

Table 4.1. **Share of small and medium-sized enterprises in the total number of firms and GDP, Malaysia, 2011 and 2014**

Sector	Share of SMEs (%)	Share in total SMEs (%)	Contribution to GDP (%), 2011	Contribution to GDP (%), 2014
Agriculture	76	1	3.4	4.5
Mining	71.5	0.1	0.1	0.1
Construction	87.1	3	0.8	2
Manufacturing	95.4	5.9	7.9	7.8
Services	98.2	90	20	21.1
Total	97.3	100	32.5	35.9

Source: Department of Statistics, Malaysia.

Large firms account for an even more disproportionate share of exports since they are often export-oriented subsidiaries of MNEs operating in global value chains. The semiconductor industry, for instance, is composed of 126 foreign establishments, which together account for 80% of all semiconductor exports; the 240 smaller domestic firms account for the remaining 20% (EPU, 2014).

A key issue for SMEs is their low level of productivity. As in most developing and emerging economies, small firms' productivity lags behind that of large firms, but tends to narrow as the level of development increases. The productivity of large Malaysian firms was 3.2 times and 2.7 times higher than that of small firms in 2005 and 2013, respectively. The change over the period 2010-14 was rather small, however[6] (Figure 4.1). The gap is particularly large in services where productivity per worker in large firms is more than four times higher than in small firms, partly due to the large number of micro-enterprises (EPU, 2015a). Compared to other countries, the labour productivity of Malaysian SMEs appears particularly low – 3.6 times lower than that of Singapore's SMEs, 7 times lower than in SMEs in the United States (SME Corporation, 2015).

Figure 4.1. **Productivity of small and medium-sized enterprises and large firms, Malaysia**

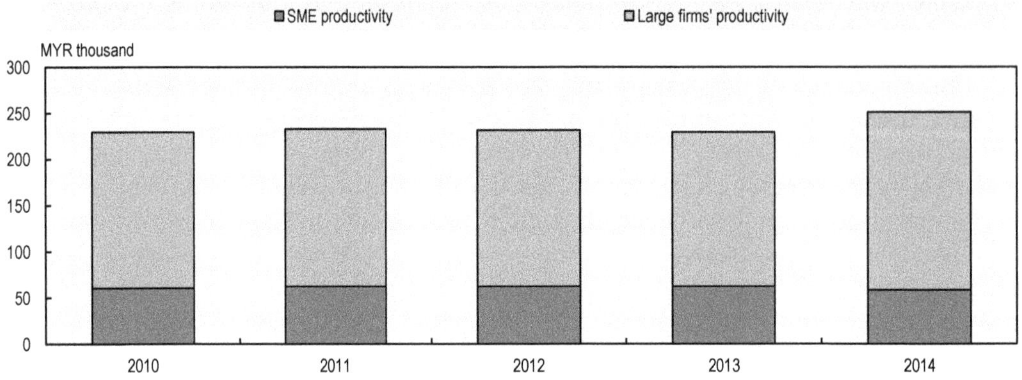

Source: OECD (2016), *Economic Outlook for Southeast Asia, China and India 2016: Enhancing Regional Ties*, http://dx.doi.org/10.1787/saeo-2016-en.

The factors hampering the performance of SMEs are plenty, and interrelated. These include the large share of unskilled workers in labour-intensive industries across all sectors of the economy, low capability and willingness to engage in human capital development, weak financial capacity and difficulty accessing external financial sources, and lock-in in low value-added segments (SME Corporation, 2012; OECD, 2016, 2014). Moreover, according to a survey of SMEs carried out in 2012,[7] only 11% of those that engage in innovation activities do so to raise their productivity (ACCCIM, 2012).

Since only a few non-financial domestic firms succeeded in growing and establishing their own brand, large firms are – in their great majority – either MNEs or government-linked companies (GLCs), with some notable exceptions. About 400 MNEs[8] were located in Malaysia in 2012, comprising many of the leaders in the E&E industry and in other industries (pharmaceuticals, biotechnology, aerospace, automotive, etc.). Giant services companies such as Temasek Holding, SAP or Frost and Sullivan have subsidiaries in Malaysia.

Only two Malaysian private (non-financial) companies[9] were listed in the United Nations Conference on Trade and Development's (UNCTAD) top 100 non-financial MNEs from developing and transition economies, ranked by foreign assets in 2013 (UNCTAD, 2013). These two companies are among the large domestic firms privately-owned by families.[10]

Government-linked companies in Asia

GLCs, or state-owned enterprises (SOEs) as defined by the OECD,[11] have significant weight in many Asian economies, where they have been assigned important roles in national economic development. The Malaysian government used GLCs to leverage its intervention in a wide range of priority industries (food, chemicals, iron, steel, petroleum transport, wood products, etc.), especially during the 1980s (Bhattacharya, 2002). For instance, PETRONAS, the national oil and gas company, financially supported several government mega-projects outside its core business, such as the development of Putrajaya and the construction of Kuala Lumpur Twin Towers, as well as industry and service endeavours such as the Bank Bumiputra, and the foundation of Proton, the national carmaker.

Despite a major privatisation programme launched in the early 1990s, GLCs still occupy a key position in the Malaysian economy, including in telecommunications, power generation and supply, ports, airports, highways, post, telecommunications, railways and sewerage (OECD, 2015b). Their share of the national value added is about 15% (5% of employment), comparable to Singapore, while they roughly contribute 25% in India and Thailand. Several of these Malaysian companies are listed on the national stock exchange, where together they represent about 50% of the total stock market capitalisation (60% in the People's Republic of China, hereafter "China") (OECD, 2015c).

GLCs operate in a variety of sectors, but are particularly dominant in utilities (including telecommunications, transportation, and oil and gas) (PGC, 2015a). They often occupy monopoly positions in these sectors (OECD, 2013a). In line with trends in other countries with strong SOEs, some Malaysian GLCs have become MNEs, investing and conquering market shares abroad. Of the four Malaysian enterprises that are listed in the 2012 UNCTAD top-100 multinationals from developing and transition economies, two are GLCs.[12]

Despite their weight and pervasiveness, there is little evidence that Malaysian SOEs have contributed much to fostering innovation activities beyond special cases such as Proton,[13] some links with higher education institutions, and some initiatives in the financial (new Islamic financing products and services) and sustainable development areas (biomass projects) (PGC, 2015b). This observation is in line with international evidence: GLCs in Malaysia, as well as in other countries such as Singapore, perform but little R&D for their size (OECD, 2013a). An assessment of the largest Malaysian GLCs' innovation capabilities was undertaken in 2011 in order to promote the innovation mind-set and culture across Malaysian companies. The results of this survey showed that while coming close to best practice level on certain dimensions, Malaysian GLCs were lagging behind the global benchmark on key innovation dimensions such as the "importance of innovation" and "innovation as an integral part of business strategy" (PGC, 2015b). Although they are not always available, the key performance indicators, which are at the core of the government programme for improving the efficiency of GLCs, tend to mostly relate to financial performance. The non-financial indicators have little to do with innovation (PGC, 2015b).

Finally, there are indications that Malaysian GLCs not only do not engage strongly in innovation activities, but that they also act as a disincentive to investment by other companies in the same sectors, in particular in those where they account for a dominant share of revenues (Menon and Hee, 2013).

Innovation and R&D performance of business firms

R&D activities of business firms

Starting from a low level, business expenditure on research and development (BERD) increased rapidly during the 1990s; it slowed in the mid-2000s and turned negative in 2011 before rising again a year later (Figure 4.2). The business sector stands out, accounting for 64.5% of Malaysia's gross expenditure on research and development (GERD) in 2012, down from a peak at 85% in 2006 (MASTIC, 2014a). In absolute terms, R&D has stagnated since 2010.[14]

The breakdown of BERD by field of research broadly reflects the structure of the business sector: the largest R&D effort was in engineering, technology and ICT (48%), followed by natural science, agriculture and forestry (31%). Business R&D expenditure by manufacturing industries is even more concentrated. The E&E industry is by far the largest research performer, accounting for about 79% of manufacturing R&D expenditure in 2011 (71% by electronics alone). With 8% of manufacturing R&D, the automotive sector is a distant second (Table 4.2).

Table 4.2. **Business R&D expenditures by manufacturing sector, Malaysia**

MYR million

	2005	2006	2007	2008	2009	2011
Manufacture of computer, electronic and optical products	1 000.80	787.90	1 749.80	1 401.70	1 243.80	1 417.02
Manufacture of machinery and equipment and electrical equipment and fabricated metal products	101.60	309.70	322.20	147.90	215.00	162.62
Manufacture of food products and beverage	29.90	36.60	70.30	72.10	66.90	71.48
Manufacture of rubber and plastic products	56.80	71.70	104.60	75.40	58.80	75.40
Manufacture of chemicals and chemical products	810.00	48.50	48.00	38.90	48.60	38.93
Manufacture of motor vehicles, trailers and semi-trailers and other transport equipment	265.70	175.40	50.70	160.70	94.90	160.71
Others (including manufacture of wearing apparel and other non-mineral products)	98.30	92.00	85.00	107.80	119.30	77.00
Total	2 363.10	1 521.80	2 430.60	2 004.50	1 847.30	2 003.16

Source: Department of Statistics, Malaysia.

The lion's share of expenditure is for applied research (80% in 2011), followed by experimental research (17%) and basic research (3%) (Figure 4.2). Basic research increased by 92% between 2011 and 2012 (now accounting for 34% of total R&D expenditures) due, according to the Ministry of Science, Technology and Innovation (MOSTI), to various new government initiatives launched to support this kind of research (MASTIC, 2014a).[15] However, as soon as 2014, the distribution of business expenditure went back to its earlier distribution, with an even greater share of applied research due to a decrease in experimental development (MASTIC, 2016).

Figure 4.2. **BERD, total amount and share of total by type of research, Malaysia, 1992-2014**

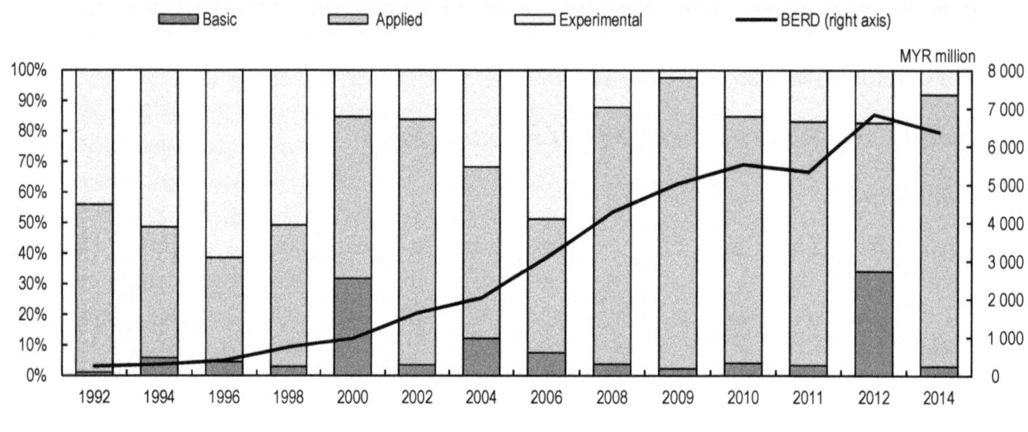

Note: BERD = business expenditure on research and development.

Sources: MASTIC (2001, 2005, 2009, 2013, 2016), *National Surveys of Research and Development*.

In international comparison, the business expenditures of the main Malaysian business R&D investors appear low, even when accounting for the difference in level of development (Figure 4.3).

Figure 4.3. **Number of top 500 corporate R&D investors, per GDP, 2013 or latest year available**

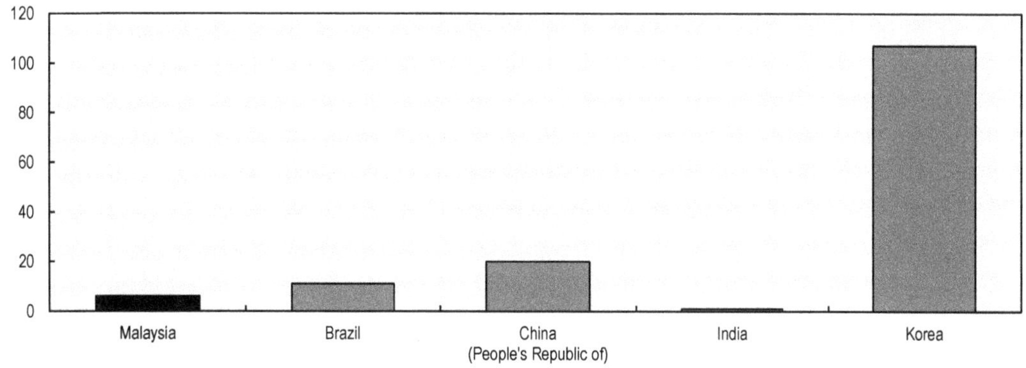

Source: OECD (2014), *OECD Science, Technology and Industry Outlook 2014*, http://dx.doi.org/10.1787/sti_outlook-2014-en.

Business firms' engagement in innovation

According to the 6th National Survey on Innovation conducted in 2012 (MASTIC, 2014b), 70% of responding companies stated that they had engaged in innovation activities during 2009-11. These "innovative firms" were mainly in the service sector (62% of all innovative firms), far exceeding those in manufacturing (38%). Service companies were also proportionally more inclined to carry out innovation activities, as 78% of them declared they were innovative, compared to 60% of manufacturing firms. However, the service firms' innovation activities were of smaller scale in terms of innovation expenditures: only 2% declared expenditures above MYR 250 000, which is consistent with the fact that the predominant activities consisted of small-scale innovation by travel and tour agencies. In contrast, 76% of manufacturing firms were above this threshold, and 42% spent more than MYR 1 million. The most strongly represented sector among innovative manufacturing firms was the computer, electronic and optical products industry, followed by food products and machinery and equipment.

While this survey provides valuable information on the features of innovative firms, it almost certainly overestimates the overall propensity of business firms to innovate. Other available data, although scarce, often dated and not very precise, suggest, for example, that the proportion of firms involved in R&D in Malaysia around 2005 was closer to 5% (OECD, 2013a).

Although somewhat dated, the surveys on investment climate conducted by the World Bank in 2002 and 2007 provide concordant evidence on the limited extent and depth of innovation activities in Malaysian manufacturing firms (World Bank, 2010). Furthermore, efforts of manufacturing firms declined between 2002 and 2007 across all types of innovation, except for those engaging external partners (subcontracting of R&D and joint ventures with a foreign partner). A comparison with the results of similar surveys conducted in a large group of other countries shows that the level of Malaysian firms' engagement in innovation activities was among the lowest and appeared to be significantly below the level achieved by its Asian counterparts (e.g. Indonesia, the Philippines, Thailand, Viet Nam, etc.) (World Bank, 2010). Distinguishing between three types of "technological capabilities", the results of the surveys also indicate that the investment capabilities (selection and preparation of technological projects) and production capabilities (conduct of process and product innovation) barely improved between 2002 and 2007, while "linkages capabilities" (exchange of technologies and knowledge) declined. One of the most remarkable results is that less than 30% of firms have carried out activities relevant to the three types of technological capabilities in recent years. SMEs, which account for the bulk of domestically-owned companies, score significantly lower than large companies (World Bank, 2009). Most Malaysian firms are considered "adapters" (50% in 2002, 40% in 2007) while few are "creators" (10% in 2002, 15% in 2007). More than 40% are only considered "adopters" or had not reported any of these activities in the two years prior to the surveys (World Bank, 2009).[16]

These results are confirmed by detailed studies of the characteristics of R&D activities performed by firms, for instance in the E&E industry, which have demonstrated that, for the most part the most sophisticated forms of innovation remain confined to a small group of firms. The most widespread form of innovation is the upgrading of existing product lines or machinery and equipment, as opposed to the development of a new product line or the introduction of a new technology. A study of 53 MNEs and local E&E firms show that, although they have increased their capability over time, two-thirds of sampled firms in the E&E industry had reached (at the beginning of the year 2000) a basic or intermediate level of innovative capability, mainly in relation to improvement of equipment, tooling, stamping, moulding, as well as process and production organisation capability (Ariffin and Figueiredo, 2003).

Using a different technological framework and more recent data than the World Bank survey, a study conducted on 103 E&E firms concluded that electronic firms experienced the most significant increase in technological capabilities of all firms over the period 2000-07 and R&D intensity over the period 2000-07, reaching ratios of 5.6% of sales in 2007 (up from 3.7% in 2000) and 8.3% of sales (up from 1.1% in 2000), respectively. However, despite progress, two-thirds of these firms performed activities pertaining to the level of "engineering" (process and product adaptation). A third of these firms only reached the highest stages of "early R&D" (process or product development) and only one firm that of "mature R&D" (new process or product) (Rasiah, 2010).

Business firms' human resources for R&D

The number of R&D personnel in business firms increased drastically between 1992 and 2004, stagnated until around the end of the 2000s and then increased again, at a slower pace, until 2012. The majority of R&D personnel are researchers (53% in 2012), rather than technicians (22%) or support staff (25%) (Figure 4.4); 69% are male. The latest data available for 2014 show a new decrease of R&D personnel due to a dramatic reduction of support staff (MASTIC, 2016).

Innovation performance of business firms

The available patent statistics for Malaysia do not provide a breakdown with regard to public institutions and private companies. However, it is possible to draw some conclusions from the list of top applicants for PCT (Patent Cooperation Treaty) applications (Table 4.3) and European patent applications (Table 4.4):

- Public institutions are by far the main category of applicants, whether universities, such as Universiti Sains Malaysia, or research institutes/public agencies (Malaysian Palm Oil Board, National R&D Centre in ICT of Malaysia [MIMOS]).
- Some Malaysian firms do engage in patenting activities, but the number of patents remains low; examples are IQ Group (supplier of security and convenience products) and Widetech Manufacturing (manufacturer of correction fluid products), both are Malaysian technology-based firms created in the 1980s.
- Some Malaysian firms that were granted patents are GLCs (PETRONAS and its Institute of Technology, Universiti Teknologi PETRONAS).

Figure 4.4. **Business R&D personnel, total number and share of total by type of post, Malaysia**

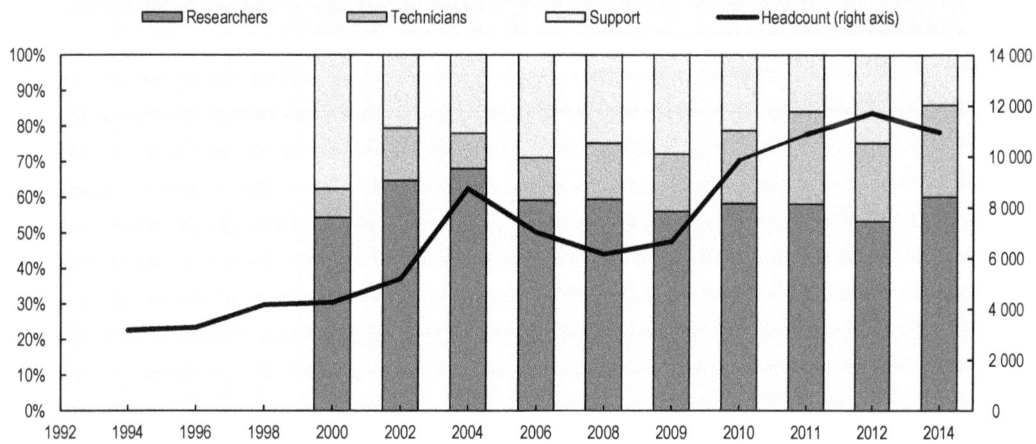

Note: Breakdown by type of post not available for the period 1992-98.

Sources: MASTIC (2001, 2005, 2009, 2013, 2016), *National Surveys of Research and Development*.

Table 4.3. **Top ten Malaysian PCT applicants, publication year 2012**

Applicant	Type	PCT filings
MIMOS Berhad	Government-owned company/agency	146
Universiti Sains Malaysia (USM)	Public university	39
Universiti Putra Malaysia (UPM)	Public university	15
PETRONAS	Government-owned company	8
Malaysian Palm Oil Board (MPOB)	Government agency	7
IQ Group	Private company	4
Universiti Malaya (UM)	Public university	4
Widetech Manufacturing	Private company	4
Universiti Teknologi PETRONAS	Government-owned company	3
Malaysian Rubber Board (MRB)	Government agency	3

Source: OECD (2015a), *Boosting Malaysia's National Intellectual Property System for Innovation*, http://dx.doi.org/10.1787/9789264239227-6-en, based on WIPO (2015b), *WIPO IP Statistics Data Center* (database), http://ipstats.wipo.int/ipstatv2.

Table 4.4. **Top 30 Malaysian European Patent Office patent applicants, filing years 2000-11**

Rank	Applicant	Filings	Rank	Applicant	Filings
1	Malaysian Palm Oil Board (MPOB)	38	16	Simplex Major	4
2	Universiti Putra Malaysia (UPM)	37	17	Universiti Malaya (UM)	4
3	MIMOS Berhad	29	18	Universiti Teknologi Malaysia (UTM)	4
4	PETRONAS	18	19	WRP Asia Pacific	4
5	**Harn Marketing**	16	20	Borneo Tsang Furnishing	3
6	**Sime Darby**	15	21	Easycup International	3
7	**IQ Group**	14	22	**Inqpharm Group**	3
8	**Shimano Components**	13	23	Koosan	3
9	**Oyl R&D Centre**	11	24	**Pure Circle**	3
10	**Biolitec Pharma Marketing**	10	25	**Quantum Electro Opto Systems (Qeon)**	3
11	Universiti Sains Malaysia (USM)	8	26	Sirim Berhad	3
12	Government of Malaysia	6	27	**Texchem**	3
13	**Neuramatix**	6	28	**TMS Technologies**	3
14	**Easy Pack International**	6	29	**Widetech Manufacturing**	3
15	**Gha Brands Limited**	4	30	**Advanced Pyrotech**	2

Note: Purely private companies, excluding public research organisations, universities and companies that are government-owned or government-linked, are highlighted in bold.

Source: OECD (2015a), *Boosting Malaysia's National Intellectual Property System for Innovation*, http://dx.doi.org/10.1787/9789264239227-6-en, based on EPO (2015) *EPO Worldwide Patent Statistical Database* (database), www.epo.org/searching/subscription/raw/product-14-24.html.

Upgrading Malaysian manufacturing and service industries

Broad consensus has emerged that firms, including domestic firms and SMEs, need to shift towards the production of more elaborate, higher value-added products and services. There is some debate, however, to what extent Malaysia has already advanced towards this goal and what might be the main obstacles on this path. This section reviews the main arguments and evidence used in this debate, following a simple analytical framework (Figure 4.5). This framework builds on the idea that Malaysia should not only pursue a shift towards more knowledge-intensive manufacturing and service industries, but also expand the range of tasks performed within these industries and, more precisely, within each relevant global value chain. Finally, if the country is to reinforce and reap the full benefits of this challenging shift, it is critical that domestic firms become partners, if not leaders, in these activities. The increase of skills and capabilities of the public and private actors necessary at each stage of this upgrading process feeds back into the country's position in former stages.

Is Malaysia moving towards higher technology manufacturing?

The success of Malaysian development during the period 1970-98 was largely based on a diversification of its production and exports, driven by manufacturing. The government has played an important role in facilitating and guiding this structural shift with varying success, from the import-substitution industrialisation strategy in the 1960s, which was replaced by Malaysia's defining export-oriented model, the intermittent orientation towards heavy industries and, since the 1980s, initiatives to attract high-technology multinationals.

Although the development of manufacturing was not linear – some MNEs even left Malaysia during times of economic slowdown or because of changes in the labour market or the financial incentives – the virtuous cycle of cluster agglomeration in areas such as

Penang is firmly established. The favourable financial conditions as well as the prospects of synergies and increasing returns of producer networks with the established firms led new companies to move to Malaysia. As a result, the share of manufacturing in total value added increased from less than 10%[17] at the time of independence when it was merely processing agricultural and mining output, to 31% in 2000.

Figure 4.5. **Schematic question tree for analysing the upgrade of the manufacturing and service sectors in Malaysia**

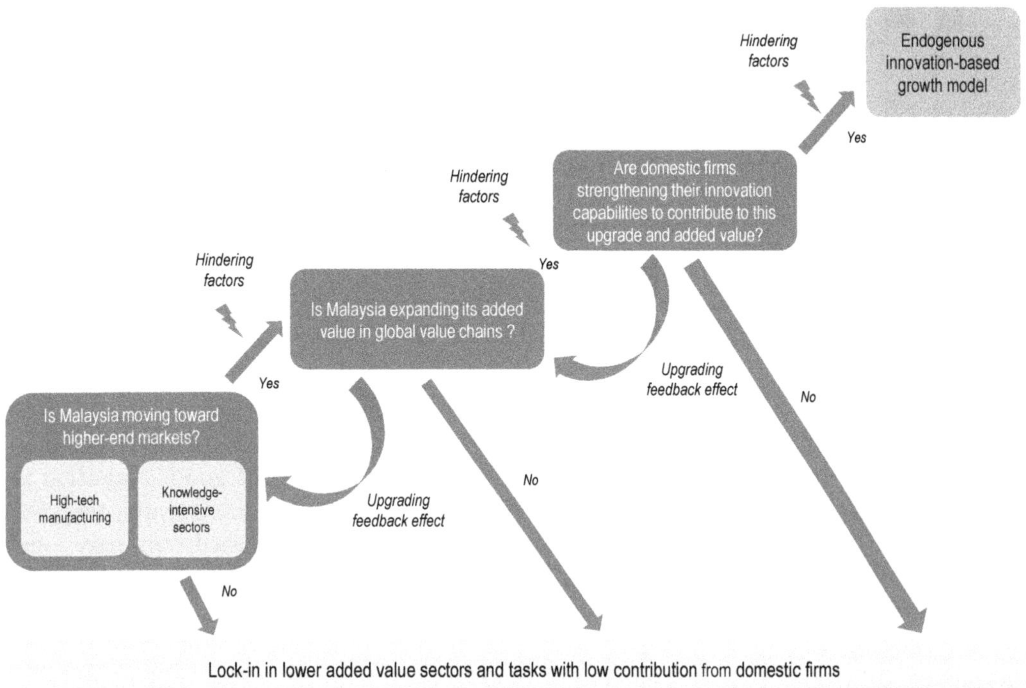

During these years, Malaysia experienced rapid growth of its manufacturing sector, a progressive transformation of the sector toward higher value-added activities, and an increase in manufacturing capabilities (Yusuf and Nabeshima, 2009). The degree of sophistication of production, especially exports, increased continuously throughout the period 1980-2000. Aggregate "high-technology" manufacturing value added grew rapidly until 2000, when it reached MYR 34.1 billion (representing 31% of the total manufacturing output, or 9.5% of GDP). It has since decreased, to MYR 23.6 billion in 2010 (11% of total manufacturing output, 3.1% of GDP). What is more, the "high-technology" sub-sectors that experienced the most dramatic relative decline are those which were at the core of the high-growth regime.

The decomposition of the manufacturing sector into a suitable group of sub-sectors reflects the important upgrade achieved during the four decades that followed Malaysia's independence and the slowdown since around 2000. In 2000, about half of the manufacturing value added was produced by higher-end sub-sectors ("global innovation for local markets" and "global technologies/innovator"),[18] which require more skills and intangible assets than labour- or energy-intensive sub-sectors. However, this structural evolution seems to have stalled since then; the share of regional processing and resource-based sub-sectors even slightly increased between 2000 and 2011 (Figure 4.6).

Figure 4.6. **Sector share of total manufacturing value added in selected Asian countries, 2000 and 2011 (or closest year available)**

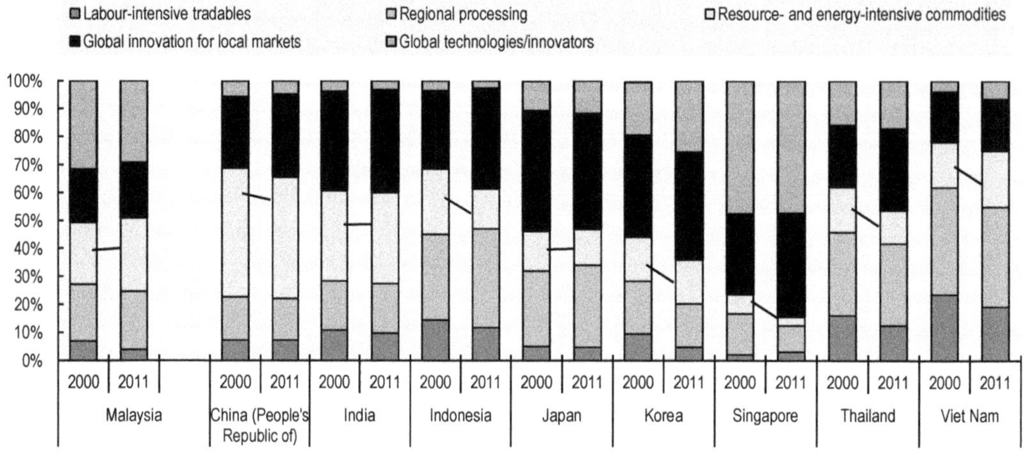

Sources: OECD (2013c), *Southeast Asian Economic Outlook 2013: With Perspectives on China and India*, http://dx.doi.org/10.1787/saeo-2013-en; ADB (2013), "Beyond factory Asia: Fuelling growth in a changing world", http://adb.org/sites/default/files/pub/2013/beyond-factory-asia.pdf.

The same trend can be observed for exports, which have been by far the main "destination" of manufacturing value added. The share of exports of goods classified as "high-technology" increased from 38% in 1990 to 58% in 2000. Subsequently, they fell sharply to 31% in 2013, whereas the share of resource-based, primary and medium-technology goods in total exports has increased significantly since 2000 (World Bank, 2014). The level of diversification of exports, which marked the development of the Malaysian economy during its high-growth years, stagnated at the 1990 level in 2000 and 2010 (EPU, 2015a). The composition of exports in 2012 was rather similar to the one prevailing in the 1990s (EPU, 2014). The stagnation and subsequent decline of high-technology manufacturing value added and exports since 2000, combined with sluggish productivity growth in manufacturing industries, is typical of a country undergoing de-industrialisation largely caused by slow upgrading (Rasiah, 2011).

Is Malaysia moving toward knowledge-intensive services?

One of the most important recent changes in the structure of the Malaysian and other Asian economies has been the rise of the services sector. Services have grown rapidly and are now the largest contributor to Malaysia's GDP. While manufacturing is widely held to remain a cornerstone of the Malaysian economy, the role of services in the economy is expected to expand further (ADB, 2013).

The service sector can further contribute – partly in conjunction with the evolution of manufacturing – to Malaysia's goal of becoming a high-income economy by upgrading through the development of knowledge-intensive services.[19] These services are distinguished by higher productivity and stronger synergies with other sectors, and they are more amenable to international trade (ADB, 2013). They can exert a positive impact on the productivity of a wide range of industries that are at the core of Malaysia's economic performance, from resource-based industries and manufacturing to other types of services, including tourism (Box 4.1).

Box 4.1. The interaction between knowledge-intensive services and high-tech manufacturing

Knowledge-intensive services can play a key role in the innovation of developing and emerging economies. By providing specialised knowledge and information to other business organisations, they act as initiators or facilitators of innovation activities, and foster knowledge transfers among or within organisations, industries or networks (OECD, 2006). Business services are of particular importance in supporting the manufacturing sector by providing essential inputs in the production process, such as R&D services, finance, legal services, human resource recruitment, marketing and information technology. The contribution of services is even stronger in advanced high-technology manufacturing, where production processes are more complex, hence requiring R&D, engineering and other business services (Nordås and Kim, 2013). By extension, services with higher productivity and higher technology content are critical in facilitating countries' participation and upgrading in value chains (OECD, 2013c).

The outsourcing of these activities to specialised service companies allows manufacturing firms to concentrate on improving and upgrading their production processes and products. It also enhances the competition between the specialised service providers, which are also under pressure to improve their offer and innovate, which will lead to further increases in productivity in manufacturing and the economy as a whole (OECD, 2006). Although difficult to measure precisely, the synergies between the service and manufacturing sectors are proven to have significant effects not only on these two sectors, but also on the economy as a whole, notably through an increase in productivity, employment and value added (Pilat and Wölfl, 2005).[1] An important result for policy making is that the contribution of better services to moving up the value chain is particularly strong in industries where a country already has technological capacity and comparative advantage (Nordås and Kim, 2013).

However, the effect of knowledge-intensive services on innovation and productivity in the manufacturing sector and elsewhere in the economy cannot be taken for granted. It depends on several conditions at micro- and macroeconomic levels. The client firms' strategy with regards to their service suppliers as well as their internal knowledge management practices and absorption capacity will determine the scale of the benefits they can draw from this relationship (OECD, 2006). On the sectoral level, the ability of the country to provide conducive framework conditions, in particular to eliminate the regulations that hinder investment, competition and innovation in services play an important role (Noland, Park and Estrada, 2012). Regulatory barriers,[2] which tend to be even more prominent in services than manufacturing, are especially detrimental in modern services such as finance, business services and ICT. Given the importance of multinational enterprises for expansion and upgrading, restrictions on foreign direct investment (FDI) are particularly critical.

1. Although not focused on knowledge-intensive services, a measure of linkages between services and other sectors in the Malaysian economy using input-output tables show the intensity of forward linkages of services with the food and beverage as well as with resource-based and E&E industries. The E&E industry is the first client manufacturing sector when it comes to professional, scientific and technical (PST) services (MPC, 2015).

2. For instance red tape, weak contract enforcement and FDI restrictions in services.

The heterogeneity of definitions and method of measurement makes it difficult to get a clear picture of the level of development of knowledge-intensive services. According to OECD calculations based on Asian Development Bank data (Table 4.5), Malaysia is one of the few Asian countries to have a share of "modern services"[20] that is comparable to that of advanced economies, which usually stand at about 30% (OECD, 2013c). Singapore, a leading offshore financial service centre records an even higher share (41%). While slightly decreasing between 1990 and 2010, Malaysia's share of "modern services" remained significantly above that of other Asian countries.

Table 4.5. **Share of sub-sectors in total services value added, 1990 and 2010**

In %

	Traditional services			Wholesale and retail trade			Modern services		
	1990	2010		1990	2010		1990	2010	
Malaysia	67.9	68.3	↗	29.2	30.9	↗	32.1	31.7	↘
China (People's Republic of)	70.2	78.3	↗	26.7	24.4	↘	29.8	21.7	↘
India	80.9	79.5	↘	27.8	30.2	↗	19.1	20.5	↗
Indonesia	84.7	79.3	↘	39.4	36.3	↘	15.3	20.7	↗
Japan	77.3	76.3	↘	21.4	16.9	↘	22.7	23.7	↗
Korea	78.3	72.5	↘	27.6	18.6	↘	21.7	27.5	↗
Philippines	77.4	74.8	↘	28.9	31.6	↗	22.6	25.2	↗
Thailand	77.8	82.1	↗	45.6	41.4	↘	22.2	17.9	↘
Singapore	60.8	58.7	↘	24.5	26.1	↗	39.2	41.3	↗

Source: OECD (2013c), *Southeast Asian Economic Outlook 2013: With Perspectives on China and India*, http://dx.doi.org/10.1787/saeo-2013-en.

ICT services can be used as one possible indicator of the shift towards higher value-added services. The contribution of ICT services to GDP increased from 5.2% in 2010 to 5.5% in 2015, while ICT manufacturing decreased, from 4.6% to 3.9% (EPU, 2015a).

Malaysia has already nurtured some segments in which it takes a leading position. The country is currently the world's largest Islamic banking and financial centre (Box 4.2). Another example is halal food.

A World Bank analysis of export data provides a more morose picture. Modern services, although growing, account for a lower share in total exports than in Singapore and Hong Kong (China) (two offshore services centres) as well as in the Philippines (World Bank, 2014). Some lower income Asian countries have rapidly developed activities based on these services. Indonesia, for instance, more than doubled its value added between 2003 and 2012 (National Science Board, 2014).

As in other countries, knowledge-intensive services still represent a relatively low share of Malaysian service value added. The services sector remains dominated by the lower value-added industries such as wholesale and retail trade, accommodation and restaurants (32% of services value added in 2015) (EPU, 2015a). Exports of services show the same focus on traditional, lower value-added segments. Transport and tourism represented the largest share of foreign exchange in 2013.

Is Malaysia increasing its value added in high-technology manufacturing and knowledge-intensive services?

While there is empirical evidence that there has been considerable expansion of the local supplier base, driven in particular by the outsourcing strategies of US-based MNEs in the late 1980s and early 1990s, and a rise of high-technology manufacturing up to around 2000, the shift towards higher value-added tasks and activities in these high-tech sectors is still very much on the agenda in Malaysia. MNEs often start their operations in a recipient country with assembly and testing lines. Therefore, the process of upgrading in value chains is usually understood as upstream or downstream expansion, starting from elementary (assembly) tasks. However, upgrading can also take other forms. Figure 4.7 shows the different options for firms to increase their value added within GVCs.

Box 4.2. The development of Islamic finance and insurance in Malaysia

Although Islamic financing first emerged in Egypt, Malaysia also benefited from an early start and is now the world's leading location for Islamic finance and insurance. The first Islamic finance institution was founded in 1963 for Muslims to save for their future expenses during their pilgrimage to Mecca (Hajj). From a very rudimentary form of co-operative banking at the start, it has since specialised and been professionalised. It accounted for 25.6% of the total banking system's assets in 2014 (22.4% in 2011). The Islamic capital market also grew significantly, rising at a rate of 11.2% per year during the period of the Tenth Malaysia Plan (2011-15).

Malaysia holds a leading position with 10% of Islamic banking assets in 2012 (43% for Iran, 12% for Saudi Arabia) and 16 fully-fledged Islamic banks including 5 foreign ones. More comprehensive indicators, which include qualitative dimensions, such as the Global Islamic Economy Indicator (GIEI), place Malaysia in an even better position. Malaysia is leading on this index that evaluates the quality of the national overall Islamic economy ecosystem, including social considerations relative to their size. In 2014/15, it was leading the 70 other countries on 4 of the 6 sub-sector indicators (halal food, Islamic finance, travel, fashion, media and recreation, and pharmaceuticals and cosmetics).

In the aftermath of the 2008 financial crisis, to which Islamic finance products are said to have been more resilient than conventional products, and the decrease of manufacturing employment, the government has made Islamic finance and insurance a national priority. There are also synergies with halal food, another policy priority and leading sector, since halal food is required to be financed by Islamic banking.

An important advantage for Malaysia was its mature governance, with a strong regulatory framework. The country passed an authoritative Islamic Financial Services Act in 2013 to oversee Islamic banking operations, whereas competing countries such as the United Arab Emirates and the United Kingdom still rely on their common banking law, completed by some Islamic finance add-ons. Both as an acknowledgment of its leading position and a further advantage, Malaysia hosts international organisations such as the Islamic Financial Services Board (IFSB) and the International Islamic Liquidity Management Centre (IILMC).

In terms of educational infrastructure, Malaysia is also well-placed, although it lags slightly behind the United Kingdom. Malaysia has 50 course providers and 18 universities offering degree programmes in Islamic finance, compared to 60 course providers and 22 universities in the United Kingdom. The International Islamic Financial Centre (INCEIF) established in 2005 was the world's first international university specialising in Islamic finance.

Malaysian universities, however, are ahead of UK ones when it comes to research in Islamic banking and insurance: Malaysia leads internationally in terms of the number of outputs, with more than 100 peer-reviewed research papers released during 2012-14, against 56 in the United Kingdom. However, innovation in this sector tends to remain marginal and imitative. Most new products in fact originate from commercial banks and are subsequently made compatible with the Islamic rules (*Shari'ah*). There are therefore important opportunities for innovation and product differentiation in this sector. In the "Financial sector blueprint" launched by the Malaysian central bank in 2011, product innovation is considered a key condition to achieving the target of Islamic financing, accounting for 40% of total financing by 2020. It was 29% in 2010. Innovation can be determinant in this sector where competition is rapidly growing, as shown by the example of *Shari'ah*-compliant bonds (*sukuk*). Malaysia pioneered the market of *sukuk* in 1990 and is now the world leader, accounting for more than two-thirds of total gross value of this growing market in 2014. In addition to new financial products to attract clients well beyond the Muslim population, many other areas for innovations are currently being explored, such as mobile Islamic banking, micro-financing, digital currencies, *Shari'ah*-compliant crowdfunding platforms, SME financing initiatives, etc.

Sources: Hussain, Shahmoradi and Turk (2015), "An overview of Islamic finance", www.imf.org/external/pubs/ft/wp/2015/wp15120.pdf; EPU (2015a), *Eleventh Malaysia Plan*, http://rmk11.epu.gov.my/index.php/en; Thomson Reuters (2015), "State of the global Islamic economy: 2014-2015 report", www.iedcdubai.ae/assets/uploads/files/ar_20142015_1448266389.pdf; Bank Negara Malaysia (2011), "Financial sector blueprint 2011-2020: Strengthening our future", www.bnm.gov.my/files/publication/fsbp/en/BNM_FSBP_FULL_en.pdf.

Box 4.3. A typology of global value chain upgrading

In general terms, upgrading refers to the process of increasing value added in production or shifting to higher value activities in global production operations. Six different types of upgrading can be distinguished (Figure 4.7):

- Entry into the value chain, when a new actor begins to participate in the value chain.
- Product upgrading, which describes the shift to the production of a higher value added, i.e. more sophisticated product in the same activity. A manufacturer in the E&E industry would skip to a new generation of integrated circuit.
- Process upgrading describes improvements in efficiency in the production systems, such as the incorporation of more sophisticated technology via the purchase of new equipment, or a better organisation of production.
- Functional upgrading describes the movement of taking up higher value, i.e. more sophisticated, stages in the chain. The highest value added being generally in intangible activities, functional upgrading involves a shift from assembly upward to design and R&D, or downward to marketing and services, such as advertising and aftersales. This shift calls for the development of knowledge-intensive services.
- Chain upgrading and end-market upgrading, which describes the entry into a new value chain by leveraging the knowledge and skills acquired in the current chain, or the entry in new higher value end-market segments.

Countries often pursue functional upgrading as the most direct way of increasing the value of their participation in these chains. An example is the palm oil industry in Malaysia, which started with cultivation, simple oil refining, and now comprises stages of the entire value chain.

However, especially in emerging economies, product and process upgrading tend to be more easily attainable, since they may require relatively minor adjustments in production and skills development with lower overall investment. Chain upgrading is also very difficult to achieve since it requires significant investment.

Figure 4.7. **Different types of upgrading in global value chains**

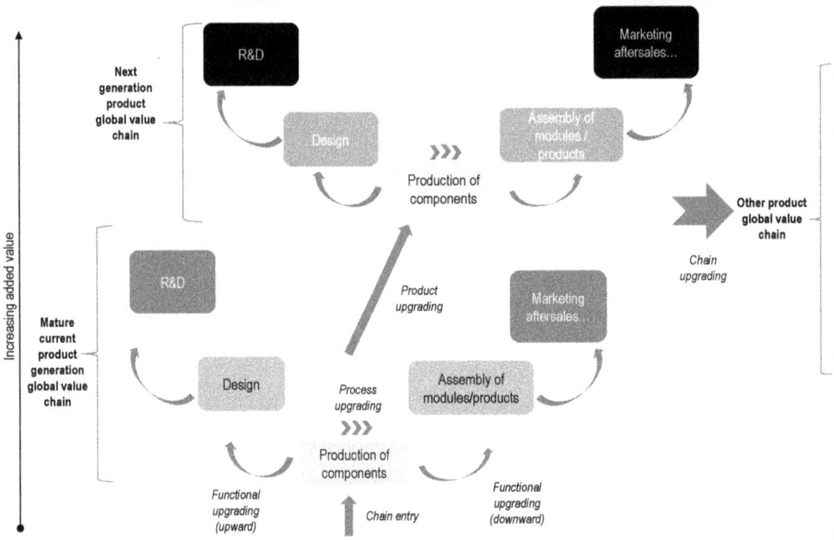

Sources: OECD (2013b), *Interconnected Economies: Benefiting from Global Value Chains*, http://dx.doi.org/10.1787/9789264189560-en; Fernandez-Stark, Bamber and Gereffi (2012), "Upgrading in global value chains: Addressing the skills challenge in developing countries", www.cggc.duke.edu/pdfs/2012-09-26_Duke_CGGC_OECD_background_paper_Skills_Upgrading_inGVCs.pdf.

MNE activities with the highest value added, including major R&D centres, mainly remain in "headquarter" countries (and, with increasing globalisation of R&D, in a restricted set of other international hubs of R&D and innovation). Currently available corporate information does not permit an accurate assessment of the level of R&D performed by MNEs on their Malaysian sites, even if the FDI project is publicised as including an R&D or design centre.

An analysis of the domestic value added shows that since 2000, as in most other Southeast Asian countries, although the integration of the Malaysian manufacturing sector in GVCs has continued to increase, it has moved upstream in these chains, i.e. further away from final demand. Malaysia has, in fact, one of the most upstream manufacturing sectors of all emerging economies.[21] While the position of imports is stable, the length of the stages of the value chain operated in Malaysia has shortened, which means that the country seems confined to very specific segments, namely those with the lowest value added. This is particularly the case in the E&E sector where domestic value added of exports is smaller than in many developing and emerging economies, including Thailand, the Philippines and, of course, China (World Bank, 2014).

Malaysia was very successful in attracting leading export-oriented MNEs in high growth sectors from 1970 to 2000. Even in recent years, MNEs still represent the bulk of investment (flows) in the E&E industry, for instance through greenfield or expansion/diversification projects.[22] Starting with mere components assembly and packaging tasks, some slightly more elaborate types of tasks have been progressively performed in these factories or in the surrounding clusters. Also, production has taken up new generations of technologies, with several semiconductor companies manufacturing their high-end components in Malaysia. However, low value-added, less sophisticated activities in these "high-technology" industries have remained dominant. Very few MNEs or domestic firms have decided to perform significant R&D in Malaysia. If at all, the R&D departments of these firms have remained mainly confined to process improvement and adaptation or testing in most cases.[23] A review of the most significant recent investment projects in the E&E industry approved by the Malaysian Investment Development Authority indicates that the majority of projects still relate to the assembly and testing of components.[24] In the meantime, previous sources of Malaysian competitiveness of the E&E industry have eroded, while the position of competing countries with lower labour cost (i.e. Viet Nam) in E&E GVCs has strengthened (World Bank, 2014).

In clear contrast with the situation prevailing in the E&E industry, Malaysia's global leadership in palm oil rests on its position at the technological frontier in this area and its control over the entire value chain, from raw materials to final products. Starting from cultivation and oil processing, the main players in the sector have succeeded in developing new products as well as expanding and upgrading their role in the various segments of the value chain (Rasiah, 2006b). R&D started to become significant as early as the 1960s but remained concentrated on palm oil at the start. Nowadays, innovation projects in this area, some of which are supported by the Economic Transformation Programme as part of the Palm Oil and Rubber NKEA (national key economic area), span the whole value chain, from improving the fruit yield and smallholders' productivity to increasing the efficiency of oil processing, valorising the resource (biogas, second-generation biofuels) and expanding the range of applications (palm-based derivatives in food and health-based products) (PEMANDU, 2014).

Further initiatives to attract MNEs with higher value-added activities and to support the development of the innovation capabilities of domestic firms were implemented in the 1990s and 2000s. Tax allowances have been granted to firms located in high-technology parks, while training programmes and incentives and new R&D grant schemes have been put in place by the government.

Another interesting avenue pursued by the government to support the upgrading of the E&E industry is to support the establishment of the physical and knowledge infrastructure for test measurement as shown by the content of the E&E projects in the Economic Transformation Programme. The rationale put forward is to make Malaysia a test and measurement hub in order to lower barriers to entry and support new investment (PEMANDU, 2014).

As a result of government efforts and industry cluster dynamics, new industry segments are emerging, most often building upon the resources of the E&E industry, such as the solar (Box 4.4) and LED sectors. These two industries remain, to a great extent, focused on low value-added segments such as the production of solar panels, while R&D is retained in the headquarter countries (MPC, 2015). Other new areas derive from Malaysia's resource-based industries. This is the case for the biomass industry that partly draws upon Malaysia's leading position in palm oil. Although significant progress has been made in some of these emerging areas, these have yet to be considered as new sources of growth. A detailed analysis using the framework of economic complexity shows that Malaysia has succeeded in moving to new "product spaces", in general towards more sophisticated products (e.g. precision instruments based on E&E capabilities, certain chemicals, certain metal products), which means it has achieved product upgrading. On the other hand, the production of some low value-added products (garments, simple ceramic and wood products) was progressively abandoned. The progress made since around 2000 has been mostly incremental and falls short of the process of upgrading and diversification that underpinned growth during the previous decades (EPU, 2014).

Are Malaysian domestic firms improving their innovation capability?

The importance of FDI to stimulate and enable innovation through market opportunities and various types of spillovers in domestic firms has been widely documented in the economic development and innovation literature through detailed case studies of various economies and sectors. With the gradual outsourcing of increasingly complex components and services, the multiplication of forward and, especially, backward linkages of MNEs generates demand that induces domestic firms located upstream and downstream to enhance their capabilities and engage in innovation.[25] Given the degree of internationalisation of these large firms, their presence in the country can also offer domestic firms a shortcut for a more rapid integration into global value chains, starting with low value-added activities before entering their upgrading process.

The spillovers from MNEs are all the more important as they are often among the leading firms in their sector. They therefore master cutting-edge skills and operate at the highest technological level. Their presence can therefore, in principle, facilitate the transfer of various types of technological knowledge as well as managerial and business skills and competences. Such effects can be expected to be potentially strong in Southeast Asian countries, such as Malaysia, Singapore and Thailand, where MNEs account for the bulk of manufacturing production and exports. However, this process is by no means automatic.

Box 4.4. An emergent new source of growth: The Malaysian solar industry

The Third Industrial Master Plan (IMP3) identified solar energy as a new industrial opportunity in 2006. While there was not any production of solar panels at that time, Malaysia is now one of the world's largest producers of solar equipment (wafers, cells and modules), behind China and the European Union. The Malaysian solar module production increased by 41% in 2013, reaching 3.3 GW in 2014. This production capacity is derived from foreign manufacturers – mostly American, European, Korean and Japanese companies – that installed their facilities in Malaysia.[1] In 2013 and 2014, the Malaysian Investment Development Authority granted permission to five new foreign companies to set up their production factories in Malaysia. Meeting the target of 12.9 GW by 2020 will therefore require significant investments, both from new gigawatt scale manufacturing plants and expansion of existing ones.

According to the solar panel manufacturers, Malaysia's two main comparative advantages are the generous tax incentives (for instance, the leading global firm FirstSolar received a 15-year income tax holiday) and the existence of a cost competitive, skilled labour force, partly developed in relation with the semiconductor industry which builds upon similar production processes. However, despite these strengths, which allow Malaysia to compete with other Asian countries such as China, India and Chinese Taipei, the nascent Malaysian solar industry is still fragile as competitive positions are rapidly shifting. The market growth has been supported significantly by the restrictions to Chinese exports of solar panels to the United States and the European Union, which led companies not to locate their factories in China. In addition, domestic demand for solar panels, and more generally a climate favourable to renewable energy, contributes to Malaysia being considered an attractive manufacturing base.

Apart from production capacity, it remains to be seen, as for semiconductors, whether Malaysian activities in solar panels will extend beyond component manufacturing towards vertically integrating a greater proportion of the value chain in the country. Another uncertainty concerns the location chosen by the manufacturers to produce the latest and future generations of solar technologies. So far, in most cases, foreign manufacturers have kept not only R&D, but also their pre-production and downstream operations at their headquarters, where a significant proportion of value added accrues. Some research activities are carried out by laboratories, such as at the Solar Energy Research Institute, the National University of Malaysia and the Standards and Industrial Research Institute of Malaysia. Since its creation in 2005, the Solar Energy Research Institute has performed numerous, mostly small-scale, research projects financed through the competitive grant schemes of the Ministry of Science, Technology and Innovation (MOSTI) and the Ministry of Research, as well as some funding under the Economic Transformation Programme. Only limited research is carried out with private companies, mostly for application and demonstration of technologies. The Standards and Industrial Research Institute of Malaysia is also involved mainly in downstream development and testing.

Government-led initiatives will be essential to support the growth of the Malaysian industry, both on the supply and demand side: support to staff training, the establishment of a domestic accreditation and certification body, incentives for solar panel installation, and connection to the grid.

1. Among those manufacturers are FirstSolar, Flextronics, MSR, SolarTif, PV HiTech, Panasonic Energy, EXT, Hanwa Q Cells.

Sources: Bradsher (2014), "Solar rises in Malaysia during Ttrade wars over panels", www.nytimes.com/2014/12/12/business/energy-environment/solar-rises-in-malaysia-during-trade-wars-over-panels.html?_r=1; News 24 (2015), "Malaysia feels heat as its solar industry soars", www.news24.com/Green/News/Malaysia-feels-heat-as-its-solar-industry-soars-20150818; EPU (2011), "Moving up the value chain: A study of Malaysia's solar and medical device industries, final report", www.epu.gov.my/c/document_library/get_file?uuid=e205228c-67e9-4477-b06f-bbc3e8abc2d8&groupId=283545; PEMANDU (2014), *Economic Transformation Programme 2014 Annual Report*, http://etp.pemandu.gov.my/annualreport2014; Chua and Oh (2012), "Solar energy outlook in Malaysia", http://dx.doi.org/10.1016/j.rser.2011.08.022.

Three main conditions come into play at the level of MNEs and that of the recipient country, respectively:

- MNEs must enter a process of upgrading and externalisation of their activities in the recipient country. As discussed previously, this process has slowed down in the last 15 years in Malaysia.
- The possibilities of upgrading the domestic industry are largely determined by the strategies of the lead MNEs in the value chain. Case studies show that some firms tap into the resources of host countries without transferring any knowledge, whereas others offer genuine upgrading prospects (OECD, 2013b).
- Domestic companies need to have the required absorption capacity to enter a partnership with MNEs and valorise the resources being transferred in the course of the relationship. As shown by many surveys of business firms in Malaysia, both foreign and domestic, a lack of skills is one of the main barriers to innovation (MASTIC, 2014b). MNEs in many instances request a certain level of certification of their supplier base to ensure quality throughout the value chain. The level of capability enhancement needed to achieve upgrading depends on the type of shift across and within value chains (Box 4.3). Process and product upgrading typically leverage the existing labour force through incremental capability enhancements (on-the-job training, short-term courses and specific certifications, etc.). Functional upgrading, on the other hand, generally requires a substantially different set of capabilities, including a high proportion of the workforce with a tertiary education, and is therefore more challenging.

It has been argued by various experts that these conditions have not been fully realised in Malaysia, resulting in an industry structure that bears features of "duality" with insufficient interlinkages between the export-oriented MNEs and the domestic SMEs in import competing sectors (Bhattacharya, 2002). More recent and detailed data analyses focused on the E&E industry provide more nuanced results: Malaysian firms themselves have a high propensity to export, but their share of value added in total exports is comparatively small due to the fact that MNEs have less linkages with domestic suppliers than those located in many other countries (World Bank, 2014).

Case studies suggest that the transfer of technological capabilities through FDI has been limited in Malaysia. The tasks externalised to domestic firms have been mainly in the area of logistics, aiming at cost reduction and delivery timeliness rather than improvement of the product quality (OECD, 2013a). Only a relatively small number of domestic firms, such as Dell and Intel, have succeeded in using linkages with MNEs as a stepping-stone to upgrade their own innovation capabilities (Yusuf and Nabeshima, 2009). In addition, few local firms have succeeded in establishing their own OEM/local brands. In most other cases, the clusters of domestic firms that benefit from forward and, to a lesser extent backward, linkages have remained confined to logistical tasks aiming at cost reduction via proximity relationships within the value chain (World Bank, 2010). However, although knowledge clusters are far less common, some upgrading of domestic capabilities has occurred indirectly, i.e. not in the framework of an institutionalised transaction but through economies of agglomeration and cluster synergies. In the Penang E&E industry notably, local firms have been able to improve their production process by hiring former employees of MNEs that are well trained and experienced (Rasiah, 2006a). Cluster synergies, albeit not founded on knowledge spillovers, were also critical in the success of the palm oil industry (Rasiah, 2006b) and the furniture industry (Ng, Chandran and Thiruchelvam, 2015).

Although imperfect and incomplete, information on R&D inputs and outputs offer some proxy of the extent of technological improvement of the domestic industry. Unfortunately, MASTIC, the Malaysian STI statistics agency, has not published data on R&D expenditures by type of ownership/control of firms for many years. In 2006, the share of foreign-owned and foreign-controlled companies were 65% and 4%, respectively, i.e. close to 70% in total (MASTIC, 2008). Based on raw data from the Malaysian Annual Manufacturing Survey 2008, Chandran, Veera and Santhidran (2014) also show that despite strong variation across industries, local firms invest on average only a small portion of the foreign-owned companies' expenditures on R&D. For instance, in the manufacture of radio, television and communication equipment and apparatus, local firms invest 5 times less than the foreign companies located in Malaysia, while the gap is about 88 times in the manufacture of office, accounting and computing machinery. The gap is much lower in some sectors such as the manufacture of other transport equipment and the manufacture of electrical machinery and apparatus (not elsewhere classified).

Data on the United States Patent and Trademark Office's (USPTO) patents granted to business firms with Malaysian inventors (Table 4.6), which provide an indication of international-level R&D performed in Malaysia, show that in the great majority of cases, the research has been performed within MNEs rather than in domestic firms. Although, as discussed earlier, MNEs are still reluctant to relocate their R&D next to their manufacturing facilities, companies such as Intel and Motorola, which invested very early in applied research in Malaysia, seem to be notable exceptions: both of these two companies applied for about 60 utility patents between 1990 and 2007 (Chandran and Wong, 2011). Only two of the top ten applicants are Malaysian entities, including the Malaysian Palm Oil Board which defines itself as a government agency under the Ministry of Plantation Industries and Commodities.

Only 14% of patents of the Malaysian Intellectual Property Office were granted to Malaysian organisations (including Malaysian universities and research institutes) in 2015.[26] This share is likely to be even smaller when only business applicants are considered since they represent only about 40% of local patent applications (MASTIC, 2014a).[27] Likewise, there was no Malaysian company among the top 100 PCT patent applicants in 2014 (WIPO, 2015b)[28] and only 2 private companies, IQ Group (lighting products) and Widetech Manufacturing (correction fluid), and 2 public companies[29] were among the top ten Malaysian PCT applicants in 2012 (MASTIC, 2014a). There is no automotive company among the top applicants. The government-owned carmaker Proton as well as Perodua Sdn Bhd rely substantially on intellectual property owned by Japanese companies, in particular Mitsubishi Motors (WIPO, 2008). These results are consistent with the analysis of patenting activities in Malaysia by Chandran and Wong (2011). They show that local firms are struggling to improve their technological sophistication and mainly perform incremental process innovation, if any. The authors conclude that the low level of innovation, in particular of domestic firms, is a major barrier to economic upgrading.

Factors hindering the upgrading of the Malaysian industry

According to the perceptions of business firms, as reported in the Sixth Innovation Survey, the main factors limiting innovation, both in services and manufacturing, are cost factors (Table 4.7), closely followed by market and knowledge factors. Across all categories, the factors are considered more constraining by manufacturing firms than by firms operating in services. These results, at least in terms of ranking of the different types of factors, are generally consistent with those obtained in previous surveys (see for instance the Fifth Innovation Survey in MASTIC [2011]).

Table 4.6. **Top 15 business USPTO patent applicants, Malaysian inventors, 2010-14**

First-named assignee	Country of origin	Main sector	Activities in relation with patents	Number of patents granted	
				2014	2010-14
Avago technologies ECBU IP PTE. Ltd. and Avago Technologies General IP PTE. Ltd.	Singapore (Penang)	Electronics	R&D, manufacture and marketing of various electronic products	0	165
Altera Corporation	United States (Penang)	Electronics	R&D, research and development of VLSI design, layout, test and software development	35	98
Intel Corporation	United States (Penang)	Electronics	Assembly and testing of processors	19	91
Freescale Semiconductor, Inc.	United States (Dutch since 2015) (Petaling Jaya)	Electronics	Design, manufacturing, assembly and testing of semiconductors	18	48
Infineon Technologies AG	Germany (Malacca)	Electronics	Assembly and testing	9	45
Western Digital Technologies, Inc.	United States (Petaling Jaya)	Electronics	Manufacturing of computer storage devices	18	40
Malaysian Palm Oil Board	Malaysia (Kuala Lumpur)	Palm oil	Conduct and promote R&D activities relating to the palm oil industry	12	36
Purecircle Sdn Bhd	Malaysia (Negeri Sembilan)	Biotechnology	R&D and refinery of sweetener for food and beverage	1	34
Spansion LLC	United States (Penang)	Electronics	Design centre (design, layout, computer-aided design and verification services)	4	20
Motorola Solutions, Inc.	United States (Penang)	Electronics	Manufacturing, design, development and distribution	5	18

Note: Patent origin is determined by the residence of the first-named inventor listed on the patent grant.

Sources: USPTO (2015), "Patenting by geographic region (state and country): Breakout by organization: Malaysia", *General Patent Statistics Reports* (database), www.uspto.gov/web/offices/ac/ido/oeip/taf/stcasg/myx_stcorg.htm.

Table 4.7. **Factors hampering innovation activities, average results by factor type**

	Services	Manufacturing
Cost factors	1.66	1.88
Knowledge factors	1.44	1.54
Market factors	1.27	1.72
Organisational factors	1.31	1.51
Regulatory factors/public policy	1.03	1.2
Other factors	0.78	0.73

Note: Mean indicator: 0 = not relevant; 3 = highly important.

Source: MASTIC (2014b), *National Survey of Innovation 2012*.

A look at the detailed results reveals that the lack of qualified personnel follows closely after the high cost and lack of funds associated with innovation activities, in particular for manufacturing firms (Figure 4.8). Furthermore, judging by former surveys when distributions of responses were provided over the whole rating scale (as opposed to mean results), a higher proportion of respondents considered the lack of qualified personnel as the highest barrier to innovation.

Figure 4.8. **Factors hampering innovation activities, all factors**

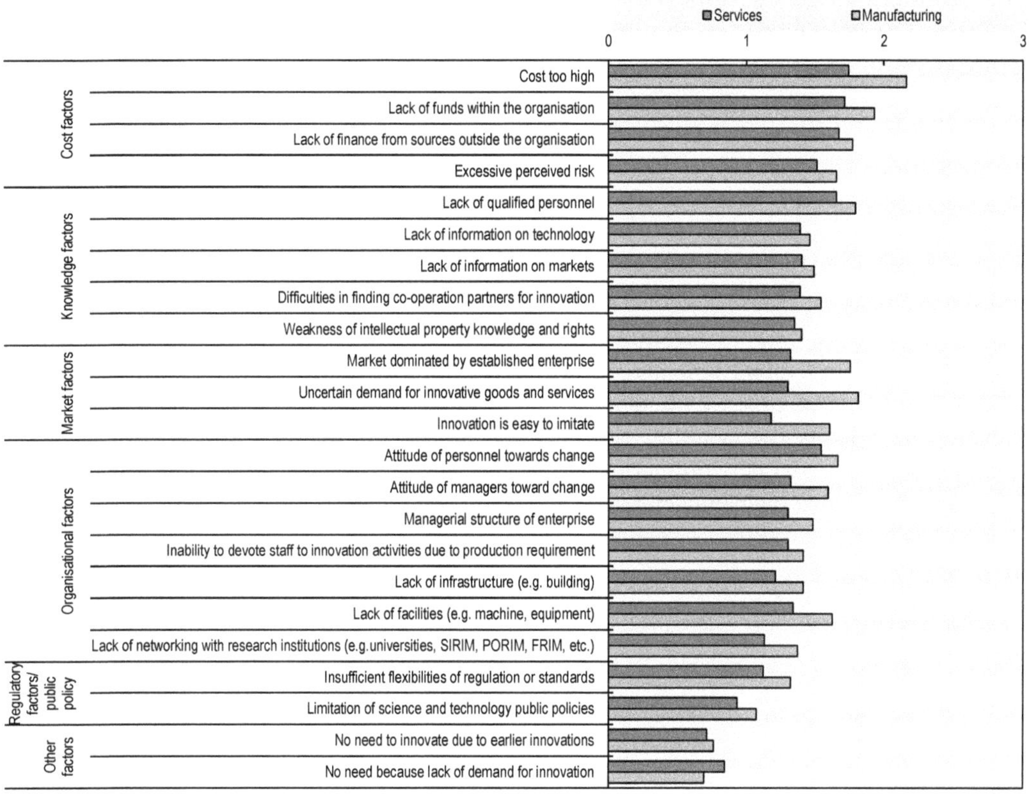

Note: Mean indicator: 0 = not relevant; 3 = highly important.

Source: MASTIC (2014b), *National Survey of Innovation 2012*.

Skills shortage and mismatch has received much attention due to its negative impact on the industry's ability to upgrade its innovation capability. As mentioned previously, this is the root of the problem of attracting FDI in higher end activities and improving the absorption capacity of domestic firms.

Two surveys conducted in 2002 and 2007 (respectively, MyKe 1 and MyKe II, commissioned by the EPU) attempted to assess the knowledge content of business firms in 21 sectors. One of the main results of these surveys is that, overall, although the knowledge content of Malaysian business firms has increased, it is modest.

Another important finding with regard to the upgrading of the domestic industry is that the gap between the MNEs and local firms, although confirmed, is narrowing. The same results emerge for the gap between large and small firms. In the manufacturing sector, except for the E&E, machinery, chemical, rubber and automotive industries, knowledge generation was found to be typically low. This can be explained by the fact that most firms in this sector acquire knowledge solely by adapting and adopting foreign technology (Shapira et al., 2008). The surveys also identified the most important factors constraining knowledge development in three so-called "knowledge contexts" (knowledge acquisition, generation, utilisation and management), technology and human capabilities. The most important factor constraining knowledge acquisition is the lack of funds to finance the plans to improve knowledge capabilities. With regard to workers' skills and knowledge specifically, the lack of English proficiency appears to be the most cited main hindrance to knowledge acquisition, followed by the cost of training and the higher turnover after training (Shapira et al., 2008).[30]

Higher education institutions

The higher education sector of Malaysia has evolved dynamically since its independence. The number of higher education institutions (HEIs) has multiplied and important reforms in terms of funding (e.g. moving to performance-based funding mechanisms) and governance have been or are currently being implemented with the goal of strengthening quality and delivery and fostering excellence in higher education. These reforms are already showing signs of change and important results have been achieved, notably in terms of higher education enrolment rates (at all levels) as well as in terms of enhanced R&D personnel and the research performance of public universities, among other major achievements. Challenges remain in terms of governance (e.g. autonomy) and relevance to industry (connecting with demand), as well as growing funding constraints. The latter relates to the new obligations for HEIs to diversify their sources of funding and find ways to enhance their impact on the economy and society.

Historical evolution

The history of higher education in Malaysia can be broadly divided into four main phases (Lee, 2005; Grapragasem, Krishnan and Norhaini Mansor, 2014):

- Until the 1970s, higher education was restricted to a single university, with access limited to a selected proportion of (usually well-off) elite students.
- The second phase, between 1970 and 1990, saw the start of the democratisation of higher education driven by the state, with the creation of the general higher education structure which is still largely valid to date: several new public universities were created, together with polytechnics institutions (offering certificate and diploma level programmes) and a number of community colleges (providing a wide range of technical and vocational education training courses). Private institutions were also created during this period, offering a wide range of courses at the certificate and diploma levels. These new institutions dramatically increased student access to higher education, in response to the rapid population and economic growth of the country.
- The third phase, from 1990 to mid-2000, was marked by the consolidation of the structure set up during the second phase, with new legislations providing a better defined framework for the whole system.[31] More public institutions were set up (the number of public universities reached 20) and several private colleges were awarded university status. The main objective during this period was to foster the rapid transition of the country towards an upper middle-income economy.
- The last phase, since mid-2000, has been characterised by a number of dramatic changes in the character and functions of higher education in Malaysia. These changes are largely linked to the evolution of the economic nature of the Malaysian economy, to globalisation and to increased competition worldwide. First, the Private Higher Educational Act 1996 was amended in 2003 which subsequently lead to the restructuring of private higher learning institutions in order to make them more competitive globally. The Ministry of Higher Education was created shortly thereafter (in 2004) and in 2007 two plans were launched: the

National Higher Education Strategic Plan (NHESP) Beyond 2020 and the National Higher Education Action Plan (NHEAP), whose objectives were to facilitate the transition of Malaysia to a knowledge economy. These plans were followed by a series of updates and national strategic reforms.

Structure

Malaysia possesses over 20 public HEIs, as well as private universities, foreign university branch campuses and colleges that have substantially expanded in the recent past (OECD, 2013a). The number of public universities rose from 11 in 2002 to 20 in 2008, and private universities expanded from a handful in the 1980s to 51 in 2010. Today there are 24 national private universities, 23 university-colleges and 4 branch campuses of foreign universities. Table 4.8 displays the current composition of the sector.

Table 4.8. **Higher education landscape of Malaysia**

	Number of HEIs	Enrolment	Graduates
Public institutions			
Universities	20	508 526	104 291
Polytechnics	30	89 292	33 310
Community colleges	70	6 319	6 624
Private institutions			
Universities	24	202 714	29 139
University-colleges	23	40 651	1 269
Branch campuses of foreign universities	4	8 107	1 353
Colleges	500	177 501	22 456

Source: Ministry of Higher Education (2011), *Statistics of Higher Education 2011.*

The expansion of private HEIs was spurred by the adoption of the Private Higher Educational Institutions Act and the National Accreditation Board Act in 1996, which allowed private operators to provide higher education programmes under discretionary tuition fees and management. Specifically, the amended act provided the provision for the establishment and upgrading of private universities, university colleges and branch campuses of foreign universities in Malaysia. In this configuration, public universities registered the largest student enrolment with about half a million students and 104 291 graduates in 2010. Public universities reported 54% of enrolment compared to 46.4% in private universities in 2013. In the first three years of the NHESP, enrolment in public universities increased by 21%, making these the main providers of higher education in Malaysia.

The Higher Education Department within the Ministry of Education co-ordinates and monitors the activities of public and private universities and colleges. Public universities are categorised by the Ministry of Education in three groups: 5 research universities (with a focus on research, competitive entry, quality lecturers and a ratio of undergraduates to postgraduates of 50:50), 11 technical/specialised universities (with a focus on technical, education, management and defence research issues, competitive entry, quality lecturers and a ratio of undergraduates to postgraduates of 50:50) and 4 comprehensive/teaching universities (with a focus on teaching, competitive entry, quality lecturers and a ratio of undergraduates to postgraduates of 70:30) (OECD, 2015a). Table 4.9 provides an overview of public universities in Malaysia. The largest public university of the country is the University Teknologi Mara, with 34% of all tertiary students in 2013. Ten public universities were either newly created or granted university status in the 1990s.

Table 4.9. **Size and type of public universities in Malaysia**

Type of university	Acronym	Year of creation	Name	Student enrolment	% of total enrolment	Top 10 PCT Malaysian applicant 2012
Research	UM	1949	Universiti Malaya	27 091	5	Yes
Research	USM	1969	Universiti Sains Malaysia	29 065	5	Yes
Research	UKM	1970	Universiti Kebangsaan Malaysia	30 041	5	No
Research	UPM	1931	Universiti Putra Malaysia	32 092	6	Yes
Research	UTM	1904	Universiti Teknologi Malaysia	33 361	6	Yes
Focused	UUM	1984	Universiti Utara Malaysia	30 837	6	No
Comprehensive	UIAM	1983	Universiti Islam Antarabangsa Malaysia[1]	32 086	6	No
Comprehensive	UNIMAS	1992	Universiti Malaysia Sarawak	17 198	3	No
Comprehensive	UMS	1994	Universiti Malaysia Sabah	25 207	4	No
Focused	UPSI	1922	Universiti Pendidikan Sultan Idris	27 659	5	No
Comprehensive	UiTM	1956	Universiti Teknologi MARA	189 551	34	No
Focused	UniSZA	2005	Universiti Sultan Zainal Abidin	7 977	1	No
Focused	UMT	1979	Universiti Malaysia Terengganu	8 715	2	No
Focused	USIM	1998	Universiti Sains Islam Malaysia	13 022	2	No
Focused	UTHM	1993	Universiti Tun Hussein Onn Malaysia	15 319	3	No
Focused	UTeM	2000	Universiti Teknikal Malaysia Melaka	12 593	2	No
Focused	UMP	2002	Universiti Malaysia Pahang	8 904	2	No
Focused	UniMAP	2001	Universiti Malaysia Perlis	10 415	2	No
Focused	UMK	2007	Universiti Malaysia Kelantan	6 443	1	No
Focused	UPNM	2006	Universiti Pertahanan Nasional Malaysia	2 783	0	No
			Total enrolment	**560 359**	**100**	

1. Also known as the International Islamic University Malaysia.

Sources: MOE (2015a), "Public institutions of higher education (PIHE)", www.moe.gov.my/en/ipta for the list of public universities and their type, as well as the enrolment data; WIPO (2014), *Patent Cooperation Treaty Yearly Review*, www.wipo.int/pct/en/activity for top ten PCT applicants and Internet search for the year of creation of each university.

General trends

Overall, Malaysia invests much more in tertiary education than its peers in the region. Malaysia's government expenditure for tertiary education relative to GDP stood at 2% in 2009 and 1.5% in 2013, whereas Korea invests around 0.6% and Singapore 1%. Enrolment rates in both public and private universities have increased substantially. For undergraduate programmes, enrolment has surpassed the half million mark, which represents an increase of 7% (EPU, 2015a). The enrolment for PhD degrees increased by 56.3% from 2010 to 2013, while at the master's level, enrolment increased by 31.7% (EPU, 2015a) (Figure 4.10). Academic performance for students at the bachelor level in public HEIs has improved, with 17.5% of graduates attaining cumulative grade point average scores of 3.49 and above in 2013, compared to 13.6% in 2010.

However, in terms of overall quality of university education as measured by international rankings, Malaysia's position has improved within the region but is still far from joining the top 100 universities of Asia or the world according to the QS World University rankings. This is in great contrast to universities of a similar age in

Hong Kong (China), India, Singapore and even Saudi Arabia, which have made the top 100 in the Asian rankings over the last few years. In the QS World University Rankings (2014/15) report, Universiti Malaya was ranked 151st and rated with five stars and is generally described as a world-class university in a broad range of areas, enjoys a high reputation and has cutting-edge facilities and an internationally renowned research and teaching faculty.[32] In the Times Higher Education World University Rankings 2015-16, Universiti Tecknologi Malaysia ranked in the 401-500 range, while the Universiti Kebangsaan Malaysia, the Universiti Putra Malaysia and Universiti Sains Malaysia rank in the 601-800 interval.

R&D activities and funding

Research

HEIs play a central role in Malaysia's innovation system: 80% of the nation's R&D research personnel are found in HEIs, accounting for 28.67% of the total R&D expenditure in 2012 (MASTIC, 2014c). More than half of the R&D infrastructure is located at university labs. Within the NHESP Beyond 2020, the government developed a plan to enhance the R&D capacity of universities. With this new development, the government has set goals to develop and strengthen research capacity and innovation to international standards.[33] In an effort to enhance the research capacity of universities as well as their role in building a knowledge economy, HEIs have seen their R&D expenditure growing steadily over the last decade (Figures 4.9 and 4.10). Research expenditure was multiplied by 11 between 2000 and 2012. In 2014, it reached MYR 6 445.48 million – which was twice the amount invested in 2012. The increase could be due to the number of participating higher learning institutions, which was 58 in 2014, as compared to 49 in 2012 (MASTIC, 2016).

From 2006 onwards (e.g. passage of the Ninth Malaysia Plan, 2006-10), R&D expenditure at HEIs grew at an average annual growth rate of 27.6%, reaching MYR 6445.48 million (about USD 1.659 billion) in 2014. Of this, about 38% went to capital expenditure.

An important strategic change in the orientation of R&D occurred between 2012 and 2014. In 2014, applied research increased significantly – doubling the amount of basic research, whereas two years earlier applied and basic research displayed similar levels of funding. In relative terms, the importance of basic research (44.36% to 29.64%) and experimental development research (13.62% to 7.80%) have decreased over the 2008-14 period to the benefit of applied research. This trend is explained by the increased focus on applied research in government funding of university research.

In tandem with R&D funding, the number of R&D personnel employed at HEIs has expanded rapidly since 2006 (Figure 4.10). Before 2006, the numbers were fairly stagnant, with a total headcount of 13 007 (of which 12 152 were researchers). The total number of full-time equivalent (FTE) researchers almost tripled from 2008 to 2010 and continued increasing from 2010 to 2014, reaching 51 097.26. The headcount of R&D personnel reached 92 975 – almost three times the figure reported in 2008 (34 859). Malaysia now surpasses Indonesia, Singapore and Thailand – the latter of which actually substantially decreased the number of researchers. The proportion of female to male researchers has been almost equal since 2010 (50.46% in 2014) – much higher than other ASEAN economies. The percentage of PhDs in total researchers has recently decreased, from 51% in 2012 to 22.34 % in 2014 (MASTIC, 2016).

Figure 4.9. **Evolution of R&D expenditure in higher education institutions**

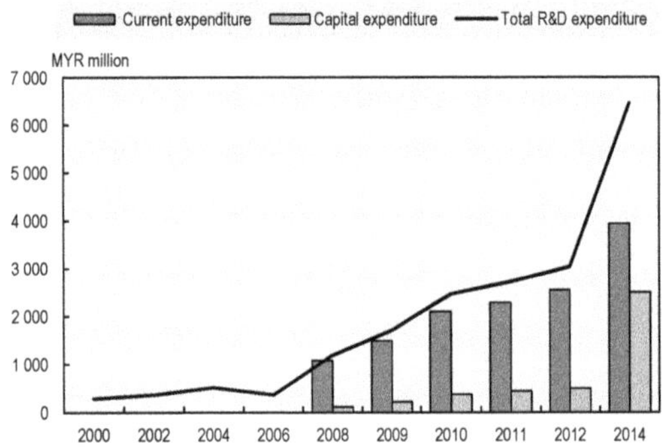

Sources: MASTIC (2001, 2005, 2009, 2013, 2016), *National Surveys of Research and Development.*

Figure 4.10. **Evolution of R&D personnel and researchers (FTE and headcount) in higher education institutions**

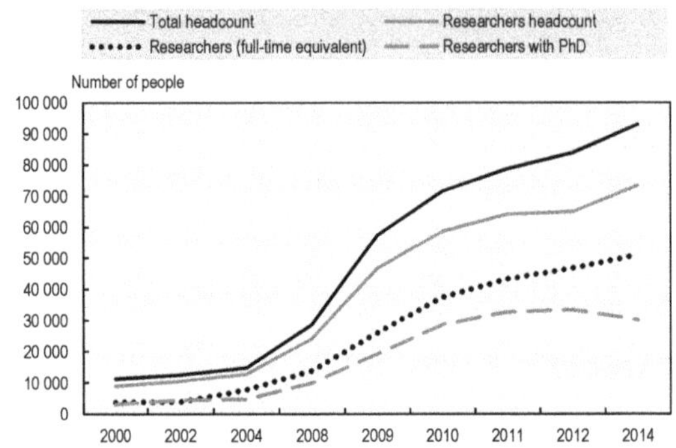

Sources: MASTIC (2001, 2005, 2009, 2013, 2016), *National Surveys of Research and Development.*

The ratio of R&D expenditure per researcher, however, is much lower compared to Malaysia's counterparts (Figure 4.12). In other words, university researchers in countries like Singapore or Thailand have much more resources at the individual level – e.g. four times more in Singapore and twice the amount in Korea. This is essentially due to the substantial expansion of R&D funding for higher education institutions, an increase that has been higher than the number of R&D personnel. This trend may suggest that the R&D resource allocation is weakly linked to planning of human resources for R&D. This may reflect a weak interaction between policy design and actual implementation of programmes at institutions.

The main source of funding for R&D (Figures 4.13 and 4.14) remains the government, although its importance is in decline – from 91.3% in 2008 to 58.22% in 2014). The part of HEIs has also decreased, from 17% in 2009 to 8.7% in 2012 (data for 2014 are not available). The second and third most important sources of funding for R&D in 2012 were internal sources (8.7%) and foreign sources (7.87%). Compared to previous years, foreign sources and other sources have gained in importance, moving from less than 1% in 2011 to 7% and 8% in 2012. Business enterprise remains a weak source of financing for R&D (4.76% in 2014). This is a sign of a weak connection with industry in the undertaking of research activities. OECD countries on average display lower ratios of government funding (39% on average in 2013) and higher internal financing (48% of R&D comes from the HEIs themselves) (Figure 4.14) A higher ratio of funding by the business sector also prevails in more advanced economies (7%).

According to MASTIC indicators (MASTIC, 2014a), 37% of R&D conducted at HEIs in 2012 was allocated to engineering and technology research, followed by natural sciences (17%) and social sciences (10%). These were the three top areas in R&D. In terms of publication activity (total national), engineering and technology is also the first domain of publication (23% for the period 2010-14), followed by computer sciences and medicine (12% each in total publications).

Figure 4.11. **Total researchers in higher education institutions, 2002 and 2012**

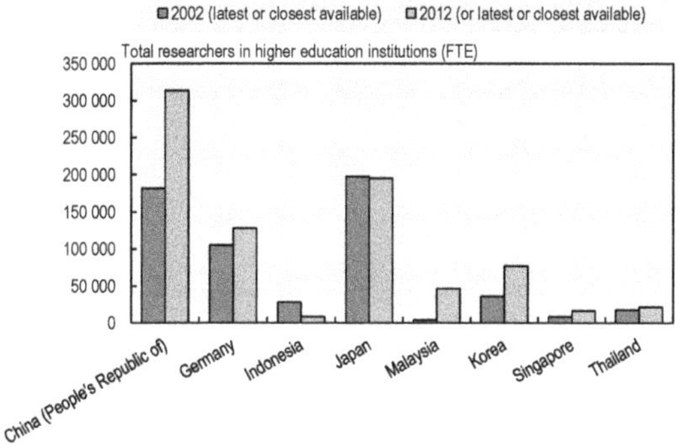

Note: Data for Malaysia correspond to 2014. Data for Indonesia and Thailand correspond to 2009 and 2011, respectively. For the start of the period (2002), data for Indonesia and Thailand correspond to 2001 and 2003, respectively.

Source: UNESCO (2016), *UIS.Stat* (database), http://data.uis.unesco.org.

Figure 4.12. **R&D expenditure per researcher in higher education institutions, 2002 and 2012**

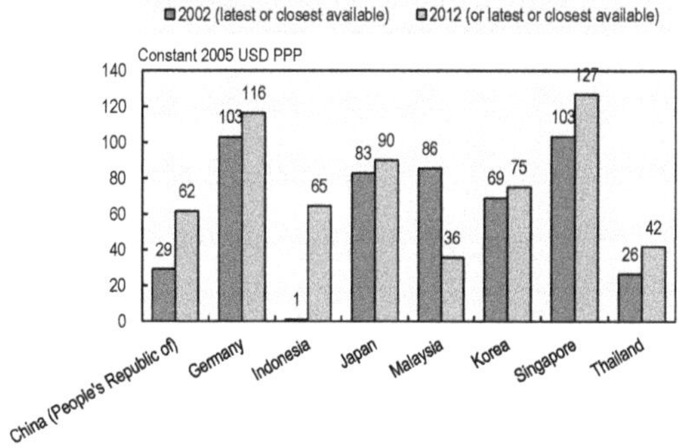

Note: For Malaysia, expenditures refer to 2003 whereas researchers to 2002. For the second period, data refer to 2012 in order to compare with other country data. For Thailand, expenditure in the first period refer to 2004 and researchers to 2003. For the second period, researchers refer to 2009 and expenditure to 2010. For Indonesia, expenditure reported for 2012 refer to expenditure of 2010 and researchers of 2009.

Source: UNESCO (2016), *UIS.Stat* (database), http://data.uis.unesco.org .

Figure 4.13. **Sources of funding for R&D performed by higher education institutions, evolution over the period 2006-16**

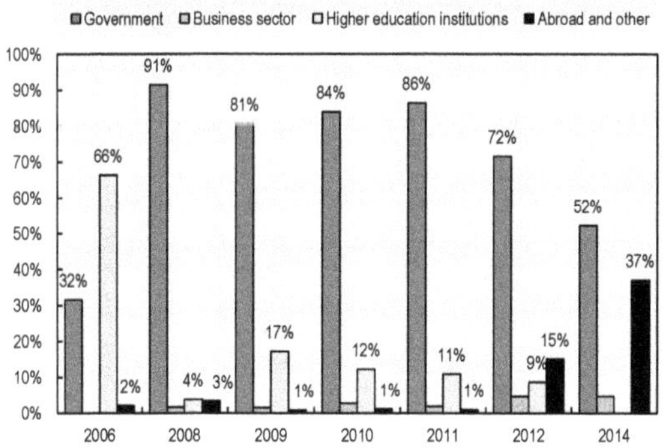

Sources: MASTIC (2001, 2005, 2009, 2013, 2016), *National Surveys of Research and Development.*

Figure 4.14. **Sources of funding for R&D performed by higher education institutions in 2013 or latest available**

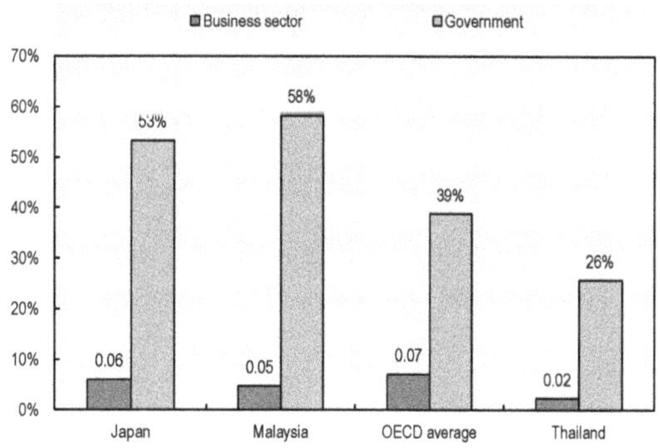

Note: Data for Japan and the OECD average refer to 2013; data for Malaysia refer to 2014; data for Thailand refer to 2011.

Source: UNESCO (2016), *UIS.Stat* (database), http://data.uis.unesco.org; OECD (2014), *OECD Science, Technology and Industry Outlook 2014*, http://dx.doi.org/10.1787/sti_outlook-2014-en.

Results

In terms of scientific performance, Malaysia has dramatically expanded its number of scientific publications over the last decade. However, scientific publication is highly concentrated in a few universities (Figure 4.15), with the Universiti Malaya, the Universiti Sains Malaysia and the Universiti Putra Malaysia representing 76% of the total output produced by the top 15 institutions over the period 2001-11. The Malaysian Palm Oil Board is the prime research organisation, which has moved up to rank 13, according to a recent bibliometrics study (MASTIC, 2012).

Yet in spite of the increased scientific production, the quality of publications remains low compared to other countries. In 2011, there were 4.85 cites per document (according to SCImago and based on Scopus data) whereas Singapore recorded an average of 12.7 cites (per paper), Thailand 6.82, Indonesia 5.99 and Korea 8.33. Malaysian researchers need to improve the quality and impact of their research.

In addition, growth in scientific publication has not been accompanied by a significant increase in international collaboration in science (Figure 4.15). According to SCImago (data from Scopus), the percentage of international co-authorship actually decreased between the early 2000s and 2010s. Over the period 2000-04, 35.6% of publications involved international co-authorship whereas in 2010-14 this figure decreased to 32.6%. Furthermore, the h-index indicates that most of Malaysia's top universities have a lower ranking than those of international collaborators with a comparable article output. This is consistent with the lower cites per document (than peer countries) discussed above.

Figure 4.15. **International collaboration in science: International co-publication ratio (relative to total publications), 2000-14**

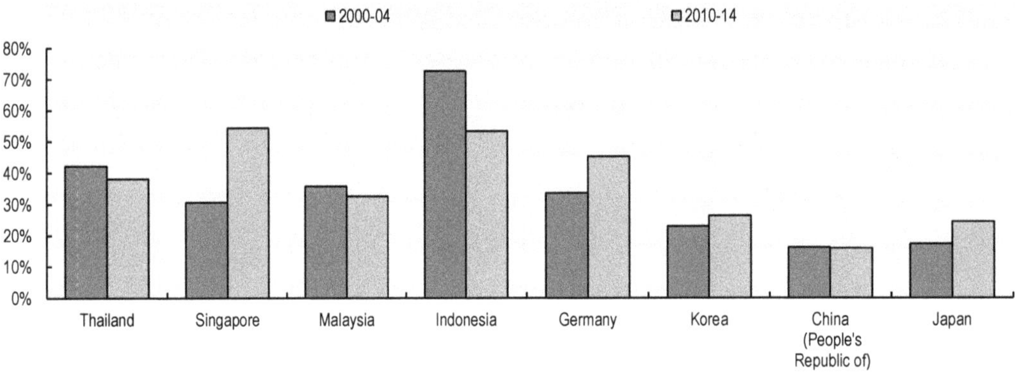

Source: SCImago (2007), *Country Rankings* (database), www.scimagojr.com/countryrank.php.

There has also been an enormous increase in university patenting in recent years. Universities applied for 81 local patent applications in 2005, whereas in 2012 this figure jumped to 407, thereby increasing the share of university patenting from 16% in 2005 to 35% in 2012 (Table 4.10). Furthermore, 314 patents were granted between 2010 and 2013. The leading universities in terms of patent applications include Universiti Sains Malaysia, University Malaya, Universiti Putra Malaysia and Universiti Teknologi Malaysia.[34] Two public research institutions are amongst the top patent applicants of the country: the National R&D Centre in ICT of Malaysia and the Malaysian Palm Oil Board. In particular, the National R&D Centre in ICT of Malaysia has been the top PCT

Malaysian applicant in the past few years, with a difference of more than 100 PCT applications.

Table 4.10. **Local patent applications by type of applicant, 2005-12**

	Total applications by residents	Universities (public and private)	Share	Public research institutes	Share
2005	522	81	16%	38	7%
2006	531	94	18%	40	8%
2007	670	165	25%	109	16%
2008	864	272	31%	151	17%
2009	1 234	547	44%	204	17%
2010	1 275	574	45%	222	17%
2011	1 136	442	39%	164	14%
2012	1 160	407	35%	177	15%

Source: MASTIC (2014a), *Malaysia Science, Technology and Innovation (STI) Indicators Report 2013*, http://mastic.mosti.gov.my/documents/10156/38ae84ca-b8a0-4edb-a5b8-d30aa8c016e6.

Malaysia ranks high among developing countries in terms of patenting by universities and public research universities (Figure 4.16). For the period 1980-2010, the highest rates of university patenting as measured by international patenting indicators (e.g. patent filings through the Patent Cooperation Treaty [PCT]) were for Singapore (13% of total PCT filings), Malaysia (13%), Ireland (11%) and Israel (10%). The countries with the highest participation of public research institutes (PRIs) in PCT patent filings were Malaysia (27%), Singapore (19%), India (14%) and France (10%). China and South Africa reported the highest university rates within middle-income countries with 5% of PCT filings (Zuniga, 2011; WIPO, 2011).

Figure 4.16. **Patenting by universities and public research organisations in PCT applications, 1980-2010**

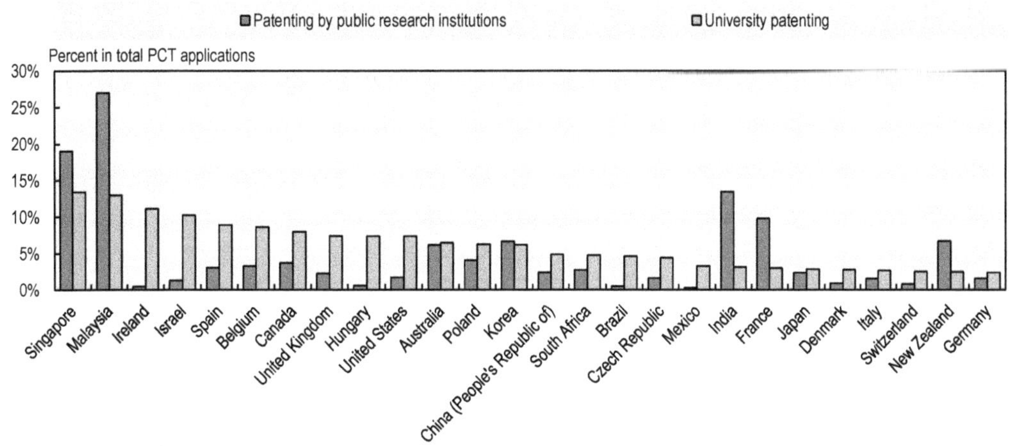

Note: Only countries having at least 1 000 PCT filings were included with at least 2.4% of university patenting in total patent applications (PCT filings).

Source: WIPO (2015b), *WIPO IP Statistics Data Center* (database), http://ipstats.wipo.int/ipstatv2.

Technology transfer and commercialisation

In Malaysia, commercialisation of public research began with the Sixth Malaysia Plan (1991-95) (EPU, 1990), which emphasised that public R&D programmes should become more market oriented by exploiting the commercialisation of research and technology (Chandran, 2010). Several funding programmes have been launched since to support and facilitate technology commercialisation and technology transfer at publicly-funded research institutions.

Despite a much larger and increasing number of patent applications (and other intellectual property rights), the commercialisation rate of research from universities and public institutions has until recently remained limited. Exceptions are to be found in the intellectual property rights (IPR) portfolio of some Malaysian key research actors, such as the Universiti Sains Malaysia and Universiti Putra Malaysia, as well as, on the public research institute (PRI) side, the Malaysian Palm Oil Board and the Rubber Research Institute of Malaysia (Chandran, 2010). For instance, the Malaysian Palm Oil Board generated USD 1.43 billion and has the highest commercialisation rate, at 30.6%.

Universities face a variety of challenges in the pursuit of technology transfer and commercialisation activities (OECD, 2015a):[35]

- poorly structured technology transfer offices and information process
- lack of demand-oriented research and poor intellectual property management
- bureaucracy
- lack of relevance of university R&D to industry
- lack of co-operation with industry in general
- lack of information on technology and appropriate markets for inventions
- insufficient government support and incentives, including financial ones
- lack of skilled personnel, absorptive capacity and human capital in SMEs that hamper university-industry knowledge flows and innovation more generally
- lack of funding at various stages of the commercialisation process (e.g. prototype, marketing, etc.).[36]

With recent advances in university autonomy and wider flexibility in their intellectual property policy, commercialisation has been eased to some extent but some obstacles remain (OECD, 2015c). Among the most important barriers to improving the rate of commercialisation are the lack of relevance of R&D projects to industry and the lack of funding at the various stages of the commercialisation process (Chandran, 2010). Strengthening links with industry through governing and steering committees (e.g. research boards and strategies) should be leveraged not only because of financial constraints, but more fundamentally because curricula research should address economic (and societal) demands.

Among the knowledge factors, the limited pool of qualified personnel is also seen as particularly detrimental to innovation activities. The lack of solid intermediary support at some universities implies that technology transfer and commercialisation initiatives fall under the responsibility of scientists themselves – in potential detriment of teaching and the pursuit of research activities per se. To reduce administrative hurdles derived from being part of the public administration, they should establish their own wholly owned subsidiary holding to operate more flexibly with industry. Leading universities have also started to adopt new strategies, moving from previous efforts aimed more at creating spin-offs to licensing, an activity that is often done by universities' subsidiaries. The reason for moving away from spin-offs was the high cost involved (OECD, 2015a).

Governance

Malaysian HEIs are governed by legislation, including the Universities and University Colleges Act (1971, amended 1996), the National Higher Education Council Act (1996), and the Malaysian Qualifications Agency Act (2007), which is in charge of accreditation and quality control. The first two were enacted with the purpose of providing for the establishment, organisation and management of public HEIs and to plan and formulate national policies and strategies for the development of HEIs. The education system overall is highly centralised and follows a top-down approach, with the federal government led by the Ministry of Education. The Council for Science and Education controls and regulates most of the operational decisions and policy strategy of the sector.

The Ministry of Education oversees HEIs (both public universities and private higher educational institutions), community colleges, polytechnics and other government agencies involved in higher education activities, such as the Malaysian Qualifications Agency, the National Higher Education Fund Corporation (Perbadanan Tabung Pendidikan Tinggi Nasional, PTPTN), the Tunku Abdul Rahman Foundation (Yayasan Tunku Abdul Rahman) and others.

Major reforms in the governance and strategy of the higher education sector started in 2007 with the launch of the National Higher Education Strategic Plan (NHESP) Beyond 2020 and the National Higher Education Action Plan 2007-2010.[37] These policy programmes outlined detailed strategic plans for the transformation of higher education in Malaysia with the purpose of fostering academic excellence in education and achieving global standards. A major goal of this programme is to make Malaysia an international hub for higher education in Southeast Asia. The roadmap contained in the NHESP has focused on reinforcing the delivery system via three key areas: 1) strengthening HEIs by giving them more autonomy; 2) enhancing research and innovation and improving the quality of teaching and learning; and 3) encouraging lifelong learning and increasing access to and equity in higher education.

Autonomy of universities

The autonomy of public universities has been enhanced over time but remains weak, as only a few universities have been granted autonomy. Strategic decisions are mostly taken at the ministry level, particularly concerning financial matters, tuition fees and hiring procedures. Since the Universities and University Colleges Act of 1971 came into effect, the Ministry of Education is responsible for closely regulating student admissions, course structures and curricula, staff appointments, remunerations, and financial management. The current practice of centralised administration has hindered the potential of change in higher education institutions and limited (or slowed down) their capacity to implement reforms and institutional strategies. Supervisory burdens and inefficiencies still continue to hinder the responsiveness of universities.

Measures have been undertaken through the legal framework to transfer administrative powers to HEIs through their boards of directors (ADB, 2012). The Universities and University Colleges Act replaced university councils with university boards of directors. This, however, only had a mild success. The board of directors continues to function as a university council and has neither the status nor the authority to act as a true corporate board (ADB, 2012). The amendments to the Universities and University Colleges Act in 2008 also intended to provide a greater level of autonomy and accountability to public universities. More recently, the *Malaysia Education Blueprint 2015-2025 (Higher Education)* (hereafter "Higher Education Blueprint 2015-25) (MOE, 2015b) envisages enhancing the decision-making power of universities (transferring competences from the ministry) and building the capacity and capabilities of university boards and institutional leaders to take on increased responsibilities.

In recent years, the government has been promoting autonomy on a merit-based approach in which being granted autonomy depends on institutional performance and governance achievements, as reported by quality rankings and governance assessments. The University Code of Good Governance and the University Good Governance Index have been adopted to help measure the level of readiness of Malaysian public universities for greater autonomy. The purpose of the University Code of Good Governance is to measure university governance best practices, while the University Good Governance Index measures the readiness for autonomy implemented in management, academic management and admissions.[38]

Autonomy is now linked to new internal funding obligations. Enhancing the autonomy of universities is one of the proposed strategies for enhancing the cost-effectiveness of higher education funding in Malaysia and for dealing with the expected reduction in government funding. The two other proposed reforms to enhance cost-effectiveness in HEIs focus on: 1) strengthening industry and research collaboration; and 2) enhancing the performance culture in teaching and research. The NHESP Beyond 2020 outlines the strategies needed for universities to subsidise their income from internal resources and directly link these achievements with autonomy concession.[39] Strategy Paper 10 (EPU, 2015c) emphasises the financial sustainability of HEIs. Within public universities, a more commercial and entrepreneurial approach has become prominent, but this has taken time to be formally implemented.[40]

Since August 2015, UNIMASS has been given more autonomy for deciding what to do and how to accomplish it (including the level of wages of professors, etc.). In exchange, new funding rules apply. Now 70% of funding comes from the government's annual block funding (covering operational expenses, and including staff salaries) and 30% is self-generated (industry, Ministry of Education and MOSTI grants, some post-graduate education fees).[41] Likewise, the qualification as "research university" involves (enhanced) autonomy, in addition to facilitating access to additional funding (for R&D). As a result, autonomy is not uniform across the sector; the best-performing institutions are able to persevere with more ease compared to new and smaller institutions.

In 2012, autonomous status was accorded to five research universities, namely the Universiti Malaya, Universiti Kebangsaan Malaysia, Universiti Sains Malaysia, Universiti Putra Malaysia and Universiti Teknologi Malaysia. These universities are empowered to manage student admissions directly, including intake announcements, receiving and processing applications, student selection and appeals. In 2013, three more universities – the Universiti Utara Malaysia, International Islamic University Malaysia and Universiti Malaysia Sarawak – became autonomous. In 2014, the number of public universities granted autonomy reached 12, with the addition of the Universiti Teknologi Mara, Universiti Teknikal Malaysia Melaka, Universiti Sains Islam Malaysia and Universiti Malaysia Terengganu.

Although these research institutions have been granted autonomy, this has not yet translated into any meaningful improvement of their operations, management or financial sustainability. It may, however, be too early to detect any major improvements. Furthermore, the governing boards of most of these universities still lack representation by professionals and captains of industry. Continued dependence on government funding and exigencies to gradually increase self-funding might pose complications for many universities.

Funding and evaluation

Funding from the government comes mainly from Ministry of Education and MOSTI grant schemes, although sometimes it is from other sources (i.e. the Ministry of Environment for renewable energy projects). The annual block funding provided by the Ministry of Education covers full professors' and associate professors' salaries. This includes research, as professors are expected to spend about 50% of their time conducting research. Every year a detailed proposal is made to the government for the following year's budget in order to obtain block funding.

The Tenth Malaysia Plan stated the necessity of reducing the proportion of government funding to public universities – in line with the government's objective to decrease the public deficit to 3% of GDP. It went on to say that public universities must seek alternative funds to improve the quality of teaching and research (EPU, 2010). Block funding will be decreased and internal sources of finance are expected to gradually compensate and finance operating costs. New funding mechanisms will link the allocation of block funding to performance outcomes, such as the number of undergraduates and postgraduates, research projects and commercialisation (Box 4.5). New funding schemes (performance-based funding) were announced in 2010 and 2014 with the release of the Higher Education Blueprint 2015-25 (MOE, 2015b) and the Eleventh Malaysia Plan (Box 4.5). Key initiatives of the Higher Education Blueprint 2015-25 include: improving the funding formulae for public HEIs by replacing block grants with performance-based and per student funding; implementing five-year (3 + 2 years) performance (outcome-based) contracts and targeting government investment in priority areas.

The government has emphasised that these financial reforms are crucial for achieving the desired transformation in HEIs as envisioned in the National Higher Education Plan Beyond 2020. Starting in 2015, all public universities are now required to generate 25% of their own operating costs (self-finance + funds obtained from competitive grant schemes). This obligation will increase to generating 75% of their own budgets by 2025. Concerns have been expressed regarding whether these percentages and the timeline are realistic and whether such an approach is feasible for all types of universities.

The Malaysian higher education sector has recently taken some important steps in evaluating its universities. Several assessment instruments have been introduced, such as rating mechanisms including SETARA and MyQUEST,[42] to assess the quality of undergraduate education and provide transparency. Introduced in 2011, MyQUEST (Malaysian Quality Evaluation System for Private Colleges) evaluates private colleges in terms of the quality of students, programmes, graduates, resources and governance. It is expected that the use of these ratings will help to ensure that financial flows to HEIs are transparent, thereby promoting accountability. Following international practice, SETERA (Rating System for Higher Education Institutions in Malaysia) looks at new performance indicators in addition to student enrolment and quality of teaching and learning, publications, R&D, patents, and licenses, among others.

Box 4.5. Performance-based funding of higher education institutions: Current reforms

For the years to come, the government will continue reforming the funding and governance of higher education institutions (HEIs) and will strengthen performance-based funding. According to the Higher Education Blueprint 2015-25 (MOE, 2015b), key initiatives for reform include: improving the funding formulae for public HEIs by replacing block grants with performance-based and per student funding; implementing five-year (3 + 2 years) performance (outcome-based) contracts and targeting government investment in priority areas; strengthening quality assurance in the private sector; linking access to student loans with the performance and quality standards of HEIs; and incentivising the creation of endowment funds, as well as encouraging contributions to higher education, for example through the provision of matching grants for higher learning institutes during the initial fundraising period.

Starting in 2016, the government will withhold 5% of the total funding for universities. This reserve fund will be given to the universities after they meet their key performance index (KPI) and have complied with extra competency, productivity, performance and success. The fund will comprise input-based funding (3%) and performance-based funding (2%). The current 5% reserved fund will be increased on a yearly basis and is expected to reach 40% in 2025 when the Malaysia Higher Education Blueprint 2015-25 (MOE, 2015b) will be fully implemented. In addition, a portion of the direct block grant for R&D and innovation given to HEIs will be converted into a voucher scheme for the industry to outsource its R&D and innovation to industry centres of excellence (ICoEs).

Sources: EPU (2015a), *Eleventh Malaysia Plan*, http://rmk11.epu.gov.my/index.php/en.

Another evaluation instrument is the Malaysian Research Assessment Instrument (MyRA). MyRA helps the Ministry of Education monitor the annual block funding. It covers a comprehensive set of key performance indicators (post-graduate education, research publications, citations, consulting fees, industry contracts, etc.).[43] This assessment determines the amount of annual block funding a university can obtain the following year. Six universities – five public and one private – received the six-star rating of the MyRA for the year 2014-15.[44] In 2015, for the first time, a MyRA audit panel visited all public universities on-site to complement the 2014 performance assessment.[45]

According to a study by Ahmad, Farley and Naidoo (2014), the funding reforms have had a positive impact on public universities and their organisation. In particular, their study found that the funding reforms have enabled public universities to be more proactive in implementing government programmes. Focus group interviews revealed that public universities seem to have embraced the changes brought about by the funding reforms. In spite of difficulties in implementing the NHESP Beyond 2020 and the National Higher Education Plan 2007-2010, the majority of the participants viewed these reforms as necessary for improving the standard of higher education and displayed positive and optimistic attitudes (ibid.).

Research strategies

To foster excellence in research and competition among universities for research funding, the Ministry of Education created the qualification of "research university" (Table 4.9) following a research and governance assessment of universities in 2012. Today there are five research universities where the research capacity of the higher education sector is concentrated; the remaining universities are classed as non-research universities, which means they concentrate on teaching. The five research-focused public universities receive between USD 26.5 million and USD 53 million annually (MYR 50-100 million) in block grants; 5-10% of that money is dedicated to technology transfer (OECD, 2015a).

Overall, many of Malaysia's HEIs are quite new, particularly private universities, and only a few have recently developed sophisticated research capabilities. A number of university research programmes are classified as "centres of excellence", which have to meet selective performance criteria and are evaluated periodically using traditional academic indicators, such as the number of publications in peer reviewed journals with high impact factors. Centres of excellence have undergone a rigorous evaluation by the Ministry of Education and meet certain performance indicators.

An additional classification, the Higher Institution Centre of Excellence (HICoE), was created in 2009, whereby a small number of centres of excellence have been selected based on the quality of their research and outputs produced. The first evaluation exercise was undertaken in 2008. Out of 142 applications, 6 centres of excellence in 5 public HEIs met the stringent requirements for becoming an HICoE. The purpose of the HICoE qualification is to identify the best of the best centres of excellence in HEIs at the national level and encourage them to work towards becoming global leaders in their research areas. This implies that HICoEs will be supported financially and will pioneer R&D and innovation agendas in key areas, particularly in fundamental research and human capital development.

The Ministry of Education's strategy is to push these six HICoEs to make a quantum leap towards internationalisation. These centres of excellence include the UM Centre of Research for Power Electronics, Drives, Automation and Control at the University of Malaya; the National University of Malaysia's (UKM) Medical Molecular Biology Institute at the National University of Malaysia; the Institute for Research in Molecular Medicine; the Institute of Biosciences at Putra University of Malaysia; the Centre for Drug Research at the Science University of Malaysia; and the Accounting Research Institute at the MARA University of Technology.

To conclude, HEIs have undergone a radical transformation to foster excellence in higher education and research. Measures have been taken to improve the quality of the education system and encourage institutional reforms in universities through the promotion of a new culture of performance and result-driven management. These efforts are part of a wider policy agenda to continuously upgrade HEIs and their quality, as well as the impact of higher education on Malaysian society and the economy.

Among the key challenges and issues that HEIs encounter on their path to establishing academic excellence, competitive research and technology transfer, as expressed in new policy directives, are:

- Growing financial constraints: Decreasing federal funding will require more focus on internal and industry funding, which will entail additional resources or competencies that many universities (especially non-research ones) might still not have – e.g. industry partners and networks, spinoffs, etc. It is important therefore to help universities find the appropriate and realistic financial model according to their competencies and ambitions.
- Weak involvement of industry in governance and curricula: Participation of industry on governing boards is still a pending task as well as industry's involvement in the definition of curricula (and programmes). Strengthening links

with industry through governing and steering committees (e.g. research boards and strategies) should be leveraged not only because of financial constraints, but more fundamentally because curricula and knowledge produced should address economic (and societal) demands.

- Incipient collaboration with industry in innovation activities: Enhancing universities' impact on economic development will entail strengthening industry-science linkages, more relevant research for industry and widening the array of interactions. The latter involves increasing collaboration in research and widening the channels of knowledge transfer – e.g. joint PhDs, training, consulting services, product development and engineering activities, among others.
- Race to patent, growing costs of protection and lack of technology strategy: Although greater intellectual property (IP) activity is an encouraging factor for commercialisation, a growing patent portfolio may also be the sign of a lack of an IP strategy. An increase in patent grants will require new financial means to cover the costs of protection (renewal fees). A strategy for selecting and filtering inventions for patenting is lacking and this may require policy action at a higher level. More fundamentally, the definition of a technology transfer strategy (and policy framework at the institutional level) that correctly balances IP and non-IP forms of technology transfer and realistically addresses business needs is yet to be developed in most institutions.

Public research institutes

Structure

Public research institutes (PRIs) play a critical role in the process of innovation and technology diffusion in Malaysia and are key components of sectorial innovation systems, such as agriculture, electronics, health and forestry, among others. Malaysia's PRIs perform mainly downstream or applied research and their objectives are essentially to serve the needs of their respective Malaysian stakeholders or departmental remits. By 2011, there were 29 PRIs, which share the mandate to act as the interface between science, industry and society (Table 4.11). Of the 29 PRIs, 1 is a company under MOSTI, 3 are statutory bodies with a governing board reporting to sectorial ministries, 2 are cess funded, and the remainder are departments or institutes of ministries.

The PRI landscape is much more complex and irregular than that of public universities. PRIs differ with regard to institutional forms and governance, size and resources, and performance. Some institutions have a long scientific tradition but diverse public missions and disciplinary specialisations. They are extremely diverse in size, age, fields of research and oversight. MOSTI has no direct authority in determining their research agendas. Most of them have a sectorial focus covering a wide range of areas including natural resources (agriculture, palm oil, rubber, cocoa, forest, etc.); industry and engineering (electronics, industrial productivity); healthcare (medical research); or other selected fields (nuclear technology, remote sensing, economics, etc.).

The Malaysian Agricultural Research and Development Institute, Malaysian Palm Oil Board, Malaysian Rubber Board, Malaysian Cocoa Board and Forest Research Institutions Malaysia are key PRIs that support the commodity sector at the technological frontier. In order to strengthen the local technological capability and capacity in the manufacturing sector, several PRIs and their complementary institutions have been established to provide research and services related to industry and engineering. For example, the Malaysia's national R&D centre in ICT (MIMOS) focuses on electronics and information technology development, while the Standards and Industrial Research Institute of Malaysia and the Malaysia Productivity Corporation were established to help improve productivity.

Table 4.11. **Selected public research institutes in Malaysia**

Name	Research field	Institutional status	Ministry in charge
MIMOS Berhard	ICT	Corporate	MOSTI
Malaysian Agricultural Research and Development Institute (MARDI)	Agriculture	Government	MAABI
Malaysian Palm Oil Board (MPOB)	Palm oil	Government	MPIC
Malaysian Rubber Board (MRB)	Rubber	Government	MPIC
Malaysian Cocoa Board (MCB)	Cocoa	Government	MPIC
Forest Research Institutions Malaysia (FRIM)	Forest	Government	MNRE
Standards and Industrial Research Institute of Malaysia (SIRIM)	Standards	Corporate	MOF
Malaysia Productivity Corporation (MPC)	Management research	Corporate	MITI
Institute for Medical Research (IMR)	Medicine	Government	MOH
Institute for Health Systems Research (IHSR)	Medicine	Government	MOH
Institute for Public Health (IPH)	Medicine	Government	MOH
Institute for Health Management (IHM)	Medicine	Government	MOH
Clinical Research Centres (CRC)	Medicine	Government	MOH
Institute for Health Behavioural Research (IHBR)	Medicine	Government	MOH
National Heart Institute (IJN)	Medicine	Corporate	MOF
Agro Biotechnology Institute	Biotechnology	..	MOSTI

Note: MOSTI = Ministry of Science, Technology and Industry; MOH = Ministry of Health; MPIC = Ministry of Plantations Industries and Commodities, MNRE = Ministry of Natural Resources and Environment; MAABI = Ministry of Agriculture and Agro-based Industry; MOF = Ministry of Finance; MITI = Ministry of International Trade and Industry.

Sources: Thiruchelvam, Mohamad and Ng (2011), "Higher educational reforms and institutional responses: The role of public universities in promoting innovation in Malaysia"; relevant institutional web pages.

There are also a number of PRIs that have been assigned to safeguard the quality of healthcare of Malaysians, such as the Institute for Medical Research and the National Heart Institute. In addition to the extensive number of PRIs mentioned above, there are also numerous PRIs that have been established for the advancement of science, technology and innovation in selected fields, such as Nuclear Malaysia which provides nuclear technology research facilities; the Malaysian Remote Sensing Agency for the use of remote sensing technology in national planning, development and resource management; and the Malaysian Institute of Economic Research, which provides expertise in economic, financial and business-related issues.

Governance and funding

In terms of governance/oversight, PRIs can be classified into three different categories: ministry division, statutory and corporations limited by guarantee. Their autonomy is subject to their status. For a ministry division PRI, the governing ministry has complete oversight regarding the management, funding and regulatory issues governing the individual institutions (NSRC, 2013). Statutory PRIs are created by an act of the Malaysian parliament (e.g. the Malaysian Agricultural Research and Development Institute was created by the MARDI Act of 1969) that stipulates how the PRI is managed and funded. Statutory PRIs are usually governed by an independent board of trustees though they may receive their funding from a number of sources, including agencies and "cess", which is a tax applied to particular industries. While statutory PRIs are typically seen as having much more autonomy than ministry division PRIs, both are subject to personnel policies and practices as stipulated by the Public Service Department. Governed by the Company Act of 1965, corporations limited by guarantee are government-owned corporations and are considered to have the highest degree of autonomy among PRIs; they are not subject to the Public Service Department's hiring and personnel policies. For example, corporations limited by guarantee are also governed by an independent board of trustees (NSRC, 2013).

Over the years, several PRIs have expanded their scope by engaging in new activities and disciplines, albeit somewhat missing the focus of the original mission for which they were created. Changing policy priorities and regulations, the multiplication of funding sources and agencies, as well as pressure to strengthen commercialisation have contributed to this trend. As a result, PRIs have encountered more difficulties than universities in ensuring consistency and expanding R&D capacity over the years.

This context has hindered overall performance and undermined specialisation and focus in core competencies. Although a number of PRIs have demonstrated their capacity to develop useful technologies, particularly those dedicated to commodities, connection with the economic sector remains very uneven and unsatisfactory. The purpose and role of PRIs (develop tools for policies, monitor regulations, facilitate technology transfer, etc.) is, in fact, not always clearly defined.

In an effort to enhance the efficacy and efficiency of public sector organisations, the government has initiated the corporatisation of several public research-related institutions since the 1990s, such as the Standards and Industrial Research Institute of Malaysia, the MIMOS and Technology Park Malaysia. With this restructuring, research organisations were expected to enhance infrastructure and equipment and better provide R&D services to the private sector. The Malaysia Institute of Microlectronics System has clearly expanded capacity and become a major technology provider for a wide array of sectors, from government (e.g. education) and the private sector.

A major handicap to the evolution of PRIs is the lack of clarity in the specific role that they should play in national strategic plans. As discussed in the National Science and Research Council's Public Research Assets (PRA) Performance Assessment conducted in 2012 (NSRC, 2013), the Tenth Malaysia Plan did not mention a clear responsibility for public research organisations in the implementation of the plan's recommendations. Goals and a definition of means are thus left up to individual ministries and programmes.

The National Science and Research Council made several recommendations in its 2013 PRA assessment, including: the need to create a Research Management Agency under the National Science and Research Council in order to improve the management of public research; to establish an industry research nexus as a platform for public research and industry collaboration in order to improve the relevance and marketability of public research; to review, restructure and realign PRIs; and to enhance human capital and related funding, and improve the research ecosystem and culture. A new Science Act, linked to the creation of a Research Management Agency, is also on the agenda. The Prime Minister also announced the Science to Action (S2A) initiative for the implementation of the National Policy on Science, Technology and Innovation (NSTIP) as one of the key strategic thrusts of the forthcoming Eleventh Malaysia Plan (2016-20). One of the objectives of S2A is to strengthen public services and governance to ensure an environment that will facilitate the development and uptake of science and technology. The government recently established the National Science, Technology and Industry Council, which aims to rationalise the many science- and industry-based councils (OECD, 2014).

Research and development

The role of PRIs in R&D activities in Malaysia has remained low since the early 2000s. In 2014, only 8.21% of R&D conducted in Malaysia was performed in PRI labs. This can be explained, in several cases, by the higher relative importance of advisory and monitoring services (and technology transfer activities) in many of these institutions. This situation also reflects a weaker position of the sector in embracing new national innovation and technology plans, and a lack of upgrading *vis-à-vis* global standards of PRIs.

PRIs in Malaysia essentially focus on applied R&D, which accounts for 74% of their research (MASTIC, 2014). Expenditure for experimental development decreased from MYR 371.56 million in 2011 to MYR 36.3 million in 2012 but then increased in 2014, reaching MYR 58.70 million. This trend widely differs from the situation in 2000 when both applied and experimental development registered similar levels of expense (MYR 191.2 and MYR 184.95 million).

Compared to higher education institutions, the evolution of the R&D expenditure of PRIs has been less dramatic – flows contracted in 2004 and 2006, as well as in 2009 after a mild increase in 2008 (MASTIC, 2014c). This trend is explained by a lack of consistency in funding schemes (e.g. limited medium- and long-term funding), as well as difficulties in ensuring medium-term funding given the multiplicity of sources on which PRIs depend. Several public institutions were reclassified as private or semi-government agencies,[46] which might have also affected the contraction registered in 2012. PRIs have unfortunately held a weak position or a non-explicit role in the design of national strategies and funding programmes.

According to the National R&D Survey, the three most important areas of research of PRIs are natural sciences – representing 28.1% of expenditure in 2012 – followed by biotechnology (27.4%), and agriculture and forestry (26.3%). Following these fields are medical and health sciences (9.30) and engineering and technology (6.6%). This pattern differs from 2008 when agricultural sciences dominated the R&D expenditure of PRIs (Thiruchelvam, Mohamad and Ng, 2011).

The government is the main source of finance for R&D in PRIs, providing, on average, more than 90% of funding over the years (MASTIC, 2014a). In 2012, the federal government contributed 97% of funding. In 2014, this figure fell to 60.4%. Although increasing in importance, the business sector and foreign sources only play a minor role: they represented 0.38% and 0.56% of the funding sources, respectively. While mainly reliant on public funding, some institutions have also received important additional funding from the private sector. For example, Malaysia's Cancer Research Initiatives Foundation has individual and corporate donors such as Sime Darby and PETRONAS (OECD, 2013a).

The evolution in terms of research personnel is also less consistent than in the case of HEIs. From 7 777 headcounts recorded in 2000, total research personnel was 4 556 in 2006, and has shown an upward trend since, reaching 8 339 in 2012. Of this amount, about half are researchers (4 045), followed by support staff (2 386) and technicians (1 908). The proportion of female researchers reveals steady growth since 2000, reaching 53.4% of research personnel in 2012 – a substantial increase since 2000 when it was 29.8%.

Expenditure in public agricultural research has also encountered fluctuations over the years, but more modestly than other areas and sectors. Growth in public agricultural research capacity occurred across all institutional categories from 2007 to 2010 (ASTI, 2015). In 2010, the country's main public agricultural R&D agency, the Malaysian Agricultural Research and Development Institute (MARDI), accounted for a quarter of national agricultural research investments, while commodity boards accounted for almost half (ibid.) and 36% of human resource capacity. MARDI, administered by the Ministry of Agriculture and Agro-based Industry, encompasses 3 branches (research, technology transfer and commercialisation, and operations) and oversees 29 regional research stations. In 2010, MARDI's expenditures totalled MYR 183 million (USD 106 million; PPP, both in 2005 constant prices) (Flaherty and Abu Dardak, 2013). Research capacity levels remained fairly stable throughout the 1980s and early 1990s, but declined slightly in the late 1990s. In 2004, staffing levels began to increase, although inconsistently, and reached 578 full-time equivalents (FTEs) in 2010.

Despite MARDI's central role in agricultural R&D, the commodity-based research agencies spent twice as much on agricultural research, representing almost half the national total. These centres include the Malaysian Palm Oil Board, the Malaysian Cocoa Board and the Malaysian Rubber Board. These agencies are better funded than MARDI due to the high value of export crops and related commodity-based resources (e.g. cesses), but they employ fewer researchers (a combined 305 FTEs in 2010). Employing 207 FTE researchers in 2010, the Malaysian Palm Oil Board is the largest of the three agencies; the Malaysian Cocoa Board and the Malaysian Rubber Board are similarly sized, employing 53 and 45 FTE researchers in 2010, respectively. Two of Malaysia's states, Sabah and Sarawak, exercise a greater degree of autonomy and, as such, operate their own research agencies.[47] A number of other government research agencies operate in Malaysia, the largest being the Forestry Research Institute Malaysia, which employed 202 FTE researchers in 2010. Other agencies include the Department of Veterinary Services (44 FTEs) and the Malaysian Institute for Nuclear Technology Research (22 FTEs).

Evaluation and performance-based management

To date there is no equivalent of MyRA, the research assessment instrument by the Ministry of Higher Education for universities, for PRIs. This is clearly an example of the disparity in the rhythm of modernisation between universities and PRIs, and is largely rooted in the lack of a co-ordinating agency of the public research system and policies. A monitoring and performance evaluation mechanism has not yet been established – a step that relates to the need to redefine and clarify the mission and objectives (expected outputs and activities) of PRIs. Instruments for evaluating improvements in governance do not yet exist either. Evaluation of R&D allocations has started moving from R&D disbursements (expenditure approach) to outputs.

However, as in many other respects, there is a wide heterogeneity between PRIs. Some of them have established some monitoring and evaluation processes. For instance, at the MPOB, all the research projects are evaluated and approved by the Programme Advisory Committee (PAC), comprised of local and international experts and palm oil industry scientists. This committee, which meets every year, is tasked with ensuring that the research carried out by MPOB researchers are based on the industry's needs and is scientifically sound. This committee also evaluates the progress of research. When problems are identified, the PAC can recommend an International Review Panel to critically evaluate the programme and provide recommendations.

Results

In terms of scientific and technological performance – according to the new metrics such as patents, licensing revenue and contracts – PRIs appear to lag behind universities. This is not surprising given the lower level of importance placed on scientific production at many of these research institutions. The total number of papers published by PRIs over the period 2001-11 was 1 778 in the Thomson Reuters' *Web of Science Database* (MASTIC, 2014a). The leading institution is the Malaysian Palm Oil Board (395 papers), followed by the Forestry Research Institute Malaysia (357 papers), the Institute for Medical Research (321) and Agensi Nuklear Malaysia (256) (MASTIC, 2014a).

PRIs also show fewer numbers of patents than universities. In 2012, local patent filings by PRIs represented only 15% of total patent applications made in MyPO (MASTIC, 2014a). This is, however, more than a twofold increase from 2005 (7% of national patent filings). In 2012, PRIs had 39 patents granted while HEIs received 158. In total, the portfolio of granted patents summed 187 patents, whereas HEIs owned 680 in total (MASTIC, 2014c). In terms of other IP rights, HEIs declared 416 trademarks and 44 industrial designs while PRIs claimed 47 and 4, respectively.

A remarkable institution with growing patenting and technology applications is the National R&D Centre in ICT of Malaysia (MIMOS), a PRI corporatised in the 1990s. Today, MIMOS Berhad is Malaysia's forefront technology provider of information and communications technology, industrial electronics technology, and nano-semiconductor technology. In 2013, it ranked 12th among the top public research institutes in the world in terms of PCT filings. Over the past ten years, MIMOS has filed more than 900 intellectual property rights in various technology domains and across key socio-economic areas. In 2011, it represented 43% of Malaysian PCT filings. PCT patent filing has steadily been growing since 2007, when there were not any PCT patent applications. MIMOS remains a strategic agency under the umbrella of the Ministry of Science, Technology and Innovation (MOSTI).

Behind this patenting performance is the change in strategy experienced by MIMOS in 2006 with the redefinition of its mission[48] and increased emphasis on IP generation and commercialisation activities. The institution's key performance indicators call for it to make 100-120 patent filings per year from its three areas of R&D: applied research, advanced technology and application development – no basic research. With increased threats of budget cuts in the future, the incentive for MIMOS to raise revenue from commercialisation has increased even further. Another critical challenge for MIMOS is ensuring the successful adoption of its technologies along with the limited capacity of national SMEs to take advantage of inventions.

In practice, the nature of technology transfer undertaken at many PRIs may differ somewhat from that at universities given the different approach to research and objectives. It is also quite diverse in the types of modes and intensity across PRIs. According to several studies, PRIs have a better success rate than universities in transferring the results of (applied) research to industry and agricultural producers. MARDI, for instance has a good track record, commercialising 14.3% of its products. It has a division for technology transfer and commercialisation that provides technical services and scales up the new technologies it has developed. MARDI collaborates with private companies, undertaking contract research and providing test beds to entrepreneurs. Its Entrepreneur Development Programme has involved 200 SMEs, helping them to develop businesses based on agri-technology.

Figure 4.17. **Evolution in the number of scientific papers by public research institutes in Malaysia**

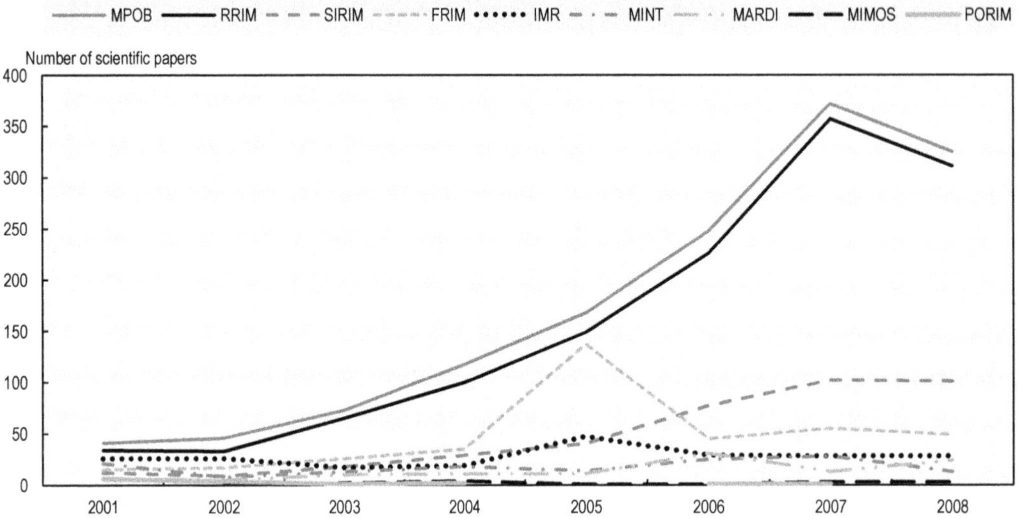

Note: MPOB = Malaysian Palm Oil Board; RIIM = Rubber Research Institute of Malaysia; SIRIM = Standards and Industrial Research Institute of Malaysia; FRIM = Forest Research Institutions Malaysia; IMR = Institute for Medical Research; MINT = Malaysian Institute for Nuclear Technology Research; MARDI = Malaysian Agricultural Research and Development Institute; MIMOS = National R&D Centre in ICT of Malaysia; PORIM = Palm Oil Research Institute of Malaysia.

Source: MASTIC (2012), *Science and Technology Knowledge Productivity in Malaysia: Bibliometrics Study.*

Yet according to metrics, only a few PRIs are formally engaged in technology commercialisation and other technology transfer activities. A recent evaluation has noted some improvements in performance, but also highlighted some overlaps and institutional inflexibilities that prevent scale-dependent research and more long-term collaboration with industry (NRSC, 2013).

In general terms and with the exception of a few cases, research institutes seem to be less prepared to pursue commercialisation and IP activity than universities (OECD, 2015a). PRIs face greater administrative barriers, budget cuts on research and a less adaptive culture that until recently put little emphasis either on collaboration with the private sector or on producing IP. These institutions, however, have very different profiles, and this situation calls for a careful appreciation of their outcomes and achievements. The focus on IP and its revenue might not necessarily be the most pertinent way to evaluate the technology transfer activities in PRIs, while comparison with universities should be made with care and achievements should probably not be measured under the same criteria. Several PRIs undertake transfer of technologies of a public good nature, which are distributed freely or at a low price, especially when serving the purposes of ministries/departments. As an example, MARDI distinguishes between two different types of technology. It does not charge a licence fee for "public good" technologies, whereas "industrial good" technologies bring in royalties (ibid.).

An in-depth assessment of PRIs' knowledge and technological activities should help determine their focus and activities, as well as the best ways to impact stakeholders through the transfer of knowledge and technology. For some PRIs, traditional forms of knowledge transfer such as advisory services and technology extension (e.g. adaptation of existing technologies and their diffusion) might remain highly demanded by customers/stakeholders while for others enhancing technology commercialisation through IP and licensing (those with growing research capacity) may be a new step within their revised strategic plan and mission. Overall, an assessment (or audit) of their activities and mission, and potential for evolution, should help clarify their roles and engagements and help define budget planning for their modernisation. Again, reforming governance and moving to new steering funding through performance-driven mechanisms and evaluation in PRIs is critical for research and commercialisation outcomes.

To summarise, the pace at which PRIs have been evolving in terms of governance reforms and modernisation has been varying across institutions. Universities have been pushed towards adopting international standards, diversifying their sources of funding, and new institutional reforms with respect to governance and autonomy are recently being implemented. Funding for research has increased dramatically, following a strategic plan. In contrast, PRIs have been largely left to themselves to define their trajectories.

PRIs have encountered the following difficulties in improving their efficiency and moving to global standards:

- persistent deficiencies in funding (e.g. dispersion of sources and unstable trend) and high fluctuations in the availability of funding streams have been detrimental to the accumulation of experience and the stability necessary to build vibrant research communities and long-term research agendas
- changing missions (widening scope) or unclear objectives as defined in their regulatory framework and mission statements have contributed to a growing dispersion in activities and hampered PRIs from concentrating on core competencies
- the lack of a national strategy (and action plan) for their modernisation and for replenishing their resources has slowed the process of transformation
- the lack of accountability and performance evaluation (e.g. including audits by international experts and definition of performance objectives and metrics to monitor results periodically).

Without a revision of their regulatory frameworks and governance, as well as a comprehensive reinforcement of their capabilities and relevance, PRIs' impact could remain weak and uneven across institutions. The reform of PRIs needs to entail efforts at the individual and sectorial level. At the institutional level, PRIs urgently need to update/redefine their mission and roles, revise their governance and efficiency, and improve their research management and accountability.

With regard to capacity replenishment, research, technology and human capital resources need to be strengthened based on an in-depth assessment of public research institutes' technological competences, bottlenecks and potential. A study on "Enhancing the Effectiveness of Research and Development Institutions" has recently been launched by the EPU and the Prime Minister's Department. On the basis of the results of this in-depth assessment, which are expected by the end of December 2016, strategies will be proposed to enhance the effectiveness of these institutions and eliminate overlapping of functions of the R&D institutions as stipulated in the Eleventh Malaysia Plan. It is also pivotal to provide the means and funding resources in a more efficient way, particularly avoiding duplication and fragmentation. Strengthening equipment and infrastructure would benefit from collective co-ordination and planning – via a co-ordinating agency –

that would allow tracking the inventory, their (shared) use and increase the cost-benefit ratio by avoiding duplication. Monitoring of technology transfer activities and institutional reforms (and skills) to foster technology transfer at public research institutes might also benefit from a central entity to facilitate the even acceleration of progress in these areas.

Notes

1. In particular electronics, which accounted for 88.3% of the E&E value added in 2014. Electrical equipment contributed the rest.
2. This sector includes primary, agro-based and other resource-based industries.
3. This includes the manufacture of petrochemicals, oleochemicals, refined petroleum, palm oil, rubber gloves, tyres and prophylactic products.
4. The upward trend at the beginning of the year 2000 is partly related to the rise of commodity prices. The fall of the price of oil has changed the distribution since.
5. Since 2014, the definition of SMEs has been broadened so that more domestic firms can benefit from the specific government support programmes and schemes. Since 2014, the companies in manufacturing with sales below MYR 50 million (previously MYR 25 million) or less than 200 employees (previously 150 employees) fall under the SME category. Service sector SMEs are companies with sales turnover below MYR 20 million or less than 75 employees.
6. It even increased in 2014 (to a difference of factor 3.3) but the change of definition of SMEs does not allow for meaningful comparisons.
7. Improving the quality of products/services is the main motive for 31% of SMEs surveyed by the Associated Chinese Chambers of Commerce and Industry of Malaysia (ACCCIM, 2012).
8. Out of a total of 8 000 foreign-owned companies located in Malaysia.
9. Genting Bhd (other consumer services – including tourism and casino business) and YTL Corporation Bhd (electricity, gas and water utilities) employing, respectively, 58 000 and 9 000 workers, over 70% of which are located abroad.
10. All sectors considered, financial institutions and investment holdings are the largest Malaysian companies, in particular Maybank (sales of USD 8.1 billion in 2014), CIMB Group (USD 6.6 billion) and Public Bank (USD 4.9 billion), which range respectively 1st, 2nd and 4th in terms of market capitalisation, see Forbes (2016).
11. State-owned enterprises are defined by the OECD as enterprises where the state has significant control, through full, majority or significant minority ownership (OECD, 2015c). Government-linked companies are defined as companies that have a primary commercial objective and in which the Malaysian government has a direct controlling stake (PGC, 2015a).
12. Petroliam Nasional Bhd (PETRONAS) and Sime Darby Bhd.

13. Proton's R&D expenditure accounted for 8% of its sales in 2005 and nearly 76% of the total R&D expenditure of industry. In 2014, its R&D expenditure amounted to MYR 66.9 million and it employed 600 research engineers in its R&D centre.

14. The increase of business expenditures in absolute and relative terms from 56.7% in 2011 to 64.5% in 2012 is due to the reclassification of five former government research institutes as business companies (MASTIC, 2014a).

15. The previously mentioned change of classification of five government research institutes as business companies in 2012 might also have affected the structure of expenditures.

16. Adapters are defined as firms that only upgraded machinery and equipment or introduced new technology in the last two years; an adopter has upgraded an existing product line or entered new markets; a creator has undertaken some of these activities and has filed patents/utility models or copyright protected materials.

17. 9% of GDP according to Jomo and Edwards (1993), compared with 40% for agriculture and 6% for mining (Peninsular Malaysia only).

18. The sub-sector "global innovation for local markets" comprises chemicals and pharmaceuticals, transport equipment, machinery, and electrical appliances. The sub-sector "global technologies/innovator" includes computers and office machinery; semiconductors and electronics; medical, optical and other precision equipment.

19. These services include research and development (R&D), management consulting, information and communications services, human resource management and employment services, legal services (including those related to intellectual property rights), accounting, financing, and marketing-related service activities (OECD, 2006).

20. "Modern services" comprises knowledge-intensive financial, business and ICT services.

21. In the region, only Indonesia has a higher measure of "upstreamness", whereas latecomer Viet Nam moved significantly downstream between 2000 and 2012.

22. In 2015 (January-September), 93% of the cumulated volume of the 62 investment projects in the E&E industry came from foreign sources (MIDA statistics: www.mida.gov.my/env3/uploads/FactsFiguresPDF/JanSept2015/byIndustry.pdf).

23. See, for instance, the case of SanDisk, which recently established an R&D facility in Penang for the development of advanced packaging and testing. In the same sector, Carsem Malaysia is reported to have upgraded its technology and R&D in advanced semiconductor packaging and testing (EPU, 2014). The most ambitious R&D activities, such as the development of new integrated circuits designs, seems to happen mostly in the MIMOS research institutes available for companies to adopt commercially (ibid.).

24. See the Malaysian Investment Development Authority website at: www.mida.gov.my/home/industry-news/posts.

25. Research surveys and case studies of vertical "productivity spillovers" within GVCs tend to show that backward linkages have a stronger positive effect on the suppliers positioned upstream from the MNEs than forward linkages toward customer sectors (see Havranek and Irsova, 2011). The review and reprocessing of the data of a wide number of studies indicates that recipient countries' firms benefit from greater spillovers when the technological gap to the multinationals' headquarter countries is smaller (ibid.). This might be interpreted in terms of required absorption capacity.

26. Data until November. See: www.myipo.gov.my/web/guest/paten-statistik (accessed 8 January 2016).

27. 50% in 2012 and 36% in 2011. However, these figures include the research institutes incorporated as legal companies (in particular the top local applicants MIMOS, the Malaysian Palm Oil Board and the Malaysian Rubber Board), hence significantly inflating the proportion of companies.

28. With 4 companies among the top 100 applicants, Chinese Taipei is the only Southeast Asian country represented on this list.

29. The oil and gas company PETRONAS and its R&D subsidiary, the Universiti Teknologi PETRONAS. MIMOS, the Malaysian Palm Oil Board and the Malaysian Rubber Board, although legally incorporated, are considered as research institutes here.

30. See also the following related publications: Newman, Shapira and A. Porter (2004); Shapira et al. (2006); Hegde and Shapira (2007); Kay, Youtie and Shapira (2014).

31. The Education Act 1996 (Act 550), the Private Higher Educational Institutions Act 1996 and the National Council of Higher Education Act 1996.

32. Universiti Kebangsaan Malaysia and Universiti Teknologi Malaysia were ranked 259th and 294th while Universiti Sains Malaysia and Universiti Putra Malaysia were 309th and 376th. As for the QS World University Rankings by subject, in 2014, Universiti Sains Malaysia ranked 31st in environmental studies, while Universiti Malaya, Universiti Kebangsaan Malaysia and Universiti Putra Malaysia were ranked within 51-100 for various subjects.

33. The government's goal is to ensure that at least 6 public universities are able to be classified as research universities by 2020, with 20 centres of excellence receiving international recognition and 10% of the research commercialised (Ministry of Higher Education, 2007).

34. In 2012, USM was among the top 50 university applicants, with 39 PCT applications, one position behind Duke University (also with 39) and 6 positions higher than Cambridge University (with 36). USM moved from 10 and 16 PCT applications in 2010 and 2011 respectively, to 39 in 2012 (MASTIC, 2014a).

35. See also Chandran, Farha and Veera (2008); Chandran and Wong (2011); Thiruchelvam, Mohamad and Ng (2011); and Chandran (2010).

36. This is confirmed by the results of the National R&D Survey 2012 (MASTIC, 2014a), where the lack of funding for and the high costs of innovation activities are considered by innovating Malaysian companies to be the main factors hampering innovation activities.

37. This plan was organised in four phases: Phase 1: Laying the foundation (2007-10); Phase 2: Strengthening and enhancement (2011-15); Phase 3: Excellence (2016-20); and Phase 4: Glory and sustainability (beyond 2020).

38. Public universities are audited in four designated areas, namely governance, finance, wealth creation, human resources. Based on the results of these evaluations, the government determines their readiness for autonomous status.

39. In Phase 3 (from 2016 to 2020) the government will expect comprehensive/focused universities to supplement 25% of their operating expenditure and 5% of development expenditure, with research universities supplementing 30% of their operating expenditure and 10% of development expenditure.

40. The authorisation to engage in commercial activities started in the mid-1990s. In 1995, five of the oldest public universities in Malaysia were corporatised, which allowed them to enter into business ventures with the aim of generating their own funds. Such a commercial approach permitted academics to become involved in income generation through consultancy activities.

41. So far it has not been difficult for UNIMAS to fulfil the 30% self-financing requirement. Overall financing has remained stable. Although the 70/30 ratio objective is new, the university is confident that its funding will remain stable, since in the past it has consistently achieved the 30% self-financing goal.

42. SETARA was implemented in 2009 to measure the performance of undergraduate teaching and learning in universities and university colleges in Malaysia. It uses a six-tier scale, with Tier 6 identified as "outstanding" and Tier 1 as "weak".

43. Four main parameters are used for the purpose of evaluation: 1) human capital; 2) publication; 3) patents and intellectual property rights; and 4) income generation.

44. The public universities are: Universiti Malaya, Universiti Sains Malaysia, Universiti Kebangsaan Malaysia, Universiti Putra Malaysia and Universiti Teknologi Malaysia, while the private university is Universiti Teknologi PETRONAS.

45. Previously this system operated through self-assessment and reporting to the Ministry of Education's Department of Higher Education every six months.

46. The following organisations were reclassified as business enterprises: Astronautic Technology, SIRIM, Cyber Security Malaysia, Sarawak Biodiversity Centre and Craun Research.

47. Sarawak's public agencies include the Department of Agriculture (14 FTEs), the Forest Research Centre (6 FTEs), the Fisheries Research Institute-Sarawak (10 FTEs) and an autonomous non-profit agency, the Sarawak Biodiversity Centre (32 FTEs), established to advise the government on policy. Research activities in Sabah are conducted at the Department of Agriculture (27 FTEs) and the Department of Fisheries (2 FTEs). Further information is provided in ASTI (2015).

48. Redefined in 2006, MIMOS' vision is to become the premier applied research centre in frontier technologies, and to transform the landscape of the Malaysian indigenous industries. Towards this end, MIMOS' mission is to pioneer information and communication technologies (ICT) to grow globally competitive indigenous industries. MIMOS' R&D activities are focused on ten technology thrust areas: advanced analysis and modelling, advanced computing, intelligent informatics, information security, knowledge technology, microenergy, microelectronics, nano-electronics, psychometrics, and wireless communications.

References

ACCCIM (2012), *The Associated Chinese Chambers of Commerce & Industry of Malaysia (ACCCIM) Report of 2012 SMEs Survey*, Associated Chinese Chambers of Commerce and Industry of Malaysia, Kuala Lumpur, www.acccim.org.my/file/2012%20SME_EN.pdf.

ADB (2013), "Beyond factory Asia: Fuelling growth in a changing world", Background Paper for the Asian Development Bank 2013 Annual Meeting Governors' Seminar, Asian Development Bank, Manila, http://adb.org/sites/default/files/pub/2013/beyond-factory-asia.pdf.

ADB (2012), *Administration and Governance of Higher Education in Asia: Patterns and Implications*, Asian Development Bank, Manila, www.adb.org/sites/default/files/publication/29956/administration-governance-higher-education.pdf.

Ahmad, A.R., A. Farley and M. Naidoo (2014), "An examination of the implementation federal government strategic plans in Malaysian public universities", *International Journal of Business and Social Science*, Vol. 3/15, August, pp. 290-301, http://ijbssnet.com/journals/Vol_3_No_15_August_2012/33.pdf.

APO (2015), *APO Productivity Databook 2015*, Asian Productivity Organisation, Tokyo, www.apo-tokyo.org/publications/ebooks/apo-productivity-databook-2015.

Ariffin, N. and P.N. Figueiredo (2004), "Internationalization of innovative capabilities: Counter-evidence from the electronics industry in Malaysia and Brazil", *Oxford Development Studies*, Vol. 32/4, pp. 559-583, http://dx.doi.org/10.1080/1360081042000293344.

ASTI (2015), *Agricultural Science and Technology Indicators* (database), www.asti.cgiar.org.

Bank Negara Malaysia (2013), "Annual report 2013", Bank Negara Malaysia, Kuala Lumpur, www.bnm.gov.my/files/publication/ar/en/2013/ar2013_book.pdf.

Bank Negara Malaysia (2011), "Financial Sector Blueprint 2011-2020: Strengthening our Future", Bank Negara Malaysia Publishing, Kuala Lumpur, www.bnm.gov.my/files/publication/fsbp/en/BNM_FSBP_FULL_en.pdf.

Bhattacharya, M. (2002), "Industrial concentration and competition in Malaysian manufacturing", *Applied Economics*, Vol. 34/17, pp. 2 127-2 134, http://dx.doi.org/10.1080/00036840210135683.

Bradsher, K. (2014), "Solar rises in Malaysia during trade wars over panels", *The New York Times*, 11 December, www.nytimes.com/2014/12/12/business/energy-environment/solar-rises-in-malaysia-during-trade-wars-over-panels.html?_r=1.

Chandran, V.G.R. (2010), "R&D commercialization challenges for developing countries: The case of Malaysia", *TechMonitor*, Nov-Dec, pp. 25-30, www.techmonitor.net/tm/images/d/dd/10nov_dec_sf3.pdf.

Chandran V.G.R. and C.-Y. Wong (2011), "Patenting activities by developing countries: The case of Malaysia", *World Patent Information*, Vol. 33/1, March, pp. 51-57, http://dx.doi.org/10.1016/j.wpi.2010.01.001.

Chandran V.G.R., A.G. Farha and P. Veera (2008), "The commercialization of research results among researchers in public universities and research institutions", *Asian Profile*, Vol. 36/3, pp. 235-250.

Chandran, V.G.R., P. Veera and S. Santhidran (2014), "Innovation systems in Malaysia: A perspective of university-industry R&D collaboration", *AI and Society*, Vol. 29/3, pp. 435-444, http://dx.doi.org/10.1007/s00146-013-0468-9.

Chua, S.C. and T.H. Oh (2012), "Solar energy outlook in Malaysia", *Renewable and Sustainable Energy Reviews*, Vol. 16/1, January, pp. 564-574, http://dx.doi.org/10.1016/j.rser.2011.08.022.

EPU (2015a), *Eleventh Malaysia Plan*, Economic Planning Unit, Putrajaya, http://rmk11.epu.gov.my/index.php/en.

EPU (2015b), "Services sector blueprint", Economic Planning Unit, Putrajaya, www.epu.gov.my/documents/10124/284bf88c-1aa1-4e3a-b43e-3b4b91fa2d1b.

EPU (2015c), "Transforming education system", Chapter 6, Strategy Paper 10, *Eleventh Malaysia Plan*, Economic Planning Unit, Putrajaya, http://rmk11.epu.gov.my/pdf/strategy-paper/Strategy%20Paper%2010.pdf.

EPU (2014), "Complexity analysis study of Malaysia's manufacturing industries: Final report", Economic Planning Unit, Putrajaya, www.epu.gov.my/documents/10124/99b3e588-9607-4d10-a5de-85141413d2aa.

EPU (2011), "Moving up the value chain: A study of Malaysia's solar and medical device industries, final report", *Science, Technology and Innovation Report*, Economic Planning Unit, Putrajaya, and The World Bank, Washington, DC, www.epu.gov.my/c/document_library/get_file?uuid=e205228c-67e9-4477-b06f-bbc3e8abc2d8&groupId=283545.

EPU (2010), *Tenth Malaysia Plan 2011-2015*, Economic Planning Unit, Prime Minister's Department, Putrajaya, http://onlineapps.epu.gov.my/rmke10/rmke10_english.html.

EPU (1990), *Sixth Malaysia Plan*, Economic Planning Unit, Prime Minister's Department, Putrajaya, www.epu.gov.my/en/sixth-malaysia-plan-1990-19951.

Fernandez-Stark, K., P. Bamber and G. Gereffi (2012), "Upgrading in global value chains: Addressing the skills challenge in developing countries", OECD Background Paper, OECD, Paris, www.cggc.duke.edu/pdfs/2012-09-26_Duke_CGGC_OECD_background_paper_Skills_Upgrading_inGVCs.pdf.

Flaherty, K. and R. Abu Dardak (2013), "Recent developments in agricultural research: Malaysia", *Country Note*, May, Agriculture Science and Technology Indicators (ASTI), IFPRI, Washington, DC, www.asti.cgiar.org/pdf/Malaysia-Note.pdf.

Forbes (2016), *Forbes World Top-2000 Listed Companies* (database), www.forbes.com/global2000/list (last accessed on 13 January 2016).

Grapragasem, S., A. Krishnan and A. Norhaini Mansor (2014), "Current trends in Malaysian higher education and the effect on education policy and practice: An overview", *International Journal of Higher Education*, Vol. 3/1, pp. 85-93.

Havranek, T. and Z. Irsova (2011), "Estimating vertical spillovers from FDI: Why results vary and what the true effect is", *Journal of International Economics*, Vol. 85/2, pp. 234-244, http://dx.doi.org/10.1016/j.jinteco.2011.07.004.

Hegde, D. and P. Shapira (2007), "Knowledge, technology trajectories, and innovation in a developing country context: Evidence from a survey of Malaysian firms", *International Journal of Technology Management*, Vol. 40/4, http://dx.doi.org/10.1504/IJTM.2007.015757.

Hussain, M., A. Shahmoradi and R. Turk (2015), "An overview of Islamic finance", *IMF Working Paper*, WP/15/120, International Monetary Fund, Washington, DC, www.imf.org/external/pubs/ft/wp/2015/wp15120.pdf.

Jomo, K.S. and C. Edwards (1993), "Malaysian industrialisation in historical perspective", in: Jomo, K.S., *Industrializing Malaysia: Policy, Performance, Prospects*, Routledge Publishing, Abingdon-on-Thames.

Kay, L., J. Youtie and P. Shapira (2014), "Inter-industry knowledge flows and sectoral networks in the economy of Malaysia", *Knowledge Management Research & Practice*, 1 September, http://dx.doi.org/10.1057/kmrp.2014.30.

Lee, M. (2005), "Global trends, national policies and institutional responses: Restructuring higher education in Malaysia", *Educational Research for Policy and Practice*, Vol. 3, pp. 31-46, http://dx.doi.org/10.1007/s10671-004-6034-y.

MASTIC (2014a), *Malaysia Science, Technology and Innovation (STI) Indicators Report 2013*, Ministry of Science, Technology and Innovation, Putrajaya, http://mastic.mosti.gov.my/documents/10156/38ae84ca-b8a0-4edb-a5b8-d30aa8c016e6.

MASTIC (2014b), *National Survey of Innovation 2012*, Ministry of Science, Technology and Innovation, Putrajaya.

MASTIC (2012), *Science and Technology Knowledge Productivity in Malaysia: Bibliometrics Study*, Malaysian Science and Technology Information Centre, Putrajaya.

MASTIC (2011), *National Survey of Innovation 2005-2008*, Ministry of Science, Technology and Innovation, Putrajaya.

MASTIC (2001, 2005, 2009, 2013, 2016), *National Surveys of Research and Development*, Ministry of Science, Technology and Innovation, Putrajaya.

Menon, J. and N.T. Hee (2013), "Are government-linked corporations crowding out private investment in Malaysia?", *ADB Economics Working Paper Series*, No. 345, Asian Development Bank, Manila.

Ministry of Higher Education (2011), *Statistics of Higher Education 2011*, Ministry of Higher Education, Putrajaya.

Ministry of Higher Education (2007), "National Higher Education Action Plan 2007-2010", Ministry of Higher Education, Putrajaya, http://planipolis.iiep.unesco.org/upload/Malaysia/Malaysia%20Higher%20education%20action%20plan%202007-2010.pdf.

MOE (2015a), "Public institutions of higher education (PIHE)", Ministry of Education website, www.moe.gov.my/en/ipta.

MOE (2015b), *Malaysia Education Blueprint 2015-2025 (Higher Education)*, Ministry of Education, Putrajaya, www.moe.gov.my/cms/upload_files/files/3_%20Malaysia%20Education%20Blueprint%202015-2025%20(Higher%20Education).pdf.

MOE (2012), *Malaysia Education Blueprint 2013-2025: Preliminary Report*, Ministry of Higher Education, Putrajaya.

MPC (2015), *Productivity Report 2014-15*, Malaysia Productivity Corporation.

National Science Board (2014), *Science and Engineering Indicators 2014*, National Science Foundation, www.nsf.gov/statistics/seind14/content/overview/overview.pdf.

Newman, N., P. Shapira and A. Porter (2004), *Knowledge Content in Key Economic Sectors in Malaysia*, Intelligent Information Services Corporation and Georgia Tech Technology Policy and Assessment Center, Atlanta, Georgia, March, www.epu.gov.my/en/knowledge-content-in-key-economic-sectors-in-malaysia.

News 24 (2015), "Malaysia feels heat as its solar industry soars", News 24, 18 August, www.news24.com/Green/News/Malaysia-feels-heat-as-its-solar-industry-soars-20150818.

Ng, B.K., V.G.R. Chandran and K. Thiruchelvam (2015), "Technological knowledge, learning and linkages in the wooden furniture industry in Malaysia: A spatial innovation perspective", *Asian Journal of Technology Innovation*, Vol. 20/2, pp. 187-200, http://dx.doi.org/10.1080/19761597.2012.726417.

Noland, M., D. Park and G.B. Estrada (2012), "Developing the service sector as engine of growth for Asia: An overview", *ADB Economics Working Paper Series*, No. 320, Asian Development Bank, Manila, www.adb.org/sites/default/files/publication/31114/developing-service-sector-engine-growth-asia.pdf.

Nordås, H.K. and Y. Kim (2013), "The role of services for competitiveness in manufacturing", *OECD Trade Policy Papers*, No. 148, OECD Publishing, Paris, http://dx.doi.org/10.1787/5k484xb7cx6b-en.

NSRC (2013), *PRA Performance Evaluation. Unlocking Vast Potentials, Fast-Tracking the Future*, UiTM Press, National Science and Research Council, Shah Alam, http://umexpert.um.edu.my/file/publication/00012427_86127.pdf.

OECD (2016), *Economic Outlook for Southeast Asia, China and India 2016: Enhancing Regional Ties*, OECD Publishing, Paris, http://dx.doi.org/10.1787/saeo-2016-en.

OECD (2015a), *Boosting Malaysia's National Intellectual Property System for Innovation*, OECD Publishing, Paris, http://dx.doi.org/10.1787/9789264239227-6-en.

OECD (2015b), *Implementing Good Regulatory Practice in Malaysia*, OECD Publishing, Paris, http://dx.doi.org/10.1787/9789264230620-en.

OECD (2015c), *State-Owned Enterprises in the Development Process*, OECD Publishing, Paris, http://dx.doi.org/10.1787/9789264229617-en.

OECD (2014), *OECD Science, Technology and Industry Outlook 2014*, OECD Publishing, Paris, http://dx.doi.org/10.1787/sti_outlook-2014-en.

OECD (2013a), *Innovation in Southeast Asia*, OECD Publishing, Paris, http://dx.doi.org/10.1787/9789264128712-en.

OECD (2013b), *Interconnected Economies: Benefiting from Global Value Chains*, OECD Publishing, Paris, http://dx.doi.org/10.1787/9789264189560-en.

OECD (2013c), *Southeast Asian Economic Outlook 2013: With Perspectives on China and India*, OECD Publishing, Paris, http://dx.doi.org/10.1787/saeo-2013-en.

OECD (2006), *Innovation and Knowledge-Intensive Service Activities*, OECD Publishing, Paris, http://dx.doi.org/10.1787/9789264022744-en.

PEMANDU (2014), *Economic Transformation Programme 2014 Annual Report*, Performance Management & Delivery Unit, Putrajaya, http://etp.pemandu.gov.my/annualreport2014.

PGC (2015a), "GLC Transformation Programme Report Card, April 2015", Putrajaya Committee on GLC High Performance, Kuala Lumpur, www.pcg.gov.my/PDF/20150423%20Report%20Card%20April%202015.pdf.

PGC (2015b), *GLC Transformation Programme: Graduation Report*, Putrajaya Committee on GLC High Performance, Kuala Lumpur, www.pcg.gov.my/PDF/GLCTP%20Vol%201%20Graduation%20Report.pdf.

Pilat, D. and A. Wölfl (2005), "Measuring the interaction between manufacturing and services", *OECD Science, Technology and Industry Working Papers*, No. 2005/5, OECD Publishing, Paris, http://dx.doi.org/10.1787/882376471514.

Rasiah, R. (2011), "Is Malaysia facing negative deindustrialization?", *Pacific Affairs*, Vol. 84/4, pp. 715-736, www.jstor.org/stable/23056129.

Rasiah, R. (2010), "Are electronics firms in Malaysia catching up in the technology ladder?", *Journal of the Asia Pacific Economy*, Vol. 15/3, Special Issue: Innovation and Catch-Up Experiences in Automotive and Electronics Industries in Asia, pp. 301-319, http://dx.doi.org/10.1080/13547860.2010.494910.

Rasiah, R. (2006a), "Electronics in Malaysia: Export expansion but slow technical change", in: World Bank, *Technology, Adaptation, and Exports: How Some Developing Countries Got It*, The World Bank, Washington, DC.

Rasiah, R. (2006b), "Explaining Malaysia's export expansion in palm oil and related products", in: World Bank, *Technology, Adaptation, and Exports: How Some Developing Countries Got It*, The World Bank, Washington, DC.

SCImago (2007), *Country Rankings* (database), www.scimagojr.com/countryrank.php.

Shapira, P. et al. (2008), "Knowledge content in key economic sectors in Malaysia: Phase 2 (Myke 2) – Final report", prepared for the Economic Planning Unit, by the IIS and Georgia Tech Program in Science, Technology and Innovation Policy, Atlanta, Georgia.

Shapira, P. et al. (2006), "Knowledge economy measurement: Methods, results and insights from the Malaysian knowledge content study", *Research Policy*, Vol. 35/10, pp. 1 522-1 537, http://dx.doi.org/10.1016/j.respol.2006.09.015.

SME Corporation (2015), "SME annual report 2014/15", SME Corporation, www.smecorp.gov.my/index.php/en/resources/2015-12-21-11-07-06/sme-annual-report/book/7-annual-report-2014/2-annual-report.

SME Corporation (2012), *SME Masterplan 2012-2020*, SME Corporation.

Thiruchelvam, K., Z.F. Mohamad and B.K. Ng (2011), "Higher educational reforms and institutional responses: The role of public universities in promoting innovation in Malaysia", in: Krishna, V.V. and S. Ramakrishna (eds.), *Impacting Economy and Society: Role of Universities in Asia-Pacific*, NUS Press, Singapore.

Thomson Reuters (2015), "State of the global Islamic economy: 2014-2015 report", Commissioned by Dubai - The Capital of Islamic Economy, www.iedcdubai.ae/assets/uploads/files/ar_20142015_1448266389.pdf.

UNCTAD (2013), *World Investment Report 2013: Global Value Chains: Investment and Trade for Development*, United Nations Conference on Trade and Development, Geneva, http://unctad.org/en/PublicationsLibrary/wir2013_en.pdf.

UNESCO (2016), *UIS.Stat* (database), http://data.uis.unesco.org.

USPTO (2015), "Patenting by geographic region (state and country): Breakout by organization: Malaysia", *General Patent Statistics Reports* (database), www.uspto.gov/web/offices/ac/ido/oeip/taf/stcasg/myx_stcorg.htm.

WIPO (2015a), *World Intellectual Property Indicators: 2015 Edition*, Economics & Statistics Series, World Intellectual Property Organization, Geneva, www.wipo.int/edocs/pubdocs/en/wipo_pub_941_2015.pdf.

WIPO (2015b), *WIPO IP Statistics Data Center* (database), http://ipstats.wipo.int/ipstatv2.

WIPO (2014), *Patent Cooperation Treaty Yearly Review*, World Intellectual Property Organization, Geneva, www.wipo.int/pct/en/activity.

WIPO (2011), *World Intellectual Property Report 2011*, World Intellectual Property Organization, Geneva.

WIPO (2008), "Impact of the intellectual property system on economic growth: Fact-finding surveys and analysis in the Asian region: Country report – Malaysia", WIPO-UNU Joint Research Project, World Intellectual Property Organization, Geneva, www.wipo.int/export/sites/www/about-ip/en/studies/pdf/wipo_unu_07_malaysia.pdf.

World Bank (2014), "Malaysia economic monitor: Boosting trade competitiveness", The World Bank, Bangkok, www-wds.worldbank.org/external/default/WDSContentServer/WDSP/IB/2014/06/27/000350881_20140627082245/Rendered/PDF/891020WP0P14640B00PUBLIC00MEM100web.pdf.

World Bank (2010), "Malaysia economic monitor: Growth through innovation", The World Bank, Bangkok, http://siteresources.worldbank.org/INTMALAYSIA/Resources/324392-1271308532887/mem_april2010_fullreport.pdf.

World Bank (2009), "Malaysia: Productivity and investment climate assessment update", The World Bank, Washington, DC, http://documents.worldbank.org/curated/en/2009/08/11321562/malaysia-productivity-investment-climate-assessment-update.

Yusuf, S. and K. Nabeshima (2009), "Tiger economies under threat: A comparative analysis of Malaysia's industrial prospects and policy options", The World Bank, Washington, DC, http://documents.worldbank.org/curated/en/2009/01/11261234/tiger-economies-under-threat-comparative-analysis-malaysias-industrial-prospects-policy-options.

Zuniga, P. (2011), "The state of academic patenting in developing countries: Policy models and approaches", *WIPO Economics Working Papers,* No. 4, World Intellectual Property Organization, Geneva.

Chapter 5.

Innovation policy and governance in Malaysia

This chapter examines public activities that have a bearing on the Malaysian innovation system. It begins with an overview of the historical evolution of science, technology and innovation policy in Malaysia. It next examines the main policy actors, governance arrangements and national plans. The chapter then reviews current policies under the light of the observations made in earlier chapters and concludes with a summary note on the strengths and weaknesses of the country's STI governance and policy mix.

Science, technology and innovation policy in Malaysia: A historical perspective

The Malaysian "innovation imperative" to move up the value-added ladder in global value chains (GVCs) and to adapt to the more sophisticated demand of the emerging domestic middle class has been increasingly acknowledged in the successive five-year national development plans (the "Malaysia plans"). In line with the growing interest for these activities as a driver of growth, science, technology and innovation (STI) activities became prominent in these plans and strategies in the mid-1980s. A detailed examination of the early policy initiatives – in particular since the mid-1980s when Malaysia started to develop a distinct STI strategy framework, governance structure and policy – helps to better understand some of the current strengths and weaknesses of the national innovation system and related policies.

The early rise of industrial policy

The Malaysian innovation system was outward-oriented from the outset, with the public authorities playing a strong role. While the country was still a British colony, the increasing needs of industrialised countries for raw materials spurred the growth of Malaysian production and exports of tin and rubber. Malaysia accounted for half of the world production of tin at the end of the 19th century and of rubber in the 1920s. In 1957, a few years after its independence, these two resources together still represented 85% of exports and 48% of gross domestic product (GDP) (MIGHT, 2009).

However, the limitation of and the risk inherent to an almost exclusive dependence on the export of resource-based commodities led the country to explore and develop new sources of growth. As early as 1958, the government launched an import-substitution industrialisation strategy, complemented by protectionist measures and the first initiatives to attract foreign firms, principally through the improvement of infrastructures. This effort was aimed at encouraging the production on Malaysian territories by domestic or foreign firms of goods which were previously imported. The few foreign companies to locate their manufacturing activities in Malaysia, such as Matsushita Electric in 1965, which previously only had a small-scale trading company, did so to supply the Malaysian domestic market. They started with only minor, labour-intensive assembly operations in Malaysia.

Like in several other developing countries before Malaysia, this import-substitution strategy marked the beginning of the country's industrialisation but fell short of expectations in terms of economic growth. In particular, the size of the domestic market was not sufficiently attractive for multinational enterprises (MNEs) to set up subsidiaries in Malaysia and no policy was in place to support capability building of human resources. Rising unemployment and inequalities called for a change in direction. From the mid-1960s, the government decided to complement the import-substitution policy with various reforms to promote Malaysian exports, at first of products of resource-based labour-intensive industries (rubber, tin, palm oil and timber).

In the 1970s, as industry developed and matured progressively, non-resource based manufacturing (in particular of electrical and electronic [E&E] components) took the lead, encouraged by state regulations and tax incentives to attract FDI in free trade zones and export processing zones. The firms located in these zones enjoyed various advantages, such as financial incentives for firms exporting a significant part of their production, as well as exemptions on import tariffs and social equity obligations associated with the application of the New Economic Policy. It is only with the opening of the first free trade zones in 1972 that the pioneering export-oriented E&E companies established their assembly lines in Malaysia and that the Malaysian E&E export industry really took off.[1] The nascent E&E industry was specialised in semiconductors, remained focused on highly labour-intensive assembly tasks and included almost no domestic firms. The second wave of entrants, starting from 1986, was composed of giant consumer electronic firms attracted by generous tax incentives, soon to be followed by leaders in the disk drive and computer segments (Rasiah, 2006).

In the 1980s, in parallel to these efforts, large projects in heavy industries such as steel production, machinery and equipment, petrochemical, cement, and automobile manufacturing were launched, with direct intervention from the government. Apart from protection, the state was instrumental in providing subsidies for acquiring foreign technologies, e.g. for the national car project "Proton" and its engine and gear-box technologies from Mitsubishi.

The building of a strategic framework for industrial policy

The Industrial Master Plan (IMP1) launched in 1986 by the Ministry of International Trade and Industry was in line with this new policy development. It renewed and strengthened the financial incentives to export-oriented firms and complemented these with specific stimuli for higher value-added activities,[2] such as tax allowances on firms' training and R&D expenditures (UNIDO, 2003). IMP1 also provided distinct long-term indicative development roadmaps for targeted sectors, including seven sectors stemming from the transformation of basic resources, i.e. food processing, rubber and palm oil, etc., and five non-resource based sectors, including E&E, transport equipment, ferrous metals and textiles. The fiscal incentives were focused on priority activities (R&D, training and exports) as well as key products, whose list was decided upon and updated by the Ministry of International Trade and Industry. However, the figures on reclaimed tax credits demonstrate that very few firms were engaged in product or process R&D at that time. These incentives consequently had only a limited effect on MNEs' willingness to significantly upgrade their activities in Malaysia. Specific schemes were also launched to support R&D[3] but suffered from a lack of beneficiaries since MNEs were not eligible to benefit from these grants and most local firms lacked the capabilities to engage in these activities (Rasiah, 2006).

The Action Plan for Industrial Technology Development (APIDT, 1990-2011) was launched in 1990 as a follow up on the implementation of IMP1. This plan set the ground for a strategic and integrated steering of innovation activities in specific sectors. The APIDT advocated an increase of industrial R&D, supported by greater public resources via matching grants and soft loans, to reorient part of the activities of existing research laboratories and institutes toward industry-oriented and market-driven research (EPU, 1990).

The Second Industrial Master Plan (IMP2), launched in 1996, built upon the actions initiated as part of its predecessor and put more emphasis on the functional, product and value chain upgrade of key manufacturing sectors:[4] shift toward activities upstream and downstream on the value chain, i.e. R&D or distribution and marketing services; moving toward higher technology operations (e.g. production of wafers); developing the information technology and multimedia industry. The plan aimed to promote cluster approaches where small and medium-sized enterprises (SMEs) could build upon their relationships with the MNEs they supply to enhance their capability (called "cluster-based industrial development" strategy). The Multimedia Super Corridor (MSC) can be seen as a key initiative in that regard: world-class infrastructure is made available on a specific territory to attract the E&E leaders. Selected local SMEs can receive specific

MSC funds to conduct R&D activities. On the whole, IMP2 featured several initiatives to develop the capabilities of domestic firms, in the context of the MSC and beyond.

The Third Industrial Master Plan (IMP3) was introduced in 2006 in a context of significant manufacturing growth slow-down and a decrease of this sector's productivity and exports. The plan prolonged the momentum of the first two plans, with an additional focus on services. This has triggered a debate on a possible "premature de-industrialisation" of Malaysia (Basu Das and Lee, 2014; Rasiah, 2011). Such debates have been led in other developing and emerging economies, e.g. in Latin American countries, some of which had recorded a massive decline of manufacturing on various measures.

The emergence of a distinct science, technology and innovation policy aligned with national development goals

Important reforms of the national innovation system were implemented during the mid-1980s, illustrating the attempts to set up an STI policy in Malaysia as a distinct and more centralised policy field at the core of the national development endeavour, with integrated co-ordination mechanisms (Table 5.1). The rationales for these initiatives were not only to improve the efficiency of the R&D public schemes by avoiding overlaps and inconsistencies, but also to better align the allocation of R&D funds with national industrial development goals.

The government made concerted and concentrated efforts to provide a guided governance and strategic framework for STI activities. In 1984, the Office of the Science Advisor was created, headed by a Science Advisor appointed to advise the Prime Minister on STI policy issues. He was instrumental in the launch of the first National Science and Technology Policy (NSTP, 1986-89), under the aegis of the Ministry of Science, Technology and Environment (MOSTE, created in 1973, which became MOSTI in 2004). This first STI strategic document set the broad directions and framework to encourage national development based on science and innovation, and scientific creativity and awareness in general.

The addition in the Fifth Malaysia Plan (1986-90) of a first chapter dedicated to "science and technology" (S&T) was another critical step toward better institutionalisation of STI policy. Since no specific funds were earmarked for the NSTP, the S&T chapter represented the first comprehensive and integrated orientation in terms of the size and management of public R&D expenditure, since a new specific line was added in the national five-year budgetary allocations (EPU, 1990). A central Research and Development Fund was also announced during the Fifth Malaysia Plan to finance all STI public policy initiatives. This allowed, for instance, a strategic reflection on the right balance to strike between basic, applied and developmental research, as well as between the different research operators, in particular the research institutes and higher education institutions (EPU, 1990). Prior to this, R&D funds were allowed directly from the Treasury to research institutions (MOSTI, 2009).

The NSTP and the Fifth Malaysia Plan marked the beginning of STI policy in Malaysia. Prior to this period there was no overall strategic direction for STI (EPU, 1990). A textual analysis of 81 policy documents before and after the release of the NSTP and the Fifth Malaysia Plan shows the extent of the "paradigm shift": prior to 1986 only 20% of policy documents made explicit reference to STI issues, in sharp contrast with the 91% since then.

Although the National Council for Scientific Research and Development (NCSRD), in charge of advising the government on STI orientation, had already been created, in 1975, it was not able to fully play its role in the promotion of national STI development "due to certain circumstances" (EPU, 1986).

The Second National S&T Policy (2002-10) put an emphasis on the results of STI activities on growth and competitiveness. It set ambitious targets to be met by 2010[5] along with a number of actions covering a wide range of issues related to STI activities, from research commercialisation to research awareness.[6] Regarding governance more specifically, it paved the way towards initiatives and reforms that were to be implemented during or even after its mandate.

Table 5.1 presents an overview of several of the significant initiatives that were launched between the mid-1980s and 2010 towards creating better co-ordination and/or greater centralisation of STI policy. It should be noted that based on its own experience of building a national STI policy, Malaysia has engaged significantly in supporting developing countries faced with similar challenges.[7]

As mentioned earlier in this review (see Chapter 2), the Malaysian economy has undergone a remarkable transformation over the decades, from being dependent on primary commodities to manufacturing, including, for some time, heavy industrialisation and since the 1990s, to a more diversified and knowledge-intensive or innovation-driven economy. These distinct phases were marked by the adoption of specific policies, programmes and strategies governing the development of the macroeconomy, STI, education and industrial development, as shown in Table 5.2.

Strengths and weaknesses of early industrial policies and science, technology and innovation policy frameworks

The list of the main initiatives by governance function carried out during the building up of the STI policy framework (Table 5.2) sheds light upon one of the main systemic difficulties faced by the Malaysian innovation policy, i.e. ensuring overall co-ordination of policy formulation and implementation. As regards policy formulation, national science councils were regularly changed, reviewed and reformed to re-empower them as their legitimacy tended to fade after some years. With regards to policy implementation, it proved difficult to mandate one key public actor to be the "natural leader" of science and technology policy. Some progress was made in that respect through the two STI strategies initiated by MOSTE, which were intended to confirm this ministry in its role by strengthening its resources, legitimacy and authority. Some research institutes were brought under MOSTI, its budget increased and new funds were created. The creation of the Research in Priority Areas programme (IRPA) was also a significant step in that direction. National science and technology policies could thus be understood to reassert MOSTI's leading position within the Malaysian system of innovation. The second National S&T Policy, for instance, announced the strengthening of MOSTE's resources and mandate so that it could take charge of the central task of STI policy formulation and implementation (MOSTI, 2003). However, its central role remained disputed between different public actors and MOSTE's institutional weakness did not allow it to co-ordinate the policies of the different ministries at that time (Kondo, 1999).

Table 5.1. **Main science, technology and innovation governance-related initiatives and events in Malaysia, 1985-2010**

Main governance functions	Main initiatives fully or partially implemented
Policy advice and steering	– Strengthen of the National Council for Scientific Research and Development (NCSRD)[1] to allow intersectoral co-ordination (1986-90)
	– Transfer of the responsibilities for technology transfer from the Co-ordinating Council for Industrial Technology Transfer (CCITT, created in 1982) to the NCSRD (1985)
	– Establishment of a higher level Cabinet Committee chaired by the Prime Minister to authorise STI-related legislation and programmes (1991-95)
	– Review of the role and governance of the NCRSD to allow it to perform effectively its role of an STI advisory and co-ordination system (1996-2000)
	– Creation of the National Innovation Council (2004) to advise on STI policy and devise key strategies to stimulate innovation
Policy formulation	– Launch of the First National S&T Policy (1986-89)
	– Launch of the Second National S&T Policy (2002-10)
	– Distinct STI chapter in the national development plans for the first time in the Fifth Malaysia Plan (1986-90)
Policy implementation	– Creation of a National Innovation Implementation Co-ordination Committee to oversee the implementation of resolutions from the National Innovation Council (2006)
	– Creation of a central R&D fund to finance all public support to STI activities
	– Creation of the Intensification of Research in Priority Areas programme (IRPA) to gather all public R&D funding schemes for higher education institutions and research institutes (not firms) under an integrated allocation and review process (1987)
	– Revision of the IRPA funding mechanisms to increase effectiveness (2000)
	– Transfer of the main research institutes under the supervision of the Ministry of Science, Technology and Environment (1991-95)
	– Creation of new research support schemes to support private companies (Commercialisation of R&D Fund, Technology Acquisition Fund, etc.)
	– Establishment of the Malaysian Technology Development Corporation to promote the creation and development of technology businesses (1992)
Policy information, analysis, monitoring and evaluation	– Build the infrastructure for STI information gathering and analysis, as well as Malaysian STI performance evaluation and monitoring (creation of the Malaysian Science and Technology Information Centre)
	– Creation of the Malaysian Industry-Government Group for High Technology, Prime Minister's Department (1993)
Policy framework	– Review and reform of the national intellectual property rights system, legislation, practice and institution
	– Establishment of the intellectual corporation of Malaysia (Pejabat Cap Dagangan dan Jaminhak/Paten, which then became known as "MyPo") (2003)

Note: 1. Also often referred to in the literature as the MPKSN under its Malaysian acronym.

Sources: Felker and Jomo (2007), "Technology policy in Malaysia"; MIGHT (2009), "Malaysia high technology 2009"; EPU (1985), *Fifth Malaysia Plan*, www.epu.gov.my/en/fifth-malaysia-plan-1986-1990; EPU (1990), *Sixth Malaysia Plan*, www.epu.gov.my/en/sixth-malaysia-plan-1990-19951; EPU (1996), *Seventh Malaysia Plan*, www.epu.gov.my/en/seventh-malaysia-plan-1996-2000; EPU (2001), *Eighth Malaysia Plan*, www.epu.gov.my/en/eighth-malaysia-plan-2001-2005; EPU (2006), *Ninth Malaysia Plan*, www.epu.gov.my/epu-theme/rm9/html/english.htm.

The fact that the NSPT, the Industrial Master Plan and various Malaysia plans and strategic framework made little, if any, mutual references to each other might also be illustrative of the limits of overall STI co-ordination. For instance, although the Fifth Malaysia Plan's S&T chapter covers almost exactly the same period and policy field as the NSPT, it did not make any reference to it. Only the IMP1 is mentioned in the document. Likewise, the subsequent Malaysia Plan, when reviewing the S&T policy progress made during the Fifth Malaysia Plan, only referred to the ATIPD, the follow up to IMP1.

Table 5.2. **Role of government and focus of the science, technology and innovation system according to development stages, Malaysia**

	1960s	1970s	1980s	1990s	2000s	2010	2015
Population	8.1 million	10.9 million	13.8 million	18.1 million	23.3 million	28.3 million	>30.7 million
GDP (at current USD)	USD 2.4 billion	USD 4.3 billion	USD 24.9 billion	USD 44 billion	USD 93.8 billion	USD 192.8 billion	USD 313 billion
R&D budget as a % of GDP	..	..	..	0.22	0.47	1.07	1.13
Development stage of the National Innovation Strategy	Primary commodities, agriculture, provision of basic infrastructure as well as developing operational capabilities		Investment-driven stage; shift to manufacturing; focus on learning as well as developing duplicative imitation and adaptive capabilities		Focused on knowledge-based/innovation economy		
Major industrial policy direction	Heavy dependence on primary export commodities; decline of rubber prices; beginning of import substitutions	Move from net oil importer to exporter as petroleum prices rose sharply; free trade zones attracting multinational companies; export-led industrialisation	Regulatory reforms that led to more liberalised private sector investment; gradual shift to heavy industries; Industrial Master Plan 1 (1986-95)	Growth strategies favouring modernisation/ industrialisation, shift to new and emerging technologies e.g. ICT; Industrial Master Plan 2 (1996-2005); promotion of clusters	Focus on productivity-driven growth; stimulating knowledge-based indigenous innovation; Industrial Master Plan 3 (2006-20); Knowledge-based Economy Master Plan	Greater emphasis on knowledge-based, innovative economic growth	Focus on increasing manufacturing value added, down-streaming activities, indigenous innovation capacity and capability; and global market access
STI policy and role of government	Limited focus	Dedicated Ministry for Science established as well as the National Council for Scientific Research and Development	1st National S&T Policy; first chapter on STI in Malaysia plans; Intensification of Research in Priority Areas (IRPA) grants; double-deduction incentives for R&D	Multimedia Super Corridor established; National IT Council; mega-projects era; Returning Scientist Programme	2nd National S&T Policy; National Innovation Council; Biotech Strategy announced; IRPAs streamlined; Brain Gain Programme launched	Year of Innovation; Talent Corporation established; UNIK, Performance Management and Delivery Unit	Science to Action (S2A): Mainstreaming STI – raising the profile of STI and infusing STI into nation building; National Policy on Science, Technology & Innovation (2013-20)
Macroeconomic policy framework/conditions	First Malaysia Plan (1966-70) launched; substantial increases in public sector expenditure	New economic policy focused on national unity, restructuring society for greater Malay urbanisation and employment	Large investments in heavy industries; significant growth in foreign direct investment; major recession in mid-1980s	Vision 2020 announced; Action Plan for Industrial Technology Development; Asian economic crisis	National Economic Advisory Council, National Innovation Model; second phase of Vision 2020, focused on key strategic thrusts for sustainable growth	New Economic Model; Tenth Malaysia Plan (2011-15) followed by the Economic Transformation Program; global economic crisis	Last leg towards Vision 2020 – Eleventh Malaysia Plan (2016-20); final phase of the Economic Transformation Program; implementation of Goods and Services Tax (GST)

Table 5.2. **Role of government and focus of the science, technology and innovation system according to development stages, Malaysia** (*continued*)

	1960s	1970s	1980s	1990s	2000s	2010	2015
Education policy	Becomes federal responsibility; focus on basic education for all	Focus on improving quality; system begins adjusting to economic needs	Continued focus on improving quality and access; National Vocational Training Council	Rapid transformation/ reform; opening of private sector institutions; Human Resource Development Fund	Ministry of Higher Education established; National Higher Education Action Plan; creation of research universities; APEX university; University Grading System; implementation of Malaysian Qualifications Framework; National Dual Training System	Science and maths to be taught in Bahasa Malaysia (the official language of Malaysia) from 2012	*Malaysia Education Blueprint 2015-2025 (Higher Education)*,[1] whose main aim is to produce holistic and balanced graduates with an entrepreneurial mind

Note: .. = not available.

1. Hereafter "Higher Education Blueprint 2015-25".

Sources: Adapted from OECD (2013a), *Innovation in Southeast Asia*, http://dx.doi.org/10.1787/9789264128712-en.

The reasons for the limited success of the government's effort to support the upgrade of the domestic industry via effective STI policies since the mid-1980s have been widely documented in many studies. The policy factors most frequently found in the literature are listed in Box 5.1.

Box 5.1. Mixed results of government policies supporting the upgrade of the Malaysian economy (1970-2000): Lessons from the literature

The reasons for the limited success of government efforts to support the upgrade of domestic industry since the mid-1980s have been widely documented. The most frequently mentioned policy factors include:

- An inadequate balance between the measures aimed at deepening and broadening foreign direct investment (FDI). The incentives and obligations for multinational enterprises to build stronger linkages with the domestic economy have been applied sparingly, so as not to discourage FDI. For instance, the tax holidays for companies undertaking R&D activities in Malaysia were, to a great extent, overshadowed by the more traditional and very generous incentives supporting manufacturing exports.
- Top-down industrial and innovation policies combined with a "passive" over-reliance on FDI. Some authors have suggested that, apart from exceptional cases such as the Penang E&E cluster, the massive inflows of FDI have hindered the development of domestic industrialisation more than they have encouraged it.
- Social equity rules associated with the New Economic Policy, affecting a wide range of domains including education and businesses, did not allow sufficient mobility of resources which, in the end, hindered innovation activities.
- Oligopolistic industry structures not conducive to competition and entrepreneurship. Particularly prior to the more recent liberalisations, many sectors were dominated by major family-owned conglomerates or government-linked companies that tended to prevent new entrants from challenging their position through innovation.
- Limited cohesion and co-ordination in regional networks. Although initiatives aimed at strengthening the weaving of regional and sectoral linkages are often run by businesses themselves, experience shows that public authorities, most often at local level, play an important role initiating them, including by establishing intermediary organisations.
- Lack of emphasis on secondary and tertiary education, which resulted in low absorption capacity of domestic industry and, more generally, shortage of skills. Other Asian countries such as Korea, Singapore and Chinese Taipei put much more emphasis on the quality of teaching, chiefly in science, technology, engineering and mathematics, and now pay increasing attention to creativity.
- The easy access to low-skilled foreign workers, creating little incentive for firms to switch to more innovative production modes.
- Weak capacity to implement well-designed strategies and plans. Even the best initiatives have suffered from a lack of sustainable efforts, political interference or, in some cases, clientelism and corruption.
- Limited government capacity to monitor the effect of state incentives and initiatives on beneficiaries' activities. This was said to be the case for technological transfers between foreign suppliers and local firms, where the state authorities merely registered transactions instead of evaluating them *ex ante* and *ex post* as it has been done in other Asian countries (Korea, Chinese Taipei). The same applies to R&D grants, which are not evaluated properly when projects come to an end.
- Other East Asian countries (Japan, Korea, Chinese Taipei, and later the People's Republic of China [hereafter: China]) exposing their "champions" more rigorously to the discipline of international (export) markets to "weed out losers".

Box 5.1. **Mixed results of government policies supporting the upgrade of the Malaysian economy (1970-2000): Lessons from the literature** *(continued)*

- Frequent shifts in strategic direction and unpredictability of early industrial support policies; government's lack of patience and tenacity to implement a consistent policy over time.
- Too little interaction between public and private STI actors in policy formulation and implementation; in higher level advisory committees as well as in lower level programme boards, business tends to be under-represented; some research schemes such as the Intensification of Research in Priority Areas programme could not allocate funds to private enterprises. *De facto*, Malaysian technology policy has long been inadequately informed or too heavily influenced by some academics.

Sources: Basu Das and Lee (2014), *Malaysia's Socio-Economic Transformation,*; Jomo (2014), "Malaysia's economic development and transformation"; Yusuf and Nabeshima (2009), "Tiger economies under threat: A comparative analysis of Malaysia's industrial prospects and policy options", http://documents.worldbank.org/curated/en/2009/01/11261234/tiger-economies-under-threat-comparative-analysis-malaysias-industrial-prospects-policy-options; Rasiah (2006), "Electronics in Malaysia: Export expansion but slow technical change"; Rasiah (2011), "Is Malaysia facing negative deindustrialization?", www.jstor.org/stable/23056129; MIGHT (2009), "Malaysia high technology 2009"; UNIDO (2003), "Malaysian electronics: At the crossroads"; Kondo (1999), "Improving Malaysian industrial technology policies and institutions"; Studwell (2013), *How Asia Works. Success and Failure in the World's Most Dynamic Region.*

Main policy actors

The first ministry dedicated to STI matters was established in 1973 under the name of the Ministry of Technology, Research and Local Government. In 1976 it became the Ministry of Science, Technology and Environment (MOSTE) and, finally, in 2004, the Ministry of Science, Technology and Innovation (MOSTI). It is the general administrator of STI policy which oversees a great number of agencies, R&D centres, institutes and government-linked companies in a number of high-tech sectors (nanotech, biotech, nuclear, etc.). MOSTI operates several STI R&D support schemes, either directly or via its agencies, mainly focusing on the commercialisation stage and support to start-ups (including the InnoFund, the ScienceFund and the TechnoFund). MOSTI is also responsible for infrastructural institutions (such as the Malaysian standards-setting agency), plus directorates for specific technologies – including biotech, nano, marine sciences and ICT). Finally, it is in charge of the secretariat of the National Science and Research Council (NSRC), one of the key councils advising the Prime Minister on R&D priorities.

The Ministry of Finance is another key player, not only through its authority on public budget expenditure as Treasury, but also via specific tax incentives, export promotion and, less typically, schemes dedicated to support collaborative research and technology commercialisation. With regards to science policy, the Ministry of Education operates a number of schemes to support basic and applied research, mainly in the universities to which it has awarded specific excellence status (research university, centre of excellence, etc.). To a lesser extent, the various ministries which have public research institutions (PRIs) or relevant government-linked companies under their jurisdiction also intervene in the STI arena in their respective sector (agriculture, environment, IT, etc.).

The Ministry of Higher Education was established in 2004[8] with the intention of developing and creating a higher education environment appropriate to meeting the national development goals. It is supported by key related agencies responsible for higher education, such as the Malaysian Qualification Agency (co-ordinates and supervises the quality assurance and accreditation of higher education) and the National Higher Education Fund Corporation (manages funding for higher education purposes).

The main mission of the Ministry of International Trade and Industry is to develop and implement the strategy to make Malaysia an attractive investment destination and a globally competitive trading nation. It is also tasked with the development of industrial activities in line with the goal of achieving the status of developed nation by 2020.

The Ministry of Energy, Green Technology and Water was established in 2009. Prior to that it was known as the Ministry of Energy, Water and Communications. The ministry, in its new configuration, received the new function of supporting environmental technologies. Simultaneously, "communication" moved to the Ministry of Information, Communications and Culture.

The Prime Minister is also directly involved via its department and specific implementing agencies such as the Performance Management and Delivery Unit (PEMANDU) and the Unit Peneraju Agenda Bumiputera (TERAJU). These agencies make it possible to operate government-wide programmes such as the Economic Transformation Programme (see Chapter 4). Also located under the Prime Minister, the National Innovation Agency of Malaysia was given a broad mandate in 2010 that ranges from the formulation of national policies, strategies and directions relating to innovation to the conduct of the analysis and surveys relating to innovation, the promotion of the culture of innovation and entrepreneurship, and advising the government on matters relating to innovation. In reality its role is more modest with regards to higher level STI orientation, being more focused on the implementation of various programmes to support a broad environment conducive to innovation and entrepreneurship.

In addition, the Economic Planning Unit (EPU) co-ordinates R&D financing from various ministries via its review of their STI budget applications. Since 2012, the EPU is assisted in this task by the Investment Committee for Public Funds (Box 5.2).

The post of the Science Advisor was established in 1984 to advise the Prime Minister on all STI matters, from the prioritisation of STI activities and public support to the promotion of business innovation and science diplomacy. One of the Science Advisor's key tasks is to facilitate inter-sectoral co-ordination of STI policy, using its centre of government position in the Prime Minister's Office and his position at the head of several councils and boards.[9] The Science Advisor set up the Malaysian Industry-Government Group for High Technology (MIGHT) in 1993 as an independent, industry-driven non-profit organisation, before being formally incorporated the year after, firstly to provide support to the Science Advisor in his/her role to plan and strategise on high technology. Currently, MIGHT mainly acts as a think tank for discussing strategies and policies for high-tech industries, partly relying on foresight studies carried out by the Malaysian Foresight Institute. It also intervenes directly in nurturing of high-tech industries via its support to the building of strategic partnerships and alliances, technology acquisition, and capacity-building initiatives. Finally, MIGHT is the co-secretariat of the Global Science and Innovation Advisory Council (GSIAC).

The Academy of Sciences Malaysia was established by an act of parliament in 1994. Its functions are wide-ranging, from the promotion of the development of science, engineering and technology to the drafting of reports to advise the government and research operators and more generally to promote science in society. It therefore acts both as a think tank and a platform to support interactions among key actors in the science arena.

Box 5.2. The Investment Committee for Public Funds (ICPF/JKPDA)

The Investment Committee for Public Funds is the committee responsible for co-ordinating publically funded research, development and commercialisation projects in the framework of the five-year national planning process. It is composed of 15 representatives of all science, technology and innovation-related ministries (Ministry of Education; Ministry of Science, Technology and Innovation; Ministry of International Trade and Industry, etc.) as well as technical experts in STI areas.

The establishment of the Investment Committee for Public Funds aims at:

- Ensuring effective and efficient utilisation of public funds in the planning and execution of research, development and commercialisation by fund managers at ministries and government agencies.
- Ensuring adherence to sectoral focus in line with the national priority areas and the National Science and Research Council.
- Facilitating collaboration, streamlining and minimising duplication of projects/programmes between ministries and agencies. For instance, in 2014, during the review of development projects worth MRY 1.2 billion, the Investment Committee for Public Funds claims to have streamlined 26 applications, resulting in savings of MRY 432 million which were then allocated to other research applications.
- Diffusing information on R&D activities and schemes (i.e. manages the 1Dana database of all R&D funding opportunities).

The National Innovation Agency of Malaysia and the National Science and Research Council jointly take charge of the Secretariat of the JKPDA.

Source: AIM (2013), *Corporation Annual Report 2013.*

The Investment Committee for Public Funds is one of many bodies providing advice to the Prime Minister's Department or to specific ministries. Although these bodies can differ according to their scope and precise function, their role is generally to consult various experts and stakeholders, including from abroad, in STI policy decision making and to facilitate co-ordination of the different Malaysian public actors. In addition to those already mentioned, there are numerous other councils, some of which have a sectoral focus, others which are dedicated to specific parts or functions. These councils include the ICT International Advisory Council or the Malaysian Aerospace Council or National SME Development Council (Table 5.3). As mentioned above, MIGHT also support the steering of the innovation system, acting as a think tank, supporting strategic and foresight activities, and providing various intelligence and capacity-building services. The Academy of Sciences Malaysia, created in 1995, fosters general science across Malaysia and provides independent advice to the government on matters related to science, technology and engineering. Finally, the Science Advisor to the Prime Minister provides advice on all STI matters, including prioritisation and STI policy support.

A new advisory council, the National Science Council, held its inaugural meeting on 27 January 2016. It will be in charge of the overall STI agenda. Since the mandate of this council is not yet available, it is not known what its connection will be with other committees, in particular the NSRC, the Investment Committee for Public Funds, and the Global Science and Innovation Advisory Council,[10] and with other key STI organisations such as the National Innovation Agency of Malaysia and the future Research Management Agency.

Figure 5.1. **Main public actors of the Malaysian science, technology and innovation system, 2015**

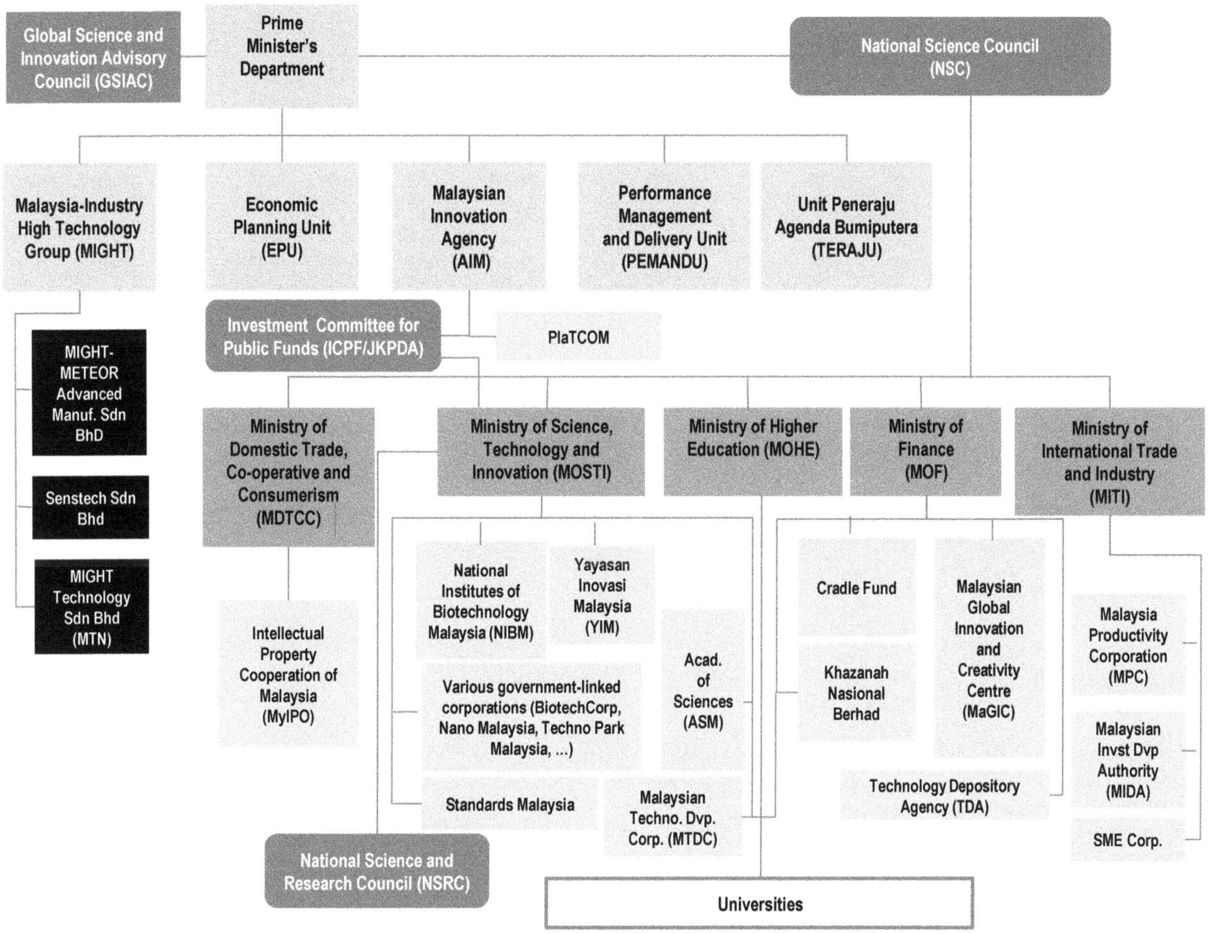

Note: Several other ministries involved in science, technology and innovation related activities are not represented in this figure, such as the Ministry of Energy, Green Technology and Water.

Overall national plans and strategies currently in action

The Malaysian government has played an important role in supporting and guiding the development path that transformed it from a low-income to an upper middle-income country, by implementing policies and support measures adapted to the different stages of its development.

Malaysia's current development strategy consists of a hierarchy of four major strategic components, each of which is led at the strategic policy level by the Prime Minister's Office or by a specific ministry or set of ministries, each of which has a primary agency responsible for implementation and the transformation of the objectives into programmes. Within the strategy as a whole, there is a very strong emphasis on innovation as a primary driver of development, and it seems clear that this will be the central focus for innovation policy makers in the years ahead. The focus here is on the overall strategy and its implications for innovation policy and governance.

Table 5.3. **Main non-sectoral science, technology and innovation councils and committees in Malaysia**

	Function	Secretariat	Membership
Investment Committee for Public Funds (ICPF/JKPDA) (2014)	Responsible for co-ordinating public funds associated with research, development and commercialisation Manage the 1Dana portal	Joint secretariat by the National Innovation Agency of Malaysia and the National Science and Research Council	Headed by the Minister of Science, Technology and Innovation and the CEO of the National Innovation Agency of Malaysia 15 representatives of all science, technology and innovation-related ministries (Ministry of Education; Ministry of Science, Technology and Innovation; Ministry of International Trade and Industry, etc.) as well as technical experts in STI areas
Global Science and Innovation Advisory Council (GSIAC) (2010)	Provide strategic advice to support Malaysia's development through science and innovation Benchmark Malaysia's ranking and competitiveness in science and innovation against technologically advanced countries	Joint Secretariat by the Malaysian Industry-Government Group for High Technology and the New York Academy of Sciences (NYAS)	Headed by the Prime Minister Joint secretaries: Science Advisor to the Prime Minister and the President and CEO of the New York Academy of Sciences International experts, industry leaders Relevant ministers (Ministry of Education; Ministry of Science, Technology and Innovation; Ministry of International Trade and Industry, etc.)
National Innovation Council (NIC) (2004-11)	Provide strategic leadership and support policy decision making	Secretariat by the Prime Minister's Office	Headed by the Prime Minister 28 members in 2011 Supported since 2006 by a National Innovation Implementation Co-ordination Committee to oversee the implementation of resolutions from the National Innovation Council
National Science and Research Council (NSRC) (2010, replaced the National Council for Scientific Research and Development [NCSRD] created in 1975)	Set priorities for R&D investment ("one-stop shop for R&D priority-setting") Encourage interdisciplinary research Ensure integration between government departments and organisations Evaluate R&D programmes and monitor outcomes	Secretariat by the Ministry of Science, Technology and Innovation	Nine *ex officio* members: heads of Treasury; Ministry of Science, Technology and Innovation; Academy of Sciences Malaysia; Economic Planning Unit; Ministry of Higher Education; Protem President of Academy of Social Sciences and Humanities; Council of University Vice-Chancellors; National Innovation Agency of Malaysia; National Defense Research Council The council is assisted by ten expert working groups in R&D focus areas (environmental sciences, advanced material sciences, etc.)
National SME Development Council (established in 2004)	Policy-making body responsible for the development of small and medium-sized enterprises (SMEs) in Malaysia. Its main goal is to ensure the comprehensive and co-ordinated development of SMEs across all sectors	SME Corporation	Headed by the Prime Minister; includes 13 ministers, the Chief Secretary to the Government, Director-General of Economic Planning Unit and the Governor of Bank Negara Malaysia
National Green Technology and Climate Change Council (established in 2009)	Provide high-level co-ordination between ministries, agencies and other stakeholders in the implementation of green technology policies and climate change issues	Secretariat by the Ministry of Energy, Green Technology and Water	Headed by the Prime Minister Steering Committee together with eight specific working committees (Industry, Human Capital, Research and Innovation, Promotion and Public Awareness, Transportation, Green Neighbourhood, Adaptation and Green Development) supports the functioning of the council
National ICT Implementation Design Council (established in 1993)	Non-profit agency responsible for the design industry and promotion of Malaysia as an international creative and innovative hub	Secretariat by the Ministry of Science, Technology and Innovation	Headed by Prof. Dr Ahmad Haji Zainuddin and has 14 members, including the Ministry of Higher Education; Ministry of Domestic Trade, Co-operatives and Consumerism; Ministry of Science, Technology and Innovation; Ministry of International Trade and Industry; and industry secretary generals

The first component of the development strategy is the New Economic Model (Box 5.3) (NEAC, 2009) unveiled in 2010, led by the Prime Minister and his office. This is the overarching strategic framework for Malaysia's development, and hence for all subordinate policy areas. It has three major objectives: 1) the transition of Malaysia into a high-income economy; 2) the creation of an inclusive society; and 3) the building of a sustainable economy and society. It has four guiding principles: 1) it should be market-led; 2) it should be well governed; 3) it should embrace an innovation perspective; and 4) it should promote an entrepreneurial society. The main framework for the New Economic Model will be the Eleventh Malaysia Plan; the implementation responsibility lies with the Economic Planning Unit (EPU).

Box 5.3. Malaysia's New Economic Model: Leveraging global value chains for structural transformation

Malaysia's New Economic Model (NEM) can be seen as a structural transformation plan that largely relies on upgrading global value chains (GVC) for achieving its main goals. A key element of the NEM is to improve the economic specialisation of Malaysia, especially in higher value-added activities and industries in GVCs. A specialisation in low value-added segments of manufacturing has come under pressure as lower income countries, China followed more recently by a new cohort of catching-up economies such as Viet Nam, have increasingly entered these activities, as discussed in Chapter 2. Malaysia can no longer compete with these countries on the basis of a high-volume, low-cost strategy. Immigration of unskilled labour to maintain these segments is not a viable strategy for sustainable growth of GDP per capita.

The NEM is implemented through the Economic Transformation Program, which identified 12 national key economic areas (NKEAs) and 6 strategic reform initiatives. The 12 NKEAs are expected to deliver almost three-quarters of the growth in Malaysia's GDP over the next decade. A so-called "lab" was convened for each of them to develop an action plan, set specific targets (job creation and GDP contribution) and determine the required resources (skills, funding, etc.). For those NKEAs characterised by a strong presence of GVCs, the labs identified the most important challenges of Malaysia's specialisation in low value-added activities; for example in the case of the electronics industry: 1) an excessive concentration in low-value assembly operations; 2) increasing competition from China; 3) a decreasing contribution to exports; and 4) too broad a focus on a broad range of subsectors. Based on this, four subsectors (semiconductors, LED, solar, and industrial electronics and home appliances) were selected to be the most attractive in terms of growth and size, and specific actions were formulated for each subsector to move Malaysia up the value chain.

Complementary to these very targeted actions at the industry level, a number of horizontal policies have been implemented:

- private investment promotion and fiscal support to attract domestic and foreign investment
- enlarging human capital through investment in vocational education, stimulating the return of Malaysians currently working abroad and better immigration rules to facilitate the arrival of foreign talent in desired areas
- improvements in the business environment to foster private investment and entrepreneurial activity: liberalisation in specific industries, easing the set-up of business operations, reducing administrative costs for SMEs and a more effective institutional setting for interaction between government and private agents
- investment in infrastructure, particularly in broadband and logistics.

Strategic reform initiatives comprise supportive public policy areas aimed at strengthening Malaysia's global competitiveness through 37 policy measures recommended by the National Economic Advisory Council (PEMANDU, 2014).

Source: Adapted from OECD (2013a), *Innovation in Southeast Asia*, http://dx.doi.org/10.1787/9789264128712-en.

The second component is the Economic Transformation Program, which focuses these overall objectives and principles on 12 national key economic areas (NKEAs), chosen on the basis of their potential to raise income and promote Malaysia's global competitiveness over the coming decade. The 12 NKEAs are: oil, gas and energy; palm oil and rubber; financial services; tourism; business services; electrical and electronics; wholesale and retail trade; education; agriculture; healthcare; communications content and infrastructure; and Greater Kuala Lumpur. Each of these NKEAs is the responsibility of a particular ministry, but the programme as a whole is overseen and monitored by PEMANDU. The primary instruments for the Economic Transformation Program are "entry point projects", which are collaborative government-business projects that aim to upgrade and transform the industry or area concerned. As PEMANDU remarks: "The NKEAs are the engines of growth, while the Entry Point Projects are the spark plugs that will fire up these engines to a new level of performance." There are currently 196 entry point projects. Policy interventions are mainly implemented in the spirit of public-private partnerships, with public agencies mandated to provide eco-systems that are conducive to innovation and commercialisation, while business entities are expected to foster business and entrepreneurial agendas (OECD, 2013b).

The third component is science transformation, under the Prime Minister's Office, overseen by the Science Advisor and implemented by MIGHT. The National Innovation Agency of Malaysia also plays an important role in this programme.

In order to provide more specific guidelines, these wide plans have been completed by dedicated mid- to long-term STI strategies. The fourth component, the National Policy on Science, Technology and Innovation 2013-2020 (Table 5.4), launched by the government in 2013, provides strategic guidelines for STI policy and investment for Malaysia's transition to an innovation economy by 2020 in the framework of the nation's Vision 2020 and the New Economic Model. These strategic plans all set bold objectives and contain significant new initiatives covering all aspects of the Malaysian innovation system, from R&D expenditures and the commercialisation of research to public awareness of S&T and the evaluation of STI policy.

Most of these four higher level strategic components do not have dedicated budgets. The allocation of funds, in STI as in any other "developmental" area, is determined in the framework of the five-year Malaysia plans, and follows the same process (Box 5.4). As mentioned earlier, STI has been singled out as a distinct policy area with a dedicated chapter and a specific budget since the Fifth Malaysia Plan.

Table 5.4. **Objectives of the National Policy on Science, Technology and Innovation 2013-2020**

Strategic thrusts	Objectives
Advancing scientific and social research, development and commercialisation	– Increase the ratio of R,D&C funds to at least 2% of GDP by 2020 – Enhance the performance of public R,D&C funding – Improve the delivery of STI services – Enhance commercialisation and increase uptake of home-grown R&D innovative products through clear guidelines and standards compliance – Intensify the integration of social sciences and humanities with pure and applied sciences
Developing, harnessing and intensifying talent	– Increase the ratio of researchers per 10 000 workforce to at least 70 by 2020 – Develop higher order cognitive, analytical, creative and innovative skills among school children, tertiary level students and teachers – Introduce new innovative skills in the workforce to advance the nation's STI capabilities – Intensify STI's brain gain and brain circulation – Enhance the talent management system to track the supply and demand of skilled human capital in STI – Develop a dynamic career path for researchers in public research institutes and institutions of higher learning – Promote and enhance meaningful, effective and equitable female participation in STI at all levels and in all sectors – Increase the skilled and competent technical workforce to manage, operate and maintain highly specialised equipment and infrastructure
Energising industries	– Maintain a minimum R&D expenditure ratio between the private and public sectors – Develop enterprises with distinctive capabilities – Initiate extensive review of fiscal and financial incentives to promote industry innovation, particularly among small and medium-sized enterprises – Stimulate and facilitate the private sector to undertake R,D&C – Engage industry associations and strengthen networking to co-create STI programmes and activities – Develop new approaches to enhance knowledge transfer to industry from public research institutions, institutes of higher learning, government organisations and regional corridor development agencies – Formulate and implement the Inclusive Innovation Roadmap (2013-20) – Encourage social, grassroots and prosumer-driven innovation – Enhance industry-driven collaboration and partnerships – Enhance innovation and inculcate a risk-taking culture among entrepreneurs to accelerate R&D commercialisation
Transforming STI governance	– Formulate an STI Act for orderly implementation of the national STI agenda – Strengthen and streamline STI-related councils – Transform and enhance public research institutions' governance to ensure efficient management and effective implementation of their core functions – Provide greater autonomy to public and private institutes of higher learning and public research institutions to spur industry collaboration and entrepreneurship – Incorporate social norms, ethical and moral values in the advancement of science – Encourage institutes of higher learning and public research institutions to comply with the Intellectual Property Commercialisation Policy for R&D Projects Funded by the government of Malaysia (2009) – Transform existing science and technology information centres to become more effective – Innovate and improve the public sector delivery system
Promoting and sensitising STI	– Establish an advisory body to guide STI public awareness and promotion – Expand and empower science centres to popularise and sensitise STI in society – Promote STI among school children, professional bodies and science-oriented societies – Conduct an outreach programme to raise awareness on ethics and humanities in society
Enhancing strategic international alliances	– Improve the R,D&C ecosystem to attract global partners – Nurture domestic talents to enable organisations and industries to penetrate global markets – Develop partners, allies and channels in key destination countries – Establish "go-global" market strategies for home-grown STI products – Strengthen the marketing and development of global brands – Continuous improvement in monitoring and evaluation – Intensify domestic and international networks for research collaboration, strategic partnerships and business relationships

Source: MOSTI (2013a), *National Policy on Science, Technology and Innovation 2013-2020.*

The Eleventh Malaysia Plan featured many new initiatives to support both technological and social innovation (Table 5.5).

Box 5.4. Science, technology and innovation in the national development budget process in Malaysia

The allocation of budget for R&D follows the same process as any other government development project. It is governed via the five-year Malaysia Plan that includes all "development projects" in a broad sense, in all policy areas categorised under economic, social, security and general administration. The five-year plan sets the directions and the main projects to be followed by the Malaysian economy during the next five years.

The budgeting process starts both at the bottom and at the top of the governance structure:

- The Economic Planning Unit, in consultation with other central agencies such as the Ministry of Finance and the central bank, define the macroeconomic framework and the growth targets and their implications in terms of public sector development expenditures.
- The 25 ministries in charge of the different policy areas draw up plans in their areas for the next 5 years through consultations with the relevant actors, including for instance, policy makers, industry and service representatives, non-governmental organisations and citizens. In practice, the breadth and depth of these consultations, conducted via a series of dedicated workshops and surveys, vary according to established practices in the different areas and institutions concerned.

These inputs are then submitted by each ministry to the Economic Planning Unit. As far as budgeting for R&D is concerned, the Investment Committee for Public Funds (ICPF/JKPDA) – which is tasked with reviewing the projects to avoid overlaps – aligns the projects with the national priorities and advises the Economic Planning Unit on the project proposals.

Based on advice from the Investment Committee for Public Funds and its own expertise, the Economic Planning Unit decides on budget allocation and provides feedback to line ministries and agencies. The budget can be adjusted accordingly when necessary.

For development expenditure budgeting as a whole, the Economic Planning Unit prioritises the development projects, as the volume of proposals exceeds the available resources, and takes the final decision based on policy priorities between sector regional balances and macroeconomic conditions. The selected projects are then integrated into the yearly budget, which is submitted to parliament by the Cabinet. The indicative total budget available for the five years is decided by the Cabinet based on advice from the Prime Minister in consultation with the Ministry of Finance.[1] The development budget of each ministry results from the consolidation of the budget of the different projects submitted to Economic Planning Unit.

The Tenth Malaysia Plan introduced a performance-based component. A fixed budget for each development project is allocated for the first year and a budget ceiling is agreed upon for two years, depending on the project cost and duration. The results of each development project are assessed at the end of each year in order to determine the budget allocation for the year to come.

This national development budget process allows the development of a whole-of-government approach to guide individual budget allocation at the ministry level – and even lower at development project level. This process also allows the Economic Planning Unit to reduce the likelihood of duplications between different ministries, including in STI.

However, this process has some limitations:

- the strong centralisation of the budgeting process can come at the detriment of very specialised and complex projects that require specific knowledge to be understood and assessed
- unplanned budget fluctuations during the course of the plan (further to yearly assessment or due to overall budget restrictions) can be particularly detrimental for R&D projects with a mid- to long-term horizon
- it is not clear how the Investment Committee for Public Funds's members can have expertise that is wide enough to cover the range of development project proposals from 24 ministries and agencies.

1. The Prime Minister is currently also the Minister of Finance.

Table 5.5. **Main initiatives to support research and innovation under the Eleventh Malaysia Plan**

Main initiatives	Actions to be implemented
Enterprise innovation	
Strengthen governance mechanisms	– Establish the Research Management Agency to decrease the number of overlaps and low-impact programmes – Expand the 1Dana Portal to become the one-stop archive for R&D&C&I projects (i.e. facilities, intellectual property or different expertise available) – Promote an innovative corporate culture in medium-sized and large companies to enable them to be sustainable and gain a competitive advantage using different existing programmes (i.e. National Corporate Innovation Index, Intellectual Capital Future Check)
Enhance demand-driven and applied research	– Streamline public sector funding for R&D&C&I projects to ensure better returns – Reinforce funding of applied research for resolving national problems and improving well-being (i.e. climate change), and contributing to the development of new products and industries – Enforce demand-driven research using science-industry strategic partnerships in order to improve companies' productivity and competitiveness as well as the R&D commercialisation rate
Development and intensification of industry-academia collaboration through intermediaries	– Continue simplification of science-industry collaboration through newly created industry-led intermediaries: Steinbeis, SIRIM-Fraunhofer and PlaTCOM – Enforce contract research conducted through the Ministry of Education's Public Private Research Network – Create a collaborative platform for a cluster of healthcare firms and research-intensive companies based at the Universiti Kebangsaan Malaysia and provide clear guidelines for remuneration, equipment use and intellectual property ownership
Promote and increase private financing of R&D&C&I	– Strengthen the participation of private financial institutions, venture capital and angel investors in R&D projects to decrease the share of public participation – Expand Technology Park Malaysia Angel Chapter and SME Investment Programme – Investigate possibilities for equity crowdfunding to broaden the number of investors and give more opportunities to innovative start-ups and SMEs to receive financing – Improve the innovation environment by giving a transparent explanation of risk mitigation and management challenges
Innovation in the manufacturing sector	
Leverage intermediaries to increase innovation and R&D activities	– Use intermediaries such as Steinbeis Malaysia Foundation; SIRIM-Fraunhofer and PlaTCOM Ventures Sdn. Bhd to leverage existing research institutions to improve the R&D component in products and processes – Promote the 1-InnoCERT programme by SME Corporation to complement intermediates' partnership
Leverage industry associations and chambers of commerce to drive innovation and productivity	– Use industry associations and chambers of commerce as a platform to disperse information on industry-related policies, obtain feedback and conduct specific trainings
Promote intellectual property rights sharing and protection	– Develop IP sharing and protection guidelines to protect interests and ensure fair returns to researches and manufacturers – Introduce a "pay per use" mechanism in public laboratories and R&D facilities in order to both reduce R&D costs for manufacturers and small research institutes and increase the returns of facilities' investments
Adopt life cycle assessment	– Encourage manufacturers to use green production processes to recover materials from waste to reduce the use of raw materials and develop the remanufacturing industry
Streamline industry development to multilateral environmental commitments	– Increase strategic co-operation with developed economics in the field of technology, innovation and R&D to ensure compliance with environmental requirements and reduce compliance-related costs
Introduce performance-based incentives	– Introduce incentives that will have clear key performance indicators, a validity period and exit policy to increase productivity and stimulate innovations.

Table 5.5. **Main initiatives to support research and innovation under the Eleventh Malaysia Plan** (*continued*)

Main initiatives	Actions to be implemented
Social innovation targets	
Strengthen collaboration using a whole-society approach	– Shift from a government-centralised approach to society level in order to improve collaboration between all levels of society (government, non-governmental organisations, citizens, etc.) – Establish a task force that will include ministries, non-governmental organisations, community-based organisations and private sector representatives that will co-ordinate the design, planning and delivery of social service programmes – Define clear key performance indicators, monitoring and evaluation tools to improve the expertise of non-governmental organisations and community-based organisations
Develop a social financing model	– Facilitate public-private partnerships to promote private sector investments in social services delivery – Introduce a "payment by results" approach where investors receive reimbursement from the government when the agreed results are achieved
Promote higher order thinking skills to develop a dynamic society	– Scale-up existing higher order thinking skills programmes with the purpose to improve the critical thinking, leadership and communication skills of the current and future workforce – Give priority to science and mathematics in education in line with the "Higher Education Blueprint 2015-25" (MOE, 2015) – Increase the number of higher order thinking skills to 10 000 schools by 2020

Source: EPU (2015a), *Eleventh Malaysia Plan*, http://rmk11.epu.gov.my/index.php/en.

Numerous other strategies and policy documents aim to guide activities in STI-related sectoral or horizontal areas (Table 5.6).

Malaysia's capacity for developing well-designed, comprehensive and formally innovative strategies and plans has been widely acknowledged by domestic and foreign analysts. The level of ambition and scope of the strategic exercise also deserve to be emphasised. Far beyond a simple document, several strategies are, in fact, genuine integrated "systems" on their own, including strategic guidelines, a new inter-sectoral committee for taking collegial decisions, a dedicated organisation in charge of its implementation, with new R&D schemes and/or tax incentives to influence public and private actors' behaviour as needed. The National Green Technology Policy and the National Biotechnology Policy are illustrative of such integrated "strategic systems".

Support to R&D

The government has played an important role in supporting R&D activities, progressively diversifying the national portfolio of policy instruments to cover all the distinct needs of higher education institutions (HEIs), research institutes and business enterprises since the mid-1980s. The main public institutions have enriched their offer of support schemes, and new institutions were created or started to become active in the area of research and innovation. Although several instruments have since been discontinued or significantly modified, the set of schemes currently available under the Eleventh Malaysia Plan is largely the result of this gradual broadening and differentiation of the public R&D support infrastructure.

Table 5.6. **Main ongoing science, technology and innovation-related strategies and plans in Malaysia**

Strategy or plan	Leader and/or operator in charge of the implementation	Main science, technology and innovation component
National strategies and plans		
Vision 2020 (1991-2020)	Economic Planning Unit, Prime Minister's Department	One challenge (out of nine) aimed at creating, through 2020, a scientific and progressive innovative society that will not only consume, but also contribute to, scientific and technological development in the future
New Economic Model (NEM) (2010-20)	Economic Planning Unit, Prime Minister's Department	Three out of seven of the New Economic Model approaches to economic development take into account the importance of STI: 1) the "growth through productivity" concept includes business concentration on innovation processes and technologies supported by a high level of private investment and skills; 2) endorsement of technologically competent industries and firms through grant incentives; 3) retain and attract experienced local and foreign professionals
Eleventh Malaysia Plan (2016-20)	Economic Planning Unit, Prime Minister's Department	Its main goal is to convert innovation to wealth, by improving co-operation between all stakeholders and focusing innovation at enterprise and societal level, instead of at the national level
Research and innovation		
National Policy on Science, Technology and Innovation (NSTIP) 2013-2020	Ministry of Science, Technology and Innovation	Specify strategic guidelines for STI policy and investment for Malaysia's transition to an innovation economy by 2020
Science to Action (S2A) Program (2013-20)	Malaysian Industry-Government Group for High Technology	Implement initiatives to promote a focus and investment on science and technology through various programmes, such as the Kuala Lumpur Engineering Science Fair (KLESF), FameLab or TinkerMind
Third Industrial Master Plan (IMP3) (2006-20)	Ministry of International Trade and Industry	Reach long-term global competitiveness and industrial growth through innovation of the manufacturing and services sectors and development of innovative human capital
Knowledge-Based Economy Master Plan (2002-20)	Economic Planning Unit	Strategic framework that includes 7 crucial areas with 136 recommendations covering human resource development, information structure, incentives, science and technology development, reorientation of the private and public sectors as well as addressing the digital divide
Higher education		
Higher Education Blueprint (2015-25)	Ministry of Higher Education	Innovation is one out of six shifts aimed at facilitating the higher education system. Key initiatives are: – focus on creating scale and growth in strategic research areas linked to national priorities – play a catalytic role in securing investments motivate higher learning institutions to establish supporting systems for the commercialisation of ideas
National Higher Education Strategic Plan (NHESP) (started in 2007 and beyond 2020)	Ministry of Higher Education	Review the overall education system to build up innovative educational infrastructure and enhance technology use in the teaching and learning process
Functional plans		
SME Master Plan (2012-20)	SME Corporation	SME development framework for innovation-led and productivity-driven growth that includes the development of technology commercialisation platforms to encourage more SMEs to innovate and expansion of inclusive innovation to improve bottom 40% position
Government-Linked Companies (GLC) Transformation Programme (2005-15)	Putrajaya Committee on GLC High Performance (PCG)	Managed the ten-year transformation of government-linked companies into high-performing bodies through, *inter alia*, improvement of innovation understanding. Introduction of innovative investment *sukuk* framework in the Islamic capital market
Intellectual property commercialisation policy for research and development (R&D) projects (2009)	Ministry of Science, Technology and Innovation	Established a common framework of intellectual property (IP) regulation and management at all levels, improved the protection of IP in line with the National Intellectual Property Policy as well as IP exploitation and commercialisation from projects funded by the government

Building the portfolio of R&D support schemes

Until the Fifth Malaysia Plan, the bulk of public support to R&D activities was directly allocated to basic and applied research in research institutes and, to a much lesser extent, to universities. The gradual understanding that the growth of manufacturing FDI in the 1970s had not led to a significant increase of business R&D, as observed in different field studies and confirmed afterwards by the first R&D survey in 1990, called for a significant widening of the portfolio of support schemes. The main instrument until 1996 was the Intensification of Research in Priority Areas (IRPA) programme, which was dedicated to funding research institutes and HEIs since its creation in 1987, although one of its objectives was to enhance R&D linkages between public and private actors. This centralised scheme, which remained the only R&D support scheme for almost ten years, marked an important improvement with regard to the quality and efficiency of the research proposal selection process. It was also a significant change in terms of openness, since four thematic "IRPA panels", operating under the supervision of the National Council for Scientific Research and Development, initiated a consultation among representatives of academia, industry and public authorities about research directions (EPU, 1990). Due to the prominence of agricultural research, in particular in research institutes, and the still limited research capacity at universities during this period, agriculture received about half of the IRPA funding allocated under the Fifth and Sixth Malaysia Plans.

According to a government review undertaken in 1995, the results in terms of research commercialisation, although a key selection criterion, fell short of expectations[11] (EPU, 1996; Rasiah, 1999). It became clear when reviewing the progress of the Sixth Malaysia Plan that the financing of research institutes and HEIs would not result in innovation and that a redirection of funds toward more downstream activities was also necessary. The IRPA principles were modified over time to allow a small portion of funds to benefit private firms co-operating with public research operators, which proved far from sufficient. The linear process assumption underlying such a model had been proven wrong in Malaysia as in many other countries and more schemes were needed to support innovation in firms or in co-operative science-industry projects directly. The only instrument to support private firms was the Industrial Technical Assistance Fund launched in 1990 to support innovation and productivity improvement in SMEs (consultancy services, market research, quality improvement, etc.) (Din and Krishna, 2007). The small amounts allocated through this scheme, in total and per project,[12] were an obstacle to the potential of this programme (Rasiah, 1999).[13]

It was only from 1996 onwards and the start of the Seventh Malaysia Plan that new significant schemes dedicated to industry R&D at large were introduced. The Industry R&D Grant Scheme was launched in 1996 by MOSTI to support Malaysian-owned companies involved in R&D projects, when possible in co-operation with HEIs or research institutes.[14] The Multimedia Super Corridor R&D Grant Scheme and the Technology Acquisition Fund were both initiated in 1997. The Technology Acquisition Fund pursued the traditional "FDI-based upgrading approach" by partially covering the costs of acquisition of technology (including high-tech equipment and machinery, technology licensing, acquisition of patent rights, prototypes, etc.) by Malaysian companies. As part of the new cluster approach instilled by the Second Industrial Master Plan (IMP2) launched the year before, the Multimedia Super Corridor R&D Grant Scheme specifically aims to support private R&D projects within the Multimedia Super Corridor "mega-cluster". During the Seventh Malaysia Plan, two venture capital schemes were introduced, one administered by the Malaysian Technology Development Corporation to support firms in the Multimedia Super Corridor and the other for firms located in Technology Park Malaysia.

Further downstream in the R&D cycle, the Demonstrator Application Grant Scheme applied only to IT and multimedia companies and was managed by the National R&D Centre in ICT of Malaysia (MIMOS), at that time still playing the role of ICT agency for MOSTI. Finally, the Commercialisation of R&D Fund managed by the Malaysian Technology Development Corporation, supported, through different types of grants, the final stages before commercialisation of R&D results: market survey and research; product and process design including designs, prototypes, pilot plants; and standardisation measures including intellectual property rights.

Some more focused new schemes were introduced during the Eighth Malaysia Plan (2001-05) to complete the support infrastructure to business firms and cover their specific needs. The Business Accelerator Programme, managed by SME Corporation, focused on improving the technological capabilities of Malaysian-owned SMEs through grants and loans to finance the improvement of their processes (acquisition of equipment and machineries, improvement of packaging and advertising activities, etc.). The Cradle Investment Programme was set up in 2003 as a fund with an initial dotation of MYR 100 million, raised to MYR 150 million under the Tenth Malaysia Plan, in order to stimulate the development of Malaysian entrepreneurship in key industrial areas through conditional grants. The Biotechnology R&D Grant Scheme was established in 2001 under the National Biotechnology Directorate to support biotechnology R&D and commercialisation activities.

The Ninth Malaysia Plan (2006-10) provided for a major overhaul of the portfolio of policy instruments to support research and innovation, concomitantly to an extraordinary increase of the public funds allocated to this policy mission (Figure 5.2). MOSTI's IRPA was discontinued and replaced by a new set of funds, in particular the ScienceFund (basic research), the TechnoFund and the InnoFund (both at pre-commercialisation stage), reconducted under the Tenth Malaysia Plan (2011-15) and still in place today. In addition to other already existing schemes, this set of instruments allowed the ministry to cover research institutions' and firms' needs throughout the whole spectrum of R&D activities.

The Ministry of Higher Education (MOHE), which previously intervened as research funder mainly through the dotation to HEIs, took a much stronger role as planned in Phase 1 of the National Higher Education Strategic Plan (2008-11). It introduced its first research support scheme, the Fundamental Research Grant Scheme in 2006, to fund fundamental research projects in research institutions and HEIs. Grants are allocated bottom-up following an application and selection process of project proposals. Some projects directly identified by a dedicated committee, the Fundamental Research Grant Committee, are also financed top-down. Under the Ninth Malaysia Plan, the MOHE allocated MYR 200 billion to the Fundamental Research Grant Scheme (ORICC, 2011).

As was the case for MOSTI, the MOHE built up its set of schemes in subsequent years to respond to more specific needs. Three additional schemes were introduced in 2011, i.e. the Long Term Research Grant Scheme, the Exploratory Research Grant Scheme and the Prototype Development Grant Scheme. Specific grants were also allocated for enculturation of research such as RAGS and RACE.

The expansion of the number of schemes dedicated almost exclusively to HEIs was reflected in the increase of funds during Phase 1 of the National Higher Education Strategic Plan and beyond: HEIs' R&D expenditures rose from MYR 1.7 million in 2009 to MYR 2.7 million in 2011 (MASTIC, 2013).

The MOHE also provides incentives to individual researchers via the Young Scientist Programme, and to selected research universities. Based on a performance assessment, a few universities are awarded the status of "research university", which entitles them to receive additional funds.[15] Five research universities were designated during Phase 1 of the National Higher Education Strategic Plan. The list has not expanded since then and it seems that the MOHE intends to only generate some turnover among the five research universities according to the evolution of their performance, as measured through the MyRA assessment system (MOE, 2014).[16]

Figure 5.2. **Total amount and breakdown of financial support for R&D by Malaysia Plan period**

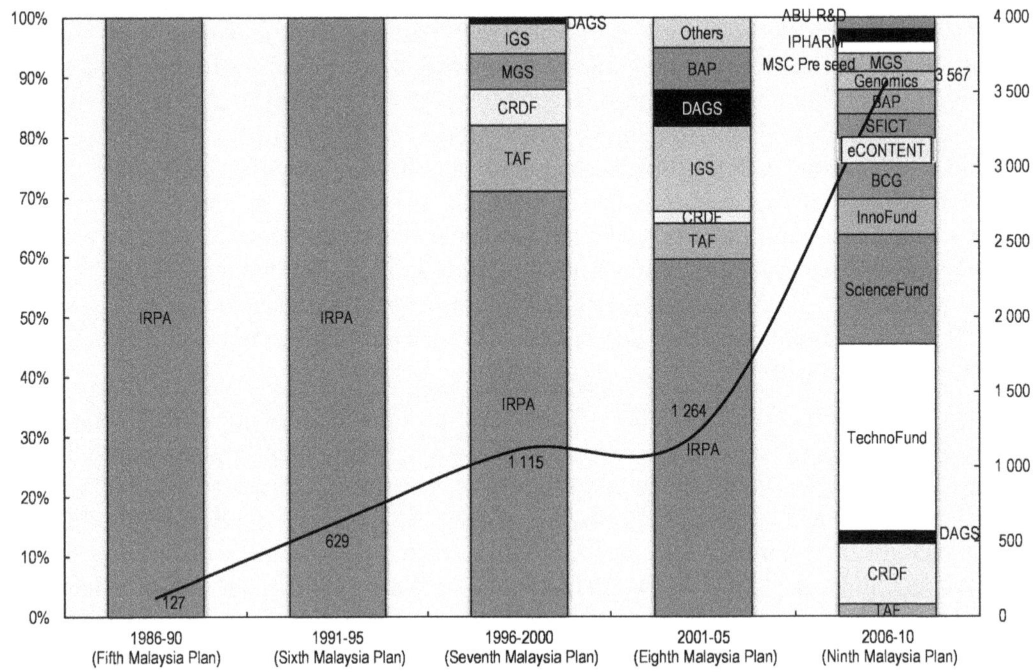

Notes: IRPA = Intensification of Research in Priority Areas; IGS = Industry R&D Grant Scheme; DAGS = Demonstrator Application Grant Scheme; MGS = Multimedia Super Corridor R&D Grant Scheme; CRDF = Commercialisation of R&D Fund; TAF = Technology Acquisition Fund; BAP = Business Accelerator Programme; IPHARM = Institut Farmaseutikal Dan Nutraseutikal Malaysia; MSC = Multimedia Super Corridor; BCG = Biotechnology Commercialisation Grant. The 2001-05 data include only the schemes managed by MOSTI. Allocated amounts are based on *ex post* expenditure data, not *ex ante* allocation announced in the Malaysia plans.

Besides the general schemes operated by the two main ministries in charge of STI matters – MOSTI and the Ministry of Higher Education, which are usually launched in the framework of a new Malaysia plan or STI strategic plan – more specific schemes have been created on the occasion of the launch of a sectoral or thematic plan. This was the case with the Biotechnology R&D Grant Scheme, created in 2001 to support the R&D and commercialisation activities of biotechnology companies. In more recent years, this scheme was completed by several other initiatives in the framework of the National Biotechnology Policy launched in 2005.

Sources: Adapted from ASM (2015), *Science Outlook: Action Towards Vision, Research & Policy*; absolute amounts taken from EPU (1985), *Fifth Malaysia Plan*, www.epu.gov.my/en/fifth-malaysia-plan-1986-1990; EPU (1990), *Sixth Malaysia Plan*, www.epu.gov.my/en/sixth-malaysia-plan-1990-19951; EPU (1996), *Seventh Malaysia Plan*, www.epu.gov.my/en/seventh-malaysia-plan-1996-2000; EPU (2001), *Eighth Malaysia Plan*, www.epu.gov.my/en/eighth-malaysia-plan-2001-2005; EPU (2006), *Ninth Malaysia Plan*, www.epu.gov.my/epu-theme/rm9/html/english.htm.

Recent R&D support schemes

Under the Ninth and Tenth Malaysia Plans, MOSTI allocated almost MYR 240 million through its main schemes, i.e. the ScienceFund and the Pre-commercialisation Fund, which gathers the TechnoFund and InnoFund (Figure 5.3). However, there was significant variation within the period, in particular a clear downward trend between 2007 and 2012, with a slight increase since then. The funds allocated in 2014 were only about a fifth of what they were in 2007. The reasons for this dramatic fall can be found partly in the number of applications, which decreased radically between 2006 and 2010, but also in the selection process, with a success rate declining from over 50% to below 20% (Figure 5.3). This evolution most likely reflects a decrease in the quality of the projects submitted to MOSTI once the stock of eligible, high-quality projects of the first years was exhausted,[17] but also the increasing pressure on the public budget in recent years.

Figure 5.3. **Amounts allocated and selection rate of the ScienceFund and Pre-commercialisation Fund, 2006-15**

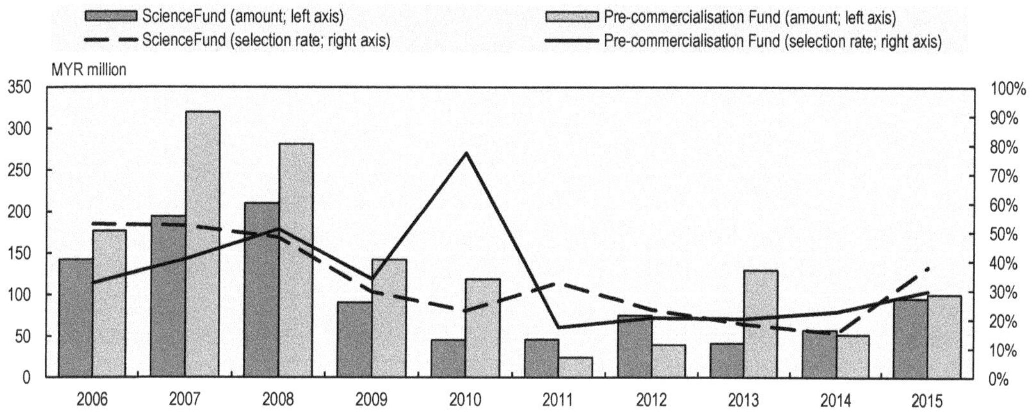

Note: The Pre-commercialisation Fund includes the TechnoFund and the InnoFund.

Source: MOSTI (2015), "Kemudahan Dana MOSTI".

MOSTI's main instrument in most of the years during this period was the Pre-commercialisation Fund. Although the number of projects selected through this fund was far lower than that of the ScienceFund, it accounted for 58% of the funds allocated, in line with what can be observed in many countries given the costly investments to be co-financed during this crucial stage (Figure 5.4).

In terms of area focus, the ScienceFund has allocated more money to industry and S&T core fields. Although there is a specific scheme to support biotechnology research projects, the ScienceFund has also significantly supported this area. The TechnoFund allocated more funds to the industry sector, followed by biotechnology and ICT (MASTIC, 2014). However, the breadth of the thematic areas used in the monitoring of these schemes does not allow precise conclusions to be drawn on the extent of prioritisation. This is particularly problematic since, whereas support for basic funding must preserve a certain breadth to be able to build the knowledge base, prioritisation is crucial for schemes intervening more downstream in the R&D chain. Some information on the extent to which such prioritisation is happening through MOSTI pre-commercialisation funds can be found in the scheme's application guidelines: TechnoFund applications must pertain to ten broad research and priority areas that cover almost all areas. In addition, the schemes also focus on 13 flagship programmes which, although more selective, still represents a vast portion of the technological landscape.[18]

Figure 5.4. **Breakdown of allocations of the ScienceFund and Pre-commercialisation Fund, 2006-15**

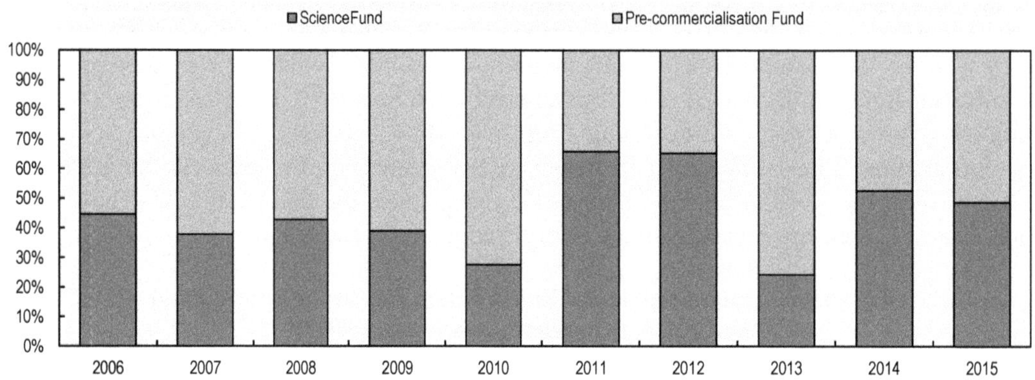

Note: The main MOSTI funds include the ScienceFund, the TechnoFund and the InnoFund.

Source: MOSTI (2015), "Kemudahan Dana MOSTI".

In 2015, the scope of MOSTI's pre-commercialisation programme was expanded through the creation of a Facilitation Fund to cover downstream activities which were previously not eligible (MOSTI, 2015).[19] The range of innovation activities was also broadened via the creation of a new MOSTI Social Innovation Fund. As its name suggests, the Social Innovation Fund aims to extend the InnoFund's "Community Innovation Fund" by supporting projects that include social innovation aspects that are usually poorly fit for traditional R&D schemes.

In 2012, the MOHE's and MOSTI's main schemes represented, respectively, about 45% and 34% of the funds allocated via the various R&D schemes, newly created or inherited from the past (Figure 5.5).

In terms of evolution of the overall amounts allocated via the R&D support schemes, the same downward trend as the one observed for MOSTI's ScienceFund and Pre-commercialisation Fund can be observed. The cumulative amounts allocated by the Technology Acquisition Fund, the Biotechnology Commercialisation Fund, the Commercialisation of R&D Fund and the Multimedia Super Corridor R&D Grant Scheme have been halved since 2010, and at least through 2012.[20] One of the few schemes which has significantly increased its activity is the Biotechnology Commercialisation Fund, created in 2011 under the BiotechCorp, which provides loans and grants to facilitate ongoing commercialisation of biotechnology products and services and/or expansion of existing biotechnology business (Figure 5.6).

R&D tax incentives

Soon after its independence, Malaysia used various mixes of restrictions, requirements and incentives to fuel its economic transition. It mostly put in place protective measures (incentives and tariff protection) when implementing its import-substitution strategy at the end of the 1950s. As early as the beginning of the 1960s, these measures were replaced by incentives for export-oriented, labour-intensive, investment, ranging from tax relief to free trade zones. At each of these stages, the government laid specific legal foundations, from the Pioneer Industries

Ordinance of 1958, the Investment Incentive Act of 1968 and the Free Trade Zone Act in 1971 to the Industrial Co-ordination Act in 1975.

Figure 5.5. **Total amount and breakdown of R&D support scheme financing in Malaysia, 2012**

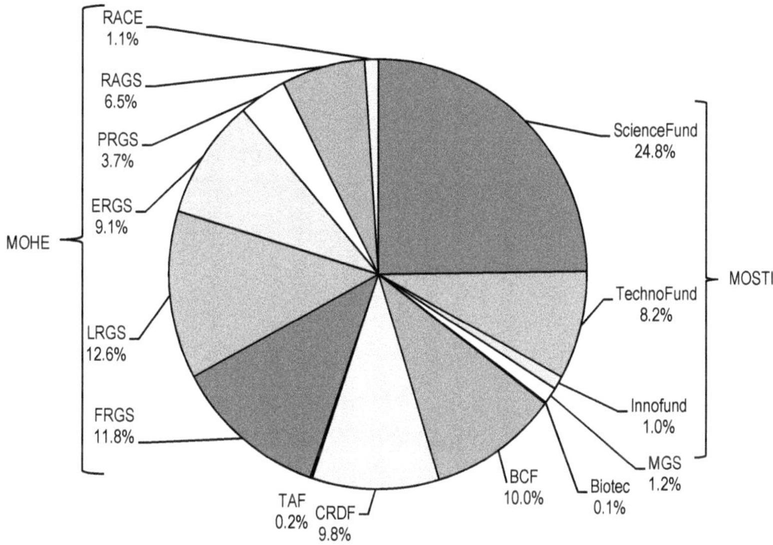

Note: MOHE = Ministry of Higher Education; RACE = Research Acculturation Collaborative Effort; RAGS = Research Acculturation Grant Scheme; PRGS = Prototype Development Grant Scheme; ERGS = Exploratory Research Grant Scheme; LRGS = Long Term Research Grant Scheme; FRGS = Fundamental Research Grant Scheme; TAF = Technology Acquisition Fund; CRDF = Commercialisation of R&D Fund; BCF = Biotechnology Commercialisation Fund; MGS = Multimedia Super Corridor R&D Grant Scheme; MOSTI = Ministry of Science, Technology and Innovation.

Sources: MASTIC (2013), *Malaysian Science & Technology Indicators Report*; MOSTI (2015), "Kemudahan Dana MOSTI"; MOSTI (2012), "R&D funding mechanisms", www.jsps.go.jp/english/asiahorcs/data/meetings/6th/malaysia.pdf.

Figure 5.6. **Total amount allocated by scheme, 2008-12**

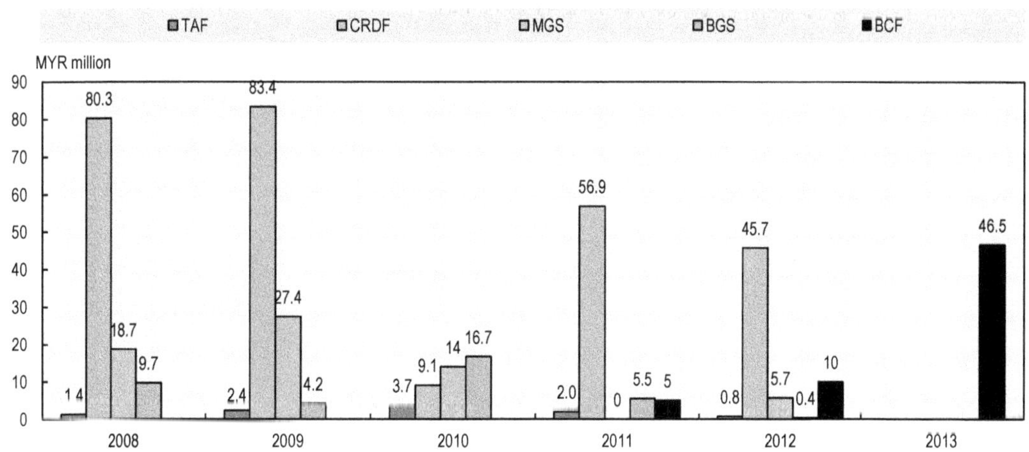

Note: TAF = Technology Acquisition Fund; CRDF = Commercialisation of R&D Fund; MGS = Multimedia Super Corridor R&D Grant Scheme; BGS = Biotechnology Commercialisation Fund; BCF = Biotechnology Commercialisation Fund.

Source: MASTIC (2013), *Malaysian Science & Technology Indicators Report.*

Table 5.7. **Main funding schemes to support research and innovation in Malaysia**

Phase	Ministry	Main support scheme	Main beneficiaries and targets
Basic research	Ministry of Higher Education	Exploratory Research Grant Scheme (ERGS)	Grants for academics for supporting untested ideas, projects in emerging areas, new approaches (up to three years, MYR 100 000 per year)
		Fundamental Research Grant Scheme (FRGS)	Grants to academics for fundamental research (up to three years, MYR 250 000 maximum per project)
		Long Term Research Grant Scheme (LRGS)	Grants to academics for fundamental research that involves extensive scope and longer duration and requires high commitment approaches (up to five years, MYR 3 million per year)
Applied R&D	Ministry of Communications and Multimedia	Creative Industry Development Fund (CIDF-SKMM)	Loans to Malaysian small and medium-sized enterprises (SMEs) for the publication, purchase of assets or other related activities for the commercialisation of local creative industries (MYR 5 million per project)
	Ministry of Health	Ministry of Health Research Grant	Grants to research and development projects whose goal is to improve health and enhance health service delivery according to national and Ministry of Health priorities
	Ministry of Higher Education	Prototype Development Grant Scheme (PRGS)	Grants to public and private institutions' academics whose research output requires prototype development, including proof of concept, evaluation, up-scaling, pre-clinical testing and field testing (up to two years, MYR 500 000 maximum per project)
	Ministry of Science, Technology and Innovation	ScienceFund	Grants for research scientists and engineers from government research institutions, government STI agencies, and public and private institutions of higher learning with accredited research programmes which carry out basic research R&D projects contributing to the discovery of new ideas and the advancement of knowledge in applied sciences, focusing on high impact and innovative research (up to 2.5 years, MYR 500 000 maximum per project)
Pre-commercialisation	Ministry of Finance	Cradle Investment Program Catalyst (CIP Catalyst) – Pre Seed	Conditional grants for entrepreneurs and individuals with innovative, technology-based ideas in the ICT, non-ICT and high growth technology industries (up to one year, MYR 150 000 maximum per application)
		Cradle Seed Venture Fund 1 (CF1)	Funding of early-stage technology start-ups with high growth potential to cultivate an entrepreneurship ecosystem and innovation and stimulate the local economy through job creation (MYR 3 million maximum per company)
		University-CIP Catalyst (U-CIP Catalyst)	Conditional grants for researchers and inventors, private and public universities, colleges, institutes of higher education and commercialisation units with technology-based ideas in the ICT, non-ICT and high growth technology industries (up to one year, MYR 150 000 maximum per application)
	Ministry of Science, Technology and Innovation	Pre-commercialisation Fund (InnoFund)	Funding for micro-business and individuals (Enterprise Innovation Fund) as well as for non-governmental organisations and community groups (Community Innovation Fund) that are involved in the development or improvement of new or existing products, processes or services with elements of innovation (12-18 months, MYR 500 000 maximum per project; MYR 50 000 for individuals)
		Pre-commercialisation Fund (TechnoFund)	Funding to researchers, SMEs, institutions of higher learning, research institutes and STI agencies involved in the development of new technologies, intellectual property registration procedures and R&D outputs commercialisation (up to 30 months, MYR 3 million maximum per application). Priority is given to projects supported by the ScienceFund or those having InnoCert recognition
	Ministry of Communications and Multimedia	Product Development and Commercialisation (PCF)	Funding for Malaysia Status Companies involved in market-driven, innovative product development with high commercial potential and realistic technical and commercial targets (up to 18 months, MYR 750 000 maximum per project)

Table 5.7. **Main funding schemes to support research and innovation in Malaysia** (*continued*)

Phase	Ministry	Main support scheme	Main beneficiaries and targets
Commercialisation	Ministry of Science, Technology and Innovation	Biotechnology Commercialisation Fund (BCF)	Grants for Malaysian BioNexus Status companies to facilitate ongoing commercialisation of biotechnology products and services and expansion of existing biotechnology business (up to six years, MYR 3 million maximum per company)
		Business Growth Fund (BGF)	Follow-on funding that acts as a transition and a bridge from grant to venture capital financing (MYR 4 million maximum per company)
		Business Start-Up Fund (BSF)	Funding for new start-up technology-based companies involved in the creation of new important strategic businesses as well as support for companies within a technology eco-system (up to eight years, including a three-year grace period; MYR 5 million maximum per company)
		Commercialisation of Research and Development Fund (CRDF)	Grants for commercialisation activities of locally developed technologies (by the public sector or R&D companies) undertaken by Malaysian-owned companies (up to two years, MYR 500 000 maximum per company)
		Technology Acquisition Fund (TAF)	Partial grants for Malaysian SMEs to facilitate the acquisition of foreign technologies for immediate incorporation into a company's manufacturing activity (up to two years, MYR 2 million maximum per company)
	Ministry of Finance	Cradle Investment Program Catalyst (CIP 500) – Seed	Conditional grant for budding companies on commercialisation activities (up to one year, MYR 500 000 maximum per company)

Sources: 1DANA (2014), *1DANA Database of Funds, Facilities, Experts and Commercialisation Opportunities* (database), www.1dana.gov.my/search-com.aspx; Ministry of Higher Education and Ministry of Science, Technology and Innovation websites.

As of the mid-1980s, the stronger focus on high value-added activities was reflected in the type of incentives made available to domestic and foreign investors. The 1986 Promotion of Investment Act included provisions for training and R&D. In 1987, the double-deduction on R&D expenditures was introduced. These early incentives, allegedly poorly designed (Rasiah, 2011; Felker and Jomo, 2007; Mani, 2002),[21] mainly subsidised the infrastructure investment of R&D institutions. These two layers of incentives co-existed until 1991, when the tax incentives for exports were phased out, and 1995, when labour-intensive projects were no longer eligible for promotion. On the contrary, additional tax incentives under the Pioneer status were granted for investment in strategic priority industries, in particular high-tech sectors (UNCTAD, 2003). As of 2004, Malaysia was the only Association of Southeast Asian Nations (ASEAN) country, besides Singapore with its "model" for investment promotion policies, to have set specific R&D contingencies (OECD, 2005).[22]

With growing awareness that attracting high-tech industries did not automatically lead to benefits for the Malaysian economy, additional incentives were provided under conditions of domestic sourcing of inputs. Another important evolution was the progressive reduction of the scope and tightening of the requirements of the most generic and generous incentives, in particular those associated with the Pioneer status, as they tended to overshadow the more focused and restrictive R&D tax incentives, and were proven to be biased toward large capital-intensive investment (Rasiah, 2011).

New tax incentives have also been created. There are now specific tax incentives managed by the Multimedia Development Corporation and by the Biotech Corp. More generally, R&D tax incentives have been the traditional reaction of the Malaysian government when considering the below-expectations progress of the country toward the long-awaited knowledge-intensive economy.

The uptake of R&D incentives was slow at the start. By 1991, less than ten companies had received the double-deduction on R&D (Felker and Jomo, 2007). This is in line with the slow growth of R&D activities in private companies, limited by skill shortages rather than financial reasons, and the strategies of MNEs, particularly interested in the low-cost Malaysian labour force rather than in additional tax discounts. It is also rooted in the flexible application of the requirements for benefiting from other more advantageous tax incentives, such as Pioneer status, even after its reform. It is worth noting that R&D requirements have always been voluntary, under the form of positive inducement, providing access to additional tax breaks under certain conditions.

It was only at the beginning of the 2000s that the amount of double-deduction increased drastically (Figure 5.7), peaking in 2006 before falling sharply until 2011, the last year for which data are available.

Despite strong variations from one year to another, applicants are mainly from the IT/electronics and the automobile industry.

The amount of double-deduction on R&D expenditures obtained by companies should also be relativised in comparison to other types of incentives. The amount of deduction granted on export promotion expenditures (overseas advertising, supply of free samples abroad, supply of technical information abroad, etc.) in particular is by far higher (Figure 5.8).

The other types of R&D incentives remain marginal, as shown in Figure 5.10. Only a handful of projects have applied for the specific incentives for companies providing R&D services to other companies in the same group or to external firms. In the absence of further information, the extent to which this is related to the low number of companies providing such services or to the lack of attractiveness of these incentives remains an open question.

Figure 5.7. **Number of projects applying for double-deduction on R&D expenditures and amount of deduction, Malaysia, 1999-2011**

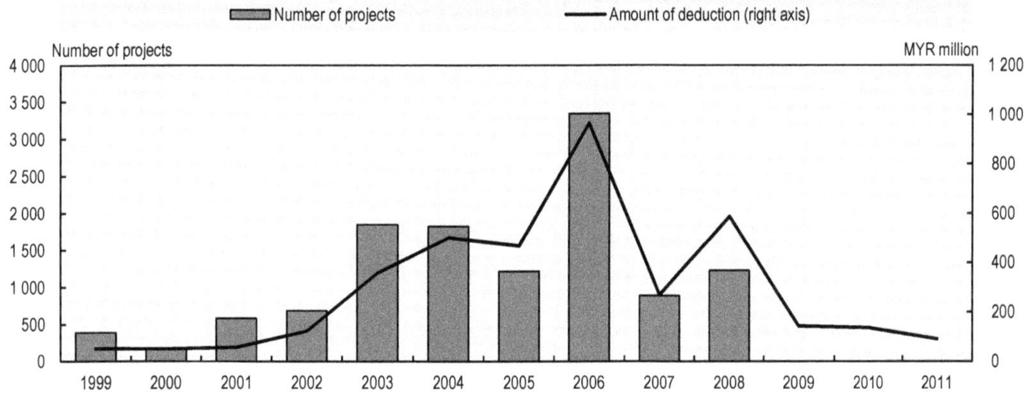

Notes: Data on the number of projects is missing for 2009-11.

Sources: MASTIC (1996, 1998, 2000, 2002, 2004, 2006, 2008, 2010, 2013), *Malaysian Science & Technology Indicators Report.*

Figure 5.8. **Number of applicants for double-deduction on R&D expenditures and export promotion, Malaysia, 2000-06**

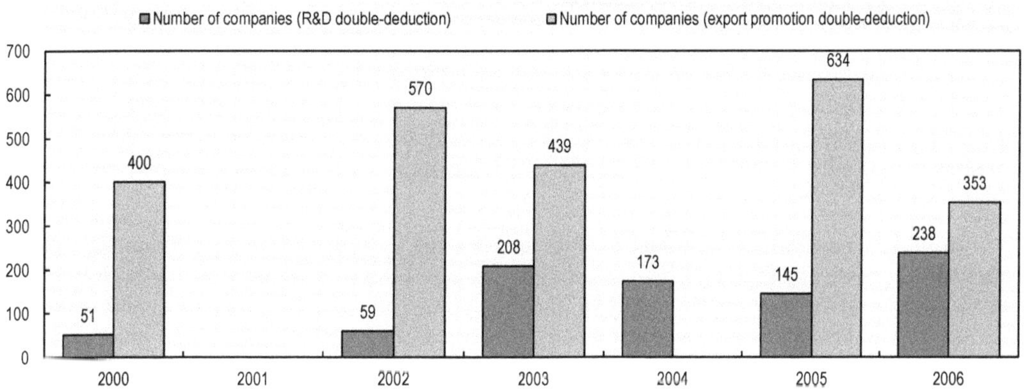

Sources: MASTIC (1996, 1998, 2000, 2002, 2004, 2006, 2008, 2010, 2013), *Malaysian Science & Technology Indicators Report.*

Figure 5.9. **Number of R&D projects by type of R&D incentives, Malaysia**

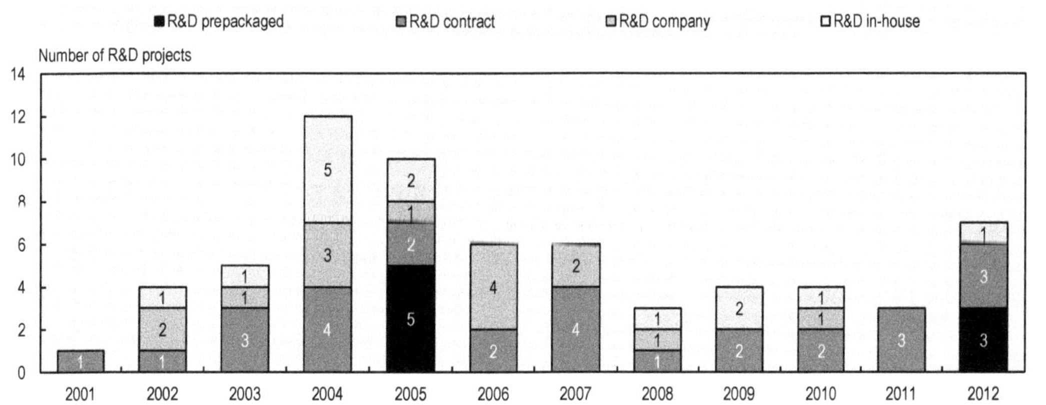

Sources: MASTIC (2008, 2010, 2013), *Malaysian Science & Technology Indicators Report.*

A recent review of Malaysia's investment policy recommended that the Malaysian Investment Development Authority's incentives be better targeted and subject to public review and reappraisal (OECD, 2013b). This could be beneficial to both the double-deduction on R&D expenditures, whose number of applicants has drastically decreased according to the latest figures available from MASTIC, and the specific schemes for R&D (contract) companies, which never took off. Other relevant recommendations from that review are presented in Box 5.5.

Box 5.5. Summary of recommendations on investment promotion and facilitation from the 2013 *OECD Investment Policy Review of Malaysia*

Enhance the Malaysian Investment Development Authority (MIDA)'s role as the government's interface with the private sector. Although MIDA is internationally recognised as an effective investment promotion agency, particularly for investors at the establishment phase, its after-care services for established investors could be enhanced in a period when the government aims to increase reinvestment and expansion by established investors.

Expand key performance indicators (KPIs) to include the impact of investment on Malaysia's economy. MIDA may consider adjusting its KPIs to support the government's objective to move the economy further up the value chain by producing more sophisticated and high-end technology products. KPIs should go beyond target investment volumes and include an evaluation of the impact of investment. KPIs could also be expanded to include the developmental effects of investment.

Undertake a cost-benefit analysis of investment incentives. Despite the efficiency with which MIDA disburses incentives, incentives could be more targeted and should be subject to adequate public review and reappraisal. Their benefits should be considered with regards to their budgetary and other costs. One estimate of forgone revenue in the 1980s amounted to 1.7% of GDP.

Improve co-operation between business and institutes of higher learning to address skills shortages. Closer collaboration between industry and institutes of higher learning on R&D and curriculum development could improve the alignment of training provisions and industry demands. The Penang Skills Development Centre could be considered as a good practice to be emulated elsewhere in the country.

Source: OECD (2013b), *OECD Investment Policy Reviews: Malaysia 2013*, http://dx.doi.org/10.1787/9789264194588-en.

Special support to industry and services

Support to innovation in small and medium-sized enterprises

The diversity of small and medium-sized enterprises' support schemes

As previously mentioned, the contribution of Malaysian SMEs to the country's economy remains small, in absolute terms and even more so relative to their share of the total number of business firms. Against this backdrop, the government has long been intervening to eliminate the bottlenecks that hinder the development of SMEs, in particular when it comes to engaging in innovation activities that would allow them to access high value-added international markets.

The history of the support to SMEs closely follows the various stages of Malaysian industrial and innovation policies: from protection of domestic markets and export promotion in the early years, new schemes introduced in the 1990s and 2000s increasingly focused on the improvement of SMEs' innovation capabilities. Early support to SMEs' technological level used the Vendor Development Programme to develop their linkages to MNEs, as a way to both learn from their higher level of capabilities – technological, managerial and others – and find a "shortcut" to global value chains (see below). The trend toward the "deepening" of tax incentives through local content requirements also automatically favoured SMEs since they represent the bulk of domestic companies. A dedicated agency was created in 1996 – the Small and Medium Industries Development Corporation (SMIDEC) – to support the development of SMEs. It intervened mainly through matching grants for development projects, capacity-building programmes, fiscal and non-fiscal incentives, linkages between SMEs and MNEs, and technical and advisory support services (SME Corporation, 2006).

The government has also launched a number of reforms to ensure a regulatory and institutional framework conducive to entrepreneurship and SME development. These efforts have been successful to a significant extent, as can been seen from the position of Malaysia in the international ranking for doing business.[23]

Like in other policy areas, the government has developed a more comprehensive and increasingly holistic approach with the multiplication of specific, tailor-made schemes to respond to the specific challenges faced by SMEs, including low technological capabilities, lack of skills and knowledge, weak ICT literacy, low awareness of innovation and R&D support schemes, limited self-financing capacity and difficult access to external finance, etc.

The main policy actor is the dedicated agency, SME Corporation, created in 2009, which operates a vast array of SME support schemes covering the main needs of SMEs (Table 5.8). Several other agencies, most of them represented in the National SME Development via their parent ministry, are involved in SME innovation-led development programmes. Three are under the Prime Minister's Office or department: the Unit Inovasi Khas' mandate includes assistance to SMEs in innovating and introducing new technologies. The National Innovation Agency of Malaysia also has a few programmes which partially or mainly address SME innovation processes. As for its subsidiary, PlaTCOM, it was conceived as a "one-stop shop for commercialisation of local IPs for SMEs" (AIM, 2014). Its capacity remains limited, however (OECD, 2015a). MIGHT and the National Innovation Agency of Malaysia's sectoral strategies and technology roadmaps usually strive to identify specific niches for SMEs and devise an upgrading trajectory, such as the Biomass Action Plan, which aimed to mobilise the participation of Malaysian SMEs along the biomass value chain (MIGHT, 2009). Other agencies not entrusted with innovation-related policy fields can also indirectly strengthen SME innovation capabilities through their interventions. This is the case, for instance, of the Malaysia External Trade Development Corporation, which implemented one of the Masterplan HIPs, the Go-Ex programme, to support SMEs willing to enter into new products or new markets.[24]

Most of the recent initiatives feature in the SME Masterplan 2012-2020, which aims to create the conditions for innovation-led and productivity-driven growth of SMEs. It has set ambitious targets to be met by 2020 in terms of SME share of GDP (41%), employment (62%) and exports (25%). Precisely, the masterplan is composed of 32 initiatives, including 6 high-impact programmes: 1) a business registration and licensing scheme to provide a single window for business registration; 2) a technology commercialisation platform to promote innovation; 3) a programme (Go-Ex) to support new exporter SMEs; 4) a capacity-building programme (Catalyst) to assist SMEs to become world-class players; 5) an inclusive innovation programme to empower the bottom 40% through innovation; and 6) an SME Investment Partner scheme to provide early-stage financing. By 2014, all of these projects with the exception of the last had been implemented (SME Corporation, 2014; OECD, 2016a).

Table 5.8. **Main support schemes for small and medium-sized enterprises in Malaysia**

Strategic framework	Measures/schemes/incentives	Modalities
Human capital development[1]		
Economic Planning Unit	Services Sector Blueprint	Action plan focused on services sector development through enhancement of existing programmes and new initiatives developed in compliance with the best global practices so as to increase the number of service providers and broaden their reach
SME Corporation	Skills Upgrading Programme	Enhance SME employees in technical and managerial capabilities such as financial, quality management and business management
	SME @ University	Provide a structured learning opportunity for CEOs of the new and existing SMEs based on the Training Model of Japan SME University to help them develop human capital capable of driving diverse management innovation and creativity in developing business
	SME-University Internship Programme	Facilitate and upgrade SMEs' performance towards including business processes, productivity and financial performance while the students are further nurtured with knowledge related to entrepreneurship
	SME Mentoring Programme	Enhance SMEs' knowledge in production, sales and marketing and halal-related matters for the food and beverage industry through sharing Nestlé's best practices
Pembangunan Sumber Manusia Berhad (PSMB)	SME Training Needs Analysis Consultancy Scheme	Assist SMEs in identifying current and future training needs on a systematic basis, resulting in the preparation and implementation of an annual training plan
Access to research and innovation		
SME Masterplan (SME Corporation)	Business Accelerator Programme (BAP)	Business and technical advice to SMEs on how to strengthen and enhance their business, improve their capacity and facilitate access to financing
	Enrichment and Enhancement (E^2)	Business and technical advice to micro enterprises on how to strengthen and enhance their business, improve their capacity and facilitate access to financing
	Catalyst Programme	Targeted approach with total support to companies with high growth potential: development of growth strategy; build internal capability; grow market; access to experts
	Green LED Programme	Provides funding for the development or improvement of commercially viable solid-state lighting products, and provides partial/matching grant for purchasing or improvements in manufacturing equipment, testing, processes or monitoring techniques, to obtain international certifications
National Innovation Agency of Malaysia (AIM)	Technology Commercialisation Platform (PlatTCOM)	Acts as commercialisation one-stop shop for SMEs: commercialisation, intellectual property and legal, capacity-building services, technology scouting, validation and verification
	Steinbeis Foundation Malaysia	Provides a network of consultants from academia to support industry projects; creates transfer centres between industry and academia; identifies industry needs
Ministry of Education (MOE)	Public-Private Research Network	A platform for academia-industry communication that also co-finances development costs
ICT literacy		
SME Corp	Enabling e-Payment for SMEs and Micro Enterprises	Providing easier access to affordable terminals and readers, integrated with e-commerce solutions, to increase the offer of e-payment services
Promotion of SME-MNE linkages		
Ministry of International Trade and Development	Vendor Development Programme (VDP)	Aims to develop SMEs to become competitive suppliers and manufacturers of component/services in domestic and global markets
Economic Transformation Programme (NKEA Business Services)	Developing SMEs in the Global Aerospace Manufacturing Industry (EPP8)	Supports SMEs to become the major distributor for leading global aerospace companies (certification, capacity building, etc.)
Services Sector Blueprint (MATRADE)	Large Corporation-SME partnership programme (2015)	Procurement of SME services by large corporations

Table 5.8. **Main support schemes for small and medium-sized enterprises in Malaysia** (*continued*)

Strategic framework	Measures/schemes/incentives	Modalities
Certification and branding		
SME Corporation	1-InnoCert certification programme	Identifies and accelerates the growth of innovative SMEs through certification and incentives to encourage entrepreneurs to engage in innovation
	SME Competitiveness Rating for Enhancement (SCORE)	Diagnostic tool which assigns star ratings to indicate the performance level of SMEs based on seven assessment criteria, such as financial strength, business performance, human resources, technology acquisition and adoption, certification and market presence
	Micro Enterprise Competitiveness Rating for Enhancement (M-CORE)	Simplified version of SCORE that identifies the performance of micro enterprises in four areas: business performance, financial capability, operation and management
SME Corporation and Deloitte Malaysia	Enterprise 50	Every year selects 50 enterprises based on key financial and non-financial factors. The companies get publicity in both the print and electronic media
Access to/development of markets		
SME Corporation	National Mark of Malaysian Brand	Certification scheme that promotes the development of Malaysian brands to meet global quality standards and compete on a global market
	Branding and Packaging Mobile Gallery	Increase the awareness of rural SMEs on the importance of branding and packaging and provision of trainings and workshops on these topics
Malaysia External Trade Development Corporation (MATRADE)	Go-Ex Programme	Direct advice from experts (market advisors and market linkers to SMEs), information on competitors to improve SMEs' export performance
Access to financing		
SME Corporation	*Shari'ah*-compliant SME Financing Scheme	Financial assistance to eligible Malaysian SMEs by participating financial institutions (13 Islamic banks)
	Soft loan for SMEs	Scheme that assists the promotion of the development of existing as well as new start-up SMEs in project, fixed assets and working capital financing
	SME Emergency Fund	Grants or loans to SMEs in case of flood, drought, beach erosion and landslide
Specific support to start ups and entrepreneurship		
Science Advisor to the Prime Minister	Malaysian Industry-Government Group for High Technology (MIGHT)	Consensus-building think tank; main platform for private-public sector co-operation through membership programme; high-tech industries maintenance via catalytic interventions programmes
Ministry of Finance (MOF)	Malaysian Global Innovation and Creativity Centre (MaGIC)	Platform for entrepreneurs to easily connect and share ideas and solutions with each other; academy for start-up education; seed accelerator programmes; success stories exposure
National Innovation Agency of Malaysia (AIM)	Mid-Tier Companies (MTCs) programme	Co-operation with high potential mid-tier companies to catalyse innovation-led growth in these companies
Venture capital		
Multimedia Development Corporation	Niche Acceleration Programme (Multimedia Development Corporation)	Accelerator programmes for entrepreneurs in specific niche areas: games, big data, Internet of Things
	Global linkages (Multimedia Development Corporation)	Platform to accelerate high-growth start-ups by linking them to the global start-up ecosystem (experts, mentors, companies, etc.)

Note: Only STI-related schemes and programmes targeting specifically or preferentially SMEs are reported in this table.

1. Other human capital development frameworks can be found at: www.smecorp.gov.my/index.php/en/programmes/2015-12-21-10-16-28/human-capital-development.

Sources: SME Corporation, Standards Malaysia, Ministry of International Trade and Development and Ministry of Education websites.

One new initiative, Steinbeis Foundation Malaysia, was launched in 2013 by the National Innovation Agency of Malaysia in collaboration with Steinbeis Foundation Germany. It is a platform through which SMEs facing specific technical and market issues can identify and interact with the relevant experts in various "transfer centres", mainly in academia. In 2015, the foundation had established partnerships with 79 public and private HEIs and 16 research institutes. The foundation acts as a broker, identifying both the needs and the relevant experts, and assists the commercial arrangement. It can also finance the SME via the Steinbeis Innovation Voucher system, a matching innovation grant for locally owned SMEs that require financial assistance to resolve their industrial problems or necessitate assistance from Steinbeis's pool of consultants from academia.

The Public-Private Research Network launched in 2015 by the Ministry of Education in collaboration with the Malaysian Technology Development Corporation and SME Corporation is a complementary programme that matches companies with researchers that can solve their specific technological problems. The contractual arrangement is partly funded by the government via the university research funding and by the company.

Given their prominence in this sector, the Services Sector Blueprint launched in 2015 also comprises several initiatives aimed at SMEs, such as the Business Accelerator Programme, which provides qualitative assistance to SMEs to support their development, or the Soft Loan Scheme for Automation and Modernisation of SMEs (EPU, 2015b).

To these programmes should also be added the schemes that give SMEs access to finance for their generic business operations (credit guarantee schemes, debt resolution mechanisms, soft loan schemes, etc.). These schemes are administered by various institutions, notably the Malaysian Industrial Development Finance Corporation (an agency of the Ministry of International Trade and Industry) and the SME Bank (SME standard banking and advisory services).

Several entry point projects (EPPs) in the Government Transformation Programme also specifically target the upgrade of SMEs, notably in the E&E and business services NKEAs. The business services EPP 8, "Developing SMEs in the global aerospace manufacturing industry", aims, as its name suggests, to create an ecosystem of dynamic manufacturing SMEs in the aerospace industry. It implements actions to facilitate the certification of SMEs so that they can become suppliers of higher added value components to the aerospace leaders. The E&E EPP 10, "Creating local solid state lighting champions", also undertakes business development programmes and grant facilitation programmes for equipment and certification of ten SMEs in the Malaysian LED Consortium (MLC). The E&E EPP 11, "Building a test and measurement hub", is also often mentioned as an example of a project that has allowed SMEs to research and develop higher value products (PEMANDU, 2014).

Co-ordination of the SME policy

The multiplication of SME support schemes has called for a significant co-ordination effort. The multiple challenges faced by SMEs are interrelated and self-reinforcing, and it is key to address them in a coherent way. The abundant literature on SMEs and innovation has demonstrated that although this holds true for all domains of policy intervention, it is especially needed for SMEs, which do not always have the necessary capabilities – either the time or willingness – to integrate internally the different schemes they benefit from into a consistent development strategy.

An important step taken by the government to improve policy coherence in this area was the establishment of the National SME Development Council in 2004. This council is mandated to formulate long-term strategies and policy direction for SME development and ensure more co-ordinated efforts and effective implementation of overall SME development programmes. It is chaired by the Prime Minister and comprised of 13 ministers as well as other high-level policy makers.[25] One of the key decisions taken by this council was to establish SME Corporation as the central co-ordinating agency for SME development (and as its secretary division) in 2009. The contact points of SME Corporation are notably the special SME unit established in each of the ministries and agencies involved in SME development.

This clear institutional infrastructure made of a well-connected, high-level body and a central agency was instrumental in developing the aforementioned SME Masterplan in 2012 and in ensuring its legitimacy and effectiveness. It is particularly noteworthy that the SME Masterplan is still the reference framework in the Eleventh Malaysia Plan focus area "Growing dynamic SMEs" (EPU, 2015a). The National SME Development Council has spearheaded other actions, such as the change of the definition of SMEs, the centralisation of training programmes,[26] the launch of additional schemes and the monitoring of the implementation of the SME Masterplan (Hashim, 2015).

The assessment of the strengths and weaknesses of such a comprehensive portfolio of instruments is beyond the scope of the current review. Table 5.8 shows that all the possible challenge areas of SMEs are covered by at least one dedicated support scheme. The institutional setting for the co-ordination of this vast array of instruments also seems well in place with the National SME Development Council and SME Corporation. The ERIA-OECD SME Policy Index shows that Malaysia's SME policy is, in all policy dimensions, ahead of most other ASEAN countries (Figure 5.10) with the exception of Singapore. The gap with the ASEAN average is the greatest for support to technology acquisition and transfer, since Malaysia has implemented well-constructed innovation policies and programmes to facilitate SMEs to embark on R&D&I activities. However, there is still room for the government to introduce and manage new promotional activities to stimulate technological upgrading, especially in the service sector (ERIA-OECD, 2014).

Figure 5.10. **SME Policy Index, all policy dimensions, Malaysia and ASEAN**

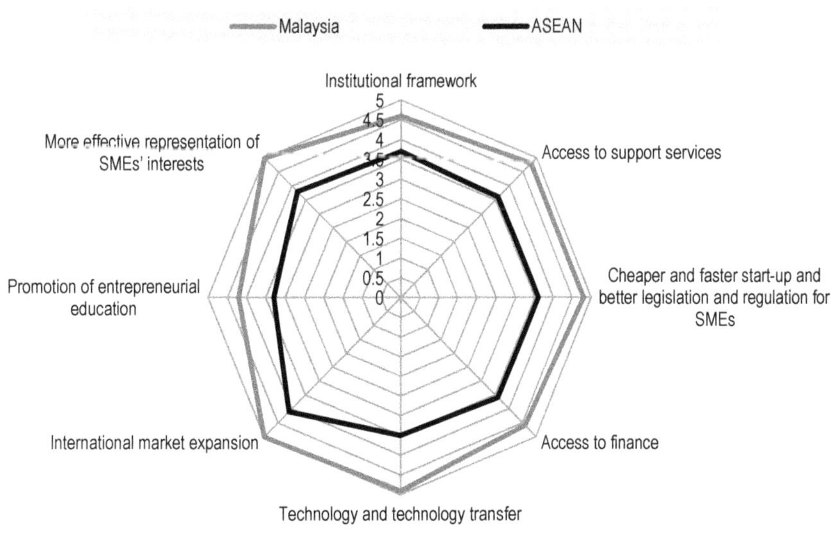

Note: The policy assessment in the SME Policy Index is conducted by an independent research team from each AMS through a questionnaire survey and in-depth interviews. All indicators are measured on 5 "levels" of policy development. Level 1 is the weakest level and level 5 the strongest.

Source: ERIA and OECD (2014), *ASEAN SME Policy Index 2014 Towards Competitive and Innovative ASEAN SMEs*, www.eria.org/publications/research_project_reports/FY2012-no.8.html.

The results for the institutional framework confirm that the Malaysian co-ordination infrastructure, with the National SME Development Council at its core, and the delivery mechanisms spearheaded by SME Corporation, are ahead of its ASEAN counterparts (Figure 5.11).

The results of this scoreboard are also consistent with the weakness in policy evaluation in Malaysia that was mentioned above. The absence of an evaluation and monitoring report, besides the SME Corporation's annual report, is emphasised. Too often the monitoring of programmes is limited to the analysis of the extent to which money is spent, with no consideration for the programme's potential impacts.

Support to low innovation capability firms

One area of uncertainty remains the support to SMEs that do no or only little innovation. In a country like Malaysia, these represent a vast untapped potential to mobilise. To the lack of knowledge and capability, and hence very limited absorption capacity, should be added the presumption that none is needed (Arnold and Thuriaux, 1997). One step higher in Arnold and Thuriaux's taxonomy of SMEs, firms have minimum technological capability. The gap with academia is such for these SMEs that no interaction is possible. Without specific hands-on support based on proximity and mid- to long-term commitment, these companies are bound to reproduce the same activity, which puts them in danger of a change of context. As rightly put by the authors, progress in policy depends not only on finding the right economic levers, but on closer engagement with firms and technological practice.

Figure 5.11. **SME Policy Index, institutional framework**

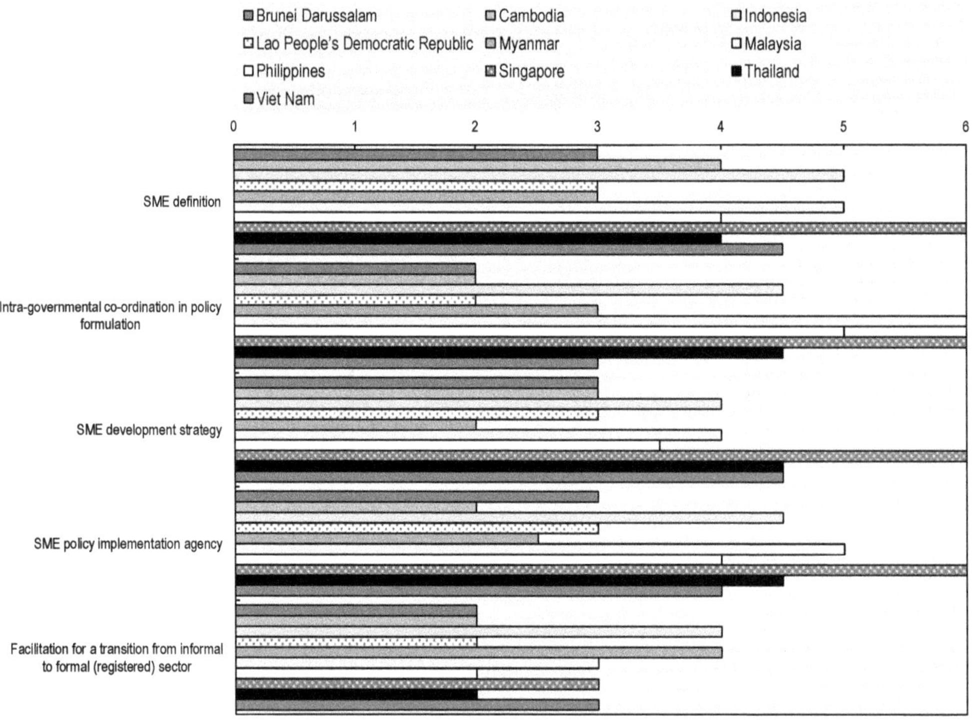

Source: ERIA and OECD (2014), *ASEAN SME Policy Index 2014 Towards Competitive and Innovative ASEAN SMEs*, www.eria.org/publications/research_project_reports/FY2012-no.8.html.

Figure 5.12. **"Staircase" for developing company capabilities**

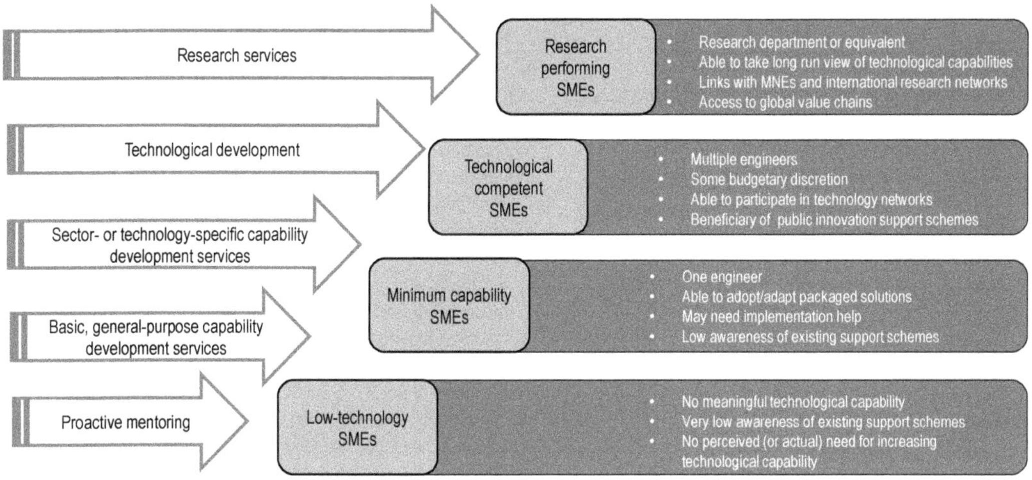

Source: Adapted from Arnold and Thuriaux (1997), "Developing firms' technological capabilities".

The Steinbeis Foundation and the Public Private Research Network are certainly important steps toward providing local and tailored – on demand – support to SMEs facing bottlenecks and linking them to academia. The risk of such initiatives is to be limited to facilitating specific transactions and projects between companies and academic consultants. It is not clear how "virtual" these programmes are, i.e. whether there is a structure, staffed with dedicated and competent personnel, or whether it is mainly an "elaborate database" with motivated academics turned to the cause of industry support.

The lack of learning capabilities and awareness of SMEs positioned at the bottom of the "staircase" (Figure 5.12) calls for "local innovation centres" to undertake some public mission background work, in addition to supporting specific firms in their innovation and improvement projects (including assisting in contractual arrangements with external experts). This public mission, carried out by experienced local staff of the centres, consists mainly in promoting innovation in a broad sense, providing information on the available schemes, liaising on an ongoing basis with companies and academia, etc. The overarching mandate of these permanent organisations should not be technology transfer from universities to firms but the enhancement of firms' absorptive capacities and learning abilities as a core determinant of innovation performance at firm level. In fact, the two dimensions, although distinct if only for the sake of sound budgeting, co-exist in the structure, i.e. the public mission background work and the project-based support to individual SMEs or group of SMEs (Table 5.9). The scope of such an organisation is defined by the areas of specialisation of the local HEIs that provide the resources and the local industrial structure. Although their focus is mainly on the respective territories where they are located, in particular for the background work mentioned above, they should be networked to multiply the opportunities of matching supply and competence needs.

Different models exist, from the various types of regional innovation agencies (OECD, 2011) to the range of technology extension service organisations. While at this stage the regional innovation agencies seem far beyond what is needed in Malaysia and might result in additional governance issues, the technology extension services gather all of the requirements to bolster innovation capabilities in SMEs with low innovation capability firms (Box 5.6).[27]

Table 5.9. **The twofold mission of local innovation centres in Malaysia**

Public mission background work	Specific support to SMEs or groups of SMEs/joint projects
– Provision of information on opportunities for improvement in existing technologies, best practices, international trends, relevant regulations, business networks, opportunities to become government suppliers and other support to contractual arrangements – Awareness raising – General capability building – Stimulation and/or running of networks and clusters – Node for local/regional partnership – Promotion of internationalisation, promotion of foreign investors – Facilitator for sharing scientific and technical equipment – Maintenance of database of experts	– Benchmarking of companies in the industry at the national and international levels to gauge performance level – Technical assistance and consulting in the context of innovation/improvement projects designed individually for interested companies (including identification of needs) – Training of plant and administrative staff for the effective use of technologies more advanced than those previously used by the company – Provision of services to a group or network of companies with common needs and challenges that are not directly related to competition among them – Joint projects of companies and public and academic laboratories for solving specific problems associated with the companies' products or processes – Advice on developing new strategies for the company and assistance in diagnosing and managing impending changes during implementation

Sources: Adapted from OECD (2011), "Maximising the impact of regional innovation agencies, http://dx.doi.org/10.1787/9789264097803-9-en; Rogers (2013), "Technology extension services".

Support to knowledge-intensive services

The Service Sector Blueprint launched in 2015 plans a wide range of actions to develop services and support their shift to knowledge-intensive services on four main axes: 1) internationalisation; 2) capital development; 3) investment; and 4) governance (EPU, 2015b). These actions have been integrated in the Eleventh Malaysia Plan, with a particular emphasis on facilitating the shift towards knowledge-intensive services whose contribution to GDP is targeted to rise from 36% in 2014 to 40% in 2020 (EPU, 2015a). The Eleventh Malaysia Plan also built upon the Service Sector Blueprint to derive specific strategies in key service sectors.[28]

Box 5.6. **Technology extension services**

Technology extension services (TES) are organisations focused on direct support to local firms.

Given the low level of awareness of small and medium-sized enterprises (SMEs), including with regards to threats and opportunities, extension services must be proactive in suggesting, promoting before providing support, hence the synergies with the public mission background work (information, awareness raising, training, stimulation) that takes place outside any specific contractual arrangement.

Once a project is initiated, either by the SME looking for help or by TES staff visiting the firms and communicating about the upgrading opportunities, a field engineer is assigned to follow the different steps: assessment of the state of operation of the company's production processes and their results; preparation of an improvement plan; assistance in implementing the improvement plan.

The cost of extension services are covered by three main sources:

- the government pays for structural costs of the TES and the public mission background work

Box 5.6. Technology extension services (*continued*)

- the first step of projects (review and diagnosis) is also usually subsidised, possibly by a system of vouchers
- the beneficiary auto-finances part of the cost of the project.

International experience suggests that the following principles should be adhered to when implementing a national technology extension service:

- The TES should be capable of providing guidance, service quality control and analysis of results of activities and services offered at regional and local levels. The TES should therefore be staffed with experts who are familiar with SMEs and the delivery of industrial extension services. It is likely that most academic researchers will not fit the purpose. Forcing academic researchers to be more relevant to industry by changing their incentives has failed in many countries. They can, and should, be part of the TES environment but cannot be the core field engineers. The ideal candidates must have knowledge of technology and of the business environment of companies, as well as the ability to communicate in interpersonal relationships, since extension services are rendered by means of direct, face-to-face interaction with company leaders and employees.
- The desired impacts of the TES should be achieved by leveraging local and regional resources through wide participation of and collaboration with all sectors of industry.
- The TES should have the analytical capacity to study demand and monitor implementation and assessments at all levels.
- It should have sufficient administrative flexibility to link with the programmes of other agencies and integrate the technology extension programme into the broader (national) innovation policy framework
- It should be demand-oriented and results-oriented in its entire operation.
- Evaluation of programme performance and its impact should be systematised.

It is recommended to start with a pilot project, with some modularity in the implementation of programme components to assess the most promising combinations before taking on the large-scale programme.

Examples of TES are, for instance, the Japanese technology service centres (offer a specific menu of services in every prefecture), the Canadian Industrial Research Assistance Program (makes field engineers available in every province), the Manufacturing Extension Partnership in the United States (supports centres in every state), productivity promotion centres in China (2 200 public productivity promotion centres across the country assisting SMEs), the French *Réseaux de développement technologique* (structuring industries, strengthening SME performance, attracting foreign investors, in every region).

Source: Rogers (2013), "Technology extension services".

These actions address the whole range of factors that traditionally hinder the development and upgrading of services (see above) as well as more generally the limitations of SMEs that account for the bulk of service providers. New initiatives aimed particularly at supporting knowledge-intensive services, and therefore also in most cases high-tech manufacturing, include, for instance, large corporation-SME partnership programmes to enhance synergies between the client and providers of specialised services, training programmes in SMEs or a dedicated research incentive scheme.

The Eleventh Malaysia Plan also features a few initiatives to create a favourable environment for the development of knowledge-intensive services, in particular the provision of necessary skills (co-funded scholarship programme between the government and SMEs) and the creation of a dedicated body to professionalise the ICT industry.

Although Malaysia made significant efforts to liberalise the service sectors during the Tenth Malaysia Plan, important barriers remain.[29] Increasing the level of education and skills both in services and client industries is also essential as it is a key condition of their positive synergies. Although Malaysia is one of the Southeast Asian countries where these services are the most developed, further efforts will be critical to its future productivity and growth performance (OECD, 2014). In the service sector, as is the case in industry, the multiplicity of relevant ministries and agencies and the lack of co-ordination between them has been detrimental to the development of services and their upgrade to knowledge-intensive segments. It has led to weak policy coherence, overlaps between initiatives and a complex landscape that hinders investment. The inadequate structure of incentives has also hampered the shift to modern services by favouring investment in capital rather than in knowledge in services (EPU, 2015a).

Support to upgrading domestic firms' innovation capabilities through linkages with multinational enterprises

Technology transfer from the early foreign investment projects of the 1970s and 1980s to domestic firms was negligible (Jomo, 2003). Apart from specific cases like the automobile industry, where the government intervened directly, the local content of manufacturing by domestic firms was still low at the beginning of the 1990s – even by Southeast Asian standards. As previously mentioned, the conditioning of R&D incentives to R&D and/or local content was implemented rather loosely and consequently had a limited impact on the "deepening" of FDI.

Since the end of the 1980s and especially in the 1990s, the Malaysian government has decided to play a new more "hands-on" role, promoting and assisting the linkages between its SMEs and MNEs to such an extent that Malaysia is now frequently cited with regards to best practices in the promotion of business linkages between local enterprises and MNEs. These efforts have been beneficial for instance in the automobile industry. Although this industry always had strong technological linkages with multinationals, about 70% of the automobile parts are currently supplied by domestic SMEs.

Beginning in the 1980s, the Malaysian government has introduced a number of initiatives in manufacturing to create greater linkages and integration between SMEs and the MNEs that located their facilities in Malaysia. That was first the case with the Subcontractor Exchange Program, which was launched in 1988 to match local firms with multinational companies.

The first Vendor Development Program (VDP) was introduced the same year, initially to encourage Malaysian infant MNEs to foster local firms' capabilities to become their suppliers of goods and services (Rasiah, 2006). This first VDP was associated with the national car project Proton, with significant results.[30] The programme was then extended to the electronics industry and by the mid-1990s made available to a wider range of Malaysian companies. PETRONAS introduced its first VDP in 1994 with the objective of creating competitive local companies in oil and gas-related manufacturing and medium and high technology technical services.[31] Malaysia's VDPs also acted as an instrument for contributing to national development and social equity goals, as they aimed to help *Bumiputera*-owned[32] SMEs in particular. Because it did not address some of the supply capacity weaknesses of the SMEs that participated in the programme, this first experiment had only limited success (OECD, 2013b).

Subsequent programmes benefited from the VDP experience and put more emphasis on strengthening the learning capabilities of SMEs. The Ministry of International Trade and Industry's Industrial Linkage Programme was a relaunch of the VDP, in 1996, which by this time had come to encompass foreign-owned as well as Malaysian-owned MNEs as buyers of indigenous firms' goods and services (Jomo, 2003). Under the Industrial Linkage Programme, both large buyers and small local vendors benefited from income tax reductions when they contributed to improving the production and service quality of local vendors. As of 2007, 906 SMEs were registered under the Industrial Linkage Programme, with 128 supplying MNEs or large companies. However, here also, the programme confronted several problems, including the lack of adequate expertise from the implementing agency (SMIDEC, later to become SME Corporation) (Jomo, 2003). More successful experiments – albeit with a more limited scope – of industrial linkage programmes were implemented in the semiconductor sector in Penang, with the Penang Development Corporation playing a key enabling role (Rasiah, 2006).

The Vendor Development Programme and Industrial Linkage Programme remain Malaysia's most important development measures linking SMEs and MNEs (OECD, 2013b). Recently, in the framework of the Services Sector Blueprint (EPU, 2015b), a new partnership programme was launched by the Malaysia External Trade Development Corporation to increase the export of the services sector and its contribution to the national economy. Under the partnership arrangement between large corporations and SMEs, the latter benefit in terms of knowledge transfer, capacity building and international exposure (MATRADE, 2015).

However, international experiences show that successful programmes follow a more hands-on approach, whereby SMEs are supported throughout the whole process of learning and transfers. This support is not only financial, but also non-financial, following a well-structured partnership approach involving the three main stakeholders of these initiatives, i.e. MNEs, SMEs and the state. The Chilean Supplier Development Programme has been very successful in this regard (Box 5.7). It has strengthened the productive capabilities of SMEs in Chile and their integration into global markets and has inspired other similar initiatives in Colombia, El Salvador, Mexico and Uruguay.

Another means to support linkage creation is by training suppliers and potential suppliers according to MNEs' needs and standards. The Penang Skills Development Centre is an example of a dedicated enterprise support centre which has adopted this approach. The Penang Skills Development Centre is a public-private partnership involving major Malaysian companies, MNEs, universities and the Malaysian government. A key focus of the centre's several hundred courses is to facilitate more effective business linkages between its member companies and their suppliers. The Penang Skills Development Centre's Global Supplier Development Programme serves to upgrade the core competencies, technologies and systems of small local enterprises through a combination of training, coaching, mentoring and business linkages with large multinational corporations (UNIDO and Harvard University, 2007). It also supplies high-end shared services facilities and promotes design and development activities to meet the current needs of industry.

Box 5.7. Key features of the Chilean Supplier Development Programme

By subsidising the cost of services such as improvement in management, professional advice, training of personnel, technical assistance and technology transfer, the Chilean government has encouraged small and medium-sized enterprises (SMEs) to formally associate with large firms' clients (buyers) and through such links take steps to improve their competitiveness and stabilise commercial linkages. Implemented by the Chilean Economic Development Agency (CORFO) since 1998, the programme was motivated by the trade agreements signed by Chile that created the need for compliance with international production standards by Chilean exporters and potential exporters. Key features of this programme include the following:

- Each project must include at least 20 SMEs in the agriculture and forestry industry, or a minimum of 110 SMEs in other economic sectors such as manufacturing, industrial services or others. There is also a limit for SMEs' net annual sales.
- The programme consists of two stages: 1) assessment of suppliers (baseline definition and programme of intervention with precise objectives for improvement); 2) intervention (up to three years) following the action plan, co-financed by demanding company and suppliers.
- Once the "sponsor firm" (large firm) approaches an intermediary agent who helps prepare the project, the firm can present its project to a CORFO regional bureau.
- CORFO pays up to 50% of the costs of the assessment and development plan (first stage), with a ceiling of USD 16 000 (data from August 2010). Then, CORFO pays up to 50% of the costs of the project implementation (second stage), with annual ceilings of USD 110 000 (USD 5 000 per supplier firm).
- The first stage lasts up to six months after the signing of a contract and aims to identify areas of intervention that the sponsor wishes to develop with its suppliers. Implementation of the development plan can last up to three years. Renewal of the project for an additional year is subject to evaluation of implementation progress.

An evaluation carried out in 2011 on the basis of 439 projects (representing 271 "sponsor" firms and 8 828 supplier firms) showed that the Supplier Development Programme has been very successful in strengthening the productive capabilities of SMEs in Chile and their integration into global markets:

- The programme had a positive effect on employment, sales and the sustainability of the SME suppliers. It also benefited both supplier and sponsor firms (large firm customers).
- In the case of suppliers in the agribusiness sector, the programme helped increase sales and employment, and positively affected their survival. As for sponsor firms, the programme contributed by increasing sales as well as having a positive impact on their ability to become exporters.
- After completing the diagnostic stage, supplier firms in the agribusiness sector witnessed, on average, an increase in sales of 16%, 11% and 9% one, two and three years, respectively, after the programme was approved. Employment followed a similar pattern by increasing 8%, 9% and 10%.

The programme has inspired other similar initiatives in Colombia, El Salvador, Mexico and Uruguay.

Sources: Zuniga (forthcoming), "Public policy for productive development in small and medium-sized enterprises in Latin America: What have we learned?"; Rivas (2012), *La experiencia de CORFO y la transformación productiva de Chile: Evolución, aprendizaje y lecciones de desarrollo*; and Arraíz, Henriquez and Stucchi (2011), "Impact of the Chilean Supplier Development Program on the performance of SME and their large-firm customers".

Building on cluster approaches to promote and facilitate matchmaking and connecting investors with potential suppliers is another means to foster linkages between MNEs and SMEs. The Collaborative Research in Engineering, Science & Technology is one of the best examples, including internationally. This platform has allowed, among several other achievements, the ten leading semiconductor companies that initiated it to develop programmes (on talent development for instance) to strengthen and connect with local companies located upstream and downstream in the value chain. Still in the Penang E&E cluster, Invest Penang has also established a database of local suppliers available online, and regularly organises "supplier days" to match MNEs with potential SME suppliers. The Malaysian Investment Development Authority and SME Corporation similarly have established SME databases for foreign MNEs looking for local suppliers.

Malaysia's measures for fostering linkages are similar in many respects to supplier development programmes in Europe, Singapore and Latin America (Box 5.8). Where Malaysia seems to differ is in the coherence and scope of its programmes. Malaysia would benefit from streamlining its Vendor Development Programme and Industrial Linkage Programme, ensuring that a single national programme encompasses all aspects of best international practice, including a process for assessing SME capabilities, company upgrading needs, the development of a network of mentors/consultants to assist in upgrading SME capabilities, and co-financing or direct assistance for SME upgrading.

Finally, in the specific case of high-value and strategic government acquisitions worth more than MYR 50 million, the offset agreements managed by the Technology Depository Agency have also been intervening since the beginning of the 2000s to allow technological transfer between MNEs and the indigenous companies (MIGHT, 2009). The first non-defence offset programme was built around Airbus A380 engine procurement. It was designed to benefit the local aerospace industry and promote new technology development. Among the several components included in this programme were a research programme on palm oil-based, bio-based gas-turbine fuel; initiatives to upgrade local aerospace industry players' capabilities to become part of the global supply chain; technology transfers on advanced materials, etc. (MIGHT, 2009). The Malaysian Industry-Government Group for High Technology is also working on developing offset projects based on green technology, nanotechnology and human capital development.

Government-linked companies as innovation agents

In recent years, several Asian economies such as China, the Philippines or Viet Nam have launched reform programmes to improve the efficiency and transparency of the governance and management of their state-owned enterprises. In Malaysia, the GLC Transformation Programme was launched in 2004 and the Committee for GLC High Performance was formed a year later to ensure its co-ordination. This ten-year programme, completed in 2015, aimed at transforming government-linked companies (GLC) into high-performing companies on an economic, social and financial level.

Beyond improving their own economic and financial performance, the contribution to national development goals featured in a good position among the GLC Transformation Programme's objectives. GLCs were, for instance, expected to "improve total factor productivity" through their role in executing government policies and initiatives and in building capabilities and knowledge in key sectors such as automotive and semiconductors (PGC, 2006). Taking stock of the programme results after its term, the Putrajaya Committee on GLC High Performance put forward that GLCs have contributed to new knowledge-based and service-oriented industries and sectors, and have therefore supported the move of the nation further up the economic value chain (PGC, 2015).

Box 5.8. International examples of programmes to foster linkages between multinational enterprises and local firms

National supplier development programmes

Supplier development programmes are designed to overcome the main barriers to developing buyer-vendor linkages between multinational enterprises (MNEs) and domestic firms (World Bank, 2014). Successful examples include the Czech Supplier Development Program from the early 2000s, the Singaporean Local Industry Upgrading Program from the 1980s, the Supplier Development Programme implemented by CORFO in Chile (see Box 5.7), the Tractor Programme in Mexico and the *Programa Encadenamientos* in Costa Rica.

Supplier development programmes typically combine the following:

- The development of relationships with local senior managers of MNEs to encourage co-ordination of purchasing plans and pool information about future demand.
- The establishment of a database of qualified domestic suppliers with information on products, customers and benchmarking of supplier performance, organised by industry/sector or commodity/product. Such a database reduces the search costs for MNEs in sourcing potential domestic suppliers.
- A process for assessing SME capabilities company upgrading needs in various aspects of company performance – management, production, sales and commercialisation, innovation, human resources and overall productivity.
- The development of a network of mentors/consultants to assist in upgrading SME capabilities e.g. through regular visits to the company to help the company monitor its implementation.
- Co-financing or direct assistance for SME upgrading, including management training and other improvements in efficiency. Eligible costs typically include the salary of the supply chain champion and the fees of the external advisors or mentors.

Programmes that rely on groups of companies working collectively together

The Scottish Technology and Collaboration Initiative (STAC) is an example of an initiative that is not primarily transactional i.e. that is not primarily a supplier-customer relationship. STAC is an initiative based on fostering relationships between SMEs and MNEs in which there is strong mutual learning for both parties involved.

In STAC's approach, firms collaborate to exploit a business opportunity by focusing on different aspects of the value chain. It involves the establishment of a "stac", that is a group of companies that work jointly towards an innovative outcome, usually a new product offering. A stac typically involves a "pillar" MNE subsidiary and two SMEs. An early learning outcome for STAC was the utility of identifying and involving a potential customer in the collaborative effort (Prashantham and McNaughton, 2006).

Dedicated small enterprise support centres

Ireland's technology centres are collaborative R&D entities established and led by industry. They are resourced by researchers associated with public research institutions which undertake market-focused R&D for the benefit of industry. The Technology Centres Programme is a joint initiative between Enterprise Ireland and IDA Ireland allowing Irish companies and multinationals to work together in these centres. There are currently 15 industry-led research centres in the Technology Centres Programme, each of which focuses on a different sector or technology area. Each technology centre can be multi-site and geographically dispersed, to bring together relevant MNEs, SMEs and public research organisations.

Sources: World Bank (2014), "Facilitating global value chain integration for competitiveness in Costa Rica"; Department of Jobs, Enterprise and Innovation (2015), "Directory of research centres and technology centres 2015", www.djei.ie/en/Publications/Publication-files/National-Directory-of-Research-Centres-and-Technology-Centres-2015.pdf.

However, GLCs have, in great majority, contributed to the building of infrastructure in their respective sector and to broad socio-economic development goals (for instance the Bumiputera Empowerment Agenda) via their employment policy[33] as well as their sourcing policy.[34] This goes against one of the main lessons learnt from international experiences, i.e. the need to define well the specific development goals assigned to each state-owned enterprise and avoid mixing them with other broader issues, such as social equity (Box 5.9). The multiplicity of objectives, including some that span far beyond the development of the sectors they intervene in, was seen as one of the main weaknesses of the way the Malaysian state has attempted to use its state-owned enterprises as development agents (OECD, 2015b).

The previously mentioned survey on GLCs, which evidenced their limited innovation activities and capabilities, was the basis for several recommendations, covering the whole innovation cycle in a company, from developing a culture of innovation within GLCs, setting objectives and priorities, assessing the strengths and weaknesses, to laying the foundation for effective implementation (Box 5.10). The results of this survey have so far received little attention and it remains unclear which public institutions have ownership of the recommendations and will take concrete actions to implement them.

The Science for Industry component of the S2A Programme is also aimed at encouraging GLCs to venture into innovation and pursue new emerging growth areas (MIGHT, 2013a, 2013b). However, no information is available on the corresponding initiatives that might have been implemented under this programme.

Enhancing the contribution of higher education institutions and public research institutes to innovation

Higher education institutions

HEIs contribute in various ways to national innovation. They provide human capital and training, and are the main producers of knowledge, which is expected to be used and transferred to the business sector and/or government to address societal challenges. Thus, HEIs are also sources of entrepreneurship and technology commercialisation – referred to as the third mission. In developing countries, public research institutes and universities are the key institutions supporting the process of economic catching up, through research but mostly through the formation of human capital, training and assistance to firms in technology absorption (Mazzoleni and Nelson, 2007).

Although Malaysian HEIs have radically improved the supply of human capital, the quality and relevance of this labour force has yet to be improved. In regards to its two other contributions to innovation – knowledge production and technology transfer – the sector has initiated important efforts in funding and organisation, but no meaningful progress in terms of results has been achieved to date. A revision of how these two contributions should better address the necessities of industries as well as the potential action by HEIs is needed. The articulation of guidelines for university technology transfer policy and their resonance at the university level through institutional policies should help advance in this direction.

Box 5.9. State-owned enterprises as development agents: Lessons drawn from emerging countries' experiences

While showing some very significant differences, several Asian countries such as Japan, Korea and Chinese Taipei have often been described in the development literature as examples of a successful intermediate policy approach that combines state intervention and a market-based environment. Despite the wide variety of approaches, owing in particular to different levels of initial development, state-owned enterprises have been deemed an important element of their respective industrial policy, beside a gradually growing private sector. They have been instrumental not only in overcoming the finance shortage in the early years of their development strategy through the forming of state-owned financial institutions, but also in some cases in kick-starting the development of manufacturing in low-tech sectors (textile, garment) and supporting their upgrade to middle technology (machinery and heavy chemicals) via dedicated workforce training programmes and vendor development programmes. Combined with well-designed tax incentives to attract higher value-added foreign direct investment (FDI) in special economic zones, this later contributed to move some of these countries beyond middle-income levels.

Three broad conditions for successful state-owned enterprise-based development strategies can be extracted from a review of successes and failures of selected emerging countries:

- A competent bureaucracy should exert its ownership function. More generally, world-class corporate governance rules and principles should be applied to govern these entities (see OECD, 2015b).
- The areas in which state-owned enterprises operate should preferably be free of concentrations of commercial, financial and other market powers. Conditions of relative equality are proven to yield better results and avoid risks of corruption or capture of developmental objectives by specific existing interest groups.
- The developmental objectives state-owned enterprises are expected to contribute to should be clearly defined and, in particular, not intermingled with broader social policy objectives unrelated to their initial, sector-specific purpose.

Singapore is considered a successful example of a proactive use of state-owned enterprises for development which broadly complied with these three conditions. Early on it reformed the corporate governance of its state-owned enterprises, a key step being the creation of Temasek as a holding company to rationalise management practices across all of the state-owned enterprises in its portfolio and separate their governance from state regulation.

Although the specificity of its city-state condition makes the replication of this model difficult, countries such as Malaysia have tried to emulate its trajectory. The creation of Kazanah Nasional, in 1993, was clearly modelled after Temasek, however, preserving a direct role of the state in its governance. Singapore has also clearly defined the development objectives of its state-owned enterprises and refrained from overburdening them with multiple objectives. State-owned enterprises are, in particular, relieved from broader social objectives (health, social equity, housing, etc.), which remain under the responsibility of the state alone through dedicated institutions.

Source: OECD (2015b), *State-Owned Enterprises in the Development Process*, http://dx.doi.org/10.1787/9789264229617-en; OECD (2010), *Policy Brief on Corporate Governance of State-owned Enterprises in Asia: Recommendations for Reform*, www.oecd.org/daf/ca/corporategovernanceofstate-ownedenterprises/45639683.pdf.

Box 5.10. Recommendations from the GLC Innovation Survey 2012 for government-linked companies to improve innovation capabilities

Develop a holistic view of innovation:

- provide stronger leadership guidance on establishing a central theme for innovation and moving towards a portfolio of ideas
- develop clear measures of innovation and incentives to reward.

Be clear on the top five innovation priorities to support business goals:

- communicate the innovation priorities across the organisation
- invest in both process/product and game changing business model innovation
- internalise the urgency to innovate and aspire to achieve global excellence – create a burning platform
- recognise areas of strength and weakness, commit to building capabilities to succeed beyond the core
- invest more deeply in communicating the role of innovation to align the organisation.

Improve the effectiveness of the innovation cycle (from ideation to execution and evaluation):

- focus on the execution of ideas, celebrate successes as role models
- make the innovation cycle as relevant and thoughtfully discussed as other core business decisions.

Source: Mohammad (2012), "National innovation strategy".

Human capital contribution

In Malaysia, the provision of human capital by HEIs as reflected in enrolment rates and number of graduates (at undergraduate and post-graduate levels) has expanded dramatically over the last decade. Important investments have been made to strengthen capacity, democratise access to and improve the quality of the sector. The large number of HEIs for the size of the country, and the high number of strategic policies dedicated to this domain, highlight the priority given to higher education by the Malaysian government. The 2007 National Higher Education Strategic Plan, which was extensively reviewed in 2014, and the recent Higher Education Blueprint 2015-25 (MOE, 2015), illustrate the commitment of the Malaysian government for adapting its higher education to its ambitious economic and societal objectives.

Yet despite considerable investments in the last decades, the quality of higher education in Malaysia remains an issue.[35] Quality has been the focus of several initiatives, from qualification requirements for staff to revised accreditation criteria for institutions or training for HEIs managers. In 2002, the government established a Quality Assurance Division within the Ministry of Education to monitor public HEIs. In 2005, the Cabinet made a major decision to establish the Malaysia Qualification Agency, which is now responsible for quality assurance in higher education and for implementing the Malaysian Qualifications Framework.[36] To encourage the competitiveness of the higher education sector and to support Malaysia's aspiration to be an education hub in the region, various indicator-based assessment mechanisms were set up, such as the SETARA performance rating system, the Malaysia Quality Evaluation System for Private Colleges (MyQUEST) and the Malaysia Research Assessment Instrument to monitor research performance (MyRA). In parallel, a progressive shift towards an increased proportion of performance-related funding is taking place.

One of the major difficulties in improving quality in the higher education sector will lie in the capacity of the system to provide a sufficient mass of qualified teachers and professors to respond to the growing number of students; a need that still has to be fully assessed. In parallel, quality of teaching, through improved pedagogic methodologies (e.g. interactive teaching and critical thinking) and adapted curricula will also require attention. Higher order thinking skills (HOTS) programmes were recently implemented in schools and tertiary institutions to inculcate creative thinking (EPU, 2015a). Special attention should be paid to private institutions. The actual quality of private institutions appears less well monitored. Some of the (sometimes rather small) private institutions might therefore not be really viable as they may not have the resources required to provide a quality education.

Malaysian institutions have yet to achieve a competitive position internationally (see QS World University Rankings). Although such a ranking, despite taking into account several criteria (including innovative curricula or career perspectives for students), often puts a strong emphasis on academic excellence (see below), which often requires many years of sustained investment to bear its fruits. It should nevertheless be underlined to identify strategic priorities for the future. More recently, Malaysia has also started to attract foreign HEIs that have set up subsidiary branches in the country. This can have a very positive impact on the Malaysian higher education system, as competition and new pedagogic processes may drive upward the quality of national institutions.

Skills: Mismatch between supply and demand

Another major challenge is improving the contribution of HEIs to innovation by better matching skills with industry demands. Different business surveys (e.g. the World Bank Enterprise Survey) have recurrently documented the lack of relevance (and lack of key skills) of skills as being one of the difficulties to improving productivity and innovation in Malaysia.

The growing number of unemployed graduates since 2000 also indicates a problem between the supply and demand for labour. Further, the still relatively low percentage of science and engineering students in Malaysian higher education remains an important handicap to increasing innovation in industry. While this situation might also be linked to the expanded supply of graduates, the constant migration of graduates and post-graduates (brain drain) has accentuated the lack of qualified professionals for local industry (World Bank, 2011).

Improving the relevance of skills implies a comprehensive revision of both education programmes (supply of skills) and their curricula. Pedagogy should also be revisited, placing a stronger emphasis on critical thinking and interactive education. In recent years, more emphasis has been put on soft skills, yet there is a need for this trend to be fully integrated into a general reform of the curriculum structure.[37] Pilot initiatives to improve the mobility between academia and industry have also been set up, but remain relatively limited in size.

Technical vocational education and training (TVET) and lifelong learning have also started to be better valorised: a National Skills Competition is conducted yearly for local TVET students to showcase their innovations and winners represent Malaysia in international skills competitions. Participation in lifelong learning programmes more than doubled between 2007 and 2013, due in part to the development of open universities. Improving and expanding TVET for industry needs remains an important task in the higher education agenda – as recognised in Strategy Paper 9: "Transforming technical and vocational education and training to meet industry" (EPU, 2010).

The number of students undertaking TVET studies remains far below that of mainstream higher education. This issue was ranked second in the priorities identified by the 2014 survey of the higher education community. For a long time, TVET remained poorly considered and underfunded compared to mainstream higher education. The need to raise its status to put it on par with higher academic education was identified in the review of the National Higher Education Strategic Plan. Nevertheless, a number of challenges remain, such as the need for improved relationships with business and industry, the sometimes insufficient skills of the staff, and the lack of identified pathways for bright TVET students to come back to high-quality mainstream HEIs (EPU, 2015a).

Research and technology transfer

Scientific excellence is an important criterion in measuring the quality and competitiveness of higher education. As described in Chapter 4, HEIs play a major role in the Malaysian research system. The Malaysian government has set up new competitive performance-based initiatives to foster research excellence – e.g. the designation of "research university" and the Higher Institution Centre of Excellence (HICoE) programme. Nevertheless, despite the existence of academic groups of excellent quality, the average scientific level among Malaysian HEIs remains relatively weak by international standards. Further, the lack of clear career prospects for scientists or the lack of research infrastructures are some of the factors that discourage the best students to undertake science studies, which are required to develop scientific academic excellence.

A major challenge remains reinforcing linkages with industry. This has to do with the lack of relevance of research to industry demands, the incipient participation of industry in the setting of R&D agendas and a weak number of joint R&D projects, as well as cultural differences and weak communication between the two actors (NSRC, 2013a). With recent advances in university autonomy and wider flexibilities in their intellectual property, policy commercialisation has been eased to some extent, although some other obstacles remain (OECD, 2015a). In addition, the lack of funding at the various stages of the commercialisation process remains an issue (Chandran, 2010).

The limited pool of qualified personnel and insufficient skills for technology management is also seen as particularly detrimental to university technology transfer (MASTIC, 2014).[38] To accelerate the learning and acquisition of new skills related to technology transfer, universities could envisage working together through a central intermediary office for technology transfer and training. This would also help to better manage resources and achieve cost-efficiency gains in technology transfer infrastructure. The creation of Khazanah Harta Intelek Malaysia, a centralised repository of intellectual property arising from government research programmes, points in that direction.

The increased emphasis given to patenting and technology commercialisation through licensing and spinoffs has somewhat been in detriment of more traditional forms of technology transfer – e.g. R&D collaboration with industry, training, R&D contract and technology extension services, two-way mobility of researchers, etc. – which could potentially have an important impact on addressing industry and societal demands. Further, the high costs of patenting impose an additional financial burden over time as granted patents need to be renewed yearly. A clear and well-articulated intellectual property strategy should help identify relevant inventions and technology priorities.

The lack of solid intermediary support at some universities implies that technology transfer and commercialisation initiatives fall under the responsibility of scientists themselves – potentially in detriment of teaching and the pursuit of research activities per se. Several steps have been recently taken to addresses these gaps. The recent creation of intermediaries such as PlaTCOM Ventures Sdn. Bhd. (PlaTCOM) and Steinbeis Malaysia Foundation (Steinbeis) addresses some of these gaps. These intermediaries aim to enhance collaboration and provide advisory services to both researchers and companies in order to connect knowledge supply with demand (EPU, 2015a).

Cross-cutting strategies to improve the performance of higher education institutions

It is worth noting that the Malaysian government has carried out a series of successive detailed national plans to achieve its ambitious objectives for higher education. The most recent Higher Education Blueprint 2015-25 was built on the achievements of the previous national plan to accompany the development of a knowledge-based economy. The goals and type of actions to be implemented take into account most of the challenges and difficulties that were identified during the review of the previous NSPHE, and propose some changes in the governance of the system to overcome the rigidity of the current structure (MOE, 2015).

The success of these successive plans depends on a number of critical elements:

- The general governance of their implementation. Oversight is currently carried out by a relatively complex structure of interconnected bodies. As was noted in the review of the previous NSPHE, a very low level of co-operation between ministries has had a negative impact on implementation. A single co-ordinating structure should probably be established (the role of the National Council for Higher Education should be clearly delineated), comprising various stakeholder representatives (including the different ministries and HEIs).
- Providing an adequate policy framework and resources. Although Malaysian plans such as the recent Higher Education Blueprint 2015-25 (MOE, 2015) include very detailed objectives, the structure and resources required to achieve those are far less described. For example, no contingency plans were devised to mitigate the impact of potential crises, such as the financial shock which took place in 2008-09, or the current crisis in oil and raw product prices. As a result, funding of critical objectives can be strongly affected to the detriment of the desired outcomes. Similarly, in the current blueprint, no plan is made for training the large number of additional higher education professors and teachers which will be required in the coming years to respond to the continuous increase in demand, and this could have a serious effect on the quality of HEIs.
- Monitoring and evaluating implementation. The Malaysian government has developed a set of useful indicators to evaluate the progress of its reforms. In addition, the Ministry of Education plans to publish performance results annually so that the public can track the progress of the implementation of the Higher

Education Blueprint 2015-25. However, there is a risk that the HEIs and government bodies involved become solely focused on achieving the key performance indicators and forget the actual strategic objectives of the reforms. The likelihood of such an indicator-focused policy is increased by the relative lack of autonomy granted to HEIs until recently. HEIs should be allowed enough flexibility to be able to innovate and develop with their own strategies to respond to the overall objectives. The role of the co-ordinating structure described above should also be to gather feedback on such innovations and share best practices among relevant stakeholders.

Supporting public research institutes

In OECD countries, the government plays a key role in the provision of public goods for innovation through knowledge and technology diffusion via public research institutions and universities. Universities are part of the national technological infrastructure and are deemed central to industrial innovation and reaching social and development objectives (e.g. water quality, health, environment, etc.). In Malaysia, the construction of this capacity through public research institutes (PRIs) and universities has gradually gained in importance in national policy agendas since the Seventh Master Plan. The Ninth Malaysia Plan greatly expanded the R&D funding and commercialisation programmes; efforts that were revised and improved with the Tenth Malaysia Plan (2011-15).

Yet real efforts to modernise PRIs and enhance their role in the national innovation system have still been partial and limited to a few institutions (e.g. MIMOS). Increased requirements have not yet been translated into institutional (or system level) strategic plans or enhanced public resources. A real upgrade and reform of the sector is still pending.

As described in Chapter 4, the Malaysian government is largely the main source of funding for the 29 PRIs – representing 97% of funding for R&D in 2012 (MASTIC, 2014). This funding mainly concerns block funding from directing ministries or project funding through the Economic Planning Unit, Ministry of Finance (or other ministries) or MOSTI. No PRI-specific statistics are available on the type of funding or types of activities financed and this hinders a more detailed analysis of the context and necessities of PRIs. Only a minor share of funding for R&D comes from competitive funding. To date, in contrast with international trends, there is no performance-based mechanism for allocating the institutional funding for R&D of PRIs. In many developed countries, research at public research institutions is financed through a combination of block funding (albeit at a decreasing rate) – of which a part consists of performance-based funding – plus funding from competitive sources.

The two salient features in funding trends for R&D in Malaysian PRIs are a lack of consistency (unstable trend) in funding and a high dispersion of funding sources. Funding of R&D has fluctuated widely over the last 15 years. The difficulties in ensuring funding consistency can, in part, be explained by the complex setting in research funding and policy prevailing in Malaysia as well as the lack of co-ordination across R&D agencies. Research funding is distributed through a multitude of sources, including managing ministries (in case of sectorial PRIs with a public good orientation), the Economic Planning Unit, the Ministry of Finance, etc. Often, the Economic Planning Unit in the Prime Minister's Department provides block grants to various PRIs to carry out top-down directive research (Olsson and Meeck, 2014).[39] Funding schemes are not always well defined or coherent between sources – which pushes institutions to lose focus and change priorities quite often.[40] As a result of this multiplicity – in both R&D funding and policy agencies – research entities often encounter conflicting directions and indicate that this undermines their capacity to sustain a research agenda and build core competencies in strategic areas (NRSC, 2013a).

In general, in spite of the increased resources for research and innovation through competitive schemes, PRIs have benefited less from these new resources than universities. This is due to several structural weaknesses as well as a potential inadequacy between policy programmes and PRIs' competencies and their orientation (which are mainly applied research, technology extension and information services).

First, not all PRIs find their discipline or area of research represented in the eligibility criteria (national strategic areas), and second, many PRIs encounter difficulties in articulating research proposals compared to academia. This situation also reflects a lack of research management skills by scientists in PRIs, which evidently hinders their capacity to leverage additional funds and foster excellence. PRIs have not benefited from an institutional research upgrading (competitive) programme, like the research university programme that exists for universities, that would allow them to compete with other PRIs for research capacity expansion.

As discussed in the National Science Research Council's Public Research Assets (PRA) Performance Assessment (NSRC, 2013a) (Box 5.11), the lack of long-term vision in public research funding has a negative impact on the research system, whose objectives can only be developed over extended periods of time. The introduction of a two-year rolling plan in funding in the Tenth Malaysia Plan, subject to a yearly performance evaluation by a ministry or public research organisation, is an example of a short-run approach to R&D. This pushes scientists to focus on projects at a very advanced stage: those with the highest potential of delivering results. As a result, ambitious research projects are currently very difficult to undertake, whether in fundamental research or for more applied objectives. Researchers also have concerns that the shorter timeframes will affect research quality.

Action by the government to foster research excellence and enhance the impact of PRIs also implies providing them with the appropriate governance and regulatory frameworks that will allow them to function more efficiently; to focus, develop and implement missions, and thereby enhance their contribution to society. For several PRIs, the current complexity in governance and the management setting leaves little room to take decisions rapidly and engage in renewed institutional strategies. As an example, there are currently eight PRIs related to agronomy/forestry/fishing in Malaysia, overseen by four different ministries. More generally, the growing dispersion (e.g. broadening mission scope and engagement in new activities) of PRIs and the lack of coherence in their function and administration hamper their efficiency.

Box 5.11. Recommendations of the 2013 PRA performance assessment concerning public research institutes

Main issues

Policy

- Confusion over the R&D roles of universities versus public research institutes (PRIs): the purpose and role of PRIs have not been clearly defined, which results in differences of expectations between actors of the national system of innovation, in particular between policy makers and the staff of PRIs.

Box 5.11. Recommendations of the 2013 PRA performance assessment concerning public research institutes (*continued*)

Several competing ministries and agencies are in charge of specification of PRIs' policy, creating a lack of co-ordination between the different types of R&D (fundamental, applied and experimental) and a need to focus at both the national and institutional levels.

Infrastructure management

- Under-utilisation of PRIs' equipment.

Funding

- R&D funding is low in absolute and relative terms in international comparison.
- Unstable public research institute (PRI) funding affects long-term investment and staff motivation.
- Multiple funding sources.
- Inconsistencies between the "base" funding (salaries and infrastructure) from the Ministry of Finance and their R&D funding from the Economic Policy Unit and grant schemes.
- Lack of R&D focus due to diverse and often competing requests from various ministries and agencies.
- Poor alignment of funding and top national R&D challenges.
- R&D granting process is not accurate or transparent (i.e. lower grant awards and unclear selection process).

Performance

- PRIs under the classification of a division/department have lower performance than other PRIs.

Main recommendations: Review, restructure and realign PRIs

- Use logic modelling to achieve realignment so that it is better designed to contribute to national priorities, and the overall PRI system is efficient and effective.
- Make certain PRIs' statutory bodies allow them to be more flexible and responsive in their decision making.
- Transform PRIs into agencies that aim to meet R&D needs through applied, experimental and collaborative research.
- Enable PRIs to monitor and evaluate R&D in order to adopt an evaluative culture and take advantage of being in direct contact with the stakeholders' questions.
- Develop strategic R&D capabilities.
- Encourage mobility, complementarity and partnership of researchers both upward (clear career pathway for researchers) and laterally (across borders between public research assets).
- Participate in the education of Masters and PhD students as a training ground to get applied research skills for solving real-work stakeholder problems.

Source: NSRC (2013a), *PRA Performance Evaluation: Unlocking Vast Potentials, Fast-Tracking the Future*, http://umexpert.um.edu.my/file/publication/00012427_86127.pdf.

PRIs' development and the accomplishment of their new roles depend strongly on the incentive structure and governance. An in-depth reform of both governance and legal frameworks has not yet taken place. It is fundamental to enrich governing directories with the participation of "principal entities" both from the public and private sector, including prestigious actors with knowledge of the business sector in which PRIs function. International experience suggests that governing laws, including organic laws and regulatory frameworks defining PRIs' relation with ministries, need to be revised to properly redefine PRIs' mission, the stakeholders, and responsibilities and competencies. An in-depth assessment of PRIs' competences and necessities (and potential) in consultation with stakeholders and an enhanced board of directors can help define new institutional strategies, the missions and mechanisms through which PRIs will generate value and impact.

Incentives to foster institutional change and impact take the form of performance-based funding in institutional (block) funding in certain countries. While the structure of finance can differ across institutions depending on the types of services and goods they deliver, it is important that institutional funding through performance schemes such as performance-based contracts be enhanced in Malaysian PRIs. Under this type of scheme, amounts of funding and time frameworks are contingent upon milestones achieved and contract targets. Performance-based institutional funding can help foster competition and incentivise PRIs to organise themselves, engage in institutional change and move towards a results-driven culture and management.

To improve efficiency in the use of public funds for research in PRIs, a channelling and co-ordinating mechanism can support the articulation of means and the implementation of new replenishment plans and modernisation strategies in institutions. A co-ordinating agency for research for PRIs can also help to oversee funding allocation and results, improve research management and conduct performance evaluation. Such institutions should be designed in accordance with the specificities and missions of PRIs, which may differ across institutions. Best practices and standards in management research and technology transfer can also be facilitated by this entity, thereby accelerating the modernisation progress of PRIs in a more unified way.

A good example of this endeavour is RISE – Research Institutes of Sweden (Box 5.12). Created in the mid-1990s, RISE AB was conceived as a co-ordinating entity to facilitate steering, unify standards and co-ordinate research policy within public research organisations. RISE AB is the state's company for ownership of the research and technology organisations of the Research Institutes of Sweden. RISE AB's task is to gather, develop and renew members of RISE to transform them into an internationally competitive and efficient Swedish force for industrial research and innovation.

Supporting system transition

Malaysia today faces the challenge of making the transition to a more sustainable development path that promotes the shift to an advanced economy by 2020 while at the same time reducing carbon emissions and maintaining the country's natural wealth (EPU, 2015a). This transition is also an opportunity, if the right policies are in place, for Malaysia to become a hub for green investment (OECD, 2014). Malaysia can even bolster its development, relying upon a sustainable use of its abundant natural endowments from fauna and flora biodiversity, to oil, gas and water.

Box 5.12. Restructuring public research institutes in Sweden: The creation of the Research Institutes of Sweden (RISE)

The Swedish public research institutes (PRIs) with a focus on industrial research were consolidated in 1997 into an umbrella holding, under the name Ireco Holding AB by the Swedish Ministry of Enterprise, Energy and Communications and the government agency The Knowledge Foundation. The company became wholly state-owned in 2007. In 2009, it changed its name to RISE Research Institutes of Sweden Holding AB and received an expanded mandate and significantly increased resources.

Its initial aims were to improve strategic orientation, pool resources and exploit complementarities. The annual budget of the 22 RISE institutes has significantly increased in recent years and currently amounts to around SEK 2.5 billion. More than 20% of the budget appears to come from international sources, including industry sources and the EU Framework Programme. In general, more than 50% of turnover comes from industry projects, 19% from government funding in the form of strategic competence funds and another 18% from various public sources. RISE has a large number of SME clients and SME-targeted activities and a large number of testing facilities for enterprises of all sizes. One of its main development goals is to strengthen the institutes as interfaces between academia and industry and as providers of useful research for firms.

RISE has four main sub-structures with a number of individual institutes clustered around broad topics, such as ICT. The institutes are all organised as non-profit, limited liability companies and have different business approaches depending on the sectors they serve. The models range from testing contracts to research consortia involving business enterprises and universities. Taken together, the institutes employ more than 2 200 people; more than a third of which have a PhD and 65 that are also university professors.

Government support for research institutes has been increasing in recent years. Specific support mechanisms include VINNOVA's Institute Excellence Programme for RISE institutes and public sector agencies such as FOI. This programme currently has eight centres, which run for six years and aim to strengthen research consortia involving the institutes, academia and various firms. At the same time, like the competence centres and excellence centres for universities, these centres support new planning and management tools in the funded institutes.

Sources: OECD (2016b), *OECD Reviews of Innovation Policy: Sweden 2016*, http://dx.doi.org/10.1787/9789264250000-en; OECD (2013c), *OECD Reviews of Innovation Policy: Sweden 2012*, http://dx.doi.org/10.1787/9789264184893-en.

Several emerging economies have included sustainable development among the priorities of their industrial policy and are thereby investing in environment-related technologies through a variety of instruments. Chinese companies, for instance, are already among the technological leaders and global top ten producers of renewable energy equipment (OECD, 2013d). While far behind China or even Singapore, Malaysia has also invested significantly in environmental technologies (Figure 5.13).[41]

The challenge of achieving and benefiting from green growth was well recognised in the Tenth Malaysia Plan, which included several initiatives to mitigate climate change and conserve ecological assets (Table 5.10). With regards to climate mitigation, in 2009 Malaysia set the ambitious voluntary target of reducing greenhouse gas emission intensity of GDP by up to 40% in the year 2020 compared to 2005 levels. Several actions were taken during the period of the Tenth Malaysia Plan, such as the implementation of the Feed-in Tariff (FiT) mechanism under the 2011 Renewable Energy Act, the SAVE programme to promote energy efficiency measures and the establishment of permanent reserved forests in the states of Pahang, Perak and Selangor. These initiatives and others have allowed significant results in several areas, in particular a reduction in greenhouse gas emission intensity of GDP as of 2013 compared to 2005 levels, and an increase in forest coverage from 56% in 2010 to 61% in 2014[42] (EPU, 2015a). New measures and instruments are planned under the Eleventh Malaysia Plan, including a review and reform of the governance system.

Figure 5.13. **Top ten PCT applicant OECD partner economies in selected environmental-related technologies**

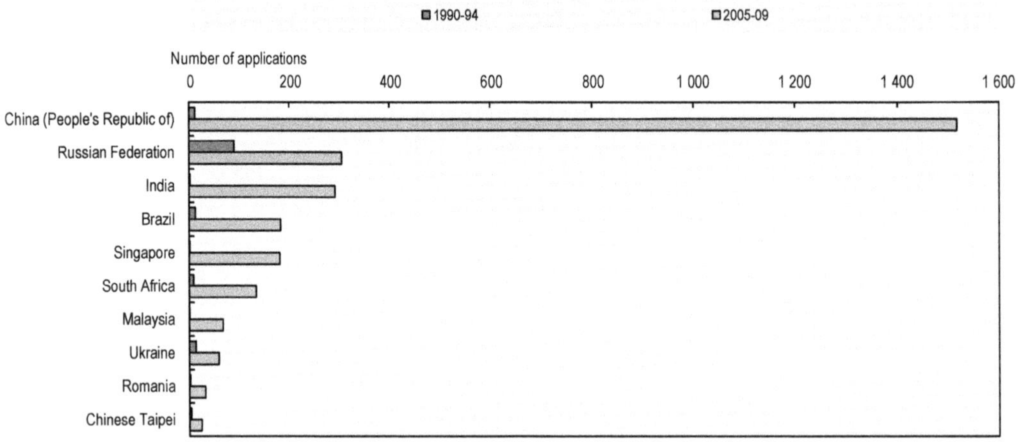

Note: According to the official OECD definition, selected environmental-related technologies include technologies in the fields of: general environmental management (air, water, waste), energy generation from renewable and non-fossil sources, combustion technologies with mitigation potential (e.g. using fossil fuels, biomass, waste, etc.), technologies specific to climate change mitigation, technologies with potential or indirect contribution to emissions mitigation, emissions abatement and fuel efficiency in transportation and energy efficiency in buildings and lighting (OECD, 2013d).

Source: OECD (2013d), *Perspectives on Global Development 2013, Industrial Policies in a Changing World*, http://dx.doi.org/10.1787/persp_glob_dev-2013-en.

Table 5.10. **Green growth initiatives under the Tenth and Eleventh Malaysia Plans**

Tenth Malaysia Plan	Eleventh Malaysia Plan
– Introducing feed-in tariffs to help finance renewable energy investments – Providing fiscal incentives and funding for green technology investments – Promoting projects eligible for carbon credits – Promoting eco-tourism to create commercial value in sustainability – Facilitating greater participation of local communities in eco-tourism activities and bio-diversity protection as a self-sustaining means to support environmental conservation – Initiating public-private corporate-social responsability initiatives around protection of flagship species as part of broader habitat conservation efforts	Strengthening governance to drive transformation: – Formulating and strengthening relevant policies – Enhancing the regulatory and institutional framework, co-ordination and capacity – Improving monitoring and evaluation mechanisms to track and assess the effectiveness of green growth initiatives Enhancing awareness to create shared responsibility: – Comprehensive communication, education and awareness programmes – Platforms for knowledge sharing and collaboration Establishing sustainable financing mechanisms: – Expanding existing economic instruments (Polluter Pays Principle and Payment for Ecosystem Services) – Funding green growth through new economic instruments (green tax, carbon tax, green bonds and REDD+ [Reducing Emissions from Deforestation and Forest Degradation])

Sources: EPU (2010), *Tenth Malaysia Plan*, http://onlineapps.epu.gov.my/rmke10/rmke10_english.html; EPU (2015a), *Eleventh Malaysia Plan*, http://rmk11.epu.gov.my/index.php/en.

In order to make the transition to sustainable development, Malaysia is also putting in place policies to foster enterprises based on emerging green technologies, introducing incentives to enable existing industries – in particular the oil, gas and rubber industries – to become more sustainable, and implementing framework conditions that foster green technologies. In this area, the government has set up an integrated strategic policy framework, which comprises a dedicated governance structure as well as specific regulations, instruments and measures (Box 5.13).

Box 5.13. An example of an integrated strategic policy framework: The National Green Technology Policy

The National Green Technology Policy was prepared by the Ministry of Energy, Green Technology and Water and launched by the Prime Minister in 2009 with the purpose of making green technology one of the essential factors for economic growth and coincidently decreasing the energy consumption rate. Its objectives span across the short, medium and long term, to be achieved under the Tenth, Eleventh and Twelfth Malaysia Plans (OECD, 2013d). Most of meeting these staged objectives entails achieving both a system transition, from a conventional one to green technology, and the building of a whole new sectoral system of innovation. To achieve the latter, the different policy actions include increasing foreign direct investment in green technology, upgrading national research capability and the domestic green tech industry in order, finally, to become a major global producer of green technology:

- expansion of local research institutes and institutions of higher learning to expand research, development and innovation activities on green technology towards commercialisation (short term)
- increased R&D of green technology by local universities and research institutions and commercialisation in collaboration with the local industry and multinational enterprises (medium term)
- expansion of international collaboration between local universities and research institutions with green technology industries (long term).

This policy is based on five strategic thrusts: a conducive environment for green technology development; human capital development in green technology; green technology R&D; promotion and public awareness; and organisational structure enhancement. The four main pillars of the National Green Technology Policy are grouped under the following headings: energy, environment, economy and social.

The fifth strategic thrust led to the creation of the GT Corporation (GreenTech Malaysia). This agency is responsible for implementation. It also resulted in the establishment of the National Green Technology Council, chaired by the Prime Minister, to provide high-level co-ordination between ministries, agencies and other stakeholders. The council is supported by a steering committee and eight specific working committees (including on human capital, green development, and research and innovation).

Under the National Green Technology Policy, a green technology roadmap was created in order to define the main challenges, indicators and mechanisms of green technology expansion (Phase 1) as well as to implement the most successful policies (Phase 2). The roadmap also defined several intermediate targets for 2015, 2020 and 2025 (number of green jobs, contribution to GDP) in the following sectors: energy, waste water, building, transportation, manufacturing and ICT.

Box 5.13. An example of an integrated strategic policy framework: The National Green Technology Policy (*continued*)

New schemes for supporting the creation and growth of green industries were also introduced under this policy. The Green Technology Financing Scheme, which was allocated MYR 1.5 billion, provides loans to Malaysian-owned companies that plan to implement (up to MYR 10 million per company for 10 years) or produce (up to MYR 50 million per company for 15 years) green technology in their business. In addition, the government provides a 60% credit guarantee for lenders that use or produce green technologies. A Green Lane Policy to support green innovative SMEs that includes loans, tax exemptions and government procurement schemes was also specified.

The other major National Green Technology Policy initiatives include:

- a pilot project on the development of low-carbon green cities (Putrajaya and Cyberjaya)
- the development of eco-labels and green public procurement guidelines
- the development of an infrastructure roadmap for low-carbon transport (i.e. electronic and hybrid vehicles)
- the integration of green topics in university curriculums, research centre studies and industries to increase the number of green technology specialists and green jobs.

According to the Eleventh Malaysia Plan, the implementation of the Green Technology Financing Scheme resulted in important greenhouse gas emission reductions. In 2015, the National Green Technology Policy was replaced by the Green Malaysia Plan 2030 that is supposed to carry through the National Green Technology Policy goals and strategic thrusts.

Sources: OECD (2013c), *OECD Reviews of Innovation Policy: Sweden 2012*, http://dx.doi.org/10.1787/9789264184893-en; EPU (2010), *Tenth Malaysia Plan*, http://onlineapps.epu.gov.my/rmke10/rmke10_english.html; www.greentechmalaysia.my; Gee (2015), "Implementation of green technology policy in Malaysia"; Muhammad (2012), "National innovation strategy".

Policy makers around the world are currently facing similar challenges in the transition to a sustainable model of economic growth. Current government policy structures and policies, however, including in R&D and innovation policy, are often ill-adapted to tackle such complex challenges. System innovation is emerging as a policy tool for helping governments and policy makers to better address complex transitions. System innovation is problem-oriented framework that focuses on mobilising the innovation system, including innovation actors, policies, policy instruments, regulations, etc., to successfully manage the transition.

System innovation has important implications for the governance of STI. Mobilising the national innovation system around a specific transition is no easy task and requires a holistic and systemic design and analysis of the STI policy mix. While technological innovation is necessary, complementary innovations in organisations and institutions are also essential, as is the acceptance of change by consumers/citizens. Improved governance mechanisms and better means of engaging a range of stakeholders are also needed to facilitate system innovations, especially because such transitions take time and sustained commitment from stakeholders.

Other issues hindering this transition relate to structural issues that were highlighted in other policy areas:

- Inter-agency co-ordination and co-operation. In 2012, the multiplicity of institutions that shared responsibility for developing and implementing green growth policies with no central body co-ordinating green policies at the federal level was highlighted (OECD, 2012). This statement was still valid in 2015. Even with the support from the National Green Technology and Climate Change Council, which is used as a platform for inter-sectoral decision making, the different institutions remain focused on their own objectives, formalised in their key performance indicators. The lack of key performance indicators set at thematic, not sectoral, level remains a problem.
- Top-down tradition of policy making. This affects not only how the policies are devised and implemented but also how stakeholders receive them, resulting for instance in a certain lack of proactivity of private sector actors and citizens.
- Mismatch of skills supplied by HEIs and the needs of green-tech companies. The imperfect communication between these actors does not allow the mid-term planning of curricula that will be necessary in three or five years.
- Lack of prioritisation and specialisation in niche areas where Malaysia can build comparative advantages.
- Inconsistency between the environmental policy ambition and other policies being implemented at the same time. Indonesia, Thailand and Malaysia have the largest fossil fuel subsidy programmes in the region, with fossil fuel consumption subsidies in 2012 amounting to about USD 25 billion, USD 10 billion and USD 7 billion respectively (IEA, 2015).

Against this backdrop, the actions set up to improve the monitoring and evaluation mechanisms that aim to track and assess the effectiveness of green growth initiatives, as announced in the Eleventh Malaysia Plan, will be a key condition of Malaysia's success in achieving its green growth ambition.

Strengths and weaknesses of STI governance and the policy mix

Strengths and weaknesses of STI governance

The history of Malaysian development, from a mining and agriculture-based economy to an upper middle-income economy, and the analysis of the main R&D schemes have shown the extent of the role of the state in strategising this shift, committing the resources and putting in place the many policy measures to implement the devised plans. Besides direct support, the government policy was also key in creating the conditions for Malaysia's transition, from the infrastructure and capabilities to the numerous and generous tax incentives. Although the industrial and STI policies have at times received severe criticisms from observers and academics, there is little doubt that the government's rather centralised and authoritarian interventions have been instrumental in guiding and supporting the successful Malaysian trajectory through the end of the 1990s.

The growth slowdown experienced by Malaysia in the wake of the Asian financial crisis and the evidence of slow technological upgrading in manufacturing industries has put in question the current policy. As stated in the New Economic Model, many of the policies and strategies Malaysia has used to achieve the current state of development are insufficient to take the country to the next stage (NEAC, 2009). Malaysia's "innovation imperative" has become increasingly pervasive and prominent in national development strategies and plans. The government, at least until the recent fiscal tightening, traditionally responded to this "imperative" by devising even more ambitious strategies and plans, associated with an increase in the quantitative and qualitative, direct and indirect, support to research and innovation activities.

However, the many commendable initiatives undertaken during this period to support the emerging knowledge economy have been confronted with weaknesses in governance, and difficulties in implementing reforms of an increasingly complex system of innovation. More co-ordination appears to be needed among actors and policies, and funding requires some prioritisation. Efficient STI governance has become all the more important at a stage where Malaysia sets out to become a developed nation, achieving high-income status by 2020.

The complexity and frequent changes of the STI policy system

Concomitant to the strong increase of STI expenditure, the STI "policy mix" has become increasingly diversified, and a wider set of instruments have come to be operated by a growing number of policy institutions with an official STI-related mandate. This process of extension and fragmentation started as early as the mid-1980s and has accelerated over the last 15 years. The introduction of a new national strategy or plan has often resulted in the creation of new STI institutions at strategic and/or implementation level (NSRC, 2013a). According to a recent study (Degelsegger et al., 2014), some 14 agencies under 8 ministries provide grants to support R&D activities. Taking a broader view, there are 44 agencies and 10 ministries engaged in initiatives to support STI activities (EPU, 2015a).

All agencies charged with the implementation of strategic plans and programmes, such as the Performance Management and Delivery Unit, are confronted with the complexity in organisational structures, programmes and instruments. As regards the overall strategic programme, the New Economic Model, (approximately) 15 ministries are responsible for implementation, and each of them has subordinate agencies; the Economic Transformation Program involves a similar number of ministries and about 61 agencies. In addition, the Science to Action Programme (S2A) operated by the Malaysian Industry-Government Group for High Technology (MIGHT) and innovation programmes of the National Innovation Agency of Malaysia are necessarily complex, and all have links to the various ministries, agencies and universities.

The multiplicity of actors with similar roles, albeit with different scopes and emphases, increases the risk of redundancies. International experience suggests that a degree of overlap and, to a certain extent, competition between schemes can improve the effectiveness of the system. However, if in excess, they tend to diminish the propensity of public and private actors to engage in R&D activities, inflict additional deadweight and lead to inconsistencies between the different support schemes that undermine their effectiveness.

The Malaysian STI policy system has been shown to be complex and characterised by a significant degree of functional overlap among actors and their respective schemes and programmes. The sources of grants to support R&D and commercialisation are particularly plentiful, which public and private actors consider to be detrimental to their activities. This kind of fragmentation implies that the funds awarded are spread thinly, which stands in the way of achieving critical mass and reaping the advantages of managing larger portfolios. The Ministry of Health, to mention just one example, has six PRIs under its purview and operates a very small research grant scheme.

Frequent changes in the system further add to its complexity and reduce transparency. The competition between institutions to keep and even sometimes extend their prerogatives in STI has triggered successive rounds of change in the STI policy landscape. This instability tends to reduce the system's effectiveness as, more than most other policy areas, it requires time to build the necessary relationships of trust, develop a shared understanding and send clear signals to all the actors in the STI system.

For example, between 2005 and 2010, MIGHT was put under the purview of the Ministry of Science, Technology and Innovation, then was transferred back to the Prime Minister's Department under the Science Advisor to the Prime Minister. In 2014, it was put under a minister in the Prime Minister's Department. The Science Advisor, whose position was established in 1984 under the Prime Minister's Department to spur economic growth through science and technology, became part of the Ministry of Science, Technology and Innovation in 2005, prior to being reinstated and placed under the auspices of the Prime Minister's Department again in 2010. In the meantime, some ministries were restructured with the Ministry of Energy, Green Technology and Water being established in 2009, following the Cabinet reshuffle from the Ministry of Energy, Water and Communications with the communications part transferred to the Ministry of Communications and Multimedia. A new Ministry of Education came back into being in 2013 after being separated into two ministries in 2004 – the Ministry of Education and the Ministry of Higher Education. In 2015, the Ministry of Education was separated again.

Multiplicity of priority-setting institutions

Conflicting guidance is also a major problem identified by Malaysian STI actors (NSRC, 2013a). As shown in Table 5.3, several STI advisories co-exist with partially overlapping remits, which include in most cases overall STI orientation. The NSRC was created to be the "one-stop centre for R&D priority-setting", while co-existing with the National Innovation Council established to provide leadership in the formulation of STI policies. Although its mandate is not yet official, it is likely that the new National Science Council, created in 2016, will be tasked to advise on innovation strategies and policies.[43] Building on domestic and international expertise, the Global Science and Innovation Advisory Council also aims to provide strategic advice on STI. The National Science Council and the Global Science and Innovation Advisory Council are expected to work together to develop the STI agenda. These STI advisory councils also have to be co-ordinated upstream with the Malaysia plan process, which itself includes its own cascading "comitology", and downstream with several sectoral or thematic strategic committees. With regards to the latter, the National Science Council is meant to be instrumental in streamlining all the sectoral committees under one single, higher level institution, partially in order to alleviate the heavy demand on the Prime Minister's time, as he chairs a significant number of these councils.[44]

The proliferation of STI governance councils to priority areas has been considered a major obstacle on the path toward integrated STI policy making in Malaysia. While there are some merits – e.g. giving more weight to certain sectoral issues and a greater proximity to action – the problems clearly outweigh the advantages (MIGHT, 2013a). These include:

- redundant and overlapping functions
- lack of co-ordination and synchronisation among the various councils
- lack of high-ranking experts involved and an adequate mix of people
- infrequent meetings.

As emphasised in OECD (2009), the turbulent history of STI councils internationally suggests both that their form and functioning are hard to get right and that some degree of experimentation is necessary. The evolution of agenda-setting councils in Malaysia illustrates quite well the difficulty to ensure this function in view of the competition between organisations already in place. Debates around the creation of such a co-ordinating institution date back to the early days of Malaysia's independence. The Pan Malayan Scientific Advisory Council was created in 1953, but soon became "remarkably ineffective" as the government allegedly refused to take notice of its recommendations, and was eliminated in 1957. It was only in 1975 that a second attempt was made, with the creation of the National Council for Scientific Research and Development.[45] It lost its power after some years and, despite its restructuring in 1990 to regain power, became dormant. It was replaced by the National Science and Research Council in 2011, in parallel with the National Innovation Council for about two years, and since 2016 is concomitant with, or replaced by, the National Science Council.

Some lessons can be drawn from confronting the Malaysian experience with STI councils with the results of two international comparative studies (Box 5.14).

- One result from international experience is that a lack of or only partial legitimacy of STI councils, e.g. due to their proliferation and limited remit, undermines their quality and strategic impact on research operators' behaviour (Box 5.16). The spread of the agenda-setting function among numerous public institutions leads to a fragmentation of investment and to efforts pulling in different directions. This reduces the opportunity to build critical mass and benefit from economies of scale. Frequent changes in priorities reduce the ability of research organisations to establish a long-term strategy and effectively make mid- to long-term commitments to the priorities corresponding to national development goals.
- Secondly, it is not always clear how comprehensive the consultations were, and how thorough the analyses on which the councils' advice or decisions were based. Few reports, if any, of previous STI councils are available, with little information on their decisions. In this regard, the progress made with the NSRC must be emphasised. The PRA performance assessment is a very comprehensive, well-documented evaluation, and is available online. It has been very influential on policy making since both the Research Management Agency, now announced in the Eleventh Malaysia Plan, stems from one of the report's detailed recommendations. Some of the NSRC's presentations that are available online indicate that the council and its numerous expert working groups have undertaken significant consultations with stakeholders, for instance prior to setting the national R&D priority areas (Rahim, 2012a, 2012b). No information has yet been made available with regard to its future role *vis-à-vis* the newly created National Science Council.

In addition to the advisory councils and committees, several other ministries or agencies have in their formal mandate a role in the orientation of the national innovation system. The Office of the Science Advisor is tasked with prioritising the role of STI for national development. One of the several functions of the National Innovation Agency of Malaysia, which replaced the National Innovation Council, is to formulate policy strategies and direction relating to innovation. Last but not least, MOSTI's "vision" is to lead the "National STI Agenda",[46] including by developing the national STI strategies.

Box 5.14. Lessons learnt from international comparisons of national science, technology and innovation councils

Science, technology and innovation councils are used as a mechanism in many countries to respond to the growing need for more effective innovation governance by fulfilling the functions not only of priority setting and advising, but also policy co-ordination and strategic planning. The majority of the councils examined in a recent benchmarking serve primarily an advisory function (Austria, Canada, Denmark, Germany's EFI, Singapore, Switzerland, the United Kingdom and the United States). Some councils also have a co-ordination function (China, Finland, Germany's Innovationsdialog and Wissenschaftsrat, Japan and Korea) and/or priority-setting (China, Finland, Japan and Korea) or even policy planning function (Finland). Their role in evaluation tends to be limited, but this is mostly due to a lack of institutionalisation of evaluation rather than for reasons of "good design". International experience also shows that the co-ordination function is the most difficult to achieve.

Against the backdrop of these different mandates, four main types of councils can be distinguished:

- joint planning model: the government uses the council as a virtual "horizontal ministry of innovation", much as engineering companies build project teams by bringing together people across different disciplines
- co-ordination model: the council communicates horizontally across ministry responsibilities so as to align policies in support of innovation, without this alignment always being binding
- advice model: the council provides non-binding advice to the government
- platform model: the council functions as a "sounding board", providing the government with a forum for interacting with a selection of representative high-level stakeholders, usually from industry and academia, but also at times including labour unions, research institutes or other actors.

Identifying best practices and generating transferable lessons is a risky task given that so many aspects of these councils' performance are conditioned by the contexts of their respective national innovation systems. These councils deal with nothing less than the very "DNA" of national STI policies and are thus highly country-specific. However, some broad lessons can be drawn from two international comparisons of STI councils:

- The chairing by the prime minister and the presence of ministers is generally positively associated with a council's ability to ensure co-ordination and communication between the different sectors; but statutory participation should be underpinned by genuine commitment.
- Their ability to affect innovation policy as a whole is limited when their legitimacy is only partial, i.e. if their scope is not systems-wide and/or there are parallel bodies acting in their sphere.
- The policy elaboration, co-ordination and advising roles of councils must not get entangled in resource allocation or budgeting; this might undermine their neutrality and independence, and also generate strong opposition from ministries who might see the council as a threat.

Box 5.14. **Lessons learnt from international comparisons of national science, technology and innovation councils** (*continued*)

- STI councils should consult and co-operate with the other actors of the system to access the strategic intelligence distributed across the system. Regardless of their power and legitimacy, councils must create an evidence base on which consensus can be built. Their decisions should therefore be based on wide and transparent consultations, as well as thorough analysis. If possible, these analyses should not be carried out only by one ministry. Most councils have analytical resources (a secretariat, budget for analyses).
- Councils' form and processes should be robust against changes of government by being sufficiently flexible to accommodate some change priorities while maintaining continuity of strategic intelligence and advice.
- Councils should make their mark quickly, both as a "thought leader" in policy making and through successful intervention. This also implies good communication and dissemination of reports.
- Realistic expectations should drive the design of STI councils' mandates. Councils cannot be tasked to address all national needs for innovation policy, i.e. provide relevant advice, oversee policy implementation, direct or guide investments, evaluate policy, encourage experimentation and learning, and mobilise stakeholders.

Sources: Schwaag Serger, Wise and Arnold (2015), *National Research & Innovation Councils as an Instrument of Innovation Governance: Characteristics & Challenges*, www.vinnova.se/upload/EPiStorePDF/va_15_07_T.pdf; OECD (2009), "Chile's National Innovation Council for Competitiveness".

Various levels of overlap between these institutions and little mutual consideration result in multiple priorities, set in the aftermath of different government programmes. The Economic Transformation Programme has identified 12 national key economic areas, the Tenth Malaysia Plan has 11 development areas, the Third Industrial Master Plan (2006-20) has 12 manufacturing sectors and MOSTI has prioritised several national technology foresight areas in the framework of its Mega Science programme. The National Science and Research Council has selected nine R&D focus areas. Before doing so, it had to review and compare the established priorities and focus areas of some of the previous strategic plans and programmes (MOSTI, 2012; NSRC, 2013b).[47] Also, more recently, in the framework of the Prime Minister's Science to Action programme, some targeted areas have been set, with science governance or governance for science high on the list. To these should be added the priorities set at the level of the different programmes or instruments, such as MOSTI's TechnoFund.

The investigations undertaken as part of the PRA performance assessment have made it clear that the diversity of priorities is exacerbated by the competition between the numerous STI actors involved in the STI decision-making and funding process for influence and control. The managers and researchers in HEIs and PRIs claimed that they received conflicting direction from different ministries and agencies. Furthermore, these organisations tended to shift their R&D priorities (NSRC, 2013a).

Lack of central co-ordination

The negative effect of the multiplication of STI institutions could, in principle, be alleviated by effective co-ordination of the different plans. However, this has not happened in Malaysia. The co-ordination function, like the agenda-setting one, is shared among various actors, the already mentioned committees and councils, which most of the time cumulate both functions, some agencies like the National Innovation Agency of Malaysia (AIM), as well as additional institutions such as the Investment Committee for Public Funds in the backdrop of the Malaysia plan process.

The absence of an organisation with clear responsibilities and the necessary legitimacy and authority to ensure central co-ordination has been underlined by many domestic and international analysts and actors (Box 5.15).

This problem was also clearly emphasised in the Tenth Malaysia Plan, which proposed giving a more prominent role to the Prime Minister's Office to head the new overall institutional structure of the innovation system. Taking advantage of its authority and the breadth of its scope, this department was considered appropriate to take into account innovation across all sectors and all parts of the value chain (EPU, 2010). For that purpose, a dedicated unit was established, the Unit Inovasi Khas, tasked to oversee and drive innovation across the entire system. This unit was later replaced by a dedicated agency, the National Innovation Agency of Malaysia. The Prime Minister himself chaired up to nine STI-related councils under the Tenth Malaysia Plan, some transversal, covering the whole STI system, others sectoral, ranging from biotech and aerospace to brain technologies. Besides increased legitimacy, the objective of the engagement of the Prime Minister in these councils and committees is to reduce the numerous "STI governance silos", and thus fragmentation. The Science Advisor to the Prime Minister also chairs several committees and councils.

One approach to achieve co-ordination between actors was the creation of a central organisation to co-ordinate the implementation of the various STI initiatives. From the outset, the National Innovation Agency of Malaysia was designed to fulfil policy formulation, co-ordination and implementation missions. Whereas in most countries innovation agencies tend to report to one specific ministry (Schwaag Serger, Wise and Arnold, 2015), the National Innovation Agency of Malaysia was established under the Agensi Inovasi Malaysia Act 2010 specifically as a cross-sectoral, cross-cutting agency that could take a "horizontal" view on STI issues and break free from ties and vested interests of already existing departmental responsibilities. Furthermore, it is administered by a Governing Council, a high-level committee chaired by the Prime Minister and composed of minister-level members (including the Minister of Science, Technology and Innovation and the Minister of Higher Education), and CEOs and presidents of public and private institutions. However, it appears that its role consists mainly of acting as a co-secretariat for the Investment Committee for Public Funds, along with policy implementation through its own programmes and initiatives.

More recently, the Malaysian government has discussed the creation of a central national research agency under the purview of the NSRC, the Research Management Agency, recommended in the 2013 NSRC study (NSRC, 2013a). It was recommended that this agency be tasked with tracking evolving social needs, co-ordinating the advancement of R&D priority areas identified by the NSRC, overseeing the management and operation of Malaysia's public R&D enterprise, and evaluating the performance of public research assets and individual research programmes (NSRC, 2013a). The government has followed this recommendation and made plans for the creation of an agency that would manage all R&D funding.[48] This agency has for over two years been the subject of lively debates between the different actors of the STI system who see their prerogatives in the matter affected by its creation. It has now been officially announced in the Eleventh Malaysia Plan (EPU, 2015a).

Box 5.15. Selected extracts from recent reports recommending a reform to improve prioritisation and co-ordination of science, technology and innovation policy in Malaysia

There are 44 agencies and 10 ministries engaged in R&D&C&I initiatives This has resulted in competition for resources as well as overlapping and conflicting priorities in some research areas (EPU, 2015a).

While the STI and its implementation are manifested in various national blueprints such as the National Policy on Science, Technology & Innovation 2013-2020 (NPSTI), Malaysia "Higher Education Blueprint 2015-25" , SME Masterplan 2012-20 and the aforementioned ETP, there is no unified approach or execution strategy. This poses a challenge to efficient and effective application of STI solutions for national development. It also underscores the need for a sound governance framework to address complex socio-cultural and fundamental policy measurement issues as we continue in our efforts to make possible an STI-powered economy by the year 2020 (ASM, 2015).

The Ministry of Science, Technology and Innovation (MoSTI) and the Ministry of Education are the principal drivers of Malaysia's national innovation system. There seems to be some agreement that applied research is the purview of MOSTI, whereas basic research falls under the Ministry of Education, but there is no mechanism for co-ordinating basic and applied research (Rasiah and Chandran 2015).

There are a wide range of support measures incorporating a large number of STI stakeholders, which are undoubtedly beneficial to STI development. Further synergies among the 14 agencies under the 8 ministries which are involved in funding, initiatives and other STI-related activities would be beneficial (Degelsegger et al., 2014).

The study found that Malaysia lacks a co-ordinating body that can effectively implement the nation's R&D priorities by funding, managing, co-ordinating, monitoring, and evaluating its R&D investments. Part of this challenge lies in the fact that there exists a multitude of plans and institutions that relate to R&D funding, programmes, and policies. (...) The constant spawning of new programmes and PRAs has resulted in competition for resources, influence and control and, in some cases, overlapping and conflicting direction from different ministries (NSRC, 2013a).

It seems that ample fiscal incentives and financing schemes have failed to have significant impact, due to: 1) lack of co-ordination among too many agencies and schemes; 2) cumbersome procedures; and 3) restrictive conditions and definition (Thiruchelvam, 2013).

With so many ministries, agencies, schemes, grants and initiatives within Malaysia's STI system, there is an urgent need for consolidation and streamlining to ensure maximum impact and value for money. This could include the fostering of greater integration between departments, through the re-establishment of a high-level cross-departmental committee and secondments, as well as a rationalisation of schemes and incentives for R&D and technology development (Day and Muhammad, 2011).

In 2013, the Prime Minister announced the creation of a wide-ranging programme, Science to Action, that aims "to streamline and monitor STI projects, policies and achievements towards sustainable growth beyond 2020" under the authority of the Science Advisor.[49]

In order to avoid this new agency being caught in "territorial disputes" between established actors or its budget – whether it is centralised or not – from being too volatile, it was proposed to establish it by a National Science Act, thus providing it with a solid legal foundation (MOSTI, 2013a; ASM, 2015). The National Science Act was conceived as a way to enshrine STI policy more generally. It was, for instance, envisaged by some to include in the act a minimum public R&D intensity. This initiative has been the object of long and controversial debates in the STI policy arena and administration. Although it seemed to be close to completion (Yusoff and Pillai, 2014), the National Science Act has more recently been abandoned.

An attempt to represent the overall process for policy development, co-ordination, planification and implementation under the new governance structure, including the National Science Council, is proposed in Figure 5.14. Further efforts to streamline this process will be needed to take full advantage of the recent and ongoing reforms. The example of the reform of China's STI governance and funding system could be interesting in that regard (Box 5.16).

Figure 5.14. **Policy development, co-ordination, planification and implementation in Malaysia**

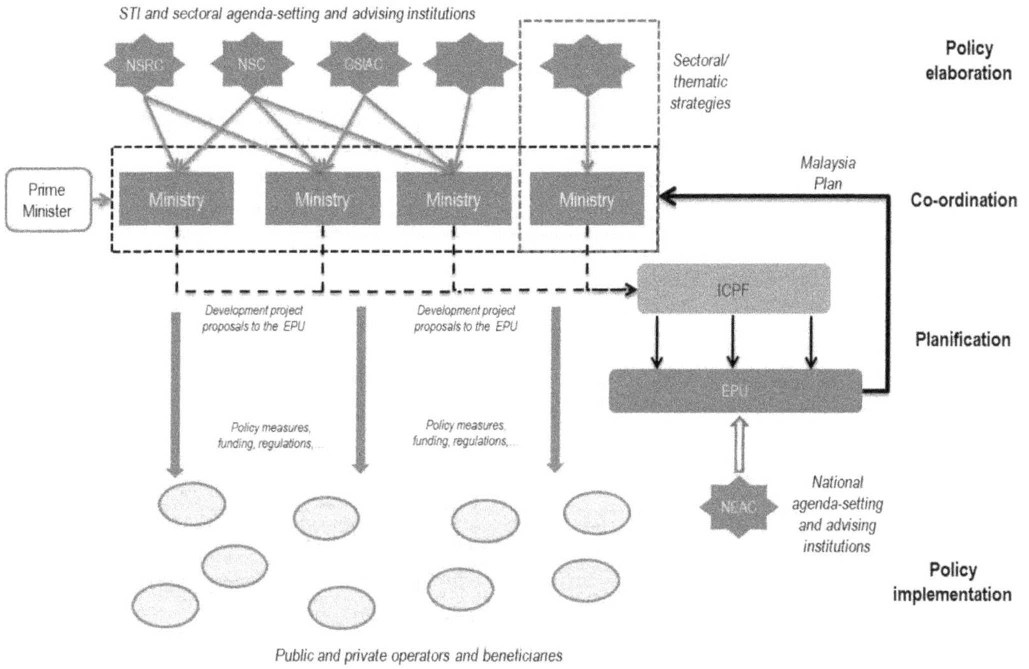

Note: NSRC = National Science and Research Council; NSC = National Science Council; GSIAC = Global Science and Innovation Advisory Council; EPU = Economic Policy Unit; ICPF = Investment Committee for Public Funds; NEAC = National Economic Advisory Council.

Strengths and weaknesses of the R&D support instrument portfolio

Fluctuating and decreasing R&D budget to support research and innovation activities

Public support for research and innovation activities through grants has been fluctuating. From one Malaysia plan to another, the budget allocation to any fund can change dramatically for reasons that appear not clearly related to an assessment of the strengths and weaknesses of the instrument concerned and in contradiction to announced priorities. More recently, "intra-plan" variations added to the traditional variation across the Malaysia plans. This is a result of the newly implemented two-year rolling plans. These fluctuations can act as a strong disincentive for potential public and private beneficiaries to engage in ambitious research projects of mid- to long-term time horizons. On top of the fluctuation of funding, the budget of most schemes has undergone a downward trend since the Tenth Malaysia Plan. Unfortunately, since the Tenth Malaysia Plan, consolidated information on the different streams of budgeted and expensed funds in the different sectors of the economy is unavailable.

Box 5.16. An ongoing reform – Streamlining China's STI governance and funding system

China has set up numerous STI programmes and foundations which have played a significant role in enhancing national scientific and technological strength, improving the country's competitiveness, and supporting economic and social development. However, due to a lack of high-level design, co-ordination and funding mechanisms, these initiatives resulted in significant duplication, dispersion and inefficiency in these programmes, and a fragmentation of science and technology resource allocation. China initiated a new round of reform of its science and technology system in order to implement the innovation-driven development strategy proposed in 2012. In 2014, two significant policies were announced: "Opinions on Improving and Strengthening the Management of National Government-Funded Projects and Funds" (Guofa [2014] No. 11) and "Scheme of Deepening Management Reform of National Science and Technology Programs (Special Projects and Foundations etc.)" (Guofa [2014] No. 64).

According to these reforms, about 100 national S&T programmes managed by different ministries and departments will be classified into 5 categories: the National Natural Science Foundation, the National Science and Technology Major Projects, the National Key R&D Programme, the Special Foundation for Technological Innovation, and the Excellence Centre and Talent Programme. The most important change is that ministries and government departments no longer directly manage specific projects. An open and unified national science and technology management platform will be established, which consists of the following six components:

1. Establishment of the Inter-Ministerial Joint Conference (IMJC) for the management of S&T programmes (special projects and foundations), led by the Ministry of Science and Technology with the participation of the Ministry of Finance, the National Development and Reform Commission and other relevant ministries. It is responsible for making rules of procedure and deliberating on S&T development strategies and plans, priorities and guidelines of S&T programmes, the formation of the Strategic Consulting and Comprehensive Review Committee, and the selection of professional agencies for managing S&T programmes.
2. The existing qualified public institutions of S&T management will be transformed into standardised professional agencies for S&T project management. Professional agencies are responsible for receiving applications and organising project review, process management, and final evaluation.
3. Establishment of the Strategic Consulting and Comprehensive Review Committee, composed of senior experts from the science and technology community, industry and specialists in economics. It provides consultation for S&T development strategies, plans, priorities and tasks of S&T programmes, which will inform the decision making of the Inter-Ministerial Joint Conference. It will also make recommendations on project review regulations, a national S&T project reviewer database, and standardised procedure of Professional agencies. In some cases it will be commissioned by the Inter-Ministerial Joint Conference to carry out the review of key and major S&T projects.
4. Establishment of a unified evaluation and inspection mechanism for S&T programmes and the performance of the Strategic Consulting and Comprehensive Review Committee and Professional agencies, spearheaded by MOST and the Ministry of Finance. The performance evaluation of S&T programmes will be commissioned to a third party by way of open competition and its result will inform the budget allocation by the Ministry of Finance.
5. Establishment of a dynamic adjustment mechanism of S&T programmes based on the results of performance evaluation and supervision and recommendations of related ministries.
6. Improvement of the national S&T information system used for management of the whole cycle of STI projects, from guidelines announcement, application submitting, review, budget appraisal, supervision and final evaluation. All non-confidential information will be publicly accessible.

The proliferation of R&D schemes

Another major trend, since 1996 in particular, is the growing number of schemes available. Following a long period when the only available means to support R&D included the funding of research institutions, in particular research institutes and the IRPA programme, the number of instruments has increased significantly with each new Malaysia plan. This trend involves a growing differentiation of instruments responding to more and more specific needs as regards R&D stage, type of beneficiary and project configuration. Each instrument itself can, in fact, include several different schemes. For instance, the InnoFund consists of two schemes, the Enterprise InnoFund for individuals and small enterprises, and the Community InnoFund for registered community groups, each with different modalities (duration, maximum amounts, etc.).

This multiplicity of disbursement vehicles could be detrimental to the efficiency and effectiveness of the overall system as it increases its complexity and opacity. International experiences show that this can act as a powerful obstacle for expanding research and innovation activities as it increases the "entry cost" for any potential beneficiary, in particular in "local" universities and SMEs which do not have dedicated services to provide the necessary information and intermediary services. The National Innovation Surveys show the low level of use of government R&D grant instruments by innovative firms.[50] Even more telling are the reasons for not accessing government support: 42% of relevant companies declare that they are not aware of the existence of the available schemes (MASTIC, 2014).

The inflation of grant schemes is also often associated with a lack of political coherence, since most schemes will have their own objectives and priority areas, moreover unclearly aligned with national development goals, apart from some general mention of the importance of knowledge and innovation.

Finally, the multiplicity of schemes tends to reduce their efficiency due to scale effects. Firstly, although there are no data on the management fees of the different schemes, it is well-known that economies of scale can be generated by a centralised administration or merger of different schemes. This is one of the main rationales for the creation of the research agencies that have been established in most developed and emerging economies. Secondly, as an analysis of the funds allocated suggests, the increase in the number of schemes often comes at the expense of the budget of each individual scheme and, in the end, results in smaller grants. This is, of course, particularly true in times of budget moderation, which has been the case in Malaysia in recent years.

Weak monitoring and evaluation culture and techniques

While the strength of Malaysia to identify the main challenges and derive the diagnostics for ambitious strategic plans is widely acknowledged, its capacity to implement and deliver them appears limited (see, for example, Day and Muhammad, 2011; OECD, 2013a; Rasiah, 2011). The reasons of this weakness in implementation can be found at various levels, from inadequate governance, lack of policy sustainability and predictability and ill-conceived measures to insufficient capabilities of middle-management administrators in some ministries and agencies, as well as their "distance" from the beneficiaries and operators of their policy. Of course, none of this is unique to Malaysia.

All these weaknesses have been extensively discussed and bold institutional and practical reforms are underway in initiatives such as the Government Transformation Programme. However, a common condition to the success of any efforts to improve the government delivery ability is the establishment of a systematic evaluation system at the core of policy making. In contrast, the poor monitoring and evaluation of R&D policy instruments was underlined in the Public Research Assets (PRA) Performance Evaluation of the National Science and Research Council in 2011 (Box 5.17).

Box 5.17. Lessons on R&D grant schemes from the Public Research Assets (PRA) Performance Evaluation

Although focused on higher education institutions and research institutes specifically, the Public Research Assets (PRA) Performance Evaluation provides a detailed and comprehensive assessment of R&D grant schemes, at least from the view point of the public research operators. This study was requested by the Prime Minister in 2011 and carried out by the National Science and Research Council in co-operation with the New York Academy of Sciences in 2011-12.

It was found that several limitations hampered the performance of the public R&D schemes, both on the side of the ministries and agencies operating the instruments and on that of the beneficiaries.

Poor monitoring techniques

The Economic Planning Unit, which has the overall responsibility of tracking the efficiency of public investment, has been using monitoring tools that are at times poorly suited to research and innovation activities. In particular, it is reported to have had a narrow focus on expenditures and the consumption of the allocated funds, which can worsen the problems faced in R&D projects. The Economic Planning Unit has progressively broadened its range of metrics to include output-based indicators, in particular, patents. However, here again, the overemphasis on patents has had a detrimental effect as it led, on the one hand, to a surge of patents of poor quality, not resulting in any commercialisation of research results, and on the other hand, to overlooking all more intangible results of research, not to mention its longer term impact. Getting a grip on the latter would require going beyond monitoring and launching proper *ex post* evaluations at higher (scheme or, better, policy) level.

Inappropriate selection and awarding process

The biggest complaints among researchers interviewed or surveyed during the study were related to the R&D grant processes:

- The process for selecting the proposals is seen as unfair, not oriented toward learning from and improvement of the rejected proposals (insufficient feedback to unsuccessful applications) and lacks transparency. This is partly due to inappropriate design of the process (short reviewing timeframes, application of selection quotas, etc.), but also to the lack of competency of the review teams.
- Selected projects are financed well below not only what was demanded in the budget proposal, but also what was announced in the initial grant award notice.
- The grant award process is too slow and not responsive enough.

Source: NSRC (2013a), *PRA Performance Evaluation: Unlocking Vast Potentials, Fast-Tracking the Future*, http://umexpert.um.edu.my/file/publication/00012427_86127.pdf.

The PRA Performance Evaluation, a self-evaluation exercise in many respects, is by far the most comprehensive and detailed assessment of the public R&D innovation system. The closest exercises to an evaluation are the few and one-off progress reviews of strategic plans, such as the "Review of the National Higher Education Strategic Plan" (MOE, 2014). The only fairly systematic assessment exercises in Malaysia seem to be undertaken every five years in the context of developing a new Malaysia plan. Some results are provided in the "looking backward" section of the new Malaysia plan, albeit results are partial and presented without any indication about the "who", "what" and "how" of the review.

Notes

1. Clarion and National Semiconductor established their factories in 1971 in Penang, followed by several other Japanese and US MNEs over that decade.
2. For instance, to qualify for some of these incentives, firms had three years to raise the level of their R&D expenditures to at least 1% of the amount of their gross sales and have science and technical graduates as 7% of their workforce (UNIDO, 2003).
3. In particular, the Industrial Technical Assistance Fund (support to licensing strategic technology from foreign sources) and the Industry R&D Grant Scheme (support to R&D).
4. Electrical and electronics; textiles and apparel; chemicals; resource-based industries; agro-based and food products industries; transportation industry (automotive, etc.); materials industries; and machinery and equipment.
5. R&D spending of at least 1.5% (from 0.7% in 2002) and 60 researchers per 10 000 labour force (18 in 2002; 4 in 1986). The latest data available show that in 2012 these targets had not yet been met: R&D intensity was 1.13 and the number of researchers 57.5 per 10 000 labour force (EPU, 2015a).
6. The seven strategic thrusts were: 1) strengthening national research and technological capacity and capability; 2) promoting commercialisation of research outputs; 3) developing human resource capacity and capability; 4) promoting a culture for science, innovation and technology-based entrepreneurship; 5) strengthening the institutional framework and management for S&T and monitoring of S&T policy implementation; 6) ensuring widespread diffusion and application of technology, contributing towards an increase in market-driven R&D to adapt and improve technologies; and 7) building competence and expertise in emerging technologies.
7. Malaysia launched the Malaysia Technical Cooperation Program (MTCP) to promote technical co-operation amongst developing countries. In 1995, it launched the Commonwealth Partnership for Technology Management to assist Africa and the Caribbean. Malaysia is also fully financing the International Science, Technology and Innovation Centre for South-South Cooperation (ISTIC), created in 2005 under the Auspices of UNESCO. Finally, Malaysia launched the Malaysia-UNESCO Cooperation Programme in 2009 to help other developing nations and small island developing states in the areas of education, science and culture (Lee, 2016).
8. From May 2013 until July 2015, it was merged with the Ministry of Education to form a single entity.
9. The Science Advisor is Chairman of the National Science and Research Council and of the National Professors Council; Joint Secretary for the Global Science and Research Council; Joint Chairman of MIGHT; Chairman of the Malaysian Biotechnology Corporation (BiotechCorp); and Chair of the Intergovernmental Panel

on Biodiversity and Ecosystem Services. Very recently, the Science Advisor has been appointed Chair of the new National Science Council created in 2016.

10. As regards the Global Science and Innovation Advisory Council, the Prime Minister declared that the National Science Council will be "the focal point for the Global Science and Innovation Advisory Council (GSIAC) that was formed five years ago," and that "a symbiosis of both councils would have a greater effect on the STI agenda" (Abas and Aziz, 2016). As regards the Investment Committee for Public Funds, it has been announced that the committee will be placed under the aegis of the Research Management Agency.

11. A sample of 200 IRPA projects was evaluated, representing about 10% of all projects and 15% of the total budget allocation. These projects produced significant scientific and technical projects, but only 7% resulted in research outputs such as patents (applied or granted). The research commercialisation results were therefore in an even smaller proportion. Furthermore, the review showed that the linkages between industry were essentially informal and collaborative R&D was negligible. Subsequent reforms of the IRPA included a strengthening of the selection of new applications and the monitoring of ongoing projects (EPU, 1996).

12. SIRIM, which managed the funds, allocated MYR 36 million for 1 402 project approvals during the period 1990-96, i.e. MYR 25 800 per project (Rasiah, 1999).

13. The Industrial Technical Assistance Fund was discontinued in 1996 and replaced by the Multimedia Super Corridor R&D Grant Scheme (MASTIC, 2008).

14. The Industry R&D Grant Scheme was discontinued in 2005 (MASTIC, 2008).

15. Only research universities can access LGRS "top-down" grants.

16. The main criteria used in MyRA to assess the level of activity in research, development and commercialisation are the quality of researchers, quality of research, innovation indicators and postgraduate quality.

17. Out of the ten most frequent reasons for rejecting projects submitted to the TechnoFund, six relate to the weak innovation content (lack of novelty, project already in commercialisation stage or already exists, assembling of commercial components, etc.) (MOSTI, 2013b).

18. The ten broad research and priority areas are: engineering sciences, advanced material sciences, chemical sciences, physical and mathematical sciences, life sciences, agricultural sciences, medical and health sciences, environmental sciences, computer sciences and ICT, and social sciences and humanities. The 13 flagship programmes are: renewable energy, advanced manufacturing, electronics, wireless sensor network, predictive analytics, three-dimension Internet, space technology, oceanography, meteorology, production system and precision agriculture, biosurveillance, tropical diseases, and food security (MASTIC, 2014).

19. Design, accreditation/certification/technology audit, incubation, training, clinical research, market research, demonstration (market research), up-scaling, and promotion/marketing/packaging.

20. No recent data are available for these schemes.

21. MOSTI undertook a survey in 2004 which revealed that many firms faced problems when applying for R&D incentives: procedures for the application of the incentives were not clear; information requested in the application for some of the incentives were company secrets; the scope of eligibility of some of the incentives were too narrow; the definition of R&D for the incentives was not clear.

22. Full income tax exemption of five to ten years, instead of a tax reduction, with the Pioneer status for strategic projects (high-tech industries, R&D activities, strengthening industrial linkages and multimedia industries). Investment Tax Allowance (allowance on qualifying capital expenditure) of ten years instead of five for R&D companies.

23. As previously mentioned, Malaysia is well ahead of most developed and developing countries with regards to the Starting a Business Index (12th position in 2015) (World Bank Doing Business website: www.doingbusiness.org).

24. 1 400 SMEs from 8 high potential sectors for the period 2014-20.

25. The Chief Secretary to the Government, the Director-General of the Economic Planning Unit and the Governor of Bank Negara Malaysia.

26. Many agencies and other institutions at general, sectoral and regional levels offer human capital development programmes with SMEs as primary target beneficiaries. According to SMEs, 157 SME development programmes were implemented by 15 ministries and 60 agencies in 2013 for a total value amounting to about MYR 12 billion (AIM, 2014). A consolidated list of 47 of these programmes is presented on SME Corporation's website (www.smecorp.gov.my/index.php/en/programmes/2015-12-21-10-16-28/human-capital-development).

27. MIDA presented to the Economic Council (EC) on 7 March 2016 a proposal to set up Innovation Manufacturing Centers (IMC) in Malaysia, inspired by international experiences in countries such as Chinese Taipei and Korea. The main proposed roles of these centres are: undertake R&D/innovation for demand-oriented production technology; provide technology support for companies to utilise the technology, manpower and infrastructure; provide/render improvement and solutions for common technology bottlenecks (productivity); facilitate commercialisation/propagate transfer of technology.

28. Halal industry, financial services, tourism industry, wholesale and retail trade, private higher education, professional services, private healthcare, and the construction industry.

29. Liberalisation of 45 services subsectors since 2009 which can now be fully detained by up to 100% foreign equity. In addition, the government enforced the Competition Act in 2012 (EPU, 2015a; MPC, 2015).

30. Local content in Proton cars increased after the launch of the Vendor Development Program, from 18% in 1985 to 80% in 1992. Total vendors of Proton increased from 17 in 1985 to 284 in 2005. Around 50% of vendors were SMEs and of these around 50% were *Bumiputera*-owned SMEs (Rasiah, Sadoi and Busser, 2008).

31. See: www.theoilandgasyear.com/articles/go-global-petronas-vendor-development-programme and www.petronas.com.my/media-relations/media-releases/Pages/article/PETRONAS-APPOINTS-THREE-NEW-VENDORS.aspx.

32. *Bumiputera* is the Malaysian term to describe the Malay race and other indigenous peoples of Southeast Asia.

33. The 16 largest GLCs counted 225 050 employees in 2014. GLCs, along with other state institutions, were key in raising the participation of *Bumiputeras* in the economy. In 2000, 90% of the employees in government-controlled sectors were *Bumiputeras* (Rasiah, 2006).

34. There were 60 666 suppliers registered with the 16 largest GLCs in 2013, accounting for MYR 75.1 billion worth of contracts. In 2015, seven GLCs were participating in the Bumiputera Vendor Development Programme: PETRONAS, Telekom Malaysia,

Tenaga Nasional Bhd, Proton, Boustead Naval Shipyard Bhd, Keretapi Tanah Melayu Bhd and Chemical Company of Malaysia Bhd. Together they represented about 1 643 vendor companies. Several GLCs also signed Memorandums of Understanding with the Ministry of International Trade and Industry to promote *Bumiputera* entrepreneurship.

35. This topic first appeared in the priorities identified in a recent survey carried out among the Malaysian higher education community during the review of the National Higher Education Strategic Plan in 2014.

36. For instance, the Malaysian Qualification Agency has developed the Codes of Practice for Program Accreditation and Codes of Practice for Institutional Audit. These codes are benchmarked against international good practices and nationally accepted by stakeholders through various consultations (Grapragasem, Krishnan and Mansor, 2014).

37. Reforms in the HEI curricula have included more entrepreneurship and soft skills, e.g. the introduction of the Malaysian Soft Skills Scale (My3S) aimed at assessing students' soft skills attainment upon entry to and exit from HEIs.

38. Several funding schemes have been launched by the Ministry of Education and MOSTI, and several new agencies with a cluster or sectorial focus have been created (e.g. the Agro-Biotechnology Institute Malaysia). Examples include the Prototype Research Grant Scheme and the TechnoFund. The Collaborative Research in Engineering, Science and Technology also promotes industry-science linkages in research and innovation.

39. For example, the Economic Planning Unit provided the Malaysian Agriculture Research Development Institute (MARDI) with block grants amounting to MYR 86 million in 2013 and MYR 60 million in 2014 to conduct specific research on food security, agri-technology, climate change and value-added agriculture (ibid).

40. According to the PRA assessment (NRSC, 2013a), a majority of PRA leaders and researchers feel that they: 1) get conflicting direction from different ministries and agencies; and 2) must continuously respond to these shifting R&D priorities. Researchers consider that these shifting expectations impact the ability of research organisations to sustain a research agenda and build core capabilities in areas of strategic importance (ibid).

41. It is, for instance, striking that First Solar Malaysia Sdn Bhd, a company producing solar panels, was, in 2013 and 2014, the third top Malaysian PCT applicant, directly behind MIMOS and the University Malaya and ahead of well-established institutions in key historic areas such as the Malaysian Palm Oil Board or PETRONAS (oil).

42. Whereas it lost 1 039 900 ha, or 4.7%, of its forest cover between 1999 and 2008 (OECD, 2012).

43. At the opening of the National Science Council on 27 January, Prime Minister Datuk Seri Najib Razak declared that the council was created to ensure that "the STI agenda can be monitored and managed under a 'mothership' council, and avoid duplication in terms of administration, outlook and priority" (Abas and Aziz, 2016).

44. The streamlining of STI-related councils was one of the policy measures foreseen in the National Policy on Science, Technology and Innovation 2013-20 (MOSTI, 2013a).

45. See the March 1964 letter from C.H.G. Oldham (Asia expert at the Science Policy Research Unit, University of Sussex) to R.H. Nolte (Institute of Current World Affairs) where the former highlighted that "Malaysia is one of the few countries in

Asia which has no science policy-making body, no national research council nor any form of science council". This absence, according to the author, might be rooted in the British colonial tradition of individual projects without any overall co-ordination or planning. It was also, according to his field study, related to the ministry already in function (the Department of Commerce and Industry at that time), which felt that its STI prerogatives would be threatened by a potential STI council (www.icwa.org/wp-content/uploads/2015/09/CHGO-24.pdf).

46. See MOSTI corporate profile at: www.mosti.gov.my/en/corporate-profile/about-mosti.

47. The systematic comparison of the focus areas of the National Foresight, Mega Science, ETP and IMP3 undertaken in 2011 showed that the priorities were not well aligned. Agriculture and E&E were the two sectors that seemed the most shared between these programmes and plans.

48. The National Science Foundation in the United States and the National Research Foundation of Singapore are referred to as a model in that respect (see Yusoff and Pillai, 2014).

49. See the Science to Action website at: www.science2action.my.

50. Less than one in four manufacturing firms declare having used in recent years an R&D grant (23%), an innovation grant (18%) or an R&D commercialisation fund (25%). These proportions are, not surprisingly, even lower for service firms (MASTIC, 2014).

References

1DANA (2014), *1DANA Database of Funds, Facilities, Experts and Commercialisation Opportunities* (database), www.1dana.gov.my/search-com.aspx.

Abas, A. and F. Aziz (2016), "Najib wants integrated plan on STEM tabled at next NSC meeting", *New Straits Times*, 28 January, www.nst.com.my/news/2016/01/124526/najib-wants-integrated-plan-stem-tabled-next-nsc-meeting.

AIM (2014), *AIM Annual Report 2014*, Agensi Inovasi Malaysia, Putrajaya.

AIM (2013a), *AIM Annual Report 2013*, Agensi Inovasi Malaysia, Putrajaya.

AIM (2013b), *Corporation Annual Report 2013*.

Arnold, E. and B. Thuriaux (1997), "Developing firms' technological capabilities", Technopolis Group Report, Brighton.

Arraíz, I., F. Henriquez and R. Stucchi (2011), "Impact of the Chilean Supplier Development Program on the performance of SME and their large-firm customers", Working Paper, OVE/WP-04/11, Inter-American Development Bank, Washington, DC.

ASM (2015), *Science Outlook: Action Towards Vision, Research & Policy*, Recommendations Document, Academy of Sciences Malaysia.

Basu Das, S. and P.O. Lee (2014), *Malaysia's Socio-Economic Transformation*, Institute for Southeast Asian Studies, Singapore.

Chandran, V.G.R. (2010), "R&D commercialization challenges for developing countries: The case of Malaysia", *Tech Monitor*, Nov-Dec, pp. 25-30, www.techmonitor.net/tm/images/d/dd/10nov_dec_sf3.pdf.

Day, N. and A. Muhammad (2011), *Malaysia: The Atlas of Islamic-World Science and Innovation: Country Case Study No. 1*, British Council et al., www.aiwsi.org/imgs/news/image/atlas-country-case-malaysia.pdf.

Degelsegger, A. et al. (eds.) (2014), *Spotlight on: Stimulating Innovation in Southeast Asia*, SEA-EU-NET Report, Centre for Social Innovation, Vienna, https://sea-eu.net/object/news/159.

Department of Jobs, Enterprise and Innovation (2015), "Directory of research centres and technology centres 2015", Department of Jobs, Enterprise and Innovation, Dublin, www.djei.ie/en/Publications/Publication-files/National-Directory-of-Research-Centres-and-Technology-Centres-2015.pdf.

Din, F.A. and V.V. Krishna (2007), "Science, technology policy and the dynamics underlying the Malaysia innovation system", in: Turpin, T. and V.V. Krishna, *Science, Technology Policy and the Diffusion of Knowledge: Understanding the Dynamics of Innovation Systems in the Asia Pacific*, Edward Elgar Publishing, Cheltenham, United Kingdom and Northampton, Massachusetts.

EPU (2015a), *Eleventh Malaysia Plan*, Economic Planning Unit, Putrajaya, http://rmk11.epu.gov.my/index.php/en.

EPU (2015b), "Services sector blueprint", Economic Planning Unit, Putrajaya, www.epu.gov.my/documents/10124/284bf88c-1aa1-4e3a-b43e-3b4b91fa2d1b.

EPU (2013), *Malaysian Economy in Figures* 2013, Economic Planning Unit, Putrajaya, www.epu.gov.my/en/the-malaysian-economy-in-figures-2013.

EPU (2010), *Tenth Malaysia Plan*, Economic Planning Unit, Putrajaya, http://onlineapps.epu.gov.my/rmke10/rmke10_english.html.

EPU (2006), *Ninth Malaysia Plan*, Economic Planning Unit, Putrajaya, www.epu.gov.my/epu-theme/rm9/html/english.htm.

EPU (2001), *Eighth Malaysia Plan*, Economic Planning Unit, Putrajaya, www.epu.gov.my/en/eighth-malaysia-plan-2001-2005.

EPU (1996), *Seventh Malaysia Plan*, Economic Planning Unit, Putrajaya, www.epu.gov.my/en/seventh-malaysia-plan-1996-2000.

EPU (1990), *Sixth Malaysia Plan*, Economic Planning Unit, Putrajaya, www.epu.gov.my/en/sixth-malaysia-plan-1990-19951.

EPU (1986), *Fifth Malaysia Plan*, Economic Planning Unit, Putrajaya, www.epu.gov.my/en/fifth-malaysia-plan-1986-1990.

ERIA (2014), *ASEAN Rising: ASEAN and AEC Beyond 2015*, Economic Research Institute for ASEAN and East Asia, Jakarta, www.eria.org/publications/key_reports/ASEAN-Rising.html.

ERIA and OECD (2014), *ASEAN SME Policy Index 2014 Towards Competitive and Innovative ASEAN SMEs*, ERIA Research Project Report, No. 8, ERIA SME Research

Working Group, Economic Research Institute for ASEAN and East Asia, Jakarta, www.eria.org/publications/research_project_reports/FY2012-no.8.html.

Felker, G. and K.S. Jomo (2007), "Technology policy in Malaysia", in: Jomo, K.S., *Malaysian Industrial Policy*, NUS Press, Singapore.

Gee, L.T. (2015), "Implementation of green technology policy in Malaysia", presentation at the COP 21 Conference, Japan Pavilion, 7 December, Paris, Ministry of Energy, Green Technology and Water, Putrajaya.

Grapragasem, S., A. Krishnan and A.N. Mansor (2014), "Current trends in Malaysian higher education and the effect on education policy and practice: An overview", *International Journal of Higher Education*, Vol. 3/1, Ohio State University Press, Columbus, pp. 85-93, http://dx.doi.org/10.5430/ijhe.v3n1p85.

Hamzah, S. (2009), "MOSTI in the Tenth Malaysia Plan", PowerPoint presentation, Ministry of Science, Technology and Innovation, Putrajaya, http://slideplayer.com/slide/4205143.

Hashim, H. (2015), "SME development framework: The Malaysian case", presentation at the Cairo AMC-CBE-WBG SME Conference, 14-15 January, SME Corp, Kuala Lumpur.

Hashim, Y. (1991), "Role of Universities in the national agricultural research system of developing countries: A case study on University Pertanian Malaysia", in: *The Role of Universities in National Agricultural Research Systems*, FAO Research and Technology Papers, No. 5, Food and Agriculture Organization, Rome.

IEA (2015), *Southeast Asia Energy Outlook 2015*, World Energy Outlook Special Report, International Energy Agency, Paris, www.iea.org/publications/freepublications/publication/WEO2015_SouthEastAsia.pdf.

Jomo, K.S. (2014), "Malaysia's economic development and transformation", in: Basu Das, S. and P.O. Lee, *Malaysia's Socio-Economic Transformation: Ideas for the Next Decade*, Institute of Southeast Asian Studies, Singapore.

Jomo, K.S. (2003), *Southeast Asia's Paper Tigers: From Miracle To Debacle And Beyond*, Routledge Studies in the Growth Economies of Asia, Routledge, Abingdon-on-Thames.

Kondo, M. (1999), "Improving Malaysian industrial technology policies and institutions", in: Felker, G. and K.S. Jomo, *Technology, Competitiveness and the State: Malaysia's Industrial Technology Policies*, Routledge, Abingdon-on-Thames.

Lee, M.N.N. (2004), *Restructuring Higher Education in Malaysia*, Monograph Series No. 4/2004, School of Educational Studies, Universti Sains Malaysia, Penang, Malaysia.

Lee, Y.C. (2016), "The role of science technology and innovation in national vision in developing countries: Policy and implementation", Workshop on building an integrated STI governance system for Seychelles, 11-12 March, Seychelles.

Mani, S. (2002), "The Malaysian experience", in: *Government, Innovation and Technology Policy: An International Comparative*, Edward Elgar Publishing, Cheltenham, http://dx.doi.org/10.4337/1840649704.00011.

MASTIC (1994, 1996, 1998, 2000, 2002, 2004, 2006, 2008, 2010, 2013), *Malaysian Science & Technology Indicators Report*, Ministry of Science, Technology and Innovation, Putrajaya, www.mastic.gov.my/en/web/guest/27.

MASTIC (2001, 2005, 2009, 2012, 2014, 2016), *National Survey of Research and Development*, Ministry of Science, Technology and Innovation, Putrajaya.

MATRADE (2015), "Matrade introduces large corporations and SMEs Partnership Programme to stimulate services export", News release, 14 December, Kuala Lumpur, www.matrade.gov.my.

Mazzoleni, R. and R.R. Nelson (2007), "Public research institutions and economic catch-up", *Research Policy*, Vol. 36/10, December, pp. 1 512-1 528.

MIGHT (2013a), "Science to Action (S2A): Building & sustaining a developed and prosperous Malaysia", presentation at the S2A consultation 2013, 28 October, MIGHT, Putrajaya, www.might.org.my/en/Event%20Documents/MC%202013%20InfoKit%20(Final%2027Oct2013).pdf.

MIGHT (2013b), "Science for industry", presentation at the S2A consultation 2013, 28 October, MIGHT, Putrajaya.

MIGHT (2009), "Malaysia high technology 2009", MIGHT, Putrajaya.

MOE (2015), *Malaysia Education Blueprint 2015-2025 (Higher Education)*, Ministry of Higher Education, Putrajaya, www.moe.gov.my/cms/upload_files/files/3_%20Malaysia%20Education%20Blueprint%202015-2025%20(Higher%20Education).pdf.

MOE (2014), "Review of the National Higher Education Strategic Plan: Higher education leads Malaysia's future", Ministry of Education, Putrajaya.

Mohammad, A.M. (2012), "National innovation strategy", presentation at World Innovation Forum 2011, AIM, Kuala Lumpur.

Morni, F. et al. (2009), "APEX University: Is it the Malaysian way forward?", presentation at the 2009 International Conference on Computer Technology and Development, 13-15 November, Kota Kinabalu, Malaysia.

MOSTI (2015), "Kemudahan Dana MOSTI" (MOSTI Facilities Fund), Powerpoint presentation at the Technology Preview and Showcase Nuklear Malaysia, Agensi Nuklear Malaysia, Bangi, 27 October.

MOSTI (2013a), *National Policy on Science, Technology and Innovation 2013-2020*, Ministry of Science, Technology and Innovation, Putrajaya.

MOSTI (2013b), "Technofund: Grant opportunities for novel technology enterprise", Powerpoint presentation, Ministry of Science, Technology and Innovation, Putrajaya. http://biomass-sp.net/wp-content/uploads/2013/05/PCS-MOSTI.pdf.

MOSTI (2012), "R&D funding mechanisms", presentation at the Sixth ASIAHORCs General Meeting, 10 October, Beijing, www.jsps.go.jp/english/asiahorcs/data/meetings/6th/malaysia.pdf.

MOSTI (2009), "MOSTI in the Tenth Malaysia Plan", Ministry of Science, Technology and Innovation, Putrajaya.

MOSTI (2003), "Malaysia's S&T policy for the 21st century", Ministry of Science, Technology and Innovation, Putrajaya, www.mosti.gov.my/wp-content/uploads/2014/08/dstn2bi.pdf.

MPC (2015), *Productivity Report 2014-15*, Malaysia Productivity Corporation, Petaling Jaya.

Muhammad, R. (2012), "National Green Technology Policy, government initiatives & incentives", Powerpoint presentation, 26 June, Ministry of Energy, Green Technology and Water, Putrajaya.

NEAC (2009), *New Economic Model*, www.epu.gov.my/en/new-economic-model.

NSRC (2013a), *PRA Performance Evaluation: Unlocking Vast Potentials, Fast-Tracking the Future*, National Science and Research Council, UiTM Press, Shah Alam, http://umexpert.um.edu.my/file/publication/00012427_86127.pdf.

NSRC (2013b), "Identifying R&D&C priority areas", Powerpoint presentation, Ministry of Science, Technology and Innovation, Putrajaya, http://blogs.nottingham.ac.uk/malaysiaknowledgetransfer/files/2012/11/NSRC-Workshop.pdf.

OECD (2016a), *Economic Outlook for Southeast Asia, China and India 2016: Enhancing Regional Ties*, OECD Publishing, Paris, http://dx.doi.org/10.1787/saeo-2016-en.

OECD (2016b), *OECD Reviews of Innovation Policy: Sweden 2016*, OECD Publishing, Paris, http://dx.doi.org/10.1787/9789264250000-en.

OECD (2015a), *Boosting Malaysia's National Intellectual Property System for Innovation*, OECD Publishing, Paris, http://dx.doi.org/10.1787/9789264239227-en.

OECD (2015b), *State-Owned Enterprises in the Development Process*, OECD Publishing, Paris, http://dx.doi.org/10.1787/9789264229617-en.

OECD (2014), *Towards Green Growth in Southeast Asia*, OECD Green Growth Studies, OECD Publishing, Paris, http://dx.doi.org/10.1787/9789264224100-en.

OECD (2013a), *Innovation in Southeast Asia*, OECD Publishing, Paris, http://dx.doi.org/10.1787/9789264128712-en.

OECD (2013b), *OECD Investment Policy Reviews: Malaysia 2013*, OECD Publishing, Paris, http://dx.doi.org/10.1787/9789264194588-en.

OECD (2013c), *OECD Reviews of Innovation Policy: Sweden 2012*, OECD Publishing, Paris, http://dx.doi.org/10.1787/9789264184893-en.

OECD (2013d), *Perspectives on Global Development 2013, Industrial Policies in a Changing World*, OECD Publishing, Paris, http://dx.doi.org/10.1787/persp_glob_dev-2013-en.

OECD (2012), *Southeast Asian Economic Outlook 2011/12*, OECD Publishing, Paris, http://dx.doi.org/10.1787/9789264166882-en.

OECD (2011), "Maximising the impact of regional innovation agencies", in: *Regions and Innovation Policy*, OECD Publishing, Paris, http://dx.doi.org/10.1787/9789264097803-9-en.

OECD (2010), *Policy Brief on Corporate Governance of State-owned Enterprises in Asia: Recommendations for Reform*, OECD, Paris, www.oecd.org/daf/ca/corporategovernanceofstate-ownedenterprises/45639683.pdf.

OECD (2009), "Chile's National Innovation Council for Competitiveness", OECD, Paris.

OECD (2005), "Investment incentives and FDI in selected ASEAN countries", in: *International Investment Perspectives 2004*, OECD Publishing, Paris, http://dx.doi.org/10.1787/iip-2004-4-en.

Olsson, A. and L. Meeck (2014), "Effectiveness of research and innovation management at policy and institutional levels: Cambodia, Malaysia, Thailand, and Vietnam",

OECD, Paris, www.oecd.org/sti/Effectiveness%20of%20research%20and%20innovation%20management%20at%20policy%20and%20institutional%20levels_Meek%20and%20Olsson.pdf.

ORICC (2011), Office for Research, Innovation, Commercialization and Consultancy Management, University Tun Hussein Malaysia website, http://ricc.uthm.edu.my/center-or-research/65.html#MOHE (accessed on 6 February 2016).

PEMANDU (2014), *Economic Transformation Programme Annual Report 2014*, Performance Management & Delivery Unit, http://etp.pemandu.gov.my/annualreport2014.

PGC (2015), "GLC Transformation Programme report card April 2015", Putrajaya Committee on GLC High Performance, Putrajaya, www.pcg.gov.my/PDF/20150423%20Report%20Card%20April%202015.pdf.

PGC (2006), *GLC Transformation Manual*, Putrajaya Committee on GLC High Performance, Putrajaya, www.pcg.gov.my/trans_manual_update.asp.

Prashantham, S. and R.B. McNaughton (2006), "Facilitation of links between multinational subsidiaries and SMEs: The Scottish Technology and Collaboration (STAC) initiative", *International Business Review*, Vol. 15/5, October, pp. 447-462, http://dx.doi.org/10.1016/j.ibusrev.2006.05.008.

Rahim, R.A. (2012a), "Getting R&D priority right", UK-Malaysia Innovation Forum, 28 February, Kuala Lumpur, http://fr.slideshare.net/Rushdi/getting-rd-priority-areas-right.

Rahim, R.A. (2012b), "Streamlining Malaysia's national R&D areas", *Maintenance Problems*, No.°4, pp. 139-150.

Rasiah, R. (2011), "Is Malaysia facing negative deindustrialization?", *Pacific Affairs*, Vol. 84/4, December, University of British Columbia, Vancouver, pp. 715-736, www.jstor.org/stable/23056129.

Rasiah, R. (2006), "Electronics in Malaysia: Export expansion but slow technical change", in: World Bank, *Technology, Adaptation, and Exports: How Some Developing Countries Got It*, The World Bank, Washington, DC.

Rasiah, R. (1999), "Malaysia's national innovation system", in: Felker, G. and K.S. Jomo, *Technology, Competitiveness and the State: Malaysia's Industrial Technology Policies*, Routledge, Abingdon-on-Thames.

Rasiah, R. and V.G.R. Chandran (2015), "Malaysia", in: UNESCO, *UNESCO Science Report: Towards 2030*, UNESCO Publishing, Paris,http://unesdoc.unesco.org/images/0023/002354/235406e.pdf.

Rasiah, R., Y. Sadoi and R. Busser (2008), *Multinationals, Technology and Localization in Automotive Firms in Asia*, Routledge, Abingdon-on-Thames.

Rivas, G. (2012), *La experiencia de CORFO y la transformación productiva de Chile: Evolución, aprendizaje y lecciones de desarrollo* (The experience of CORFO and the productive transformation of Chile: Evolution, learning and lessons learned from development), Serie Políticas Públicas y Transformación Productiva No. 3/2012, CORFO, Caracas.

Rogers, J.D. (2013), "Technology extension services", *Innovation Policy Platform Policy Brief*, The World Bank, Washington, DC.

Schwaag Serger, S., E. Wise and E. Arnold (2015), *National Research & Innovation Councils as an Instrument of Innovation Governance: Characteristics & Challenges*, VINNOVA Analysis 2015-07, VINNOVA – Swedish Governmental Agency for Innovation Systems, Stockhom, www.vinnova.se/upload/EPiStorePDF/va_15_07_T.pdf.

SME Corporation (2014), *SME Corp Annual Report 2014*, SME Corporation, Kuala Lumpur, www.smecorp.gov.my/index.php/en/resources/2015-12-21-11-07-06/sme-annual-report/book/7/Array.

SME Corporation (2006), *SME Corporation Malaysia Innovation Development Programme*, SME Corp, Kuala Lumpur.

Studwell, J. (2013), *How Asia Works. Success and Failure in the World's Most Dynamic Region*, Grove Press, New York.

Thiruchelvam, K. (2013), "Malaysia's quest for innovation", presentation at 11th MP Kick Off conference, Pot Dickson, Universiti Teknologi Malaysia, Johor Bahru, 5 December, www.epu.gov.my/documents/10124/95dc320d-fbcb-4040-8d96-98a627d827c3.

Thiruchelvam, K. et al. (2011b), "Innovation financing in Asia: The experience of Malaysia", report prepared for The International Development Research Centre, Ottawa.

UNCTAD (2003), *Foreign Direct Investment and Performance Requirements: New Evidence from Selected Countries*, United Nations Conference on Trade and Development, New York and Geneva, http://unctad.org/en/Docs/iteiia20037_en.pdf.

UNIDO (2003), "Malaysian Electronics: At the crossroads", *SME Technical Working Papers Series*, No. 12, United Nations Industrial Development Organization, Vienna.

UNIDO and Harvard University (2007), *Building Linkages for Competitive and Responsible Entrepreneurship: Innovative Partnerships to Foster Small Enterprise, Promote Economic Growth, and Reduce Poverty in Developing Countries*, United Nations Industrial Development Organization, Geneva and the Fellows of Harvard College, Cambridge, Massachusetts, p.141.

World Bank (2014), "Facilitating global value chain integration for competitiveness in Costa Rica", Technical Assistance Summary Note TA P147207, The World Bank, Washington, DC.

World Bank (2011), "Malaysia economic monitor: Brain drain", The World Bank, Bangkok, http://documents.worldbank.org/curated/en/2011/04/14134061/malaysia-economic-monitor-brain-drain.

Yusoff, K.M. and V. Pillai (2014), "Orchestrating a synchronised STI framework", *myForesight*, January, MIGHT, Putrajaya, www.myforesight.my/download/myForesight_Issue06_web.pdf.

Yusuf, S. and K. Nabeshima (2009), "Tiger economies under threat: A comparative analysis of Malaysia's industrial prospects and policy options", The World Bank, Washington, DC, http://documents.worldbank.org/curated/en/2009/01/11261234/tiger-economies-under-threat-comparative-analysis-malaysias-industrial-prospects-policy-options.

Zuniga, P. (forthcoming), "Public policy for productive development in small and medium-sized enterprises in Latin America: What have we learned?", *UNU MERIT Working Papers*, Maastricht, Netherlands.

Annex 5.A1.
SME support measures in the Eleventh Malaysia Plan

Table 5.A1.1. **SME support measures in the Eleventh Malaysia Plan**

Strategies	Measures
S1: Enhancing productivity through automation and innovation by promoting increased use of ICT and continuing the Technology Commercialisation Platform (TCP) and Inclusive Innovation programmes	i) Enhancing productivity through automation and innovation: Encourage small and medium-sized enterprises (SMEs) to adopt greater automation in production processes and business services. Promote greater ICT utilisation, mainly in business operations, supply chain management and delivery systems. ii) Continue the implementation of the two high-impact programmes, namely the Technology Commercialisation Platform and Inclusive Innovation.
S2: Strengthening human capital development within SMEs by reskilling and upskilling workers through industry partnerships	Strengthening human capital development within SMEs: i) Strengthen the curriculum for technical vocational education and training with greater input from the industry to equip workers in SMEs with the right skill sets. ii) Intensify reskilling and upskilling of workers to enable them to fill higher-paying jobs. iii) Ensure new entrants into the workforce meet industry requirements and create an entrepreneurial culture in the society.
S3: Enhancing the ease of doing business by simplifying the process of formation and formalising of businesses as well as increasing the ease of access to financing	i) Simplify the process for formation and formalising of businesses through the ongoing integration of MyCoID and BLESS (HIP 1). ii) Engage industry experts in the preparation of proposals, particularly for technology and innovation activities, to enhance access to financing. iii) The SME Investment Partner programme will also introduce new ways of financing for early-stage companies by combining equity and loan financing. iv) Encourage SMEs to pool resources, use shared services, and purchase inputs, raw materials and services in bulk to reduce costs.
S4: Increasing demand for SMEs' products and services by reviewing policies for procurement from SMEs and encouraging SMEs to obtain international standards and certifications to increase exports	i) Increase demand for SME products and services: Review of government policy on procurement from competitive SMEs to increase the demand for high-quality local products and services. Encourage the procurement of local SME products by government-linked companies and multinationals and invest in supplier development programmes. Leverage on the consortium approach to take advantage of market opportunities for large orders. ii) Encourage SMEs to comply with international standards and certifications. iii) Scale-up the Going Export (Go-Ex) Programme to assist SMEs to venture into exports.
S5: Creating home-grown champions through the Catalyst Programme to build high-performing SMEs into regional and international players	The Catalyst Programme helps to remove barriers and provide assistance to potential SMEs to become home-grown champions. The selection of SMEs will be based on transparent and clear criteria to identify the SMEs that are the most deserving and have the highest growth potential.
S6: Developing SMEs in Sabah and Sarawak by strengthening infrastructure, encouraging market expansion through e-commerce, reducing the cost of doing business, and increasing outreach of government assistance	i) Priority to be given to infrastructure development in Sabah and Sarawak, including increased coverage and quality of the telecommunications network, supply of electricity and water as well as transportation connectivity in these states. ii) Encourage SMEs to expand their markets by adopting e-commerce, cloud computing and crowdsourcing for financing. iii) Review regulations to reduce the cost of doing business and increase the outreach of government assistance to SMEs in Sabah and Sarawak.

Annex 5.A2

Main actions of the Malaysia Education Blueprint 2015-2025 (Higher Education)

Table 5.A2.1. **Main actions of the Malaysia Education Blueprint 2015-2025 (Higher Education)**

Objectives	Examples of actions to be implemented
Holistic, entrepreneurial and balanced graduates	
Enhancing the student learning experience	Expand industry collaboration in the design and delivery of programmes; increase the use of experiential and service learning to develop 21st century skills, and leverage technology-enabled models to support more personalised learning.
Devising an integrated cumulative grade point average system	Assess knowledge and thinking skills as well as ethics and spirituality, leadership skills, national identity, and language proficiency.
Creating opportunities for students and academic staff to acquire entrepreneurial skills	Pursue their own enterprises through sabbaticals, industry secondments, business incubators and green lane policies that support student-owned businesses.
Talent excellence	
Positioning public and private higher learning institutes according to recognised areas of institutional excellence	Encourage excellence in overall research, niche areas of research, and teaching and instruction, continuously improve performance in areas of specialisation and focus.
Enabling higher learning institutes to develop multi-track career pathways	Inspire educators, accomplished researchers, experienced practitioners and transformational institutional leaders.
Providing best practice guidelines to support public and private higher learning institutes	Develop stronger end-to-end talent development strategies for both local and international talent; use the New Academia talent framework covering the resourcing, recruiting, rewarding and retention of talent.
Nation of lifelong learners	
Creating a framework for recognising prior learning	Establish clear pathways for re-entry into the education system, national credit system to enable the accumulation of modular credits over time, clear criteria for recognising prior experience.
Launching stakeholder engagement programmes	Incentivise participation and improve existing marketing infrastructure to make the research of information on available programmes (i.e. MyCC Loyalty Programme, 1Family Multiple Skills Programme) easier.
Continuing to provide financial support to disadvantaged groups	Provide tax reduction incentive schemes to companies and work with financial institutions to create financial assistance programmes for all groups.
Quality technical vocational education and training (TVET) graduates	
Enabling industry to lead curriculum design and delivery	Create new partnership models and improve the quality of delivery through increased apprenticeship, hands-on training, real-life simulations and specialised employer training programmes.
Enhancing co-ordination across the ministry's various TVET providers	Eliminate the duplication of programmes and resources, enable greater specialisation in areas of expertise and improve cost efficiency.
Co-ordinating with other ministries and agencies	Offer TVET programmes to streamline the national qualification framework, ensure alignment with major industry associations and pursue international accreditations for TVET programmes.
Financial sustainability	
Improving the funding formulae for public higher learning institutes	Replace block grants with performance-linked and per student funding, implement five-year performance contracts (3+2), target government investment in priority areas.
Enhancing the National Higher Education Fund Corporation (PTPTN) performance and sustainability	Improve repayment rates, shift to income-contingent loans, link access to student loans with the performance and quality standards of higher learning institutes.
Incentivising the creation of endowment and *waqf* (mortmain property) funds	Encourage contributions to higher education, i.e. through the provision of matching grants for higher learning institutes during the initial fund-raising period.

Table 5.A2.1. **Main actions of the Malaysia Education Blueprint 2015-2025 (Higher Education)** (*continued*)

Objectives	Examples of actions to be implemented
Empowered governance	
Defining five-year (3+2) outcome-based performance contracts	Define contracts between the ministry and higher learning institutes, with public higher learning institutes' funding at risk if performance goals are not met, and create incentives for exceeding targets.
Strengthening quality assurance in the private sector	Participate in enhanced national quality assurance frameworks (i.e. SETARA and MyQUEST) for continued access to government funding. The degree of access will be linked to their participation and level of performance against these frameworks and standards.
Moving decision rights from the ministry to the leadership of public universities	Improve governance effectiveness of higher learning institutes and build the capacity and capabilities of university boards and institutional leaders to take on these increased responsibilities.
Innovation ecosystem	
Focusing on creating scale and growth	Create scale and growth in a few strategic research areas linked to national priorities for economic growth, and where Malaysia has distinctive capabilities.
Playing a catalytic role in securing investments	Use matching schemes (i.e. Private-Public Research Network), redesign existing financing criteria and grant review processes for greater transparency and accountability.
Incentivising higher learning institutes to establish supporting systems for the commercialisation of ideas	Technology transfer offices, mechanisms for the co-utilisation of infrastructure, enhanced data monitoring systems and talent development programmes.
Global prominence	
Collaborating with ministries and agencies	Improve and streamline immigration procedures and processes to match international best practices, introduce multiple year student visas and provide an accelerated "green lane" approach for students from high-quality higher learning institutes.
Increasing the proportion of postgraduate international and high-priority markets students (ASEAN)	Diversify and raise the quality of niche programmes.
Strengthening the promotion and marketing of the higher education system	Targeted measures (i.e. hosting major international education conferences) and strengthen MyAlumni.
Globalised online learning	
Launching massive open online courses (MOOCs) in subjects of distinctiveness	Islamic banking and finance, in partnership with high-profile international MOOC consortiums like EdX and Coursera.
Making online learning an integral component of higher education and lifelong learning	Conversion of common undergraduate courses into MOOCs, require up to 70% of programmes to use blended learning models.
Establishing the required cyber infrastructure	Physical network infrastructure, info structure, platform, devices and equipment, strengthen the capabilities of academics to deliver online learning at scale.
Transformed higher education delivery	
Launching the University Transformation Programme	Close partnership with pilot higher learning institutes, identify, codify, pilot best practices and tools, disseminate "playbooks" (*buku panduan*) to all higher learning institutes on critical areas for improvement.
Restructuring the ministry organisation	Focus on core functions; make stronger links between higher learning institutes, community and industry; improve efficiency in operations (key frontline services: student admissions and international student services).
Creating greater consistency in performance standards and regulations across public and private higher learning institutes	Enhance the Malaysian Qualification Agency's processes and quality assurance frameworks, eliminate unnecessary red tape.

Source: MOE (2015), *Malaysia Education Blueprint 2015-2025 (Higher Education)*, www.moe.gov.my/cms/upload_files/files/3_%20Malaysia%20Education%20Blueprint%202015-2025%20(Higher%20Education).pdf.

Annex 5.A3
Main ongoing sectoral and thematic strategies, plans and roadmaps

Table 5.A3.1. **Main ongoing sectoral and thematic strategies, plans and roadmaps**

Strategy or plan	Leader and/or operator in charge of the implementation	Main STI component
Sectoral/thematic strategies		
National Green Technology Policy (started in 2009)	Ministry of Energy, Green Technology and Water	Long-term plan that determines a conducive environment for green technology development including the introduction and implementation of innovative economic instruments.
National Graphene Action Plan (NGAP) 2020	NanoMalaysia (nanotechnology government agency)	Propose paths, opportunities and high potential applications for the companies to invest in late-stage graphene-related R&D and prototyping as well as early commercialisation and development of its own intellectual property system.
National Biotechnology Policy (2005-2020)	National Biotechnology Division, Malaysian Biotech Corporation (MOSTI)	Aims at making biotechnology one of the key economic sectors through technology strengthening and innovation licensing as well as establishing centres of excellence, in existing or new institutions, to bring together multidisciplinary research teams in co-ordinated research and commercialisation initiatives.
National Aerospace Industry Blueprint 2030	Malaysian Industry-Government Group for High Technology	Intensify R&T application in aerospace industry to improve competitiveness and develop new capacities (creation of National Aerospace R&T Roadmap). Invest in preparing for and attracting an innovative workforce.
National IT Agenda (NITA) (1996-2020)	National IT Council (NITC)	Define ICT utilisation plan to transform Malaysia to an information society, after to a knowledge society and finally to a value-based knowledge society.
National Strategic ICT Roadmap (2011-2020)	Ministry of Science, Technology and Innovation	Enhance the productivity and promote the development of new ICT-based and knowledge-intensive industries to boost innovation and commercialisation capacity of the sector.
Various other roadmaps such as the National Wireless Communications Technology Roadmap (2008), Internet of Things (2015); NanoElectronics Technology Roadmap for Malaysia (2008); National Biometrics Technology Roadmap (2008); National Semantic Technology Roadmap; Technology Roadmap for Cyberspace Security (2011); Technology Roadmap for Microelectromechanical Systems (2011).		

Annex 5.A4

Malaysia's national innovation system: Main actors and STI functions

Table 5.A4.1. **Main actors of Malaysia's national innovation system and respective STI functions**

Organisation	STI support schemes/instruments	Main functions						
Cradle Fund Sdn (Cradle)	Cradle grant schemes (pre-seed fund, university catalyst, seed venture, ...)	R&D	COM/IP				SKILLS	
	Coach and Grow Programme			ENTP				
	Angel Tax Incentive				INV/HT			
Collaborative Research in Engineering, Science & Technology (CREST)	CREST R&D Grant	R&D						
	Other: Great Lab, Innovation Design Academy ...		COM/IP				SKILLS	
Economic Planning Unit (EPU)	Various activities, including block grants to public research institutes	R&D				PUBAW		GOVSER
Khazanah Nasional Berhad (Strategic Investment Fund)	Manage the assets held by the government and undertake strategic investments				INV/HT			GOVSER
Intellectual Property Corporation of Malaysia (MyIPO)	Various activities related to intellectual property		COM/IP			PUBAW	SKILLS	
Malaysia Productivity Commission (MPC)	Provide information and training on productivity, quality, competitiveness						SKILLS	
Malaysia-Industry High Technology Group (MIGHT)	Technology nurturing activities via MIGHT Technology Sdn Bhd (MTN)	R&D	COM/IP				SKILLS	
	Capacity building via MIGHT-METEOR Advanced Manufacturing Sdn Bhd						SKILLS	
	Offset Management Services via TDA	R&D						
	Science2Action	R&D				PUBAW	SKILLS	
	Intelligence services, via Malaysian Foresight Institute (myForesight) and others					PUBAW		GOVSER
Malaysian Biotechnology Corporation (MBC)	Bioeconomy Transformation Programme (BTP)	R&D						
	Biotechnology Commercialisation Fund (BCF)	R&D	COM/IP					
Malaysian Global Inno. and Creativity Centre (MaGIC)	Various entrepreneurship-related initiatives			ENTP			SKILLS	
Malaysian Innovation Agency (AIM)	Skills-related initiatives: International Baccalaureate (MYP), i-Think, Genovasi, ...					PUBAW	SKILLS	
	Commercialisation-related initiatives: PlaTCOM Ventures, Steinbeis Malaysia		COM/IP	ENTP				
	Newco: Equity participation in companies (commercialisation and upscaling stages)				INV/HT			
	Innovation Accelerator Projects	R&D	COM/IP					
Malaysian Technology Development Corporation (MTDC)	Management of grant schemes: Acquisition (TAF), Commercialisation (CRDF)	R&D	COM/IP					
	Management of funds: Business Start-up (BSF), Growth (BGF), Expansion (BEF)		COM/IP	ENTP	INV/HT			
	Technology centres		COM/IP				SKILLS	
	Graduate Entrepreneurship Programme (Symbiosis)			ENTP			SKILLS	
Ministry of Communications and Multimedia (KKMM)	Creative Industry Development Fund (CIDF-SKMM)	R&D						
Ministry of Finance (MOF)	Tax credits and exemptions: Pioneer status, Investment, Reinvestment				INV/HT			
Ministry of Health (MOH)	Ministry of Health (MOH) Research Grant	R&D						
Ministry of Higher Education (MOHE)	Management grant schemes: Fundamental (FRGS), Exploratory (ERGS), Long Term (LRGS),Prototype (PRGS), Research Acculturation (RAGS), ...	R&D						
	PPRN		COM/IP	ENTP				
	Block grants to the five designated research universities	R&D						
Ministry of Science, Technology and Innovation (MOSTI)	Management of several grant schemes: ScienceFund, TechnoFund, InnoFund	R&D	COM/IP					
	Flagship programmes	R&D	COM/IP					
Multimedia Development Corporation (MDeC)	Multimedia Super Corridor (MSC Malaysia)				INV/HT			
	Product development and commercialisation (PCF)	R&D	COM/IP					
	Creative Lifelong Learning Programme (CILL)						SKILLS	
Performance Management and Delivery Unit (PEMANDU)	Programme implementation (including Transformation Programme)							GOVSER
PlaTCOM			COM/IP					
Yayasan Inovasi Malaysia (YIM, Inno. Foundation)	Various activities to foster creativity and innovation among Malaysian citizens			ENTP		PUBAW	SKILLS	
Academy of Science								GOVSER

- R&D: R&D funding
- COM/IP: Support to research commercialisation/IP
- ENTP: Support to entrepreneurship and SMEs
- INV/HT: Investment/equity in high-tech companies
- PUBAW: Stakeholders facilitation and public awareness
- GOVSER: Government advice and services (priority setting, etc.), think tank
- SKILLS: Innovation skills and capacity-building

Annex 5.A5

Recent initiatives to support social innovation

Social innovation seeks new answers to social problems by identifying and delivering new services that improve the quality of life of individuals and communities and by identifying and implementing new labour market integration processes, new competencies, new jobs, and new forms of participation that help to improve the position of individuals in the workforce (OECD, 2014a).

Research and innovation systems can certainly help respond to these social problems. However, the traditional disciplinary focus of academia and public research limit opportunities for developing appropriate solutions. Policy instruments, often still overlooking the demand-side dimension, are also poorly suited for supporting social – and more generally all forms of non-technological – innovation. The specific challenges of social innovation are being increasingly acknowledged. Several countries, including Malaysia, have for instance developed some type of service innovation strategy. A few countries such as Costa Rica are developing a dedicated strategic framework for social innovation (OECD, forthcoming) or have put in place specific instruments at it is the case in Colombia (OECD, 2014b).

Moreover, in many countries, policies to support innovation have been developed mainly from an R&D or manufacturing perspective. The latest policy trends show that countries have extended the scope of their established policy instruments to include other types of innovation rather than creating new specific ones (OECD, 2014a). This is the case in Malaysia where MOSTI has included social innovation in the eligibility criteria of its R&D fund since 2015 (Bernama, 2015).

The Eleventh Malaysia Plan (EPU, 2016), which places its focus on people, aims to create a particularly favourable strategic framework for social innovation to develop. In the innovation area specifically, the emphasis is put on strengthening relational capital by improving collaboration among all stakeholders, which is a key condition to social innovation. A number of related actions are programmed in the Plan, along three main strategic thrusts (see Table 5.5):

- strengthening collaboration through a whole-society approach
- developing a social Financing model
- promoting higher order thinking skills to develop a dynamic society.

The implementation of these actions will be facilitated by already established institutions and instruments, including:

- The Social Innovation Fund. This fund, operated by MOSTI, aims to extend the InnoFund's "Community Innovation Fund" by supporting projects that include social innovation aspects (94 projects approved in 2015, worth about MYR12.3 million) (Hashim, 2015). Up to MYR20 million should be dedicated annually to MOSTI Social Innovation (MSI) Projects. The target beneficiaries of MSI projects are the students, NGOs, community groups, women's organizations and ethnic communities (MOSTI, 2015).

- The Malaysian Global Innovation and Creativity Centre (MaGIC),an organisation dedicated to social entrepreneurship created in 2014. It operates several programmes to support entrepreneurial initiatives led by communities such as the MaGIC Academy (full-time coding and design) or "@Stanford" (training programme for start-up founders at Stanford University).
- The National Innovation Agency (AIM) fulfils its mission to support innovation ecosytems using a broad definition of innovation, including social innovation and innovation in the public sector (such as for instance social public-private partnership). The AIM has also created the Social Impact Measurement Toolkit to encourage social purpose organisations (SPOs) to measure the level of successfulness of these projects.

References

Bernama (2015), "*Mosti* Fund scope expanded to include facilitation, social innovation", *Bernama.com*, 16 April, www.mosti.gov.my/wp-content/uploads/2015/02/25FEBRUARI2015.pdf.

EPU (2015), *Eleventh Malaysia Plan*, Economic Planning Unit, Putrajaya, http://rmk11.epu.gov.my/index.php/en.

Hashim, Z. M. (2015), "MOSTI's Initiatives on Social Innovation", presentation at the UNESCO Innovation Forum, Kuala Lumpur.

MOSTI (2015), "MOSTI Social innovation (MSI) di perkenal", ("Launch of MOSTI Social Innovation (MSI) projects"), *MOSTI news*, 16 April, www.mosti.gov.my/berita/16-april-2015-mosti-social-innovation-msi-di-perkenal/

OECD (forthcoming), *OECD Reviews of Innovation Policy: Costa Rica 2017,* OECD Publishing, Paris.

OECD (2014a), *OECD Science, Technology and Industry Outlook 2014*, OECD Publishing, Paris, http://dx.doi.org/10.1787/sti_outlook-2014-en.

OECD (2014b), *OECD Reviews of Innovation Policy: Colombia 2014*, OECD Publishing, Paris, http://dx.doi.org/10.1787/9789264204638-en.

Annex A.
List of people interviewed during fact-finding missions

Organisation	Name	Designation
Academy of Science Malaysia (ASM)	Hazami Habib	Acting Chief Executive Officer
	Prof. Datuk Dr Halimaton Hamdan	ASM Council Member
Advanced Micro Devices Export (M) Sdn Bhd	Neoh Soon Ee	Vice President
Altera Corporation	Dato' Dr Mohd Sofi Osman	Managing Director and Vice President
American Malaysian Chamber of Commerce (AMCHAM Malaysia)	Anne Marie Brooks	Former Executive Director
Asia Pacific Biomass Conversion Business Development	Bas Melssen	Director
Avago Technologies (M) Sdn Bhd	Boon Chye Ooi	Senior Vice President
Boustead Holdings Berhad (Boustead)	Tan Sri Dato' Seri Lodin Wok Kamaruddin	Deputy Chairman/Group Managing Director
Cahaya Mata Sarawak (CMS) Cement Sdn Bhd	Alzian Mohamad Kassim	Quality Assurance Manager
Chinese Chamber of Commerce and Industry of Kuala Lumpur and Selangor	Tan Sri Emeritus Professor Datuk Dr Augustine Ong Soon Hock	Advisor of Science, Technology and Innovations
	Datuk Ir. Hong Lee Pee	Chairman of Science, Technology and Innovations
	Peck Boon Soon	Deputy Chairman, Socio-Economic Research Committee
	Hon Jia Hui	Former Assistant Executive Secretary
	Prof. Dr Ho Chee Cheong	Member of Science, Technology and Innovations
	Dr Chua Siew Kiat	Member of Science, Technology and Innovations
	Tan Kin Wai	Member of Science, Technology and Innovations
	Dr Ong Chi King	Member of Science, Technology and Innovations
	Prof. Dr Law Chung Lim	Member of Science, Technology and Innovations
Collaborative Research in Engineering, Science and Technology Centre (CREST)	Jaffri Ibrahim	Chief Executive Officer
	Dr Khoh Soo Beng	Research and Programme Director
DK Composites Sdn Bhd	Haji Habibur Rahman Ebrahim	Director
East Asia Palm Product (EAPP)	Leong Lean Pong	Head of Corporate Finance
Economic Planning Unit (EPU)	Datuk Yogeesvaran Kumaraguru	Deputy Director General, Macro
	Liew Siew Lee	Director, Manufacturing Industry, Science and Technology Section
Federation of Malaysian Manufacturers (FMM)	Dato' Dr Ir. Andy Seo Kian Haw	Vice-President
	Dr Yeoh Oon Tean	Chief Executive Officer
	Andrew Nguang	Business Development Manager
Federation of Malaysian Manufacturers (FMM) Sarawak representative office	Haji Othman Abdul Rani	Former Chairman
	Farrez Teh	Assistant Manager
Frost & Sullivan	Hazmi Yusof	Country Head, Malaysia/Senior Vice President
Intel Malaysia Design Centre	Chris Kelly	General Manager
Intel Technology Sdn Bhd	Robin Martin	Managing Director
International Centre for Education in Islamic Finance (INCEIF)	Emeritus Professor Datuk Dr Mohamed Ariff	Professor of Economics and Governance

Organisation	Name	Designation
International Science, Technology and Innovation Centre for South-South Cooperation under the Auspices of UNESCO (ISTIC)	Dato Ir. Dr Lee Yee Cheong	Chairman of ISTIC Governing Board
ItraMAS Corporation	Anura Don	Senior R&D Manager
Khazanah Nasional Berhad	Tengku Dato' Sri Azmil Zahruddin Raja Abdul Aziz	Executive Director, Investments
Khazanah Research Institute	Dr Muhammed Abdul Khalid	Director of Research
Kontron Design Manufacturing Services	Shanmuganathan Palanisamy	Managing Director
	Seeni Mohamed	Head of Project Management Office APAC, Research and Development
	Tan Yeun Nee	Manager, Head of Hardware Engineering Global, Research and Development
Kota Kinabalu Industrial Park (KKIP)	Ir. Melvin Disimond	Deputy Chief Executive Officer
Kulim Technology Park Corporation (KTPC)	Dato' Dr Annuar Mohd Saffar	President
	Muhamad Sabri Said	Senior Manager
	Saidin Abd Rahman	Senior Manager
	Ahmad Zaidi Md Zain	Senior Manager
Kumpulan Melaka Berhad	Ir. Khairul Ezuan Harun	Former Chief Operating Officer
Malaysia Automotive Institute (MAI)	Leon Lai Leong Chong	Senior Manager, Human Capital Development
Malaysian Green Technology Corporation	Ir. Ahmad Hadri Haris	Chief Executive Officer
	Norhasliza Mohd Mokhtar	Vice President, Green Econometrics
Malaysia Productivity Corporation (MPC)	Dato' Mohd. Razali Hussain	Director General
	Lee Saw Hoon	Senior Director, Global Competitiveness
Malaysia Rubber Board	Datuk Dr Mohd Akbar Md Said	Director General
	Dr Zairossani Mohd. Nor	Deputy Director General, Research and Innovation
	Nurul Huda Abdul Hamid	Former Head, Administration Unit
Malaysian Foundation for Innovation (YIM)	Muhammad Aziph Dato' Mustapha	Chief Executive Officer
Malaysian Furniture Promotion Council	Sarimah Hj. Mohamad Sabudin	Chief Executive Officer
Malaysian Industry-Government Group for High Technology (MIGHT)	Datuk Dr Mohd Yusoff Sulaiman	President and Chief Executive Officer
	Dr Raslan Ahmad	Senior Vice President, MIGHT International
	Datuk Ir. Kamarulzaman Zainal	Former Senior Vice President, Industry Intelligence
	Shamsul Kamar Abu Samah	Former Assistant Vice President, Industry Intelligence
Malaysian Palm Oil Board (MPOB)	Datuk Dr Choo Yuen May	Director General
Malaysian Technology Development Corporation (MTDC)	Dato' Norhalim Yunus	Chief Executive Officer
Melaka Green Tech Corporation	Datuk Haji Kamarudin Md Shah	Chief Executive Officer
MIMOS Berhad	Dr Chandran Elamvazuthi	Senior Director, Research Strategy and Engagement
	Foo Lai Ning	Director, Corporate Performance Excellence
	Ramesh Kumar Nadarajah	General Manager
Ministry of Foreign Affairs (MOFA)	H.E. Ambassador Cheah Choong Kit	Former Undersecretary Department of Multilateral Affairs, Multilateral Economic and Environment Division
	Wan Maisarah Mohamed Idrus	Former Department of Multilateral Affairs, Multilateral Economic and Environment Division
Ministry of Health (MOH)	Datuk Dr Noor Hisham Abdullah	Director General, Health
	Datuk Dr Lokman Hakim B. Sulaiman	Deputy Director General, Health, Public Health

Organisation	Name	Designation
Ministry of Higher Education (MOHE)	Dato' Seri Ir. Dr Zaini Ujang	Secretary General
	Dato' Prof. Dr Asma Ismail	Director General, Department of Higher Education
	Prof. Madya Dr Arham Abdullah	Director, Industrial Relation Division
	Prof. Dr Raha Abdul Rahim	Director, Higher Education Excellence Planning Division
	Dr Faridah Abu Hassan	Former Director, Division of Educational Planning and Policy Research
Ministry of International Trade and Industry (MITI)	Khoo Boo Seng	Senior Director, Strategic Planning
Ministry of Science, Technology and Innovation (MOSTI)	Dato' Sri Dr Noorul Ainur Mohd. Nur	Secretary General
	Dato' Dr Mohd Azhar Haji Yahaya	Deputy Secretary General (Policy)
	Dr Zulkifli Mohamed Hashim	Former Deputy Secretary General (Science)
	Kamel Mohamad	Senior Undersecretary, Planning
	Kamaruhzaman Mat Zin	Undersecretary, Malaysian Science and Technology Information Centre (MASTIC)
	Ho Koon Seng	Undersecretary, National Science Research Council (NSRC)
	Dr Nor Azlina Ariffin	Undersecretary, International Division
	Dr Vilasini Pillai	Former Undersecretary, National Science Research Council (NSRC)
	Nordina Idris	Undersecretary, Fund Division
	Chan Hong Jin	Deputy Undersecretary, RSE Unit, Planning Division
	Siva Kumar Solay Rajah	Deputy Undersecretary, National Biotechnology Division
Motorola Solution Malaysia Sdn Bhd	Dr Hari Narayanan	Managing Director, Penang Operation
Multimedia Development Corporation (MDEC)	Dato' Ng Wan Peng	Chief Operating Officer
Multimedia University (MMU)	Prof. Dato' Dr Muhamad Rasat Mohamad	Former President
MyBiomass Sdn Bhd	Puvaneswari Ramasamy	Chief Executive Officer
	Winson Chong Wen Shan	Assistant Manager, Business Development Division
National Innovation Agency Malaysia (AIM)	Naser Jaafar	Chief Operating Office
National Instrument Malaysia	Kit Yong	Former Director, Research and Development
Penang Skills Development Centre (PSDC)	Muhamed Ali Hajah Mydin	Chief Executive Officer
Penchem Technologies Sdn. Bhd.	Ng Chee Mang	Managing Director
Performance Management and Delivery Unit (PEMANDU)	Yong Yoon Kit	Director, NKEA (Business Services and Electronics and Electrical)
	Ku Kok Peng	Director, NKEA (Palm Oil & Rubber) and ETP Investment & Innovation
PERMATA Foundation Malaysia	Prof. Tan Sri Dato' Seri Dr Sharifah Hapsah Syed Hasan Shahabudin	Board Member
Prime Minister's Office	Prof. Tan Sri Zakri Abdul Hamid	Science Advisor to the Prime Minister of Malaysia
Puncak Deras Sdn Bhd	Su Ken Chu	Managing Director
Roll-Royce International Limited	Saji Raghavan	Country Director
Royal Selangor Pewter	Tan Sri Yong Poh Kon	Managing Director
	Yong Yoon Li	Executive Director
	Datin Paduka Chen Mun Kuen	Director

Organisation	Name	Designation
Sabah Economic Development and Investment Authority (SEDIA)	Datuk Dr Mohd Yaakub Haji Johari	Chief Executive/President
Sabah Rubber Industry Board	Datuk Harris Mathews	General Manager
Silterra Malaysia Sdn Bhd	Dr Kamarulzaman Mohamed Zin	Former Chief Executive Officer
Standards Malaysia	Datuk Fadilah Baharin	Director General
Sultan Idris Education University (UPSI)	Prof. Dato' Dr Noraini Idris	Deputy Vice Chancellor Research and Innovation
Tradewinds Corporation	Datuk Wira Azhar Abdul Hamid	President/Group Managing Director
UCSI University	Senior Prof. Dato' Dr Khalid Yusoff, FASc	Vice-Chancellor and President
UEM Group Berhad	Tan Sri Dr Ir. Ahmad Tajuddin Ali, FASc.	Chairman
UKM Technology Sdn Bhd	Mohd. Zamri Ismail	Chief Executive Officer
United Nations University International Institute for Global Health (UNU-IIGH)	Prof. Anthony Capon	Director
Universiti Kebangsaan Malaysia (UKM)	Prof. Dato' Dr Mazlin Mokhtar	Deputy Vice-Chancellor, Research and Innovation
	Prof. Dr Muhammad Fauzi Mohd. Zain	Deputy Dean (Research)/Director, Advanced Engineering Centre Faculty of Engineering and Built Environment
	Mohamad Nasir Raki	Technology Transfer (Senior) Manager, Centre for Collaborative Innovation
Universiti Malaysia Sarawak (UNIMAS)	Prof. Dr Fasihuddin Badruddin Ahmad	Director, Research and Innovation Management Centre (RIMC)
	Assoc. Prof. Dr Lo May Chiun	Deputy Director, Research and Innovation Management Centre (RIMC)
Universiti Putra Malaysia (UPM)	Prof. Datin Paduka Dr Khatijah Mohd. Yusoff	Professor, Faculty of Biotechnology and Biomolecular Science
Universiti Sains Malaysia (USM)	Prof. Dr Muhamad Jantan	Deputy Vice-Chancellor, Research and Innovation
	Prof. Dr Rahmat Awang	Director, Innovation Office
	Khairul Anuar Che Azmi	USM Legal Adviser
Universiti Teknologi Malaysia (UTM)	Prof. Zamri Mohamed	Former Dean UTM Perdana School
	Prof. Thiruchelvam Kanagasundram	Former Professor Perdana School of Science, Technology and Innovation Policy
Universiti Tunku Abdul Rahman (UTAR)	Prof. Ir. Dr Lee Sze Wei	Vice President, R&D and Commercialization
University College Sabah Foundation (UCSF)	Prof. Datuk Dr Ghazally Ismail	Vice-Chancellor
University of Malaya (UM)	Prof. Dr Rajah Rasiah	Professor, Department of Development Studies
	Assoc. Prof. Dr VGR Chandran	Associate Professor, Department of Development Studies

ORGANISATION FOR ECONOMIC CO-OPERATION AND DEVELOPMENT

The OECD is a unique forum where governments work together to address the economic, social and environmental challenges of globalisation. The OECD is also at the forefront of efforts to understand and to help governments respond to new developments and concerns, such as corporate governance, the information economy and the challenges of an ageing population. The Organisation provides a setting where governments can compare policy experiences, seek answers to common problems, identify good practice and work to co-ordinate domestic and international policies.

The OECD member countries are: Australia, Austria, Belgium, Canada, Chile, the Czech Republic, Denmark, Estonia, Finland, France, Germany, Greece, Hungary, Iceland, Ireland, Israel, Italy, Japan, Korea, Luxembourg, Mexico, the Netherlands, New Zealand, Norway, Poland, Portugal, the Slovak Republic, Slovenia, Spain, Sweden, Switzerland, Turkey, the United Kingdom and the United States. The European Union takes part in the work of the OECD.

OECD Publishing disseminates widely the results of the Organisation's statistics gathering and research on economic, social and environmental issues, as well as the conventions, guidelines and standards agreed by its members.

OECD PUBLISHING, 2, rue André-Pascal, 75775 PARIS CEDEX 16
(92 2016 03 1 P) ISBN 978-92-64-25533-3 – 2016

www.ingramcontent.com/pod-product-compliance
Ingram Content Group UK Ltd.
Pitfield, Milton Keynes, MK11 3LW, UK
UKHW051500290926
15471UKWH00008B/1313

9 789264 255333